THEY

MORE WILDSIDE CLASSICS

Dacobra, or The White Priests of Ahriman, by Harris Burland
The Nabob, by Alphonse Daudet
Out of the Wreck, by Captain A. E. Dingle
The Elm-Tree on the Mall, by Anatole France
The Lance of Kanana, by Harry W. French
Amazon Nights, by Arthur O. Friel
Caught in the Net, by Emile Gaboriau
The Gentle Grafter, by O. Henry
Raffles, by E. W. Hornung
Gates of Empire, by Robert E. Howard
Tom Brown's School Days, by Thomas Hughes
The Opium Ship, by H. Bedford Jones
The Miracles of Antichrist, by Selma Lagerlof
Arsène Lupin, by Maurice LeBlanc
A Phantom Lover, by Vernon Lee
The Iron Heel, by Jack London
The Witness for the Defence, by A.E.W. Mason
The Spider Strain and Other Tales, by Johnston McCulley
Tales of Thubway Tham, by Johnston McCulley
The Prince of Graustark, by George McCutcheon
Bull-Dog Drummond, by Cyril McNeile
The Moon Pool, by A. Merritt
The Red House Mystery, by A. A. Milne
Blix, by Frank Norris
Wings over Tomorrow, by Philip Francis Nowlan
The Devil's Paw, by E. Phillips Oppenheim
Satan's Daughter and Other Tales, by E. Hoffmann Price
The Insidious Dr. Fu Manchu, by Sax Rohmer
Mauprat, by George Sand
The Slayer and Other Tales, by H. de Vere Stacpoole
Penrod (Gordon Grant Illustrated Edition), by Booth Tarkington
The Gilded Age, by Mark Twain
The Blockade Runners, by Jules Verne
The Gadfly, by E.L. Voynich

Please see www.wildsidepress.com for a complete list!

THEY

Three Parodies

of H. Rider Haggard's *She*

Edited by

R. Reginald
and
Douglas Melville

With an Introduction by
R. Reginald

WILDSIDE PRESS

**This one's for Richard Morris, in the fellowship of
William Morris**

THEY

Introduction Copyright © 1978 by R. Reginald. All rights reserved

This edition published in 2006 by Wildside Press, LLC.
www.wildsidepress.com

CONTENTS

[Lang, Andrew and Walter Herries Pollock], HE by the Author of "It," "King Solomon's Wives," "Bess," "Much Darker Days," "Mr. Morton's Subtler" and Other Romances, London, 1887

[De Morgan, John], HE, A COMPANION TO SHE, Being a History of the Adventures of J. Theodosius Aristophano on the Island of Rapa Nui in Search of His Immortal Ancestor, New York, 1887

[De Morgan, John], "IT," A Wild, Weird History of Marvelous, Miraculous, Phantasmagorial Adventures in Search of He, She, and Jess, and Leading to the Finding of "It"; A Haggard Conclusion, New York, 1887

H E

BY THE AUTHOR OF
'IT' 'KING SOLOMON'S WIVES' 'BESS'
'MUCH DARKER DAYS' 'MR MORTON'S SUBTLER'
AND OTHER ROMANCES

[Andrew Lang and Walter Herries Pollock]

LONDON
LONGMANS, GREEN, AND CO.
1887

All rights reserved

PRINTED BY
SPOTTISWOODE AND CO., NEW-STREET SQUARE
LONDON

'SHE.'

TO H. RIDER HAGGARD.

Not in the waste beyond the swamp and sand,
The fever-haunted forest and lagoon,
Mysterious Kôr, thy fanes forsaken stand,
With lonely towers beneath the lonely Moon!
Not there doth Ayesha linger,—rune by rune
Spelling the scriptures of a people banned,—
The world is disenchanted! oversoon
Shall Europe send her spies through all the land!

Nay, not in Kôr, but in whatever spot,
  In fields, or towns, or by the insatiate sea,
Hearts brood o'er buried Loves and unforgot,
  Or wreck themselves on some Divine decree,
Or would o'er-leap the limits of our lot,
  There in the Tombs and deathless, dwelleth SHE!

DEDICATION.

Kôr,
Jan. 30, 1887.

DEAR ALLAN QUATERMAIN,

You, who, with others, have aided so manfully in the Restoration of King Romance, know that His Majesty is a Merry Monarch.

You will not think, therefore, that the respectful Liberty we have taken with your Wondrous Tale (as Pamela did with the 137th Psalm) indicates any lack of Loyalty to our Lady Ayesha.

Her beauties are beyond the reach of danger from Burlesque, nor does her form flit across our humble pages.

May you restore to us yet the prize of her perfections, for we, at least, can never believe that she wholly perished in the place of the Pillar of Fire!

Yours ever,
TWO OF THE AMA LO-GROLLA.

CONTENTS.

CHAPTER		PAGE
I.	EDITOR'S INTRODUCTION	1
II.	POLLY'S NARRATIVE	12
III.	LEONORA'S DISCOVERY	18
IV.	THE EQUIPMENT	27
V.	DOWN THE DARK RIVER	31
VI.	THE ZÛ	41
VII.	AMONG THE LO-GROLLAS	49
VIII.	HE	59
IX.	THE POWER OF HE	76
X.	A BODY IN PAWN	81
XI.	THE WIZARD UNBOSOMS	91
XII.	THE WIZARD'S SCHEME	97
XIII.	THE PERILOUS PATH	103
XIV.	THE MAGIC CHAIR	113
XV.	THE END	116

H E.

CHAPTER I.

EDITOR'S INTRODUCTION.

As I sat, one evening, idly musing on memories of roers and Boers, and contemplating the horns of a weendigo I had shot in Labrador and the head of a Moo Cow[1] from Canada, I was roused by a ring at the door bell.

---

[1] A literary friend to whom I have shown your MS. says a weendigo is Ojibbeway for a cannibal. And why do you shoot poor Moo Cows?—PUBLISHER.

Mere slip of the pen. Meant a Cow Moose. Literary gent no sportsman.—ED,

All right.—PUBLISHER.

The hall-porter presently entered, bearing a huge parcel, which had just arrived by post. I opened it with all the excitement that an unexpected parcel can cause, and murmured, like Thackeray's sailor-man, ' Claret, perhaps, Mumm, I hope——'

It was a Mummy Case, by Jingo!

This was no common, or museum mummy case. The lid, with the gilded mask, was absent, and the under half or lower segment, painted all over with hieroglyphics of an unusual type, and *green* in colour—had obviously been used as a cradle for unconscious infancy. A baby had slept in the last sleeping-place of the dead! What an opportunity for the moralist! But I am not a collector of cradles.

Who had sent it, and why?

The question was settled by an envelope in a feminine hand, which, with a cylindrical packet, fell out of the Mummy Case, and contained a letter running as follows:—

'Lady Betty's, Oxford.

'*My dear Sir,—You have not forgotten me and my friend Leonora O'Dolite?*

'*The Mummy Case which encloses this document is the Cradle of her ancient Race.*

'*We are, for reasons you will discover in the accompanying manuscript, about to start for Treasure Island, where, if anywhere in this earth, ready money is to be found on easy terms of personal insecurity.*'

'Oh, confound it,' I cried, 'here's another fiend of a woman sending me another manuscript! They are always at it! Wants to get it into a high-class magazine, as usual.' And my guess was correct.

The letter went on:—

'*You, who are so well known, will have no difficulty in getting the editor of the Nineteenth Century, or the Quarterly Review, or Bow Bells, to accept my little contribution. I shall be glad to hear what remuneration I am to expect, and cheques may be forwarded to*

'*Yours very truly,*
'MARY MARTIN.

'P.S.—*The mummy case is very valuable. Please deposit it at the Old Bank, in the High, where it will represent my balance.*

'M. M.'

Now I get letters like this (not usually escorted by a mummy case) about thrice a day, and a pretty sum it costs me in stamps to send back the rubbish to the amateur authors. But how could I send back a manuscript to a lady already on her way to Treasure Island?

Here, perhaps, I should explain how Mary Martin, as she signed herself, came to choose *me* for her literary agent. To be sure, total strangers are always sending me their manuscripts, but Mrs. Martin had actually been introduced to me years before.

I was staying, as it happened, at one of our university towns, which I shall call Oxford, for short—not that that was *really* its name. Walking one day with a niece, a scholar of Lady Betty's Hall, we chanced to meet in the High two rather remarkable persons. One of them was the very prettiest girl I ever saw in my life. Her noble frame marked her as the victor over Girton at lawn-tennis; while her *pince-nez* indicated the student. She reminded me, in the grace of her movements, of the Artemis of the Louvre and the Psyche of Naples, while her thoughtful expression recalled the celebrated 'Reading Girl' of Donatello. Only a reading girl, indeed, could have been, as she was, Reader in English Literature on the Churton Collins Foundation.

'Who is she?' I said to my friend, the scholar of Lady Betty's; 'what a lovely creature she is!'

'Who, *that*?' she replied with some

tartness. 'Well, what you can see in *her*, *I* don't know. That's Leonora O'Dolite, and the lady with her is the Lady Superior of Lady Betty's.

'They call them Pretty and the Proctor,' my friend went on, 'as Mrs. Martin—Polly they call her too—has been Proctor twice.'[1]

Now nobody could have called Polly bewitching. Her age must really have been quite thirty-five. I dislike dwelling on this topic, but she was short, dumpy, wore blue spectacles, a green umbrella, a red and black shawl, worsted mittens and uncompromising boots. She

---

[1] I say, you know, keep clear of improbabilities! No one was ever old enough to have been Proctor *twice*. PUBLISHER.

That's all you know about it. Why, I shall bring in a character old enough to have been Proctor a thousand times.—ED.

had also the ringlets and other attractions with which French Art adorns its ideal Englishwoman.

At my request, I was introduced; but presently some thirty professors, six or seven senior dons, and a sprinkling of Heads of Houses in red and black sleeves came bounding out of University sermon, and gathered round the lovely Leonora. The master of St. Catherine's was accompanied by a hitherto Unattached student, who manifestly at once fell a victim to Leonora's charms.

This youth was of peculiar aspect. He was a member of the nearly extinct Boshman tribe of Kokoatinaland. His long silky hair, originally black, had been blanched to a permanent and snowy white by failures in the attempt to matriculate at Balliol. He was short—not above four feet nine—and was tattooed all over his dark but intelligent features.

When he was introduced I had my first opportunity of admiring Leonora's extraordinary knowledge of native customs and etiquette.

'Let me present to you,' said the Master of St. Catherine's, 'the Boshman chief, Ustâni!'

'You 'stonish me!' answered Leonora, with a smile that captivated the Boshman. It is a rule among the tribes of Kokoatinaland, and in Africa generally, to greet a new acquaintance with a verbal play on his name.[1] Owing to our

---

[1] Is this *bonâ fide* ?—PUBLISHER.

All right, see *She* (p. 145), Ayesha's elegant pun on Holly. It's always done—pun, I mean.—ED.

insular ignorance, and the difficulty of the task, this courtesy had been omitted at Oxford in Ustâni's case, even by the Professors of Comparative Philology and the learned Keeper of the Museum. From that hour to another which struck later, when *he* struck too, Ustâni was Leonora's slave.

I had no further opportunity of conversing with Leonora and Polly, nor indeed did I ever think of them again, till Polly's letter and mummy case recalled them to my memory.

Perhaps for pretty Leonora's sake I did, after all, take up and open the vast cylindrical roll of MS.[1] in the mummy

---

[1] Don't you think it would stand being cut a little? PUBLISHER.
We shall see.—ED.

case. Dawn found me still reading the following record of unparalleled adventure.¹

---

¹ There is just one thing that puzzles me. Polly and Leonora have gone, no man knows where, and, taking everything into consideration, it may be a good two thousand years before they come back.

Ought I not, then, to invest, *in my own name*, the princely cheque of the Intelligent Publishers?—ED.

CHAPTER II.

POLLY'S NARRATIVE.

I AM the plainest woman in England, bar none.[1] Even in youth I was not, strictly speaking, voluptuously lovely. Short, stumpy, with a fringe like the thatch of a newly evicted cottage, such was my appearance at twenty, and such it remains. Like Cain, I was branded.[2] But

---

[1] I may as well say at once that I *will not* be responsible for Polly's style. Sometimes it is flat, they tell me, and sometimes it is flamboyant, whatever they may mean. It is never the least like what one would expect an elderly lady don (or Donna), to write.—ED.

[2] See *The Mark of Cain* [Arrowsmith], an excellent shillingsworth.—ED.

Is this not 'log rolling'?—PUBLISHER.

enough of personalities. I had in youth but one friend, a lady of kingly descent (the kings, to be sure, were Irish), and of bewitching loveliness. When she rushed into my lonely rooms, one wild winter night, with a cradle in her arms and a baby in the cradle; when she besought me to teach that infant Hittite, Hebrew, and the Differential Calculus, and to bring it up in college, on commons (where the air is salubrious), what could I do but acquiesce? It is unusual, I know, for a student of my sex, however learned, to educate an infant in college and bring her up on commons. But for once the uncompromising nature of my charms strangled the breath of scandal in the bud, and little Leonora O'Dolite became the darling of the university. The old

Keeper of the Bodleian was a crusty bachelor, who liked nothing young but calf, and preferred morocco to *that*. But even *he* loved Leonora. One night the little girl was lost, and only after looking for her in the Hebdomadal Boardroom, in the Sheldonian, the Pusaeum, and all the barges, did we find that unprincipled old man amusing her by letting off crackers and Roman-candles among the Mexican MSS. in the Bodleian!

These were halcyon hours, happier as Leonora grew up and received the education prescribed for her by her parent. Her Hebrew was fair, and her Hittite up to a first class, but, to my distress, she mainly devoted herself to Celtic studies.

I should tell you that Leonora's chief

interest in life was the decipherment of the inscriptions on her cradle — the mummy case which had rocked her ancestors since Abraham's time, and which is now in your possession. Of itself it is a sufficient proof of the accuracy of this narrative. The mummy case is not the ordinary coffin of Egyptian commerce. The hieroglyphics have baffled Dr. Isaac Taylor, and have been variously construed as Chinese, Etruscan, and Basque, by the various professors of these learned lingoes.[1]

Now about this mummy case: you

---

[1] Don't you think this bit is a little dull? The public don't care about dead languages.—PUBLISHER.

Story can't possibly get on without it, as you'll see. You *must* have something of this sort in a romance. Look at Poe's cypher in the *Gold Beetle,* and the chart in *Treasure Island,* and the Portuguee's scroll in *King Solomon's Mines.*—ED.

must know that it had been in Leonora's family ever since her ancestress, Theodolitê, Pharaoh's daughter, left Egypt, not knowing when she was well off, and settled in Ireland, of all places, where she founded the national prosperity.[1]

The mummy case and a queer ring (see cover) inscribed with a duck, a duck's egg, and an umbrella, were about all that the O'Dolites kept of their ancient property. The older Leonora grew the more deeply she studied the inscriptions on the mummy case. She tried it as Zend, she tried it as Sanskrit, and Japanese, and the American language, and finally she tried it as Irish.

---

[1] Is not *this* a little steep?—PUBLISHER.

No; it is in all the Irish histories. See Lady Wilde's *Ancient Legends of Ireland*, if you don't believe me.—ED.

We had a very rainy season that winter even for Oxford, and the more it rained the more Leonora pored over that mummy case. I kept telling her there was nothing in it, but she would not listen to me.

CHAPTER III.

LEONORA'S DISCOVERY.

One wild winter night, when the sleet lashed the pane, my door suddenly opened. I started out of a slumber, and —could I believe my eyes? can history repeat itself?—there stood the friend of my early youth, her eyes ablaze, a cradle in her arms. Was it all coming round again? A moment's reflection showed me that it was *not* my early friend, but her daughter, Leonora.

'Leonora,' I screamed, 'don't tell me that *you*——'

LEONORA'S DISCOVERY

'I have deciphered the inscription,' said the girl proudly, setting down the cradle. The baby had *not* come round.

'Oh, is *that* all?' I replied. 'Let's have a squint at it' (in my case no mere figure of speech).

'What do you call *that*?' said Leonora, handing me the accompanying document.

𝔈cffic𝔖′f   ffini)¹s£𝑛𝑖nl hz n𝑖𝑔p g;sti∧   Mhe hffoys⁶ ffi𝐔o.ΞʀH Onч,o-St𝑎Te f£𝐖 ɛᴛ o𝑓u⍴⚡ v𝑐𝑖ξΦhnɯ d∫ɔψ bpΞbffiff   ohtt uʌ Kíû am ɯhᴍ ⁞ ᴍ omℏη𝐍𝑆!𝑓   0I7ɛ𝐦ᴺ𝑔δ fiy   dosβΘmc[Mœ[| H§n‡ωs g𝑎𝑖𝑖o𝑓qc𝑓w iξc𝑖v.𝐦 ‡edcBB𝑓 η𝐜𝐏θdC𝑟 cIDnû.ɪ vec𝐑 𝐎eu𝒽Beoᴍ nmeυsgw O'q.-δ𝐫𝐡 aϱtuz]ύ∫{ dS æffi𝐮ws)i𝐲sohne 𝛿i))   woiψ𝐥n𝐫𝑓 cə ispr𝐒an𝐜 cb[)[{S]]bffi Ooɛ𝟣)eId n𝑖nchtvcz𝐢𝐪   Ψᴀc𝐬ὼ𝑎A𝑐g𝑐η𝐝 ¦

'I call it pie,' said I, usɪng a technical term of typography. 'I can't make head or tail of it,' I said peevishly.

'Well, pie or no pie, I love it like pie, and I've broken the crust,' answered the girl, 'according to my interpretation, which I cannot mistrust.'

'Why?' I asked.

'Because,' she answered; and the response seemed sufficient when mixed with her bright smile.

'It runs thus,' she resumed with severity, ' in the only language *you* can partially understand—

'It runs thus,' she reiterated, and I could not help saying under such breath as I had left, 'Been running a long time now.'

She frowned and read—

'*I, Theodolitê, daughter of a race that has never been run out, did to the magician Jambres, whose skill was even as the skill of the gods, those things which as you have not yet heard I shall now proceed to relate to you.*

'*Of him, I say, was I jealous, for that he loved a maiden inferior—Oh how inferior!—to me in charms, wit, beauty, intellect, stature, girth, and ancestry. Therefore, being well assured of this, I made the man into a mummy, ere ever his living spirit had left him. What arts I used to this last purpose it boots not, nor do I choose to tell. When I had done this thing I put him secretly away in a fitting box, even as Set concealed Osiris. Then came my maidens and tidied him away, as is the wont of these accursed ones. From that hour, even until now, has no man nor woman known where to find him, even Jambres the magician. For though the mummifying, as thou shalt not fail to discover, was in some sort incomplete, yet the tidying away and the losing were so complete that no putting forth of precious papyri into cupboards beneath flights of stairs has ever equalled it.*

'*Now, therefore, shall I curse these*

maidens, even in Amenti, the place of their tormenting.

'Forget them, may they be eternally forgotten.

'Curse them up and down through the whole solar system.'

'This is very violent language, my dear,' said I.

'Our people swore terribly in Egypt,' answered Leonora, calmly.

'But it is vain, no woman can curse worth a daric.[1]

'But for this, the losing of the one whom I mummied, must I suffer countless penalties. For I, even the seeress, know not what the said maidens did with the said mummy, nor do you know, nor any

[1] From the use of the word *daric* I conjecture that Leonora's ancestress lived under the Persian Empire. There or thereabouts.—M. M.

other. And not to know, for I want my mummy to have a good cry over, is great part of my punishment. But this I, the seeress, do know right well, for it was revealed to me in a dream. And this I do prophesy unto thee, my daughter, or daughter's daughter, ay, this do I say, that a curse will rest upon me until He who was mummied shall be found.

'Now this also do I, the seeress, tell thee. He who was mummified shall be found in the dark country, where there is no sun, and men breathe the vapour of smoke, and light lamps at noonday, and wire themselves even with wires when the wind bloweth. And the place where the mummy dwelleth is beneath the Three Balls of Gold. And one will lead thee thither who abides hard by the great tree carven like

the head of an Ethiopian. And thou shalt come to the people who slate strangers, and to the place of the Rolling of Logs, and the music thereof.

'Thereafter shalt thou find Him, even Jambres. And when thou hast healed him the Curse shall fall from me!

'Nor, indeed, shall the unmummying be accomplished, even then, unless thou, O my daughter, or my daughter's daughter as before, shalt go with He-who-was-mummied to the Hall of Egyptian Darkness and sit in the Wizard's Chair that is thereby, even the seat which was erst the Siege Perilous. These things have I said, well knowing that they shall be accomplished.

'To thee, my daughter!

'THY GRANDMOTHER.'

'There, Polly, what do you say to *that?*' said Nora.

'Your grandmother!' I replied.

'Polly!' said Miss Nora, looking at me with quite needlessly flashing eyes, 'you and I will set out on the search for this unhappy mummied one.'

'Don't you think the critics will call the *motive* rather thin?' I demurred.

'Thin, to rescue my ancestress from a curse!' said Leonora.

'There's just one other thing,' she mused. 'Shall we take a low comedy character this time, or not?'

'Let's take Ustâni,' I proposed, 'he can double the part with that of the Faithful Black! A great saving in hotel bills and railway fares.'

CHAPTER IV.

THE EQUIPMENT.

AFTER it had been decided that we should start in search of '*He* who had been mummified alive,' the next step seemed to be to go. But Leonora demurred to this.

'We must have our things,' she said; 'what do you think we should take?'

'Scissors,' I replied; and I regret to say that at first she misinterpreted the phrase.

Leonora is a powerful as well as a pretty girl, and when the bear fight that ensued was over my rooms were a little mixed.

This suggested mixed biscuits, that invaluable refreshment of the traveller, and from one thing to another we soon made up a complete list of our needs.

The scissors, and skates, and the soap we procured at the Church and State stores,[1] but not, of course, the revolvers. The revolvers we got of the genuine Government pattern, because both Leonora and I are dreadfully afraid of fire-arms, and we knew that *these*, anyhow, would not 'go off.' The jam we got, of course, at the official car-

---

[1] Won't the critics say you are advertising the stores? And the tradesmen won't like it.—PUBLISHER.

Where would the *stern reality* of the story be (see *Spectator*), and the contrast with the later goings on, if you didn't give names?—ED.

tridge emporium, same which we did *not* shoot the Arabs. The Gladstone bag and the Bryant & May's matches we procured direct from the makers, resisting the piteous appeals of itinerant vendors. Some life-belts we laid in, and, as will presently be seen, we could have made no more judicious purchase.

As, from information received on a mummy case, we were travelling in search of a mummy, of course we laid in a case of Mumm, which was often a source of gaiety in our darkest hours. The wine was procured, as I would advise every African traveller to do, from Messrs. ——.[1]

[1] Messrs. Who? Printers in a hurry.—PUBLISHER.
Suppressed the name. Messrs. —— gave an impolite response to our suggestions as to mutual arrangements.—ED.

Being acquainted with the deleterious effects of a malarious tropical atmosphere, we secured a pair of overalls, advertised as sovran for 'all-overishness,' the dreaded curse of an African climate. These we got at the celebrated emporium of Messrs. ⸺.[1]

Our preparations being now exhaustively completed, Leonora and I returned to Oxford, packed our things, and consulted as to the route which we should adopt.

[1] Name suppressed. When eligible opportunity for advertisement as a substitute for a cheque was hinted at, Messrs. ⸺ brusquely replied, in the low Essex *patois*, 'Wadyermean?'

CHAPTER V.

DOWN THE DARK RIVER.

Down the Dark River, the mystic Isis, so Leonora had decided, we sped: Ustâni plying the long pole of the dhow, or native flat-bottomed boat, while we took it in turns to keep him up to his work by flicking him with a tandem-whip.

The moon went slowly down, and it occurred to Leonora to remark that we were 'going down' too, an unusual thing so early in term. Like some sweet bride into her chamber the moon departed, and the quivering footsteps of the Don [1] shook the planets from their places, to the consternation of the Savilian Professor of Astronomy, who, as in duty bound, was contemplating these revolutionary performances from the observatory in the Parks. A number of moral ideas occurred to Leonora and myself, but out of regard for Ustâni's feelings we denied them expression. I began, indeed, to utter a few appropriate sentiments, but the poor Boshman exclaimed, 'You floggee, floggee, Missy, or preachee, preachee, but no *both* floggee and preachee—' in a tone that would have disarmed a Bampton lecturer.

Down we drifted, ever downwards,

---

[1] Do you mean the Dawn?—PUBLISHER.
Every Oxford man knows what I mean.—ED.

obedient to the inscrutable laws of the equilibrium of fluids. Now we swept past the White Willow, now through the cruel crawling waters of the Gut, now threaded the calamitous gorge of Iffley, and then shot the perilous cataract of Sandford.

At this moment, just when the dhow was yet quivering with the strain, I noticed an expression of abject fear on the face of Ustâni. His dark countenance was positively blanched with horror, and his teeth chattered.

'Silence, chatterbox!' I cried, querulously perhaps, when he laid down his pole and seated himself in an attitude of despair.

'What's the matter, old boy?' asked

Leonora, and the reply came in faltering accents—

'*The Ama Barghîs!*'[1]

We glanced in terror down the river's edge.

There, on the path trodden by so many millions of feet that now are silent,[2] there were the burly forms of five or six splendid savages.

The character of their language—which was borne to us on the pure breeze of morning—their costume, their floating house, in which these scourges

---

[1] *Ama* is the prefix of all the tribal names; Ama Zulu, Ama Hagger. I connect it with the Greek preposition ἅμα.—ED.

Don't keep hammer hammering away at Greek! This is a boy's book, not a holiday task, this is!—PUBLISHER.

[2] *Please* don't begin moralising again. One never knows when it will come upon you.—PUBLISHER.

Couldn't help just throwing it in.—ED.

of the water highway commonly reside—everything combined to demonstrate that they belonged to the Barghîz, the most powerful and most dreaded of the native populations.

'*Me umslopogey*,' whispered Ustâni in his native language, meaning that he would retreat.

'Eyes in the boat,' cried Leonora, in her clear, commanding tones; 'paddle on all!'

The Boshman, cowed by her aspect, and the mere slave of discipline (he had pulled in the St. Catherine's second torpid), obeyed her command, and presently we were abreast of the Barghiz.

'Hi, Miss,' cried the Barghî chief, a man of colossal stature, 'Can't yer look where yer a shovin' to?'

Though his words were unintelligible, his tone was insulting.

Leonora rose to her feet, and to the occasion.

By virtue of her rare acquaintance with savage customs, she was able to taunt the Barghîz with the horrors of their tribal mystery, to divulge which is *Death*!

She openly insulted the secret orgies of the tribe.

She denounced the Dog-Feast!

'WHO ATE THE PUPPY PIE UNDER MARLOWE BRIDGE?' shrilled Leonora in her proud sweet young voice.

In a moment a shower of stones struck the dhow, and spurred the water into storm. Frank Muller, the Barghî chief, distinguished himself by the fury of his imprecations and the accuracy of his aim. A smothered groan told me that Ustâni had been hit in the mouth.

Whid, whad, crash went the stones, while Leonora plied the pole with desperate energy, and I erected the patent reversible umbrellas with which we were provided to catch any breath of favourable wind.

The fierce rapidity of the stream finally carried us out of the reach of the infuriated Barghîz (who, moreover' were providentially slain by lightning— a common enough occurrence in that favoured climate, where nobody thinks anything of it), and we rested, weary and wounded, in a sheltered backwater.[1]

[1] Are you not gliding insensibly into *Bess?*—PUBLISHER.

No; all right. It is a tremendous country for storms; can't use them too often; adds to the sense of *reality.* ED.

'The dhow's looking rather dowdy,' said Leonora, glancing at the shattered craft.

'If doughty deeds my lady please,' said I, catching her light tone, 'why, she must take the consequences. But, Leonora,' I added, shuddering, 'I'm sure my feet are damp.'

If there is one thing I dread it is damp feet.

'No wonder,' said Leonora, calmly. 'The dhow has sprung a leek.'

I searched the dhow everywhere, but could find no trace of the vegetable.

Meanwhile the water had risen above the capstan, and Ustâni, shivering audibly, had perched himself on the bowsprit.

'Now or never,' said Leonora, 'is the moment for our life-belts.'

We hurriedly put on our life-belts, regretting the absence of an experienced maid.

'I'll be Mrs. Lecks, and you'll be Mrs. Aleshine!' laughed Leonora, as the dhow, shuddering in all her timbers, collapsed.

'*Ego et Lecks mea!*' cried I, not to seem deficient in opportune gaiety of allusion, and we were in the water. We advanced briskly down stream, Ustâni propelling himself with the pole of the dhow.

Ever anxious about Ustâni's University education (interrupted by this expedition), Leonora kept 'coaching' him in the usual way.

'Bow, you're feathering under water,'

she exclaimed, when the unfortunate Ustâni disappeared in a lasher, where we, thanks to our life-belts, floated gaily enough.

Here we paused to catch a few of the perch and gudgeons, which Leonora had attracted by carefully wearing white stockings.

'Nothing like white stockings for perch,' she said.

As there were not perch enough to go round, Ustâni was told to content himself with the pole, a synonym, if not an equivalent.

Laying our trencher-caps on the water, we used them, as of old, for trenchers, and made an excellent meal.

CHAPTER VI.

THE ZÛ.

Our course was now through a series of cross streams, and finally we emerged into a long, perfectly straight, and perfectly tranquil expanse of water, bordered by a path which had every appearance of having been made by the hand of man.

Night fell: a strange, murky night, smelling of lucifer matches, and lit on the eastern horizon by a mysterious light, flaring like a dreary dawn.

Our passage was obstructed by a

thousand obstacles, and at one point we plunged into the very bowels of the earth for a distance of at least a quarter of a mile. Next we found the canal barred by a grinning row of black iron teeth, under which we dived as best we might. We were now, Ustâni whispered to us, within the strange and dreaded region known to the superstitious natives as *the Zû*. For the first time in our expedition we heard the roaring of innumerable wild beasts. The rattling trumpet of the elephant, the drum of the gorilla, the scream of the lion, the chattering of countless apes, the yells of myriads of cockatoos, the growls of bears, the sobs of walri,[1] the whistle of rhino-

---

[1] Is this plural correct?—PUBLISHER.
I can't find walrus in the Latin dictionary nor any-

cerotes, combined to make a strange pandemonium—strange, I call it, because the zoological learning I had picked up while with Nora at Oxford, informed me at once that the variety of roars, screams, grunts, skreeks, whirrings, which our footsteps seemed to awake in every kind of animal, bird, and insect, could be paralleled only in the pages of the 'Swiss Family Robinson.' Add to this, that it was *night*, yet dark as a day on the London flags when the fog creeps silently about your feet and, rising from utter blackness, grows white and whiter in its ascent, till it coils round your neck, a white choker!

Yes, the fog was playing a dark

---

thing else beginning with W somehow, but it *seems* all right.—ED.

game, but Nora could see it and go one lighter (there were several on the stream we had quitted). She produced a patent electric light.¹ Aided by this, we looked about us and saw the strange denizens of the Zû.

It was now that the presence of mind of Leonora saved us. Foreseeing the probability of an encounter with wild beasts, she had filled her practicable pocket (she belonged to the Rational Dress Association) with buns and ginger-bread nuts.

The elephant now walked round, the wolves also circulated, the bear climbed his pole, the great gorilla beat his breast and roared.

Leonora was their match.

---

[1] Patent in the first sense of the word. She has not yet received offers advantageous enough to close with in the other sense.

For the elephant she had a rusk, a bun for the bear, and the gorilla was pacified by an offering of nuts from his native Brazil.

THIS WAY TO THE CROCODILE HOUSE

we now read, on an inscription in black letters, and, following the path indicated, we reached the dank tank where the monsters dwell. We had arrived at a place which I find it difficult to describe. The floor was smooth and hard.

'What do you make of *this*?' asked Leonora, tapping her dainty foot on the floor.

'Flags,' I replied phlagmatically, and she was silent.

In the centre of the space was a dark pool, circled by crystalline palaces inhabited by the sacred snakes, from huge pythons to the terrapin proud of his tureen. Again, there was a whipsnake, and a toad, bloated as the aristocracy of old time, and puffed up as the plutocracy of to-day. For such is the lot of toads!

Now a strange thing happened.

'*Hark!*' said Ustâni; '*hark! hark! hark!* a den is opening!'

He was right; it was the den of a catawampuss, an animal whose habits are so well known that I need not delay to describe them.

In the centre of the dark pool in the middle of the vague space lay one crocodile. The rest were sleeping on the banks. The catawampuss secretly emerged from its den—horror, I am not ashamed to say, prevented me from interfering—

stealthily crept across the cold floor, and, true to the instincts of all the feline tribe,[1] made straight for the water.

'Ah!' cried Ustâni, 'he's going for him!'

The expression was ambiguous, but we understood it.

The catawampuss, cunning as the dread jerboa, crept to the edge of the pool, took a header into it, and then, still true to the feline instincts, *swimming on its back*, made its way to the crocodile. In this manner it caught the crocodile by the tail and waked it. When the tail of a crocodile awakes the head awakes also. The crocodile's head, then, waking as the catawampuss seized

---

[1] *Is* the catawampuss one of the Felidæ?—PUBLISHER. Of course he is. Look at his name!—ED.

its tail, caught the tail of the catawampuss. The interview was hurried and tumultuous.

The crocodile had one of his ears chawed off (first blood for the catawampuss), but this was a mere temporary advantage. When next we saw clearly through the tempest of flying fur and scales, the head of the catawampuss *had entirely disappeared*, and the animal was clearly much distressed.

Then, all of a sudden, the end came.

They had swallowed each other!

Not a vestige of either was left!

This duel was a wonderful and shocking sight, and was therefore withdrawn, by request, as the patrons of the Gardens are directly interested in the morality of the establishment.

CHAPTER VII.

AMONG THE LO-GROLLAS.

How to escape from our perilous position on the banks of a pestilential stream, haunted by catawampodes and other fell birds of prey, now became a subject for consideration. Our object, of course, was to reach the people of the Lo-grollas, through whose region, according to the prophecy, we must pass before finding the Magician that should guide us to the mummy. Our perplexity was only increased by the discovery that we were surrounded on every side by the walls and houses of a gigantic city. Stealing out by the canal as we had entered, we found to our comfort that this must be the very city mentioned by Theodolitê. As the seeress had declared, a deep and noisome night always prevailed, only broken here and there as a wanderer scratched one of Bryant & May's matches and painfully endeavoured to decipher the number on the door of his house. The streets, moreover, were strewn and interwoven with long strings of iron fallen from the sky.

'*The people who wire themselves with wires,*' whispered Leonora; 'what do you think of my interpretation *now*?'

'I shall inquire,' I answered, and I *did* inquire for the land of the Lo-grollas, but in vain.

Happily we chanced to meet an old man, clothed in a whitish robe of some unknown substance, not unlike paper. This fluttering vesture was marked with strange characters, in black and red, which Leonora was able to interpret. She read them thus. They were but fragmentary.

```
          SP // // AL

     VORCE      C // SE.

  WAR    // //   // URKEY.

     P // L   // // LL   // // ZETTE.
```

On the fragments the words, 'Tragedy,' 'Awful Revelations,' 'Purity,' and other apparently inconsistent hieroglyphics might be deciphered.

He had a large and ragged staff; on his back he carried a vast Budget, and he was always asking everybody, 'Won't you put something in the Budget?'

'Father,' said Leonora, in a respectful tone, 'canst thou tell us the way to the land of the people called Lo-grolla, and the place of the Rolling of Logs.'

He stroked his beautiful white beard, and smiled faintly.

'Indeed, child, we not only know it, but ourselves discovered it and wrote it up—we mean, sent our representative,' he answered.

It was a peculiarity of this man that he always spoke, like royalty, in the first person plural.

'And if a daughter may ask,' said Leonora, 'what is the name of my father?'

Stedfastly regarding her, he answered, 'Our name is Pellmelli.'

'And whither go we, my father?'

'That you shall see—as soon, that is, as the fog lifts, or as our representative has made interest with a gas company.'

With these words he furnished an unequalled supply of litter, which came, he said, 'from the office,' where there was plenty, and we were borne rapidly in a westward direction.

As we journeyed, old Pellmelli gave us a good deal of information about the Lo-grollas, whom he did not seem to like.

They were, he said, a savage and treacherous tribe, inhabiting for the most part the ruined abodes of some kingly race of old.

The names of their chief dwellings, he

told us, were still called, in some ancient and long-lost speech,

'The Academy,' and 'The Athenæum.'

Leonora, whose knowledge of languages was extensive and peculiar, told Pellmelli that these names were derived from the old Greek.

'Ah,' said he, 'you have clearly drunk of the wisdom of the past, and thy hands have held the water of the world's knowledge. Know you Latin also?'

'Yes, O Pellmelli,' replied Leonora, and Pellmelli said he preferred modern tongues, though it would often be useful to him if he did in his dealings with the Lo-grollas.

'However, if our Greek is a little to seek, our Russian is O. K.,' he said proudly.

He was very bitter against the Lo-grollas.

The Lo-grollas' favourite weapon, he told us, was the club, and he even proposed to show us this instrument.

Our litter presently stopped outside a stately palace.

The street was dark, as always in this strange city, but old Pellmelli paused, sniffed, and, bending his ear to the ground, listened intently.

'I smell the incense,' he said, 'and hear the melodious Rolling of the Logs. But they shall know their master!'

Thus speaking, he led us into a vast hall, where the Lo-grollas were sitting or standing, 'offering each other incense,' as Pellmelli remarked, from thin tubes of paper, which smoked at one end.

'Now listen,' said Pellmelli, and he cried aloud the name of a poet known to the Lo-grollas.

Instantly we heard, from I know not what recess, a rolling fire of applause and admiration, which swept past us with stately and solemn music, like a hymn of praise.

'*There*,' said Pellmelli, 'I told you so. This is the place of the Rolling of Logs, and yourselves have heard it.'

Leonora said she did not mind how often she heard it, as she quite agreed with the sentiments.

'Not so!' said Pellmelli; and he cried aloud another name—the name of a poetaster—which was almost strange to us.

Then followed through that vasty

hall a sharp and rattling crash, as of the descent of innumerable slates.

'Great heavens!' whispered Leonora, 'remember the writing; *the place where they slate strangers!*'

As *we* were strangers, and wholly unknown to the Lo-grollas, we thought they might slate *us*, and, beating a hasty retreat, soon found ourselves with Pell-melli in the dark outer air.

'They are a desperate lot,' said he; 'they won't ever put anything in the Budget.'

He was quivering with indignation; and Leonora, to soothe him, told him the story of our quest for the mummy, and asked him if he could help us.

'We are your man,' said he. 'We propose to-morrow to send our representative to interview a magician who has just arrived in this country. He is a mysterious character; his name is Asher,[1] and it is said that he is the Wandering Jew, or, at all events, has lived for many centuries. He, if any one, can direct you in your search.'

He then appointed a place where his representative should meet us next day, and we separated, Pellmelli taking his staff, and going off to lead an excursion against the Ama-Tory, a brutal and licentious tribe.

[1] Pronounced *Assha*.—ED.

CHAPTER VIII.

HE.

NEXT day Leonora was suffering from a slight feverish cold, and I don't wonder at it considering what we suffered in the Zû. I therefore went alone to the rendezvous where I was to meet 'our representative.'

To my surprise, nobody was there but old Pellmelli himself.

'Why, you said you would send your representative!' I exclaimed.

'We are our usual representative,' he answered rather sulkily. 'Come on.

for we have to call on Messrs. Apples, the famous advertisers.

'Why?' said I.

'Can you ask?' he replied. 'Can aught be more interesting than an advertiser?'

'*I* call it log rolling,' I answered; but he was silent.

He went at a great pace, and presently, in a somewhat sordid street, pointed his finger silently to an object over a door.

It was the carven head of an Ethiopian!

This new confirmation of the prophecy gave me quite a turn, especially when I read the characters inscribed beneath—

TRY OUR FINE NEGRO'S HEAD!

'Here dwells the sorcerer, even Asher,' said Pellmelli, and began to crawl upstairs on his hands and knees.

'Why do you do that?' I asked, determined, if I must follow Pellmelli, at all events not to follow his example.

'It is the manner of the tribe of Interviewers, my daughter. Ours is a blessed task, yet must we feign humility, or the savage people kick us and drive us forth with our garments rent.'

He now humbly tapped at a door, and a strange voice cried,

'*Entrez!*'

Pellmelli (whose Russian is his strong point) paused in doubt, but I explained that the word was French for 'come in.'

He crawled in on his stomach, while I followed him erect, and we found ourselves before a strange kind of tent. It had four posts, and a broidered veil was drawn all round it.

Within the veil the sorcerer was concealed, and he asked in a gruff tone,

'Wadyerwant?'

Pellmelli explained that he had come to receive a brief personal statement for the Budget.

The Voice replied, without hesitation, 'The Centuries and the Æons pass, and I too make the pass. *Je saute la coupe*,' he added, in a foreign tongue. 'While thy race wore naught but a little blue paint, I dwelt among the forgotten peoples. The Red Sea knows me, and the Nile has turned scarlet at my words. I am Khoot Hoomi, I am also the Chela of the Mountain!

'Now it is my turn to ask *you* a few easy questions.

'Who sitteth on the throne of Hokey, Pokey, Winky Wum, the Monarch of the Anthropophagi?

'Have the Jews yet come to their land, or have the owners of the land gone to the Jews?

'Doth Darius the Mede yet rule, or hath his kingdom passed to the Bassarids?'

As Pellmelli was utterly floored by these inquiries (which indicated that the sorcerer had been for a considerable time out of the range of the daily papers), I answered them as well as I could.

When his very natural curiosity had been satisfied by a course of Mangnall's Questions, I ventured to broach my own business.

He said he did not deal in mummies himself, though he had a stuffed crocodile very much at my service; but would I call to-morrow, and bring Leonora? He added that he had known of our coming by virtue of his secret art of divination. 'And thyself,' he added, 'shalt gaze without extra charge in the Fountain of Knowledge.'

Thrusting a withered yellow hand out of the mystic tent, he pointed to a table where stood a small circular dish or cup of white earthenware, containing some brown milky liquid.

'Gaze therein!' said the sorcerer.

I gazed—*There was a Stranger in the tea!*

Deeply impressed with the belief (laugh at it if you will) that I was in the presence of a being of more than mortal endowments, I was withdrawing, when my glance fell on his weird familiars, —two tailless cats. This prodigy made me shudder, and I said, in tones of the deepest awe and sympathy, 'Poor puss!'

'Yes,' came the strange voice from within the tent, 'they are *born* without tails. I bred them so; it hath taken many centuries and much trouble, but at last I have triumphed. Once, too, I reared a breed of dogs with two tails, but after a while they became a proverb for pride; Nature loathed them, and they perished. **Χαῖρε***!* *Vale!*'[1]

[1] I have consulted the authorities at the British Museum, who tell me these are the Greek and the Latin words for 'Don't you think you had better go? Get out!'—ED.

This, though not understood, of course, by Pellmelli, was as good as an invitation to withdraw, so I induced the old man to come away, promising the magician I would return on the morrow.

Who was this awful man, to whom centuries were as moments, whose very correspondence, as I had noticed, came through the Dead Letter Office, and who spoke in the tongues of the dead past?

CHAPTER IX.

THE POWER OF HE.

NEXT day Leonora, the Boshman, and I returned to the home of the mage. He stood before us, a tall thin figure enwrapped in yellowish, strange garments, of a singular and perfumed character—spicy in fact—which produced upon me a feeling which I cannot attempt to describe, and which I can only vaguely hint at by saying that the whole form conveyed to me the notion of *something wrapped up*.[1]

[1] The public will say, so is your meaning.—PUBLISHER.

Don't give it away, but that's what I mean.—ED.

With a curious swaying motion which I have never seen anything like—for he seemed less to be walking than to be impelled from behind like a perambulator, or dragged from in front like a canal-boat—he advanced to the table, where lay some pieces of a white substance like papyrus, all of the same size and oblong shape, which showed on their surfaces, some of them antique-looking figures and faces curiously stained, and others red and black dots, arranged, as it seemed to me, in some sort of design, although at first sight they looked jumbled enough. Near to these lay a book bound in brown, but with heavy black and gold lettering, amid which I thought I could make out the words *Modern Magic*, and the name *Hoffmann*.

The swathed figure poised itself a moment, resting one thin hand on the table, and then spoke.

'There is naught that is wonderful about this matter,' it said, 'could you but understand it. Prestigiation itself is wonderful, but that its phases and phrases should be changed is not wonderful. Not now, I ween, is the *gibecière* of the Ancient Wizard seen; not now the "Presto, pass!" of the less ancient conjurer heard. Nay, all things change, yet I change not; that which is not yet cannot yet have taken place—at least not its proper place; that which shall not be may yet come to a bad pass, and the blind race of man watches helpless the trammels it could shake off did it but greatly dare. My business, ladies and gentlemen, now is, as I have just explained to you, to attempt to puzzle your eyes by the quickness of my fingers. Yours, on the other hand, will be to detect the way—or *modus operandi*, as old Simon Magus used to say—in which I perform my little wonders—if you can. Will any gentleman lend me a helmet—I mean a hat?'

As the only male person present was the Boshman, this appeared to me a futile question, and even the stately Magician seemed to be struck by some dim idea of the kind, for I could discern a pair of mysterious eyes peering anxiously through his swathings, and I heard him mutter to himself in several languages, 'Ought to have thought of that. No hat present. Don't know any trick to produce one. Nothing about it in the book.'

But he recovered himself quickly, and went on in clear cheerful tones, 'Ladies and gentlemen, as no person present has a hat, I will proceed to another of the tricks on my little programme. Will any lady oblige me by drawing a card? Will you, madam?' he said, bowing with infinite grace to Leonora.

Her hand touched Asher's as she drew a card, and I saw a shiver pass over the veiled figure.

'Will the lady on your left now oblige me?' he continued, turning to me, who was indeed standing on Leonora's left hand, though how he knew it is a thing I have never been able fully to understand.

'Now, please,' he continued, 'look well at your cards, but do not show them to me or to each other. *Basta. Assez.* Κόγξ Ὄμπαξ. Now, please, still hiding the cards from me and from each other, exchange them. Now,' he continued, his form dilating with conscious power, 'see how true is it that change is perennial, even so far as magic and Nature herself can be perennial. For she who held the King of Hearts now holds the Queen of Spades, and she who held the Queen of Spades now holds the King of Hearts. Thus much among the shifting shadows of life can I, the wizard, see as a sure and accomplished fact. Is it not so, my children?'

We bowed in silence, overawed by the wonder of his presence, although Leonora whispered to me, 'He has got the cards wrong, but we had better say nothing about it.'

'And now,' he continued, 'look upon this glass (it was an ordinary wineglass) and on this silver coin,' producing a *stater* of the Eretrian Republic. 'See! I place the coin in the glass, and now can I tell you by its means what you will of the future. There is no magic in it, only a little knowledge of the secrets, mutable yet immutable, of Nature. And this is an old secret. I did not find it. It was known of yore in Atlantis and in Chichimec, in Ur and in Lycosura. Even now the rude Boshmen keep up the tradition among their medicine-men.

Vill any lady ask the coin a qvestion?' he continued, in a hoarse Semitic whisper, for all currencies and all languages were alike to him. 'Sure it's the coin 'll be afther tellun' ye what ye like. Voulez-vous demander, Mademoiselle? Wollen Sie, gnädige Signora?'

'Then,' said Leonora, in trembling accents, 'I demand to know if I shall find that which I seek.'

The figure, drawing itself up to its full height, passed its hand with a proud, impatient, and mystic gesture across the glass, and then stood in the attitude of one who awaited a response. 'Should the coin, my daughter, jump three times,' he said, 'the answer is yea. Should it jump but once, nay.'

We waited anxiously. The coin did

not jump at all! The wizard took up the glass, shook it impatiently, and put it down again. Still the coin showed no sign of animation. Then the wizard uttered some private ejaculations in Hittite, but still the coin did not move. Then he affected an air of jauntiness, and said, 'I remember a circumstance of a similar kind when I was playing odd man out (τρίτος ἄνθρωπος dear old Sokratès used to call it) with Darius the night before Marathon. Darius was the Mede. *I* was the Medium.' Then he seemed about to work another wonder, when he was interrupted by the harsh cackling laughter of the Boshman, who advanced with careless defiance and observed in his own tongue, which we all knew perfectly, that he 'could see all the tricks the wizard could do and go several better.' I waited, horror-struck, to see what would follow this insolence.

Asher made a movement so swift that I could scarcely follow it; but it seemed to me that he lightly laid his hand upon the poor Boshman's head. I looked at Ustâni, and then staggered back in wonder, for there upon his snowy hair, right across the wool-white tresses, were five finger-marks *black as coal.*

'Now go and stand in the corner,' said the magician, in a cold inhuman voice. The unhappy Boshman tremblingly did his bidding, putting his hands to his head in a dazed way as he went, and, incredible as it may seem, thus transferring—as if the curse carried double force—some of the black mark to his own fingers.

'I will now,' continued the wizard, who had regained his ordinary polished, if somewhat swaying and overbalanced, manner—'I will now, with your kyind permission, show you a little trick which was a great favourite with the late Tubal Cain when we were boys together. Observe, I take this paper-knife—it is an ordinary paper-knife—look at it for yourselves. I will place it on my down-turned hand. It is an ordinary hand—look at it for yourselves, but don't touch it; the consequences might be disastrous.'

I, for my part, having seen the consequences in the case of Ustâni's hair, had no desire to do so.

'You see,' continued the sorcerer, 'I place the paper-knife *there*! It falls. Why? Because of gravity. What is gravity? Newton, as you know well, invented the art; but what of that? Did he find that which did not exist? No, for the non-existent is as though it had never been. But now, availing myself of the resources of science, which is ever old and ever young, I clasp my wrist—the wrist of the hand on which the paper-knife rests—with the other hand, and—you see.'

As the sorcerer spoke, he deftly turned his hand palm downwards, and the paper-knife fell with a crash and a clatter on the floor. It was terrible to see the dumb wrath of the swathed figure at this new defeat.

Even in this moment the Boshman glided like a serpent among us, picked up the paper-knife, and triumphantly performed the very miracle in which the wizard had failed. A harsh cackle of laughter announced his success. But the mage was even with him, or rather he was 'odds and evens.' Rapidly he drew his forefinger across the Boshman's face, perpendicularly and horizontally—

On the skin of Ustâni, azure with terror, appeared the above diagram in lines of white! The mage then made the sign of a +, thus—

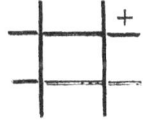

and challenged Leonora to a contest of skill in 'oughts and crosses.' But the

Boshman, catching a view of his own altered aspect in a mirror, exclaimed, 'You 'standy Ustâni? Him no standy He! Him show hisself for tin! Adults one shilling, kids tizzy. *Me Umslopoguey!*' And he sloped; nor did we ever again see this victim of an overwhelming Power (limited).

We presently took our leave of the mage, promising to call next day, and bring a policeman.

CHAPTER X.

A BODY IN PAWN.

'Gin a body meet a body!'—BURNS.

THOUGH Leonora's faith in the magician had been a good deal shaken by his failures in his black art, she admitted that, as a clairvoyant, he might be more inspired. We therefore went, as he had directed us, to the neighbourhood of Clare Market, where he had prophesied that we should find a Temple adorned with the Three Balls of Gold, which the Lombards bore with them from their far Aryan home in Frangipani. Nor did this part of the prophecy fail to coincide

with the document on the mummy case.
Through the thick and choking darkness
which has made 'The Lights of London'
a proverb, we beheld the glittering of
three aureate orbs. And now, how to
win our way, without pass-word or,
indeed, pass-book, into this home of
mystery?

Here, in these immemorial recesses,
the natives had long been wont to bury,
as we learned, their oldest objects of
interest and value. There, when we
pushed our way within the swinging
portal, lay around us, in vast and solemn
pyramids of portable property, the silent
and touching monuments of human
existence. The busy life of a nation lay
sleeping here! Here, for example, stood
that ancestral instrument for the reckon-

ing of winged Time, which in the native language is styled a 'Grandfather's Clock.' Hard by lay the pipe, fashioned of the 'foam of perilous seas in fairy lands forlorn,' the pipe on which, perchance, some swain had discoursed sweet music near the shady heights of High Holborn. The cradle of infancy, the gamp of decrepitude, the tricycle of fleeting youth, the paraffin lamp which had lighted bridal gaiety, the flask which had held the foaming malt,—all were gathered here, and the dust lay deep on all of them!

I was about to make some appropriate moral remarks, when I heard Leonora (whose command of tongues is simply *marvellous*) address an attendant priestess in the local dialect.

'Here, miss,' said she, ''ow much can yer let us 'ave on this 'ere ticker?' (producing her watch).

The priestess, whose clear-cut features and two lovely black eyes betrayed a mixture of Semitic blood, was examining the 'turnip'—as she called the watch—when Leonora, saying 'Mum's the word,' rather violently called my attention (with her elbow) to a strange parcel lying apart from the rest.

It was a long bundle, as long as a man, and was swathed in cerements of white Egyptian tissue.

''Tis you! 'tis you!' I sneezed rapturously, recognising the object of our search, the very mummy which, two thousand years ago, Theodolitê had prepared with her own fair but cruel hands.

There, beyond the shadow of doubt, lay all that was mortal of the unlucky Jambres! On the tissue which wrapped the bundle I distinctly recognised *the stencilled mark corresponding to Leonora's scarab*, a duck, the egg of a duck, and an umbrella.[1]

'How much,' said I to the priestess of the temple, 'could you afford to let me have that old bundle of rags for?'

'That old bundle of rags?' said the woman, 'Take it, dear lady, take it and keep it (if you can), and the blessing of Abraham be on your head!'

So anxious was she to part with the mummy that we could hardly get her to accept a merely nominal price. To give

---

[1] See cover. Most important to have this cover bound in *sur brochure*.—PUBLISHER.

plausibility to the purchase, we said we wanted the rags for a paper-mill. Joyously did Leonora and I call a passing chariot, and, with the mummy between us, we drove to our abode. I was surprised on the way by receiving a pettish push from Leonora's foot.

'Don't tread on my toes,' she said, though I had not even stirred. I told her as much, and we were getting a little animated when my bonnet was twitched off and thrown out into the darkness.

'Leonora,' I said severely, 'these manners are unworthy of a lady!'

'I declare, my dear Polly,' she replied, 'that I never even moved!' and as she was obviously in earnest I had to accept her word.

When we reached home, after a series

of petty but provoking accidents,¹ we first locked up the mummy very carefully in the spare bedroom. To-morrow would be time enough, we said, to consult the wizard as to our next movement. We ordered a repast of the native viands (which included, I remember, a small but savoury fish, the Blô-ta), and sought our couches, in better spirits than usual.

Next morning, long before Leonora was awake, the young but intelligent Slavî (so the common people call housemaids) crept into my chamber with a death-white face.

'Ômum,' she said (it is a term of courtesy), 'wot a night we've been having?'

'Why, what is the matter, Jemim-

---

[1] I say, are you not gliding insensibly into *The Fallen Idol*?—PUBLISHER.

Not a bit, you wait and you'll see.—ED.

aran?' I asked, for that was her melodious native name.

'There's *something* in the spare room, mum, a-carrying on horful. The bell ringing all night, and the Thing screaming and walking up and down as restless! I'm a-going to give warning, mum,' she added confidentially.

'Why, you've *given* it,' I said, to reassure her. 'Forewarned is forearmed.'

'Four-legged It do run sometimes, like a beast, mum, wailing terrible. Up and down, up and down It goes, and always ringing the bell, and crying high for a brandy-and-soda, mum, like a creature tormented.'[1]

[1] Do take care. This is copyright! Don't you remember Mr. Hyde?—PUBLISHER.

Neither Hyde nor Hidol, you're so nervous. Do wait till the end.—ED.

Wish it was come!—PUBLISHER.

'Well,' I asked, though every hair upon my head stood erect with horror (adding greatly to the peculiarity of my appearance), 'well, did you take It what It asked for?'

'Yes, mum; for very fear I dared not refuse. And when I had handed it in by a chink in the open door, first there was a sound like drinking, then an awful cry, "Potash again!" and then a heavy soft thud, as if you had knocked over a bolster stuffed with lead, mum.'

Through the brown glimmer of dawn (it was about ten A.M.) I hurried to Leonora's chamber. She was dressed, and came out. 'What do you advise?' I asked.

'Send for Mr. Urmson, the eminent lawyer, at once,' said she, 'he is used to this kind of thing. Nothing like taking Counsel's opinion. But first let me knock the door open!' She applied her magnificent white shoulder to the door, which flew into splinters.

There was not a trace of the mummy, but there, in a deprecatory attitude, stood the philosopher Asher![1]

[1] Please pronounce *Assha*.—ED.

CHAPTER XI.

THE WIZARD UNBOSOMS.

'Sir,' said Leonora, 'may I request you to inform me why we find you, rampaging an unbidden guest, in the chamber which is sacred to hospitality?'

'*Τὴν δ' ἀπαμειβόμενος προσέφη κορυθαίολος* Asher,' answered the magician, dreamily. 'Do my senses deceive me, or—that voice, that winsome bearing—am I once more with Helen on the walls of Ilion?'

'No, sir, you are in 30 Acacia Gardens,' replied Leonora, severely

'*Why*, permit me to repeat myself, do I find you here, an unbidden guest?'

'To say that I never guessed you'd find me here,' answered the magician, 'might seem a mere trifling with language and with your feelings.'

'My feelings!' exclaimed the proud girl, indignantly, 'just as if—— But answer me!'

'When a man has seen as much of life as I have,' answered the magician, 'when the Æons are to him merely as drops in a bucket which he will never kick—and when he suffers,' he added mournfully, 'from attacks of multiplex personality, he recognises the futility of personal explanations.'

'At least I can compel you to tell us *Where is the mummy?*' said Leonora.

'I am, or lately was, that mummy,' said the wizard, haughtily; then, drawing himself up to his full height, he added, 'I am the REAL JAMBRES! Old Gooseberry Jamberries,' he added solemnly. 'No other is genuine!'

'You are playing, sir, on our credulity,' replied the girl; 'no living man can be a mummy,—outside of the House of Lords or the Royal Academy.'

'You speak,' he said tenderly, 'with the haste of youth and inexperience. When you have lived as long as I have, you will know better. Hearken to my story.

'Three or four thousand years ago—for what is time?—I was the authorised magician at the Court of Ptolemy Patriarchus. I had a rival—the noted witch Theodolitê. In an evil hour she won me by a show of false affection, and, taking advantage of my passion, mummified me alive. To this I owe my remarkable state of preservation at an advanced age. *Très bien conservé,*' he added fatuously.

'But she only half accomplished her purpose. By some accident, which has never been explained, and in spite of the stress of competition, she had purchased *pure* salts of potash for the execution of her fell purpose in place of *adulterated* salts of soda.

'To this I owe it that I am now a living man; and in a moment——'

A certain stiffness of demeanour, which we had noticed, but ascribed to pride, worked an unspeakable change in the mage. As we looked at him *he hardened into our cheap mummy.*

'Here's a jolly go!' said Leonora, her mind submerged in terror.

I sprang to the bell. '*Soda water at once!*' I cried, and the *slavî* appeared with the fluid. We applied it to the parched lips of the mummy, and Jambres was himself again.

'Now will you tell me?' I asked, when he had been given a cigarette and made comfortable, 'why we found you— I mean the mummy—under the Three Balls?'

''Twas a pledge,' he replied. 'When my resources ran low, and my rent was unpaid, the landlady used to take advantage of my condition and raise a small sum on me.'

All seemed now explained; but Leonora was not yet satisfied.

'You have—' she began.

'Yes, a strawberry mark,' he replied wearily, 'on the usual place!'

'The quest is accomplished,' I said.

'Nay,' replied Jambres, to give him his real name. 'There is still the adventure of the Siege Perilous.'

CHAPTER XII.

THE WIZARD'S SCHEME.

'WE must, as you are aware, visit the Siege Perilous in the Hall of Egypt, and risk ourselves in the chair of the Viewless Maiden, of Her that is not to be seen of Man.'

'We know it,' said Leonora.

'It is,' continued the mage, ' your wish to accomplish the end for which you set forth. This seems to you an easy matter enough; young hearts are full of such illusions, and, believe me, I would willingly change my years, which are lost in geological time, for one hand's breadth of your daring. Know, then,' continued this strange creature, 'that the time has now come when matters must be brought to an end between us. It will be my business, and, I will add, my pleasure,' he continued with a lofty air which sat drolly enough upon him in his yellow duds, 'to conduct you to the Siege Perilous. From you, in return, I must exact an unquestioning obedience; and I will add a measureless *confidence*. I beg you to bear in mind that the slightest resistance to my will must be followed by consequences of which you cannot estimate either the reach or the extension.'

There was such a parrot-like pomp about the creature's tautology, and such an old-world affectation of fine manners in his constant obeisances, that I could hold it no longer, but fairly laughed out in his face.

I dreaded, it is true, lest some such fate as Ustâni's might punish me for my temerity, but for reasons which doubtless seemed sufficient to himself the wizard merely looked at me through his veil, shook himself a little in his swathings, and said in a matter-of-fact voice, 'Well, well, perhaps we have had enough of such talk as this. Let's get ahead with the business before us. That business is to reach the Siege Perilous, or Magic Chair. Thither will I guide ye, and there ye shall see what ye shall see. But first it is needful, as all sages have declared, that ye shall show your confidence in me! I value not wealth.

Gold is mere dross—nay, I have the mines of King Solomon at my disposal. But when the weary King Ecclesiast confided to me, in his palace of ivory and cedar in Jerusalem, long ago, the secret of these diamond treasures, he bade me reveal it to none who did not show their confidence in me.

'Let *them* entrust *you*,' said Solomon, 'with their paltry wealth, ere *you* place in *their* hands opulence beyond the dreams of avarice. Give me, then, merely as a sign of confidence, gold, much gold, or,' he continued in a confidential and Semitic tone, 'its equivalent in any safe securities, American railways preferred. Don't bring bank-notes, my dear—risky things, risky things! Why, when I was pals with Claude Duval—but 'tis gone, 'tis gone! Now, my dears, what have you got? what have you got?'

'I have,' answered Leonora, in her clear sweet voice and girlish trustfulness, 'as is my invariable custom, my *dot*, namely, 300,000*l.* worth of American railway shares, chiefly Chicago N.W. and L. & N., in my pocket.'

'That's right, my dear, that's right,' said the Erie wizard; 'just hand those to me, and then we can start at once.

'*And when* (he went on in italics)
o my Leonora
when that mystic change has been worked
which has been predestined
for countless ages and which shall come as
sure as fate,
then on another continent
kindred to thine yet strange, even in the land

of the railways that thy shares are in,
Thou and I,
the Magician and the Novice,
the Celebrated Wizard of the West
and his Accomplished Pupil
Mademoiselle Léonore
will make a tour that shall drag in the
dollars
by the hatful. NOW COME!'

CHAPTER XIII.

THE PERILOUS PATH.

FORTH we rushed into the darkness, through the streaming deluge of that tropic clime. For the seraphic frenzy had now come upon the mage in good earnest, and all the Thought-reader burned in his dusky eyes.

We presented, indeed, a strange spectacle, for the mage, in his silvery swathings, held Leonora by the hands, and Leonora held me, as we raced through the gloom.

In any other city our aspect and

demeanour had excited attention and claimed the interference of the authorities.

In Berlin Uhlans would have charged us, in Paris grape-shot would have ploughed through our ranks. *Here* they deemed we were but of the sacred race of Thought-readers, who, by a custom of the strange people, are permitted to run at random through the streets and even to enter private houses.

We were not even followed, in our headlong career, by a crowd, for the public had ceased to interest itself in frenzied research for hidden pins or concealed cigarettes.

After a frantic chase Jambres (late 'the **Mage**') paused, breathless, in front of a building of portentous proportions.

How it chanced I have never been

able to understand, but, as I am a living and honourable woman, this hall had the characteristics of ancient Egyptian architecture, and that (miraculous as it may appear) in perfect preservation.

There are the hypostyle halls, the two Osirid pillars—colossal figures of strange gods, in coloured relief—there is the great blue scarab, the cartouche, the *pschent*, the *pschutt*, and all that we admire in the Rameseum of the Ancient Empire.

But all was silent, all was deserted; the vast adamantine portals were closed.

Jambres paused in dismay.

'Since I last gave an exhibition of mine art in those halls,' said he, '('twas in old forgotten days, in Bosco's palmy time), much is altered. OPEN SESAME!'

he cried; but, curious to say, *nothing opened!*

At that moment a dark figure crawled submissively to our feet. It was old Pellmelli.

His instinct for 'copy' had brought him on our track, and he began—

'As our representative, I am commissioned——'

Jambres (late 'Asher') turned from him, and he fell (still making notes) prone on his face, where we left him, as the pace was too good to inquire.

The mage now reconnoitred carefully the vast façade of the Hall of Egypt, and finally fixed his gaze on a perpendicular leaden column, adorned with strange symbols, through which (for it was a rainy night) raging torrents of water were distinctly heard flowing downwards to who knows what abysmal and unfathomable depths?

In this weird climate it was the familiar yet dreaded *waterspout!*

Jambres, with the feline agility of a catapult of the mountain, began to climb the perpendicular leaden channel to which he had called our attention, and of course we had to follow him. It was perfectly marvellous to see the ease and grace with which he skipped and hopped up the seemingly naked face of the wall. There were places indeed where our position was perilous enough, and it did not add to our cheerfulness to hear the horrid roaring and gurgling of the unseen and imprisoned waters that poured down the channel with a violence which seemed as if they might at any moment burst their bonds. Helped, however, by certain ledges which projected from the wall beneath square openings filled with some transparent substance, on which ledges from time to time we rested, we arrived at the steep crest, and paused for repose beneath the leafy shade of the roof-tree, Jambres lightly leading the way.

'Now,' said Jambres, 'comes the most delicate part of our journey.'

So indeed it proved, for the mage began rapidly to divest himself of his mysterious swathings. Wrapper by wrapper he undid, cerement on cerement, till both Leonora and I wondered when he would stop.

Stop he did, however, and, with a practised hand, shot his linen into one long rope, which he carefully attached to an erect and smoking pillar, perhaps of basaltic formation, perhaps an ancient altar of St. Simeon Skylitês. When all was taut, Jambres approached a slanting slope, smooth and transparent, perhaps of glacial origin. On this he stamped, and the fragments tinkled as they fell into unknown deeps. Then he seized the rope, let himself down, and from far below we heard his voice calling to us to follow him.

Leonora and I descended with agility to some monstrous basin in the abyss— the Pit, Jambres called it. Here Jambres met us, and bade us light the railway reading-lamps which, as I forgot to mention, we had brought with us. Then, jumping off with the lead, he advanced along the floor, picking his way with great care, as indeed it was most necessary to do, for the floor was strewn with strange forms, stumbling over the legs and backs of which it would have been easy to break one's own. When we halted, brought up by a barrier, of which I did not at first discern the nature, our lamps (as is sometimes the way of some such patent lamps[1]) suddenly went out. Jambres whispered hoarsely, 'Wot are yer waitin' for? Come on; ἀλλ' ἄγε. *Nunc est scandendum.*' We saw before us a vast expanse, of which it was impossible to gauge the extent, so impenetrable, so overpowering was the gloom of its blackness. 'It is

---

[1] I think I've managed not to be libellous.—ED.
We shall see.—PUBLISHER.

the abode,' said Jambres, mysteriously, 'of my rival De Kolta!' He himself, owing to his use of his swathings, was sufficiently *décolleté*.

On the hither side was a row of *lumières à pied* which seemed *afloat* on the darkness, and in their centre a sudden chasm which looked as if it had been made by human agency. The fitful moonbeams[1] showed us a most curious and accurately shaped spur, or *run-down* as it is called in the native dialect, which connected the floor on which we stood with the darkness beyond.

What mortal, however hardy, dared cross this quivering wavering bridge in the total darkness? Beneath our feet it

---

[1] You've not mentioned them before.—PUBLISHER.
That's why I do now.—ED.

swayed and leaped like rotten ice on the magic Serpentine.

'Hush,' cried Jambres, 'it comes, it comes! Be still!'

Even as he spoke, we saw a *long shaft of yellow light* streaming from an unknown centre, and searching out the recesses of the cavern.

'Be still, as you value your liberty,' whispered Jambres. 'The Bobî is on his beat.'

Then, as the long shaft smote the swaying bridge, he lightly crossed it, and beckoned us to follow. We obeyed, and in another instant all was again darkness.

'He has gone his round,' said Jambres. 'Won't be back for hours!'

CHAPTER XIV.

THE MAGIC CHAIR.

THERE, on the plateau, or platform, we had seen, stood, in naked mystery, the Enchanted Chair.

' 'Tis the weird chair of the Viewless Maiden, the place of Her who is no more seen,' said Jambres. 'Who shall sit therein?'

'The writing said,' remarked the dauntless Leonora, 'that a descendant of Theodolitê must achieve this adventure. I am ready.'

'Nay, not so, maiden,' murmured

Jambres, 'try it not till I have made experience thereof. Me it cannot harm; in me you see the original inventor; beware of spurious imitations. But it is a dread experience; let me work it first!'

Leonora could not resist his winning manner and concern for her safety.

'I move,' she said, 'that Mr. Jambres do take the chair at this meeting.'

'I second that proposal,' said I, and there was not a dissentient voice.

'Mr. Jambres will now take the chair,' said Leonora, and the wizard, his swathing robes bulging with Leonora's securities, glided forward.

Then an awful thing occurred. No sooner had Jambres sat down than Leonora and I found ourselves—how can we expect it to be believed?—gazing on a blank, bare space!

The chair was still there, but the wizard was gone. Leonora turned to me, horror in her eyes, her golden curls changed to a pale German silver.

'It is the chair of the Vanishing Lady,' she said.

'It is the Confidence Trick,' I cried; and we both lost consciousness as the true state of the case flashed on our minds. The wizard was off with 300,000*l*. in high-class American securities.

CHAPTER XV.

THE END.

WHAT remains to be told is of little public interest. When we came to ourselves, all was darkness. Escape seemed impossible.

We could not swarm up the rope, by the way we had come.

We knew not when the shaft of yellow light might return on its beat.

We lit a Bryant & May's match, and thereby groped our way downwards, ever downwards.

Finally, as we had given up all for

lost, Leonora said, 'Don't you think the air is a little stuffy?'

We sniffed about the rocky floor, and found an iron grating.

It yielded to a strong tug, and we descended into subterranean passages, framed by the art of men, through which rolled and surged torrents of turbid water.

Through these we waded, attacked by armies of rats, till, thank goodness! we saw a moving light, flashing hither and thither on the torrent.

Half swimming, half wading, we reached the bearer of the light.

It was old Pellmelli, 'doing a Sanitary special,' as he told us.

We, somewhat deceitfully, led him to believe that we had lost ourselves on a similar errand, for a rival Budget, with which he was concerned in a Paper Mill.[1]

On our faithfully promising to give him exclusive information about our adventures, 'for an Extra,' as he said, old Pellmelli conducted us to an orifice in the rock, whence we escaped, at last, into the light of such day as dwells in the Dark City.

Our hopes now entirely rest on finding Jambres again, but it may be, of course, a good three or four thousand years before that.

Here this strange narrative closes; and as I end my editorial task, I have only one question to ask myself—Will this

---

[1] What do you mean by a Paper Mill?—PUBLISHER. A Journalistic War, then.—ED.

thing go on? will Jambres and Leonora meet? will the Americans give up Jambres under the Extradition Act? or——

Is the great drama Played Out?—Ed.

MUNRO'S LIBRARY.

VOL. 50. No. 72   APRIL 15, 1887.

Entered at the Post Office, N. Y., as Second Class Matter.
Munro's Library is issued Tri-Weekly.

HE,

A COMPANION TO

SHE.

BEING A HISTORY OF THE ADVENTURES OF J. THEODOSIUS
ARISTOPHANO ON THE ISLAND OF RAPA NUI IN
SEARCH OF HIS IMMORTAL ANCESTOR.

WITH A MAP AND NUMEROUS ILLUSTRATIONS.

[John De Morgan]

*Entered according to Act of Congress, in the year 1887, by Norman L.
Munro, in the office of the Librarian of Congress,
at Washington, D. C.*

NEW YORK:
NORMAN L. MUNRO, PUBLISHER,
24 AND 26 VANDEWATER ST.

"He," a Companion to "She."

THE ISLAND WHERE "HE" RULED.

HE,

A COMPANION TO "SHE."

INTRODUCTION.

"MANY have no happier moments than those that they pass in solitude, abandoned to their own imagination, which sometimes puts scepters in their hands or miters on their heads, shifts the scene of pleasure with endless variety, bids all the forms of beauty sparkle before them, and gluts them with every change of visionary luxury." So wrote Johnson, and I have often wondered how to draw the line between imagination and reality. That what we call imagination does convey to the mind much which our philosophy and knowledge cannot comprehend, I am ready to admit; but is the brilliancy of the mental vision original with our brains, or is it but the reflex of something which actually exists?

However wild and visionary may seem some of the things which in our solitude are borne upon our mental vision, yet the student of nature is compelled to acknowledge that the wildest, most absurd, and even most unphilosophic fiction is outdone by sober truth.

I am led to these thoughts, because I am giving to the world a narrative which, were it not for the corroboration it has received, and the high character of my informant, I should myself be inclined to look upon as the ravings of a diseased brain, or some wild and improbable fairy story.

Not many years have passed since I spent my summer vacation on a pedestrian tour through England. One day I reached the far-famed Malvern Hills.

On the Herefordshire Beacon I sat down, reflecting on

the deep trenches which marked its sides, and told of some army which had, in days gone by, intrenched itself on that point of vantage. Before my mental vision passed an army of cavaliers, quickly followed by the Parliamentarians under Cromwell. In imagination I saw the banners flying, and heard the psalm-singing of the Cromwellians.

I grew excited, and, as the sun was shining down most gloriously, I became very warm.

I lifted my hat, and as I did so, a strange creeping passed over me.

"I have got a chill," was my first thought, but that was dispelled by another feeling, a mysterious sensation which we often experience when any one approaches near us suddenly and unobserved.

I looked round quickly, and saw close to me a man whose appearance I shall never forget.

He was apparently past the allotted three score years and ten of man's life. Hair of snowy whiteness hung in long clusters round his head and fell gracefully on his shoulders; his beard, as white as his hair, reached to his waist, and gave him a patriarchal appearance.

The greatest charm of his face was his eye, which was as sharp as an eagle's, and as bright as a ray of sunshine.

"Yes, young man, those were stirring times," he said.

I had not uttered a word. Could it be that he had read my thoughts?

"What times do you refer to?" I asked, with a deference due to his years.

"The age of the conflict between the king and the Parliament," was his immediate answer, much to my astonishment.

"How did you know of what I was thinking?"

"Of what use would it be to me to explain? If I told you I could read your thoughts as easily as you can a book, you would only sneer at me."

"Perhaps so," I rejoined.

"And yet, young man, when you have acquired all the knowledge which the books can impart, you will not know much; there is a knowledge beyond all that, which only centuries of life can impart."

I looked at the old man, and began to feel that I was in the presence of a lunatic, harmless, it might be, but still *non compos mentis*.

"I knew what you would think," he continued, "but people have said that of me for years. Can you read Hebrew?"

"I must confess my ignorance," I replied.

"Learn it."

The old man walked away, with, as it appeared to me, a look of sadness on his face.

I continued my tour, but, try as I would, I could not shake off the uncanny feeling which my conversation with the strange man had left.

Three years passed, and by that time I had forgotten the strange episode.

I was seated comfortably at my home in London, when the violent ringing of the door-bell roused me from my reverie. A messenger had delivered a note to my servant which perplexed me.

It read:

"—— Hotel, London, 18—.

"MY DEAR SIR.—Three years ago I made your acquaintance on the Malvern Hills. Since that time I have watched your career, and have known that you have devoted considerable time to speculative philosophy; but as the immortal bard wrote: 'There are more things in heaven and earth than are dreamt of in your philosophy,' so I must tell you that had you passed through the same adventures I have done, your thoughts would turn in another direction. I am an old man—older than you have any idea of, but not too old to desire to benefit my fellow-men. I have passed through some strange adventures, which I am assured would prove deeply interesting if given to the world. I desire you to be my editor, and will intrust you with the MS. describing my adventures, on the condition that you publish it, without change, alteration or addition. If you decline, notify me before noon to-morrow. Should I not hear from you, the messenger who brings this letter will deliver the package to you by seven to-morrow evening. If you accept my trust and refuse to fulfill the conditions, you will never know another moment's peace, your life will drag out wearily, and your career will be blighted.

"Believe me, sincerely your friend,
"J. THEODOSIUS ARISTOPHANO."

I read this strange letter over many times, and at last determined to receive and examine the MS., and if on examination I did not care to incur the responsibility of publishing, I would return it.

The following evening the bulky MS. came. I eagerly broke the seals, and opened the parcel.

Its contents interested me strangely, but as I read the autobiography, I determined to return the copy at once.

I sent to the address the next day, and learned that the old patriarch with the Grecian name had sailed for Europe.

I had therefore no other alternative, I must publish the strange record.

Here ends my responsibility as editor.

If the philosophy seems outrageous, and the statements hard to believe, gentle reader, blame not the editor, but the author, whose character for veracity is vouched for by many respectable people in the new and old worlds.

EDITOR.

CHAPTER I.
MY EARLY LIFE.

IT may be that some day an enterprising publisher will send forth from his printing presses this story of my life and strange adventures; it will be well, therefore, that I commence at the very beginning, so that a fair and right understanding may be arrived at concerning my history. I, John Theodosius Aristophano, was born in the year—— but I had better not give any date, for did I do so, some who read this page would throw it on one side and declare the whole story to be the ravings of a lunatic.

Suffice it to say I was born—but not in the usual manner. It was only through the extraordinary skill of the physician that I ever saw the light of day, for my mother breathed out her last life-breath several minutes before I entered the world a crying, squawking, strange-looking infant.

It is not given to many to be able to say that they were born after their maternal parents' death, and that strange fact may have had a great deal to do with my after life.

My father was of a Greek family, and was born in grand old Athens. His family, however, had married and intermarried with the English for generations and had almost become Anglican. In appearance he looked like an ancient Greek philosopher, and his mind was as well stored with all the learning of the past and present as was that of any who taught at the Pantheon when Athens was the center of the philosophic world.

My mother, whose portrait never leaves me, for the small medallion I wear is the only thing which tells me of her angelic beauty and sweetness of disposition—my mother was English, and often I have heard my father say, was so perfect and good that the angels might take pattern by her. My early days differed from those of most boys, for I never attended school. My father instructing me daily in such branches of knowledge in which he desired me to become proficient.

"Theo." as he always called me, "I am rich; you will never need to work for a living; but you have a mission—what it is I cannot explain to you yet, but it is my desire to train you in such a way that when the time comes you may fulfill your destiny; and if you accomplish what I have set out for you to do, the whole creation will be your servant."

During the first fifteen years of my life I was constantly listening to speeches such as this.

I often wondered if my father was crazy; people said so, and boys pointed at me and called me the "son of a crazy fool."

One day a boy, more daring than the others, exasperated me.

He commenced by calling me a milksop—whatever that meant—a fool, and various epithets of that kind; and then he began to vilify my revered father.

"He is a crazy old fool," he said; and then seeing that my feelings were injured, and I felt ready to cry, he continued: "I say, you Greek fellow, who did your dad murder?"

Insults I could stand, but to hear my father accused of crime was more than I could endure.

Without considering that my tormenter was head and shoulders taller than I was, I dashed at him and struck him with such force that he fell down, and I on the top of him.

We got up, and he insisted that we must settle the matter by a regular, square stand-up fight.

I was quite ready to agree. My strength was not great, but as gymnastic exercises and boxing formed part of my daily study, science made up for lack of strength.

My antagonist struck out quickly but with poor effect, while many a time did he stagger under my blows.

The boys and some men had gathered round, and evidently felt interested in the contest.

"Go it, Greeky!" they called out, repeatedly, while those who took the part of my foe, who was a butcher-boy, were equally enthusiastic in their cries of:

"Give it to him, Fatty!" "Go it, Butcher!" and such like cheering encouragement.

"Here's a go, Greeky," said one of my particular friends, as he directed my attention to the sidewalk, where I saw my father standing, an interested spectator evidently of the fray.

I was more than ever determined to show my skill and prowess, and it was not long before an opportunity was presented. My antagonist had struck out with his right fist, but I saved myself from a rattler on the nose by dodging my head; my left hand came into collision with his nose with such force that a stream of blood spurted therefrom and he began to cry. His friends were heartily ashamed of his weakness of nerves, and led him away. From that day I was the champion of the town, and no one ever again breathed a word against my father.

I mention this little episode to show that my father believed in the development of the muscles as well as the mind. I was early taught to speak, read, and write the Celtic, Arabic and Hebrew languages. And long before I could construe or parse a sentence in English, I could hold a discussion in Hebrew or Arabic with my father.

When I reached the age of fifteen my father took me all over Europe. The mornings when we were not traveling were spent in study, the remainder of the day to sightseeing.

From Europe we crossed over to America and explored the States, which were then emerging from their colonial ways into the manners and habits of sovereign countries. This travel lasted three years, when a change came over my life.

My father expressed a desire to return to England. For the first time in my eighteen years of life I rebelled.

We were in Philadelphia, and had been entertained at the best houses and received by the very *elite* of the rising City of Brotherly Love.

At the house of one of the most distinguished residents I met my fate—at least, I thought so at that time.

I have not the faculty of description sufficiently developed to portray her graces and beauty.

She was my own age; but, oh, so lovely! Her eyes the brightest of dark blue, her skin fairer than was ever imitated in wax; her manner was so refined and her mind so well-cultivated, that I should have been adamant itself had I not fallen in love with her.

On the evening breeze was wafted the soft nothings which mean so much, and as we walked in the gardens at the back of her father's stately mansion, her hands clasped in mine, we wondered how any one could be unhappy in a world so bright and lovely.

We looked at the stars, and wondered which would be our home when love had transformed the mortal into the immortal. Youth and love were on our side, and no one on whom the sun had ever shone could have been more happy.

One evening we were seated in a little summer-house, and silence spoke as eloquently as words.

We gazed into each other's eyes, and in their liquid depths read the language of love.

Voices startled the silent air, and in another moment our respected fathers stood before us.

"By all the gods, but that is a pretty sight!" her father exclaimed, as he saw us both color up at their approach.

"I am sorry——" my father commenced, but whatever he was about to say was lost, for his friend, whom I loved for her sake, interposed:

"Now come, Aristo"—the short name my father's friends used when speaking to him—"young people must enjoy themselves, and there is nothing like love, now is there?"

"Not for the majority, but as we leave America to-morrow——"

"Leave to-morrow?"

Yes. A boat sails to-morrow afternoon, and as it may be very many years before we return to America, it is not wise for my son and your daughter to become attached to each other," my father said, as he walked away. We looked into each other's eyes; our hearts were too full for speech.

My darling's eyes were filled with tears, and I knew then that she loved me, even as my whole soul went out to her.

We swore to be true to our plighted faith, and vowed that no other should ever be husband to her or wife to me.

Little did I know then that I should never see her face again.

Ah, me! when I look back to those days I can see her eyes fixed on me, full of tears. One of the bitter memories of my life—and not the least—has been not to be able to render her happy and fulfill my vow of love. If there is any good feature or softness in my nature it is from memory of her that I have received it.

I am not superstitious, but in the most terrible instances of my life—when the angry billows tossed me like a cork on their bosom, and every moment I expected to be my last, when bullets whistled in my ears like the winds of the tempest—when balls showered round me like hailstones—when I stood in the awful presence of *He*, the great unnamed mystery—when surrounded by savages, each one thirsting for my blood, I have closed my eyes, and have seen in my mental vision my darling on her knees, pure as an angel, praying to the Most High for me and for my safety.

I call God to witness that the love I had for her, and the hope of one day clasping her in my arms gave me that courage, at which, sometimes, people have been astonished, and enabled me to weather every storm and overcome the difficulties in my way.

She is gone! A marble slab points out the place of her retirement until the great mystery shall be solved, and she shall come forth in all the beauty of perfect womanhood to bless and gladden the world.

But I digress, and must return to my narrative.

The next day, faithful to his word, my father insisted on sailing.

The parting with my soul's love was hard, but I had no thought of disobeying my father, and accordingly the good ship William Penn bore us across the Atlantic to England.

Steam had not then been utilized, and the mariner had to trust to wind and tide. After a long and tedious voyage we reached our destination safely, and another epoch of my life commenced.

CHAPTER II.

MY FATHER'S STORY.

A MONTH passed away quietly in our English home.

My mind was constantly dwelling on the fair and beautiful American, and I chafed a great deal at the thought that my father's object was only to separate us. The pressing business, which he gave as an excuse for his return, was a matter of but slight import, and could have been attended to later, or managed by correspondence. However, I looked up to my father with awe, and was always constrained to believe that everything he did was right.

I began, however, to lose all ambition in life. My heart was in Philadelphia and nothing was able to interest me in England.

"Theo., my boy," my father exclaimed one evening after we had been settled a month, "you are eighteen years old, and I want to tell you a story which will affect your future life."

In a moment my lethargy had gone, I was nervous and excited. Perhaps I should hear what the mystery surrounding our family was, and, who knows, perhaps I was destined to lift the shadow.

I was young and egotistic, and no one ever was so confident of success as I at that age.

"Listen to me attentively, and however strange the story seems to you, don't laugh at it, for every word can be proved. You might just as well try to prove that

Julius Cæsar never lived as to controvert any part of my story."

It was a strange commencement, and only seemed to whet my appetite. I was more than ever eager to listen.

"I should never think of laughing, father," I replied, my dignity rather touched at the suggestion of such an unwarranted frivolity.

"You may not laugh openly, but it is quite possible you will sneer at me, and laugh at my folly, mentally."

"Never, father!" I protested solemnly.

"Then listen! You are the last of a race dating back many centuries. I can trace our lineal ancestors far beyond the dawn of Christianity, back into the ages when the Pharaohs ruled Egypt with a hand of iron. Our first ancestor, of whom I can find any trace, was an Egyptian priest, though by birth a Grecian. He broke his vows and married a princess of the royal house, and fled from Egypt.

"The vessel in which he sailed was wrecked, and only the founder of our family and his wife were saved.

"They drifted on some spar to the swamps of Africa, where they were cared for by the natives. A marvelous woman is said to have ruled these people. She possessed the power of living forever, and on her favorités she could confer immortality in life.

"This wondrous woman fell in love with our ancestor, and proposed he should get rid of his wife and marry her.

"This he promptly refused to do, whereupon the sorceress tempted him by means of promised rewards, and lastly by offering him immortality.

"To all he turned a deaf ear; whereupon she blasted him by a strike of her wand, and he was carried away dead.

"His wife escaped to Greece, bearing with her an infant son. From that son we are descended."

He paused and looked at me with a puzzled expression on his face. I had listened to the story much as I should to any of the traditions and legends of the past. My father was evidently waiting for me to make some remark or express an opinion; so, not knowing whether he believed the story or not, I said:

"It is quite interesting, father; I did not know we had any mythical legends connected with our family."

"Myths! No; all I have told you is solid truth."

"Is that the whole story?" I asked.

"No; the most important is yet to come. This queen who ruled over the African tribes three thousand years ago still lives——"

My father said this with the same amount of confidence an he would use were he to tell any one that George Washington was the first President of the United States. Unmoved by my penetrating gaze, he continued:

"And what is more remarkable, I can assure you that our ancestor is living also. It appears that he was not killed by the queen, but only sent into a deep sleep, or trance, from which he awoke a few days after. He learned of his wife's escape, and the queen's absence.

"By some inward prompting, he was led to enter her private chamber—a cave hewn out of the solid rock—and there the same mysterious guiding power induced him to partake of the contents of a flagon which stood near his hand.

"No sooner did the golden liquid flow down his throat than he experienced very strange sensations. His beard, which had been of snowy whiteness, became raven black; his eyes were dim with close study, but were instantly transformed into the clearest and sharpest of optical organs, and his limbs received again the activity and lissomness of youth.

"In brief, he returned to the age of twenty-five; he had become immortal.

"He stole away from the cave, and was nearly lost in the swamp, but when he found the thick, black slime gradually rising up to his neck, he called aloud for help. A monster alligator was basking in the sun on a small island near by, and was attracted by the shout.

"The animal looked across with its great staring eyes and widely opened mouth and then leaped into the marsh.

"This was not the kind of assistance the man who had just quaffed the elixir of life desired, and he shrieked in agony.

"He had forgotten, that if the wondrous distillment gave him power over the forces of nature and physical decay, that the alligator would be powerless to injure him.

"The ugly beast reached its prey, when a dark cloud suddenly obscured the brightness of the sun, and out of the cloud appeared a face.

"The alligator looked at the beauty of the shadowy features, and instead of attempting to devour our ancestor, held him in its mouth and swam out to the open sea, the young immortal having in the meantime been able to climb on the back of this wondrous animal.

"A boat's crew, seeing the strange sight, rescued this ancestor of ours, and after wandering about for several years he found himself again in Athens.

"He found his wife dead, and his son a full-grown man, about to marry a most beautiful Athenian. Our great ancestor—whose name has been variously given as Kallikrates, Thebeisto and Isistheno—disappeared from Greece, and his son's affianced was never seen afterward.

"Kallikrates was heard of some years afterward in some far-off isle in the South Pacific, where he still resides."

My father told this legend, or tradition, with the greatest solemnity of manner, and I could not help thinking of the stories which had been whispered about, that my father was "not quite right in his head."

He looked at me quizzically, and then, as though he divined my thoughts, said:

"I am not mad. I have good evidence to offer, and if Heaven spares me, I intend finding this isle and paying a visit to our now aged ancestor."

"Do you mean it?" I asked.

"Of course I do. What do you think of the story?"

"It is very absurd, and of course not true."

"Why?"

"You talk of some woman living in Africa many thousand years, and one of your own family living three thousand years in some Pacific isle."

"I know it; what then?"

"You know, father, that none could live that length of time; death is as natural as life."

"Death! There is no such thing. What we call death is only transition from one state to another."*

"Yes, I know that; but while there is no death in a spiritual sense, there is a physical death."

"Why should there be? What we call death is caused by the wasting away of the tissues, the decay of the organs of digestion and respiration. Now, why is it not possible to discover something which would replenish the wasting energies, stop the decay, and so drive away death?"

"Why, father, that question has puzzled the scientists of all ages, but all have found its solution impossible."

"I say it is quite possible. I believe in Holy Writ, and therefore know that there was a tree in the garden of Eden, whose fruit, if eaten, would give immortality and knowledge, so that whosoever eat of it, would become like unto God."†

"I cannot argue with you about that, father, but what-

---

* Longfellow expresses the same idea:

"There is no death; what seems so is transition.
This life of mortal breath
Is but a suburb of the life elysian,
Whose portal we call death." EDITOR.

† Genesis iii., 22.

ever existed in the garden of Eden had nothing to do with our remote ancestors."

"That I admit, but it is my purpose to try and find this man, and —nay, more, I am commanded to do it."

"Commanded!" I exclaimed in astonishment.

"Yes. I will show you when I am ready, some tablets which have come into my possession, and shall ask you to swear by all that is holy, that should I fail, you will make it the business of your life to discover your ancestor, and fulfill all the behests contained on the tablet."

"How long have you known this story or legend?"

"I first heard it from my father, when I was about your age, but like you I was incredulous, and dismissed it from my mind. The year you were born, I grieved over the death of your mother. My hair became white, my body lost its strength, and I was nearly joining her in the realms beyond the river. A dream came across my troubled sleep, and in it I saw your mother. She implored me to live for your sake, and bade me fulfill the destiny of my life.

"I took courage, and traveled for a year.

"I visited South America, and in my yacht went to various islands on the Pacific coast, prompted by curiosity. I did not find any such places as my father had described to me, but when I was returning home, I was driven ashore off the coast of Chili, and my yacht was entirely destroyed.

"I spent several months on the little island known as Madre-di-Dios, while a new yacht was being prepared for me at Valparaiso. I understood the Spanish language very fairly, and listened to the conversation of the fishermen who visited the island. From them I learned that there was some island in the Pacific—but its name and location they could not give—where there lived a man of whom the people said he could never die. The inhabitants were giants, and all possessed of demoniac power.

"These legends and stories corroborated, to a great extent, the history I had heard of our family. I made many inquiries, but could not learn anything further.

"All were too much afraid to speak of the mysterious immortal. One thing I noticed, they never referred to him by any name, but always as *He*.

"Whenever they mentioned him, every hat was raised, and the devout made the sign of the cross."

"Did no one ever try to find the island?" I asked.

"Yes: I was coming to that. My host, an old fisherman, said that his great-grandfather was once wrecked on that island, and saw the mysterious *He*. His face, which was always masked, so said my host, shone with the brilliancy of the sun; and whenever any of the natives offended him, all he did was to fix his eye on them and they dropped dead.

"So frightened was the old fisherman, that even as he told the story of his great-grandfather's visit to the island, he trembled and shook like an aspen leaf."

"Well, but, father, did he tell you how to find the island?"

"That he could not do, for his great-grandfather was always too frightened to talk much about his adventure. He, however, had brought away with him some tablets of brass, said to have been written by *He*, and those tablets I have read, and together we will peruse them again."

"Have you got them?" I asked, for I had now grown very interested in the narrative.

"Yes. When I return from my northern trip I will open the casket, we will read the tablets, and you shall see the proofs of the story I have told you."

CHAPTER III.

THE TABLETS.

My father was away several weeks, and my curiosity had grown and developed so much that I could scarcely restrain it.

I have often wondered whether my father purposely stayed away, so that his story might rouse my curiosity, and, by constant remembrance, impress itself on my mind.

I verily believe that had my father tarried much longer I should have gone mad.

My imagination was at fever heat when to my great joy I heard his welcome voice.

That evening, when the house was clothed in silence, my father whispered that the time had come.

He brought from his own room a box heavily clamped with iron, and bearing about it marks of antiquity.

I had a remembrance of having seen the box once before, and wondered what its contents could be.

Drawing a heavy key from his pocket—a key the like of which I had never before seen—he inserted it in the lock, and opened the lid of the box.

Instantly a powerful, subtile perfume filled the room, and seemed to almost steal away my senses.

I discovered that it came from the woodwork of another box, which fitted neatly into the iron-clamped one.

This inner box was made of a beautiful white wood

which emitted the powerful perfume, and was inlaid with silver and mother-of-pearl.

"Where did you get the box?" I asked.

"It belonged to this wonderful creature *He*, and I got it with the tablets. In fact, I bought the box and its contents for a mere song."

The beautiful box in its turn was unlocked, and from it was taken a package.

On opening it, a small medallion or pendant such as is often worn by ladies was seen, and on it, cut deep into the red jasper, a symbol or hieroglyphic like this:

"I don't understand the meaning of the hieroglyphic," I said, "but that is a very fine piece of jasper and I would like to wear it as a pendant."

"You can do so, for I suppose it has no other use," my father quickly responded.

Carefully wrapped in a cloth as soft as silk, but evidently woven out of some kind of fine grass, my father removed three tablets or plates of brass, measuring about six inches long by four broad.

On the one side of each tablet, deeply engraved, was a mass of writing, which I quickly discovered to be Ancient Hebrew. On the other side, rudely drawn hieroglyphics were found.

The brasses looked old, though in a good state of preservation.

I was examining one of the tablets very closely, when I saw a drawing similar to the one on the jasper. My father said:

"It has some significance, but what, I cannot determine. Never lose the jasper."

I readily gave the promise.

We then sat down to read the Hebrew inscriptions, and translate them into English.

The first one read as follows:

"I, the strong and mighty Kallikrates, priest of Isis, write this, that my son, and his seed after him, may take warning, and give heed to me. Take care never to go near Libya (Africa), where dwelleth a mighty demon, a woman, who is by the powers of magic queen over the tribes. She can blast with a look, but can give immortality to those who wish it."

"So much for the first tablet; I don't see anything extraordinary in that," I said, as we finished the translation.

The second one, evidently written at another time, read:

"I, the strong and mighty Kallikrates, have drank the potion of life, and shall live forever. One thing only can release me from my burden of life. If my son, or his seed after him, will bring the talisman and declare it to be his pleasure that I shall die, I shall be free from my weight of years. Oh, the mighty and great Isis, send this writing to my son that he may deliver me."

Most people want to live, but here was one who evidently wished to die.

The third tablet was carelessly engraved, but every character was perfectly formed, and easily read.

"I, the great and might Killikrates do say to thee my son, seek out the woman, and learn the secret of her power, and from thence visit me and release me, for I want to die. I escaped the power of *She*, the mighty demon queen, and have equal power with her, except that while I take on immortality I cannot put it off."

Then followed various notes referring to the caves and swamps of Africa, and others giving a description of the island to which Killikrates had escaped.

"The old man," I said, "evidently changed his mind, for in one he tells us not to go near Africa, and in another to go there and seek out this woman."

"There is a contradiction, certainly, but I intend trying to find this island."

"I am in for the adventure, also."

To me, young and hearty, it presented a feast of unmitigated enjoyment.

I should see the world, have good hunting and fishing. There would be a chance of a sight of the noblest game, and, boy-like, I already saw myself back home with plenty of lion and tiger-skins as trophies.

My father did not disturb my meditation, but when he saw a smile pass over my face he quietly slipped into my hand a piece of parchment.

"Read that, and you will not sneer."

I unrolled it, and a saw dozen or so inscriptions on its surface.

I confess I was surprised, when, in old English black-letter, I read that for several hundred years members of my family had made searches for this wonder-land, and failed to reach it.

The black-letter inscription bore date:

"Yn ye yeere of salvacionne threeteen hundrede and fowertene."

Below it was a line:
"Dyd not goe," and signed "Theodo."
There was no date to this, but another inscription told how Theodore Aristophamus had made the attempt to find the Pacific Isle, and had been shipwrecked, only escaping with his life.

This bore date 1691.

The last entry was dated 1722, and was as follows:

"Admiral Raggewein did tell me that in one of his trips to the Southern Seas he had heard of a small island on which lived an innumerable race of giants, who dwelt mainly in caves, and that they worshiped a man who had lived on the island and reigned as king for several thousand years."

These entries were apparently genuine, and could not possibly have been forged. The color of the parchment, its fiber, and general appearance betokened age. The style of writing and the manner of pen used also varied in each entry.

I was completely staggered, and was even more desirous than my father to make the search.

Within a month we had set sail on our wild-goose crusade.

CHAPTER IV.

THE MIGHTY DEEP.

IT was a lovely morning in early summer when I stepped on board, with my father, on the good ship Patagonia, bound for South America. Like a majestic queen of the deep, she sailed from her docks down the Thames.

The air was bracing and invigorating, and as we had plenty of time to enjoy ourselves, the trip bid fair to be a pleasant one. Carefully the good ship sailed past endless lines of masts in the docks, past Wapping, past tumbledown taverns and dark arches, which could tell of many a murder and crime, past innumerable coal barges—dirty, cumbersome-looking things—away we went, passing the far-famed Greenwich Hospital and into the open sea.

Now the Patagonia spread her white wings, and with increased space was able to put on greater speed.

The Patagonia was strong and stanchly built, of some seven hundred tons burden.

She could carry a good cargo and had room for about a dozen passengers.

The captain, Mr. Leonard, was, like his ship, stout and stanch.

He had taken the Patagonia across the ocean some dozen times and had never had a mishap.

Our voyage was pleasant until we reached the Cape Verde Isles, when our first taste of Neptune's wrath was experienced.

I was standing talking to the captain, and listlessly scanning the horizon, as people at sea will do, to see if they can chance on a sight of a passing sail.

I beheld on the utmost limit of the deep blue, gently heaving water, a thin, snow-white line.

"See, Captain Leonard," I cried. "What is that strange appearance."

He hastily raised his glass, and for a moment as he looked through it, his face paled, then suddenly recovering his presence of mind: "Mr. Aristophano," he said. "Many a man has seen that white line and within an hour has been in Davy Jones' Locker. That is the white squall. If you wish to stay on deck you must lash yourself to something."

I fully resolved I would not go below. If a storm was near, I wished to see it in all its grand majesty.

Quickly lashing myself to the mast I waited.

The wind suddenly rose to a perfect hurricane, and churned the blue waters into that brilliant whiteness I had noticed first as a thin line in the distance.

Above our heads the clouds became as black as midnight, the rain descended as though a repetition of Noah's flood was about to destroy the earth, the vivid lightning flashed across the heavens, dazzling in its brilliancy, but startling in its speed through the sky, the thunder roared and crashed as I had never heard it before.

The wind howled like an angry leviathan, and as the sea dashed over the decks of the Patagonia, it made her groan like a living thing under the force of the blows.

The captain had ordered the men to furl the sails, but before they could do so the canvas was torn into a thousand ribbon-like shreds.

One half hour the tempest raged, and in that short space of time the stanch and strong ship had been buffeted by the waves until it presented a sorry appearance.

Several of the crew had been washed overboard, and the safety of the ship demanded that they should be left to their fate.

The ship was but a sheer hulk, as she lay on the breast of the waves; her masts were snapped like reeds, and her rudder was gone.

The hull held well together, and the captain expressed his firm conviction that we should be able to reach land safely.

My father had been below during the fury of the gale, and right glad I was that he was safe.

"There seems to be a fate in the matter," he said, when he looked round at the wreck on the decks.

"In what way?"

"Nearly twenty of your ancestors have set out with the same intention as ourselves, and met the same fate."

"It is a curious coincidence, but the captain says we shall reach land in safety."

"I hope so. Have you your talisman?"

"Yes, father, dear; that I will never part with."

The next morning the sun rose fierce and strong.

The captain had set the sailors to work making a rudder and two short masts, and with alertness and skill they did their work. The vessel drifted with the current, and seemed to be gradually approaching land.

Perfect good humor prevailed on board, and mutual congratulations were given and offered on our providential escape.

The fact that some of the crew lost their lives troubled us but slightly, for we are so apt to only respect the life of passengers and officers, the common seamen counting for naught.

Three days we drifted just as the current and the ever changing wind pleased.

We were powerless.

On the fourth morning the lookout announced a passing ship.

What excitement there was then!

Every one crowded to the side of the vessel. The passengers waved their hats and handkerchiefs, and the sailors shouted.

The ship was several miles away, but what cared we for that? Our hats were a good signal, and the sailors' shouts must be borne over the water to the vessel on whose promptitude we were building our hopes.

The captain fired the signal gun, and as it boomed across

the water we fancied we could discern the alteration in the course of the other ship.

Yes, its course was changed, for we gradually lost sight of it, and it had gone on its way, neglecting our signals of distress.

We felt far from lighthearted after that, and more especially did we feel depressed when the captain told us that the ship was unmanageable.

We hoped for the best, and each tried to assume the lightest heart and brightest face.

Another day slipped by, and again the darkness of night made our situation still worse.

My father kept up bravely.

His superstition was his sheet-anchor; for he declared that while many of our ancestors had been wrecked while searching for the mysterious isle, not one had been drowned.

Two days before we could see land; now, scan the horizon as we might, not the faintest glimmer of land was in sight.

Captain Leonard was anxious and nervous. To him the loss of the ship meant much, for on his return he had been promised a share if he made a good passage.

"A sail!"

The joyous shout came from one of the passengers who was early on deck the following morning.

The captain raised his glass, and looked long and steadily in the direction. Lowering his glass, he muttered a few words to his first officer, and in a few minutes a rocket went whizzing and whirring through the air.

A minute later the gun was fired, and the flag of distress hoisted and lowered repeatedly, to attract attention.

We lost sight of the sail, for a mist was rising, and we began to lose hope again.

"Boom!"

Our gun thundered out, and its noise seemed so great that we almost wondered whether the ship was strong enough to stand the shock.

"What was that?"

"Hark!"

Silence, broken only by the splashing of the waves, was observed.

Again came the noise borne across the waters.

"Hurrah!" shouted one of the seamen; "they have heard us."

Our gun sent forth one more volley, and then an answering shot was fired from the other vessel.

The mist grew denser, until we were unable to see a quarter of a mile ahead.

At intervals the firing was continued.

The answer seemed to be getting nearer and nearer every time.

How we hated that fog! What would we not have given for a clear, bright day to see our deliverer approach.

Suddenly, without the slightest warning, the mist lifted, and to our great joy we saw a finely-proportioned brig close to us, ready to tow our ship into port.

The passengers were quickly transferred to the other ship, and, as it too was bound for Rio de Janeiro, we did not lose much by our mishaps, but gained in experience and knowledge of Neptune's wrath.

In Rio we stayed a month, getting ready for our overland journey to Chile, and arranging for a good stanch whaleboat to be sent round the coast to us.

We had a pleasant time in Rio, and I for one was loath to leave it and its tropic glories.

CHAPTER V.
MADRE-DI-DIOS.

LET it not be imagined that I had forgotten my darling in Philadelphia.

Her memory was ever with me; but I must confess that the excitement of travel, and the strange mysteries I was about to investigate, and perhaps unravel, possessed for me a fascination deep and lasting. I verily believe that when we arrived at Rio, had my father proposed returning and abandoning the search, I should have openly rebelled, and gone forward alone.

One thing grieved me much, my father seemed to be failing in health, his step was not so light and active, neither could he stand so much exertion.

If he were to give way, what should I do? I asked myself many times.

There were moments when I imagined I should seize upon the pretext of his failing health to urge him to visit the States to recruit.

I should then see my darling, and once more in her presence I do not think anything would be strong enough to tear us apart. At other times I vowed that should my father abandon the search, I would let him go home alone, and proceed with the adventure as best I could.

When we were ready to leave Rio, we changed our plans somewhat and took a coaster to Monte-Video, and then arranged to cross overland to Valparaiso. We followed the course of the River de la Platte to Parana, where we were so pleased with its climate and surroundings that we rested for several days.

Then on to Cordova, in the public diligence. When reaching this place our vehicle came to a sudden stand.

On looking out of the window we saw a band of ten or twelve men of the plains, who were well armed with pistols and formidable-looking knives.

We understood their object well, and knew that whatever of value we possessed would quickly change hands.

We had six passengers, of whom two were ladies.

To these we conveyed our money and watches, which they secreted as rapidly as though they were to the manner born. The door opened, and we were ordered out. A scowl passed over the faces of the bandits as they searched us and failed to find anything of value.

The ladies, as we expected, were not searched, and we were allowed to proceed on our journey, laughing heartily as we went at the thought of how we had outwitted the bandits.

We met with no further adventure until we reached Valparaiso.

Here we found our whaleboat ready for our use, and right pleased were we with it.

We got together a crew of three men well accustomed to the sea, and having a good knowledge of the Pacific Islands.

Numbering now a party of five, we felt strong enough to invade any island and hold our own against the belligerent natives.

Our first place of inquiry was the island of Madre-di-Dios.

The old captain from whom my father had received the casket and tablets was dead, but his son reigned in his place, and had some news for us.

He told us how a number of seamen had been wrecked mysteriously when approaching an island in latitude 27 south of the equator.

"But," said he, in pure Spanish, "one of the men is here, if your excellencies would like to see him."

We intimated that such was our desire, and a few minutes later a swarthy Chilean sailor entered the room.

His looks were bad enough to sink any ship, and there was but small wonder, in my mind, that he and his comrades had been wrecked.

"I was out in a fishing-boat," he said, when we had loosened his tongue by placing some coins in his hand, "when we lost our reckoning and drifted away from all our party. The night was dark and we got into a current which, *Santa Madre!* ran in an opposite direction to the wind.

"We seemed to be carried along swiftly, and though our sails were filled, the wind was powerless to change our course."

"Do you mean to tell us," I asked, "that the wind filled your sails, and yet your boat went in an opposite direction?"

"That is just it, senor. We then tried to pull away from the land we now, for the first time, saw—but though the wind was with us, we made no headway. The more we pulled the less progress we made."

The story sounded so much like a lying yarn that I had scarcely sufficient patience to listen to him longer.

When I appealed to my father he silenced me by saying in English:

"It is just what all describe. There is a magnetic current which draws all boats toward the shore."

The Chilean stood with open mouth, listening to our conversation, but not understanding a word.

"Go on with your yarn," I said.

"Yarn, excellanza! it is all gospel truth."

"Well, proceed, then."

"The boat, as I was saying, went toward the island with a rapidity which surprised us.

"We pulled until the blood spurted from our fingers, but it was of no use. The wind itself was not strong enough. *Madre di Dios!* it was the devil himself who pushed us forward."

"What then?" I asked, impatiently.

"Then? why, we dashed on the rocks, and at once a crowd of naked savages came scudding down and surrounded us."

"What did you do then?"

"Very easy to ask that, but the very memory of it haunts me yet. I was seized by five or six of them, and notwithstanding all the resistance I could make, was stripped of all my clothing. One of the naked devils stood by receiving my garments, and as fast as they were removed he put them on.

"When this fellow, who was evidently a sort of chief, had got on all my clothing, I was handed an old palm-leaf mat, which he had just discarded.

"Darkness was fast coming on, and, knowing that the natives of all the islands in that latitude liked to sleep as long as the sun was obscured, I guessed I should soon have an interesting experience.

"I was not mistaken; for I was taken up the side of a small hill on which stood a huge image, as ugly as the devil. This image—oh, *Santa Madre!* my arms and legs were made to embrace, and my hands and feet tied round it. In this manner I was left a prisoner."

"Did you stay there long?" I asked.

"No, only a night!" he replied, with a sneer; "but seven hours in a position where you could neither lie down nor stand up is not a joke by any means.

"I cursed myself, and everybody, but it did no good.

"The sun rose, and down came the natives, singing, yelling, and shouting, as I expected they would, to take their morning bath.

"My arms and feet were untied, and I was motioned to follow the crowd.

"After I had been in the water for ten minutes, I was ordered out, and again tied to the image. I asked who was chief, and the big fellow who was wearing my clothes answered, with a deep bass voice—'*He*.'

"'*He*, which he? What he?' I asked, getting mad; but before he had time to answer, *Santa Madre!* I saw the most beautiful-shaped man who ever lived come right down close to me.

"Every one of the savages went down on their stomachs and wriggled on the ground.

"'Loose him!' this fine-looking man said, and at once I was let go."

The sailor paused. He had told a long story and told it passing well. There were many things I was desirous of knowing, so I questioned him.

"Who was this man who ordered your release?"

"*He*."

"Yes, I know, but what I desire you to answer, is, what name did the natives give him?"

"They called him *He*."

"Was he naked and white?"

"No, he was dressed well, but a thick veil was wound round his head, so I could not see his face."

"Did you hear anything about him?"

"Yes; I was told he had lived there ever since there had been an island, that he was hundreds, thousands, millions of years old. *Per Baccho!* but they did lie."

"I should say so. But how did you escape?

"*He* looked at me, and then at some of the savage brood, and they got a boat, and putting me in, pushed it out into the water.

"Then, *Santa Madre!* the current would dash me against the rocks, but *He* stood on the rock and waved his hand. Well, do you believe me, just as he waved his hand, so the boat went."

The remembrance made the sailor tremble and he devoutly crossed himself several times.

I gave him some more money and asked him if he would know the island again.

To see his look would have made an artist's fortune.

His eyes turned up toward the ceiling, and he muttered a prayer.

"Know it?" he murmured. "Yes, but, *Santa Maria!* save me from ever seeing it again."

"I and my father, have a great desire to go there; will you not accompany us?"

"No, no, no!" he shrieked, and made a dash for the door.

It was easy to see that terror held him in complete subjection.

When he had left the room my father and I looked at each other in surprise and joyful astonishment.

Here we had a certain corroboration of the stories we had heard.

A man, clothed with power, living among savages, answering to the strange cognomen of *He*, and bearing the repute of centuries of life. It was passing strange!

Means must be used to get the sailor to return to the island or at least to direct us the course to take. He would prove invaluable as a guide.

CHAPTER VI.

CAPTAIN FJORD.

THE day we had settled upon for leaving Madre-di-Dios was stormy and the wind blew in those disagreeable squalls which render traveling unpleasant.

We decided to postpone our voyage for a few days. It was fortunate we did so, for that very evening we met a man from Philadelphia, who was spending his time exploring the Pacific Coast.

Being possessed of ample funds, and having no other object than the attainment of knowledge in view, he was ready and willing to join our expedition, and offered most generously to share expenses.

We had been careful to keep the real object of our journey secret; to all we had said we were antiquarians traveling for the purpose of examining the records of the past as carved in the caves and on the monuments of antiquity.

We had told our host that we were very desirous of visiting the mysterious island, ruled over by the king or chief *He*, but at the same time we laughed at the legends and stories which we heard.

Captain Fjord, our new acquaintaince, was, as his name indicated, of Scandinavian origin, and when I asked him why he did not Americanize his name into simple Ford, he laughed and declared that the Americans thought more of a foreigner than of a native, so he kept up his ancestors' way of spelling the name.

My father was delighted with the captain, and I must confess I liked him, though there was something which I could not describe or explain, which restrained me from giving him my full confidence.

It was necessary to give Captain Fjord some little idea of the main object of our expedition, and so father told him that he had reason to believe that some of his ancestors had settled on one of the islands of the Pacific, and we desired to find whether they had left any trace.

The captain thought the object an admirable one, and as it fitted in well with his own purpose, there could be no objection to our forming a united party.

The captain had some improved guns, which were far ahead of those we had brought from England, and altogether his outfit was superior.

By the extension of our courtesy, we were therefore likely to be the gainers.

Fjord's nature was cheerful. This was to me an enigma, for his thoughts dwelt constantly on death.

I asked him to explain the anomaly, and he answered that there was no cause for astonishment, as death was far more cheerful than life, and that my astonishment arose from my ignorance of both life and death.

His ideas were strange, and I noticed him often taking notes.

I did not like to be too curious, and so I could only wait and watch for an opportunity to still further understand our new comrade.

We had resolved—acting under the captain's advice—to delay our departure for two weeks.

The time would have passed pleasantly but for one thing. My father was gradually losing his health, and I much feared that he would be unable to stand the strain of our trip.

"By the way, Theo.," said the captain, "have you any ideas of a preceding state of existence?" I laughed and answered in the negative. "But I have," he said, quite seriously; "many passing trifles have, for me, a grave significance, because they present themselves to me in the light of reminiscences of a prior existence; but, not wishing to be duped by my imagination, I note down as often as possible all that strikes me, that I may recall it, and see if these impressions which I believe to date from a previous life, have not really come to me in the course of my present existence."

"Of course they have," I answered. "You are far too sensible a man to believe in such rubbish as a prior existence."

"It is not such rubbish as you think. Reason it out, and you will admit there is a very rational foundation for such a belief."

"I don't see it."

"Perhaps not, but you will, and more than that, you will yet believe that there is a way to prevent decay, and therefore death."

I was rather startled at such an idea coming from Fjord for he seemed to be a hard headed materialist on most points. I was the more surprised because we were in search of just such proofs as would be needed to uphold his ideas.

"My meeting you," he went on, "was strange, but it was necessary. I have wandered for years to meet with just such an affinity, but accident did for me what all my designs failed to accomplish."

"It is a strange coincidence——"

"For mercy sake don't use that word. You scientists imagine all such things to be the result of fortunate accidents or chance, whereas your very science ought to tell you there is no such thing as chance."

"How do you explain it, then?"

"Don't ask me for explanations, for I may ask you to tell me why the lightning will strike one tree in a forest and leave all the rest, why one man studies and experiments for years to achieve a certain result, while another with no scientific training will go to bed and dream, and in the morning do what the other has failed to accomplish. There is no chance, there should be no death."

I began to fear the captain was not quite right in his head, and a shade of regret passed over me at the thought.

Fjord had mounted his hobby and there was no such thing as stopping him.

"You know the religion of the Druids who taught the pure ideas of Pythagoras. With them there were three stages necessary to a perfect existence. In the first stage or cycle of *Annewm*, there is only darkness or chaos, which contains all the germs of life; in the second cycle, *Abned*, we have the era in which every animated being is derived from death. This is the cycle in which we are now living; the last and glorified cycle is that of *Gwynfyd*, r perfect happiness, to which man will eventually reach when he has undergone the necessary purification. This cleansing may necessitate migrations and transmigrations; a man's soul may descend to brute life, or be reincarnated in human life. My contention is that, by stopping waste and retarding decay, we can undergo this purification by a continued existence and not die until we are sufficiently pure to enter *Gwynfyd*, the state of perfect and absolute purity and happiness."

I could not clearly follow the captain in his arguments which, while they seemed plausible, looked like a jumble of Pythagorean and Druidic ideas, as they were mixed up and mystified by the Celts in Druidic times.

My father was, however, especially interested. His eye flashed with enthusiastic brightness, and he told me that, with the captain as his companion, life would be renewed to him.

"Do you believe in th   wonderful *He*, of which the natives speak?" asked my father.

"I do most assuredly, and think we shall find him, wrest his secret from him, and learn many things of which we have not even dreamt."

I now felt inclined to sneer. I was young, and had learned so much materialistic science that such peculiar ideas were only a butt for my ridicule.

Respect for our new friend, however, restrained me, and only indulged in an occasional sneer.

"You no doubt believe in the 'Wandering Jew,' then?" I asked sneeringly.

"Believe in Ahasuerus! Yes, as much and as fully as I believe in myself."

"And you really think there is such a being walking and wandering the world to-day?"

"I believe there are three human beings to-day who count their ages by centuries, and who have seen nations rise, flourish, and fade, and are yet young. Ahasuerus is one, this marvelous *He* is another, and there is the counterpart—an immortal, never-dying *She* somewhere in Africa, I believe, who too is able to laugh to scorn the whirlwind of the ages, and will live when even England, from whence you come, is no more than a memory, like Babylon."

"Oh, stay! you are laughing at me," I could not help exclaiming.

"No," interposed my father, "Captain Fjord is only putting into words the belief of my life. He could not have expressed my ideas more clearly had he read the thoughts of my brain."

"You, too, father?"

"Yes, Theo., and when you see through the film of materialism, which obscures your vision. I verily believe you will prove the truth of these ideas to the world."

"The truth will never be taught then, for unless I become insane I shall never accept such ideas."

"Before the sun returns in its course and twelve moons have passed, you will not only accept these truths, but swear to them as well," said Captain Fjord, seriously.

"Of that I am assured," assented my father.

I was not satisfied. There was a strange fascination to me in these ideas, and I inwardly resolved to follow them up, if only to expose their shallowness.

The very next day I was walking along the sea-shore, looking at the flight of seagulls, and wishing I had my gun with me that I might wantonly destroy one of the pretty birds, when Captain Fjord, reading my thoughts, said:

"And why should you wish to destroy a bird which is beautiful while living, but of no use dead?"

I could not reply. I was staggered at this unmistakable mind-reading, so I retorted:

"Perhaps you think the bird is the casket in which the spirit of some ancestor is to be found?"

"Quite likely."

"What absurdity!" I said, almost angry.

"Why is it absurd? You go on believing that millions of *new* souls are created every year, and that not one of them is ever destroyed."

"That is the belief of our religion," I answered, shifting the responsibility as much as possible.

"Which is the most absurd idea," he asked, "to believe that all the millions and billions of people who have lived each possessed a new and specially created soul, which is now inhabiting a world of which we know nothing, or to believe that the souls of this generation may be reproduced in some succeeding generation, and so on until purified?"

"You would then believe that my individuality may have had a prior existence?"

"It is more than probable—just as you can change the breed of animals until a new race is perfected."

"Oh, Fjord, stop. The ideas are too ridiculous."

"You asked for them, and I only give them in response to your desire."

"True, forgive me; but would not these ideas destroy religion?"

"On the contrary, religion would be more generally believed in; it would become a quickening spirit instead of a form. But leaving that on one side, are you not anxious about your father?"

"I am. I fear he is weakening rapidly."

"I don't think he will leave this island alive," the captain solemnly asserted.

"You alarm me. What can be done?"

"Nothing. It is the exhaustion of every nerve and tissue, every organ of the body. Believe me, Theo., you will be fatherless before the week ends."

CHAPTER VII.

A DEATH-BED.

CAPTAIN FJORD had predicted correctly. My father was dying. The native doctors had used all their skill, but were powerless to avert the inroads of the fell destroyer.

Then it was that I longed for the secret of life. What would I not give to possess the power of rejuvenation?

I would sacrifice everything I possessed, if only I could recall the health to those cheeks and the life blood to the veins.

I was powerless.

All my science was now at fault. True, I had been taught that death was inevitable, but it was none the less hard to bear.

To stand by and see the loved father, my faithful friend, the true philosopher, pass away; to know that I should never see him more, was agony more terrible than I can describe.

He was conscious, and knew that the call had been sounded, and he had finished his course.

"My boy," he said, as I drew near his bedside, "in a few minutes, perhaps, my breath will have left me. I want you to faithfully promise that you will continue my life-work. Go on with our investigation, without ever delaying on my account. I have put it off too long, but I wanted the glory to be yours. My wish will be fulfilled. You will possess ample funds."

He paused and sunk back on the pillow exhausted.

I began to believe that the vital spark had fled, but presently the eyes opened and the lips moved.

"Come here—closer," he murmured, softly.

I put my head down close to his, and then in a voice strong as when in full health, he said:

"Swear to continue the work."

"I do, father. I promise——"

"No, no; swear it. Swear by the mother you never knew, but whom I am going to join; swear by the father whose comfort you have been; swear by all you love and cherish, that you will never cease until you have solved the mysteries we set out to probe, or death intervenes."

"I swear it, father, dear. But do not excite yourself."

"I am not excited."

My aged father fell into a sleep as calm and sweet as an infant's.

For several hours he slept, and pleasant smiles passed over his face. In dreams he saw again the faces of those he loved, and his soul seemed to be ready to join them in the "great beyond."

When he awoke, his eye seemed brighter and his voice was clearer.

He desired Captain Fjord to come to him.

"Fjord, my friend, I am going."

"Yes, I am afraid so," the captain answered, candidly.

"I have known you but a short time, but I can trust you. Look after my boy. Be a friend to him."

"I will."

"I know it. Help him in his life-work, and, however chimerical it may appear, give him your assistance. I shall die happy if you promise."

"I do promise, Aristophano. I will do all I can to help, aid, and assist your son, for I love him as a brother."

My father stretched out his hand, and with ours clasped in his, he gently passed away. The flicker of life went as easily as thistle-down floats on the summer breeze.

I was alone in the world. It was hard, for he had been my only friend, never unkind, but always faithful and true—more like a brother or friend, a true companion during all the nineteen years of my life—and now I was alone.

In the sweetly pretty Campo Santo—"God's Acre"—we laid him, and above his grave the stately palm, the lordly aloe, and the fragrant magnolia fanned the breezes and perfumed the air.

It was a charming place of burial, but even the tropical luxuriance and the majestic grandeur of the scene could not rob the rites of their solemnity. Death was always terrible to me; but then it was more so, for it had snatched away my all.

I walked away from the solemn spot, leaning heavily on the arm of my friend, and that evening we began to arrange my father's things and assort his papers. In his pocket-book we found a piece of parchment which was yellow with age; the writing was so faint with the length of years that it was scarcely legible.

After some difficulty we were able to read and translate it, for it was written in Greek.

As I dictated, Captain Fjord copied it out, so that if the

writing on the parchment entirely faded away, we might have a faithful copy.

It read as follows:

"In the days when Khung-fu-tsze* was chief magistrate in the State of Loo,† and before he had been made minister of crime, he was desirous of sending some of his friends and disciples to a land over the sea where they could put in practice the precepts he had taught. Two junks were fitted out with everything which the heart could wish, and on each junk were four hundred men. Their tremendous sails caught the four winds of heaven, and quickly skimmed the seas. They reached an island in the southern seas, which had been described to them by Khung-fu-tsze. The gods had made a perpetual fire which was to be their guide. The junks were steered by the light of the fire which came out of a rock,‡ and when two moons had passed the land was reached. Here the men who were on the two mighty vessels of the deep landed, and elected one, Hatu, as chief or king, and made him swear that he would rule them with gravity, generosity of soul, sincerity, earnestness and kindness.§

"They gave to Hatu a residence which they called Ana Quena. The rest of the island was divided, and a chief or king elected to rule over each division.

"Now in the third year of the reign of Hatu, the god, Tabu, did bring to the island a white man of commanding presence, and the great god did order that he should receive the first fruits of all the people had, and should receive the homage due to a god.

"This white man, it was said, had power of death and life, and would live forever.

"No name was given, but in awe the people spoke of him in whispers, and when he had wrought many wonders among them, they became afraid of his presence, and always spoke of him as *He*, meaning thereby 'the mighty,' 'the only one.' Some of those who had lived many years on the island declared that '*He*, the mighty one,' was always young, and could give perpetual life to those he liked. The writer never saw *He the Mighty*, but on the island knew that *He* was worshiped.

"The island can be recognized by its great mountains of fire and its strange coast. At the entrance of its river the

---
* Confucius.
† This was about the year 500 B. C.
‡ Evidently a volcano.
§ Lun Yu, xvii., 6.

Eternal has placed a monument of the great Tabu, which can never be removed."

The writing puzzled us. The parchment was old and the ink faded, yet the form of expression was comparatively modern. After studying it for some time, Captain Fjord suggested that most likely it was the copy of some old legend, and that the copyist, who either wrote from memory or transcribed from another document, had put it in his own words and made it harmonize with the time when he made the copy.

This was plausible. We noticed the curiosities of idiom, and came to the conclusion that the parchment must have been written about two hundred years ago.

Another paper we discovered which told the same story in different language, and, furthermore, spoke of the great number of images on the island.

Still another document told us that *He* lived in a cave which had been the burial-place of the great ones, and that with him was a most beautiful woman, who was so ravishingly lovely that no one who ever looked on her beauty could live. To prevent such accidents, whenever any one approached the dwelling-place of *He*, the beautiful woman was at once turned to stone. Even then, though but a marble statue, men had been known to kill themselves after looking on her form, as they considered it a desecration to look on mortal after seeing the spiritual sublimity of the statue.

Even though sad with the memory of the dear dead one whose papers we were reading, we could not restrain a laugh at the absurdity of this marble Galatea, who reserved all her glances of love, and the wisdom of her lips, for *He the Mighty*, being stone to any one else.

"It may be," said Fjord, "that it is only a legend."

"Of course; it cannot be truth."

"Wait a moment, you impatient youth. I was about to say that it was a legend, perhaps, symbolizing the chastity and purity of a true wife."

"Well, that is all it could be."

"I am not so sure of that."

"Come now, Fjord, you are not going to tell me you believe a stone figure could become warm with life?"

"No, but I know the ancients had some way of suspending animation, and giving an appearance of death, or stone, if you will, to any one they pleased. After the lapse of a certain time the animation would return, and the hue of health be again on the cheeks."

I was compelled to laugh at this whimsical absurdity, and could not resist saying that it would be an excellent way to deal with a wife who was fond of flirting in her husband's absence. I almost began to think that Fjord was so full of absurd fancies, that our explorations would be ruined by his legends and queer whimsicalities. But in spite of it all, he was a good fellow, and with him I was prepared to carry out my dead father's wishes.

CHAPTER VIII.
I BECOME A CHIEFTAIN.

Two days later we heard of a merchant vessel which had called at Madre-di-Dios, and was bound for the Friendly Islands.

We saw the captain and arranged with him for a passage as far as 100 degrees west longitude, where we could lower ourselves into our whaleboat, and cruise about as we pleased.

The captain was perfectly willing to accommodate us, and was very facetious.

He told many a yarn of the cannibals, and said that Captain Fjord was so nice and fat that he wouldn't be a bit surprised if he was salted down or eaten fresh on the first island we touched.

We had a crew of three able seamen, Captain Fjord and myself, so the five of us felt able to make a gallant fight if occasion offered.

We had been away from Madre di Dios but two days when another misfortune befell us.

There is nothing which a sailor so much dreads as a fire at sea.

All other dangers and perils are only laughed at and joked about.

Icebergs, waterspouts, and thunder-storms are often the subject of merry jest and side-splitting yarns. Sharks and whales are treated with more respect, but not a shudder passes over the seaman as he speaks of them, but with fire it is different.

The very thought fills his soul with a dread and terror which nothing else can create. A sailor will cling to a piece of spar, and though he knows that death is almost certain, he will face it cheerfully; but once let the cry of "fire" be raised and the bravest will turn coward and shake with very fear.

Two days after starting message was brought to our captain that a portion of the cargo had taken fire.

"All hands on deck!" was the order given, and immediately instructions to close the hatches were acted on.

The seams of the hatches were closed, and every precaution taken to keep the flames below from being fed with the air.

The chart was consulted and we found that land was within twenty miles of us in one direction, but the wind was contrary and we could not reach it. In another direction we should make land in forty miles, and the jib-boom was pointed toward it and all sail set.

Our whaleboat was all right, and we had taken the precaution to place all our stores—both provisions, arms and ammunition—in its water-tight compartments.

Every rag of sail that happened to be on deck was spread, and the ship's boats were got ready to launch at any moment, in case the fire should break out before we reached land.

Small jets of smoke were seen ascending through the seams of the deck.

"It's all up with her!" said one of the men.

The sailors in their terror ran to the boats, and began clambering in, when the voice of the captain was heard, loud and strong:

"Not a soul shall leave the vessel until the fire chases us. I'll shoot the first man who gets into the boat without my orders!"

The captain looked determined enough to put his threat into execution, and the sailors were awed into submission. We could distinctly hear the roaring of the flames.

"Starboard!" yelled the captain to the man at the wheel. "Keep her full!"

I moved forward among several of the crew. All were anxious to leave the ship.

The fire was gaining on us rapidly, and all hope of saving the ship was gone.

A long, loud cry, which pierced the ears and struck terror to the hearts of the whole crew, was heard.

A man had discovered that the flames were lapping round the room in which over fifty kegs of gunpowder were stored.

"Man the boats!" cried the mate.

The captain pointed his pistol at his officer, and in a tone of desperation, cried:

"I shall not leave this ship until the last moment, and I forbid any doing so."

The command was wholly disregarded, for the men clambered into the boats, and left the captain and our party all alone.

We lowered ourselves into our whaleboat, and then seeing the captain standing alone on deck, I shouted for him to join us.

He folded his arms, and stood more like a statue than a living being.

"Come with us!" shouted Fjord.

The captain shook his head, and a moment later a noise as of many thunders rent the sky, and the brig was scattered in a thousand pieces over the surrounding sea.

A shower of water, fire and burning wood was thrown up toward the sky, and from the bosom of the sea there arose a liquid rolling mountain that moved over us, tumbling in pieces as it struck our solidly built boat.

I was far from being superstitious, but I could not help recalling the various accidents which had taken place since we left the English coast in our search for the unknown. We steered due west, and after tossing about for several days without adventure we reached land.

When we were about making for port we saw for the first time a native canoe, which is the best sea-going boat on the Pacific Ocean. The one we saw leaving Naba Isle was a double canoe about eighty or ninety feet in length. A stage or platform was built across the two canoes, and on this upper deck or bridge were erected apartments for storing food and merchandise.

It was rigged with one tall spar and a yard, and was manned by twenty-five naked blacks, under the command of a copper-colored man, who evidently owned the entire cargo.

We landed at Naba, and saw a sight new to me, and one which I shall never forget.

It was feast day, and the chief was seated on a dais, or platform, raised some four feet from the ground. He had for his dress an apron made of grass fiber, and on his head an old battered hat.

About a couple of hundred savages were ranged in a circle in front of him. The men were entirely naked. The women, who were about equal in number to the men, were in full dress, which consisted of a belt or fringe made of lapels of grass fiber, about sixteen inches deep, each lapel being about two inches wide.

The single girls wore a white ovula shell, hanging by a chain made of platted grass, on their breasts. The married women were utterly devoid of any clothing but the fringe or girdle, which the natives call "Ireeree." I noticed, however, that the married women wore a huge shell ring hanging from their nostrils.

In the middle of the circle was a huge fire, and in front of it stood half a dozen plump girls, without clothing.

Their arms were tied to their sides.

They were prisoners who had been taken, or stolen from some tribe of islanders, with which the Naba tribe had been at war. They had been kept close prisoners for a month, and had been fattened on the best of food, and were to be killed and eaten.

As we approached the circle, wondering what the great gathering signified, we heard the piercing screams of one of the girls, who had been seized by the priest, who is also the executioner.

Before we were near enough to prevent the murder, the priest had dexterously plunged a flint knife into her heart, and the life-blood spurted across the grass in a crimson stream.

With a quickness which would have astonished a butcher, he had carved the body into convenient pieces and placed them on a spit, which was made to revolve in front of the fire by means of a rude crank turned by a Naba woman.

The moment the priest seized the second girl, and raised his knife to take her life, I could not resist the temptation to raise my gun and take aim.

A puff of smoke, a report, and the girl stood erect, but her would-be executioner lay dead at her feet.

The moment I fired I realized that I had, perhaps, jeopardized the lives of all our party; but when the medicine man of the tribe had proclaimed the priest to be dead, each one of the tribe, including the chief, fell flat on his face.

We intended taking to our boat, but the strange proceeding held us spell-bound.

Before we recovered from our surprise, the chief had uttered some words which we could not hear, and we were quickly surrounded and carried into the circle.

"It's all up with us!" said Fjord.

"I feel it is," was all I could answer.

I felt ashamed of myself. What business was it of mine to interfere with the feast? Imagine my surprise when I was lifted from the ground and carried to the dais. I was then seated on the chair of state. Captain Fjord and my crew were placed in positions in front of me, and then every mother's son and daughter of the tribe fell down on their faces before me, and wriggled their bodies along the grass until they had got close up to the dais.

The old chief began jabbering away in a language I did not understand.

Fortunately one of the crew I had brought ith me was able to act as interpreter.

The conversation which followed may be better understood if I transcribe a portion of it from memory

"Juarana!" shouted the chief, and instantly every native repeated the word.

"That means welcome," said my interpreter. I was astonished. I did not see how I could be so very welcome when I had killed a priest and saved the lives of some plump girls who were to be eaten.

I merely made a salaam in response.

"Mariapa! mariapa!" shouted the chief.

"He means we are to go to the Council House."

"Heaven save us!" I ejaculated, for at the Council House, I felt pretty sure, I and my friends would be killed and eaten.

We were carried on the shoulders of some brawny blacks to a peculiar building or inclosure made of young saplings, and which was roofless.

On one side stood a chair or stool; this I afterward learned was the throne.

The old chief jabbered away, and my man told me he resigned the chieftainship in my favor.

Thereupon I was lifted on the chair, and on my head was placed a knife made of flint. This was the emblem of power.

The chief then gave a grunt, and a woman, as handsome as any present, who showed by the difference of dress and the wearing of a shell ring in her nose that she was married, was pushed forward until she stood before me.

The chief explained that she was his favorite wife, and he presented her to me.

I told him that I had no desire to rob him of so great a treasure, but a scowl of displeasure passed over his face, and I became a married man by accepting his gift.

An old woman was then brought forward, and I hoped I was not to be expected to wed her also. My fears were quickly dispersed, for the chief politely requested me to shoot her.

This I firmly refused to do, and then my interpreter told me that all the chief wanted was to see how I used the gun, and by what magic I took life.

I realized at once that we owed our present position to the marvels of gunpowder, so I suggested that some animal should be procured.

A puma had been captured the day before, and the chief had this brought to the *mariapa*.

It was in a wicker trap or cage, and I, having loaded my gun, asked that it be released.

All looked aghast, but my orders had to be obeyed, and the puma made a dash for liberty.

A puff of smoke, a report, and the puma's last breath had been taken.

"A god! a god!" was the burden of the cries that ascended to the clouds.

I stipulated that the fattened girls should be returned home, and, on parting with the chief, gave him some powder, to which he gave the name of *nookoo nee bulatangi*, or the great white man's sand.

We had seen enough of this strange people, and as I did not care to settle down with a black wife—my heart being with my darling in Philadelphia—we re-entered our boat, glad to escape with our lives.

CHAPTER IX.

THE IMAGE OF TABU.

WE steered our boat in a southwesterly direction, and found ourselves borne along swiftly by the ever-changing currents of the Pacific.

Storms do not often arise in that calm and beautiful ocean, and we felt our boat to be equal to any emergency which might arise.

No event of importance need be chronicled for the first few days of our sailing.

We passed round several islands, but made no attempt to land. Our recent experiences warning us that there was danger on shore, and as we had quantities of food, and everything to make life comfortable, we felt the bosom of the ocean safer than the islands, and sharks and whales more friendly than natives might be.

One night I was on watch, and saw before me in the distance a strange undulating line.

The more I looked at it the more mysterious it appeared.

I called to Antonio Esquival, the sailor who had sailed those seas often, and asked him what he made of the strange appearance.

It looked as though a narrow strip of land a mile or so in length had been separated from some island, and was floating on the tide.

I examined it through the powerful glass with which I took care to be provided, but could not ascertain what the object was.

Antonio answered not a word, but stood in speechless amazement, devoutly crossing himself.

"Call Captain Fjord!" I commanded, and in a few minutes he was on deck.

"What do you make of that?" I asked, as I pointed to the object.

"Some driftwood, most likely," he answered, shortly, not liking to be disturbed in his short time of rest.

"Driftwood!" I sneered. "Who ever saw driftwood a mile long?"

He took my glass, and, after peering through it for some minutes, said:

"Make for it. Our trouble will be repaid."

"What is it?"

"It is alive!" he answered.

"Alive! What nonsense. Why, it is a mile long, if it is a foot."

"A mile! It is five miles—and look!"

I directed my eye in the direction of the mystery, when, to my surprise—not unmingled with horror—I saw the thing gradually rise out of the water until it towered above the hills on an island in the distance. It looked like some gigantic flag-pole.

Gradually it turned round, as though prospecting, and then with a fearful noise it fell into the water.

The waves dashed mountains high through the disturbance, and though we were ten miles away, it caused our boat to rock and roll as though in an angry sea.

"It is the sea-serpent!" said Fjord.

"I wish it had been near enough to have had a shot at it," I said in reply.

"So do I."

That was the last we saw of it, and I was not sorry. Its fall would have swamped the strongest ship.

The sea again became calm, and we continued our course.

An hour later the sun sank below the horizon, and the sky was suffused with the most gorgeous golden tints I had ever witnessed. The king of the heavens, the great orb so often worshiped, retired to rest with a majesty well fitted for its own splendor.

The shadows of night began to gather quickly, and a darkness, awful in its grandeur, hung like a pall over the broad expanse of ocean.

The moon's silvery light gradually broke through the clouds, and as its rays fell upon the water I could not help contrasting the golden sunset and the silver rising of the moon.

In all creation there is nothing grander than a sunrise and sunset at sea, unless it be the silvery glistening of the moon's rays on the blue waters.

We were out of sight of land, when the angel of dawn sent forth its bright chariots to herald the birth of the sun, and when the rays of that glorious orb appeared above the horizon, when the streaks of red and gold sped on through the darkness, like spirits of light and love and majesty, shedding a halo of glory over all, the rich and the poor, the savage as well as the civilized, I did not wonder that the untutored should bend in worship before the sun. At length the sun had risen in its sublime majesty, and flooded the earth with its wealth of light and warmth.

Our charts marked land in the near vicinity, and we kept up a sharp lookout.

On we went, eager and excited, enjoying life as never men did before. Having but few regrets—and yet how sad I ought to have been, for my love was thousands of miles away, and my father lay buried beneath the palms.

Buried? Yes, but his spirit, I felt, was with me. I could feel the presence constantly, and, laugh as one may, there was a satisfaction in the thought that he was, perhaps, guiding our lives better than he could have done if in the earth-life.

"Fjord—look! What's that?" I shouted excitedly, dropping my glass on the deck as I did so.

"Where? what is the matter?"

"See! Yonder!" I exclaimed.

Fjord looked in the direction indicated, and saw a huge rock standing out clear in the line of sight, and shaped like a human being.

"What said the writing?" he asked, not deigning to express an opinion of the wonder.

"It said that we should know the island by the monument of the god Tabu which had been erected there."

"That, then, is the place."

It seemed as if a burden had been lifted from our minds.

At last we were near the solution of the mystery, at least so we thought. Little did we know how small was our capability of knowledge.

We pointed our boat in the direction of the island, and merrily we awaited the result.

As we neared the land we saw distinctly the figure of a man of gigantic proportions standing out clearly outlined against the sky. It presented a strange appearance. Was it the work of man or a freak of nature? The lines on the face seemed perfect, and I fell to wondering whether some race of men equal in civilization to the designers of the Sphinx had once lived there, and cut the monument out of the solid stone. I made a drawing of the mammoth monument as it appeared when a mile distant. The rough lines washed away by ages, perhaps centuries, I softened down, and tried to give an accurate idea of what the head was like when the last stroke of the sculptor's chisel had been given.

If the head was a freak of nature, it was far more perfect than anything which I had ever read about.

Who could have been its designer? Not a Chinaman who went over in the time of Confucius, for the design partook more of the Assyrian. Perhaps a prior civilization had existed there.

My reverie was cut short by Captain Fjord exclaiming:

"Look here, Theo., if you are going to sketch there all day, all right; but I would like to climb to the summit of the old god's head, and take a bird's-eye view of the place we have reached."

"Just as you please. Shall we make for land?"

"No hurry for that. I propose we get a good dinner first, then look well to our guns and knives, for we may have to fight for perhaps our very lives."

"Practical as ever, Fjord! Do you know I used to think in those days at Madre-di-Dios that you were too whimsical to be of any practical use."

"Did you, my boy? But let me tell you that Norse Fjord knows just when shooting is in order as well as any one."

"Did you call yourself Norse?"

"Yes, that is the name they were pleased to give me. Funny, isn't it? North Ford, for that is what my name means."

"It was a quaint conceit, truly."

"Whew!" Captain Fjord whistled as he stood on deck staring upward.

"What's the matter now?" I asked.

"Look at those sails," and he pointed to them.

They were full. The strong wind blowing from the shore filled them to such an extent that the ropes creaked, and the masts strained and groaned until we thought they would break; but what surprised us was that the boat was being drawn as though by a strong magnetic current toward the land.

"That beats all I ever knew," exclaimed the captain. "I'm blest, but one would think the Old Harry was drawing us."

Our skipper was aghast, and gave orders to furl the sails.

Instead of going faster it really seemed that we slackened our speed.

The skipper called us all together, and, with an oath, which I don't care to record, said:

"We are going to destruction. That's a fact, and I cannot help it. Our boat is moving in some current, the like of which I have never before known."

It was well to know the fate in store for us, but it would be impossible to swim to land, so we might just as well take our chances on the boat.

Gradually, but unmistakably, her speed increased, and gradually the land grew nearer. Old King or God Tabu looked as though his head would soon be lost in cloudland.

We saw that the coast of the island was faced by an archipelago of rocky islands, small in size, but dangerous to any ship.

Only very narrow channels were between them, and through these channels the waters shrieked and roared, hissed and rushed, like so many startled demons.

"No one could steer our boat between those rocks," I said, as I looked forward.

"No mortal could; but look——" And Captain Fjord pointed to what appeared to be a miracle.

We had given up all attempt to guide or save our boat, but all stood ready when she went to pieces to leap to land, or escape the easiest way.

What now more than surprised us was the fact that, utterly unguided, the boat drifted between the rocks and threaded its way through the fury of the waters, keeping exactly in the center.

In one case the channel was so narrow that the rocks on either side could be reached by our outstretched hands; but the boat glided through, guided and steered by a mysterious power greater than we could comprehend.

Now we had reached a part of the channel where the waters were black as Erebus. This was caused by the towering above us of two gigantic rocks.

Looking up as through a telescope, we saw that the one rock was the statue of Tabu. We now perceived how perfectly it was formed. Although towering aloft several hundred feet, it was exquisitely proportioned, and what surprised us was, that the minutest detail was carved in the rock. The god's feet rested on an immense bowlder which was just above high water. Opposite was another figure of a human being, and from the difference of garb evidently a female.

This monument was broken off just above the waist, and doubtless the upper portion was buried in the waters beneath us. Here was more food for speculation and thought.

The two figures formed originally, so we judged by the appearance of Tabu, a monster arch over the water, their clasped hands and arms making the archway.

Here was a proof of a civilization possessed by some long-forgotten people for which we were entirely unprepared.

We were drawn up the river rapidly by the same mysterious power, and strangest of all, the current seemed going toward the sea, while we were being carried from it.

CHAPTER X.

A GLIMPSE OF FAIRY-LAND.

THERE were fresh surprises in store for us, for as we looked ahead we perceived that the inlet or river ran in a zigzag manner for what appeared to us to be several miles.

The further inland we went the greater our speed. This was the more remarkable because we were really going up hill.

I stood up in the boat and looked back, when to my surprise, the level of the water on which we were then sailing seemed nearly on a line with the head of Tabu.

Captain Fjord for the first time began to show symptoms of fear. Such a strange thing had never before happened, at least in his experience, although he had traveled all over the world.

The skipper was white with nervous dread, and the other sailors were on their knees praying and crossing themselves most devoutly. We rushed madly along to what appeared to be certain destruction, for straight before us was a rock right in the center of the river. Our boat was pointed straight for it, and we knew that to strike it meant certain death, for the water bubbled and boiled in such a furious manner that we were convinced a dangerous whirlpool was there situated.

The skipper called on us all to seize oars and spars and try to push ourselves away from the rock.

With our united strength we tried to swing the boat round.

Snap went the oars, like reeds in a strong wind.

Our efforts were useless. We must resign ourselves to death.

I proposed jumping into the water; but, as Fjord pointed out, that would only be death a few minutes earlier.

The huge rock was only a few yards away. I was tempted to close my eyes, the sailors were on their knees, a few moments passed, and the boat was in calm water. Fjord told me that the moment the boat struck what appeared to be the huge bowlder the rock parted and allowed us to go through.

Immediately on the other side of this very obliging rock was a clear, calm lake. As I looked round, my eyes witnessed a sight which became impressed on my mind so indelibly that no power can ever efface it.

On the banks of the lake the scene was transcendently beautiful. Flowers of the most gorgeous colors were in full bloom, and their perfume was wafted to us on the zephyr-like breeze.

The magnolia lifted its head and its beautiful blush-tint flowers seemed—after all the barrenness we had seen—like blooms of paradise.

Birds of gay plumage sang sweetly, and seemed so tame that we wondered they did not perch on our boat.

Not a human being was in sight. Had we discovered **fairy-land?**

We could easily believe it, for no mortal ever made so beautiful a paradise. The lake and gardens—for so, for want of a better name, we had to term the adjacent grounds—formed the bottom of an immense basin surrounded by high and steep hills.

There was no sign of any habitation, and nothing to indicate th presence of man. Yet the grass was short, the ground well cultivated, and the trees carefully trimmed.

"This bangs Banagher!" exclaimed Fjord, as he gazed round.

"I'm blest if I can see the way we came in," said our skipper. after he had taken a good look on every side of the lake.

There was no trace of any entrance; the rocks seemed solid, not a crevice could be seen.

I, for one, felt it was all a dream, and I rubbed my eyes, bewildered at the strangeness of the scene.

Yet everything was palpable. We heard the birds singing, we inhaled the perfume I dipped my hand into the water, but quickly withdrew it, for the water, so clear and limpid, was almost at boiling heat.

"Nonsense, Theo.!" ejaculated Fjord, when I told him. "See, there are fishes swimming about."

I saw the fishes, but still I was certain as to the heat of the water, and did not feel satisfied until Fjord had plunged his hand into its depths, and as quickly withdrawn it.

"By Jove! my boy, but we are in for it this time!" he exclaimed, his eyes wide open with astonishment.

We pulled our boat to the side, and Fjord and I landed.

We cautioned the skipper and his crew not to leave the boat, but await our return.

This they were only too glad to hear, for I could see they were too nervous to make any further explorations.

We rambled about the gardens, trying to find some entrance or exit, but were doomed to disappointment.

The day passed, and night shadows were gathering over us, when to our great surprise the water began to look bright and phosphorescent.

As we turned our eyes to the sky, we saw heavy black clouds forming a canopy over the beautiful fairy lake and garden; but below all was illumined as by the pale moonlight, only the moon was invisible, and the light came from the phosphorescence of the lake.

The monotony was relieved by the appearance of half a dozen men.

They were giants in stature, standing, I should say, seven feet high; their color was lighter than a mulatto, and yet too dark for a Caucassian.

A broad belt encircled their waist, from which hung an apron made—as I afterward learned—of cocoanut palm leaves.

A sash of many colored grasses crossed their chests, and a kind of wreath of broad leaves encircled their heads.

These strange-looking men came near to us before deigning to show that we were noticed.

One, the tallest of the six, stepped forward, and in pure Hebrew asked:

"Who are these white men who dare invade the privacy of the great Tabu and his mighty chief, *He*, the mighty one?"

Fortunately my father had taught me many languages, and, having a taste for such studies, I became proficient, more especially so in Hebrew, which had a strange fascination for me.

I replied, making an Oriental salaam:

"We are from a far country, most mighty one, in search of truth, and at the feet of the great Tabu would like to learn it."

"You are expected."

"Expected, but by whom?" I asked.

"Several suns have risen and passed since the great and mighty *He* did say to his servant, who addresses you: 'Some white men are coming—make their way smooth; let the waters bear them straight, and take heed no harm comes to them!'"

"That is very good of the great *He*. Conduct us to the presence of your master."

A look of horror passed over the giant's face, and he turned to his companions and carried on with them a whispered conversation.

"What did the fellow say?" asked Fjord, who did not understand Hebrew. "And what gibberish was he talking?"

I explained to him, and gave him a *resume* of the conversation.

"How the devil did he know we were coming?" he asked.

"That was most likely Oriental imagery," I replied.

"Not so, for I'll be jiggered if any mortal could have guided our boat up that hill, traced our way through those rocks, and even opened them to let us through."

I had to acknowledge the mystery, but our private conversation in English was interrupted by the giant turning again and making a salaam.

"No man can see the face of *He* and live," he said.

"The old fool," I muttered in English, and then in Hebrew: "Have you not seen him?"

"Your servant, his servant, has served the mighty *He* from his youth up, but has never looked upon the light of his countenance."

"Where does he live?"

"That he will reveal himself, if it so pleases him, but

your servant loves life too much to forfeit it to his displeasure."

"Then what is his pleasure?"

"A feast has been prepared, and when the most worthy pale-faced sons of the East have partaken of it, they will need rest."

"All right; conduct us to the banquet."

"Thy servant will do the bidding of *He*, for he will not be disobeyed. Bid thy boatmen to follow."

I translated the dialogue to Fjord, and he was suspicious.

"The old villain will get us all into some cave or dungeon, and seize our boat; we shall then have no chance for escape."

"I don't see any as it is," and I waved my hands round at the somber cliffs and rocks which entirely surrounded us.

"You are right; but I for one will go well armed."

"So we all will, and then treachery will meet its reward."

We went back to the boat, and found the seamen still praying.

I bade them get their weapons and plenty of ammunition, and follow us.

We armed ourselves with guns and pistols, and in our belts we placed long knives, with keen, double edges.

The skipper had made for each of the seamen a rude cross, and in high glee he held them up.

"See," he said, "the devil will be powerless when he sees this."

We walked through the gardens, still bright with the phosphorescence, and found the giants awaiting us.

They leading the way, we followed, and when the steepest cliff was reached, we noticed the first giant gradually climbing its side.

"Have we got to get up there?" asked Fjord.

"It looks like it. See, there are steps."

The climbing was not near so difficult as it seemed, for niches had been cut into the side of the rock, and with these for our hands and feet, we climbed like human monkeys up the rock.

After ascending about fifty feet or so, we saw a narrow passage-way, or crevasse in the rock.

Through this—just wide enough for one person—we walked in Indian file.

After pursuing our way in almost absolute darkness for a hundred yards, we found the passage open out into a large cave.

For a few minutes our eyes were dazzled by the brightness which suddenly flashed up as we entered.

When we became accustomed to the light we saw a huge rock or slab in the center, on which were spread rude dishes fashioned from large shells and pieces of rock.

Round the cave were shelves or benches of rock, and on these we were bidden to seat ourselves.

No sooner had we done so than the giants disappeared, how, or by what way, we were then at a loss to explain.

I must admit that I did not feel at all comfortable, and began to wish that I had never started on such a foolish expedition.

Fjord was delighted. His fears had entirely gone, and he thoroughly enjoyed the adventure.

CHAPTER XI.

THE BANQUET.

WHILE waiting for the promised banquet we took a good survey of the cave.

The table in the center we found to be a huge stone platform about thirty feet long, twelve feet wide and a yard high.

It was supported by pillars elaborately chiseled, and the top was covered with carvings of human figures in every conceivable design and attitude.

On close inspection we saw that the carvings represented scenes in the history of some people.

What seemed remarkable was that some of the men were represented as half Hebrew, half Assyrian. Others seemed to be of Mongolian origin, and reminded us much of Chinese paintings we had seen at various times.

The walls were all cut in *bas-relief*, and over each series of pictures inscriptions in hieroglyphics were placed.

A portion of the wall seemed to swing open, and in walked several girls of about sixteen years old.

They were copper-colored, and with the exception of a girdle round their waists, the fringe of which reached nearly to the knee, were naked. The upper part of their bodies was tattooed or painted in various colors, and as they moved about presented a picture as bright as can be seen in a fashionable ballroom, when it is filled with ladies dressed in varied colors and in the most *decolette* fashion.

These girls placed on the huge table shells, which we found were to be used as spoons, long sticks like Chinese chop-sticks, and flint knives.

They went out noiselessly, and others, wearing a sash of white linen across their copper-colored bodies, entered, carrying a huge slab, on which were various fruits and flowers.

This they placed on the center of the table, and retired.

They were succeeded by two men bearing a large iron pot, from which the fumes of soup were rising.

The giant who had acted as spokesman in the garden, now entered the cave, and clapped his hands. This was the signal for the entrance of several girls, fantastically dressed. Their lower limbs were naked; a girdle was fastened around the waist, from which depended a fringe made of vine leaves; across their body, from the right shoulder to the waist, they wore a sash made of vine leaves and bunches of large black grapes. Their head-dress consisted of a wreath of magnolias, heliotrope, and jasmine.

Without uttering a word they took their places, one facing each guest.

We were seated far from the table, and on the shelves round the cave.

Another clap of the chieftain's hands and the girls turned, marched in single file to the men who were standing by the pot of soup, and held out a basin made of a cocoanut shell, highly polished, and incased in a kind of wickerwork, with handles on either side.

Into each cup or basin a quantity of soup was poured, and the girl would then take a shell spoon from the table, walk to the lower end of the cave and fall on one knee, holding the cup aloft before the guest.

I was the first one to be so honored, and I was at a loss to know whether to take the cup or allow the girl to be a human table and hold it. I, therefore, waited until all were served.

It was a sight to be long remembered. A brilliantly-lighted cave, a number of men sitting or reclining on a stone seat, and in front of each a girl, remarkably pretty and well-formed, dressed in vines and fragrant flowers, kneeling.

Fjord and I watched the giant master of the ceremonies, and found that we were not expected to take the cup.

The soup was good, extraordinarily so, but I have often thought since that even a very poor quality would taste excellent when served in such a strange but pleasing way.

When all the soup was drank, the chief, or "Father," as we heard afterward he was called, clapped his hands, and the girls rose from their knees and placed the basins on the table. Another signal was given, and each of our pretty waitresses approached a guest, bearing a large trencher of fruit—bananas and pineapple, the auona and guava.

It was explained by the "Father" that those who liked grapes should pluck them from the bunches which hung so luxuriantly from the sash of the waitresses.

Another troop of younger girls entered, and each brought a cup of milk, richer in flavor than any I had ever before tasted. Later I found that it was not the product of the cow, but was the juice of *gymnema lactiferum* or cow tree, a few of which grew on the island.

After satiating ourselves with the fruit and milk the girls withdrew. For this I was sorry; I was young then, and the novelty pleased me.

The "Father" clapped his hands and the table was cleared. A few minutes later pipes were brought in; and oh, shade of Sir Walter Raleigh, such tobacco! Never before or since have I smoked anything like it.

While we were smoking the young girls re-entered and gave to each a cup of hot tea made from *mate* leaves.

It was delicious and far superior to Chinese tea.

Our human vines then entered and wore, in addition to their fruit garland, a long shawl or wrap of exquisite white muslin or linen.

They, with no other accompaniment than the clapping of their hands, executed a wild but very beautiful dance, using the linen shawl or wrap much as do the Nautch dancers of India, but were even more graceful than those girls.

While the fumes of the tobacco filled the cave, almost overpowering the rare odors from the crowns of flowers worn by the dancers, their gyrations continued, but when the first pipe gave out—my skipper was the most rapid smoker—and all laid down their pipes, the dancing ceased and we were left alone with the "Father."

He told us we were to sleep on the stone seats and hoped we should pass a good night.

He had left us only a minute before another troop of females entered. They were much older and, forgive me for saying it, in consequence not so beautiful. They were armed with soft-looking fur skins, two of which were given to each of us, and then we were left alone.

When we felt perfectly secure from interruption we commenced to talk in English.

"I tell you," said the skipper, "we shall all be killed before morning. I don't like these heathen ways."

"My dear fellow," I replied, "you have a good gun, a sharp knife and the cross. What need is there then for fear?"

Fjord was delighted, but he too argued that we had been treated too well, and evil might come of it.

I laughed at his fears, and after arranging that during the long hours of the night we should keep watch by turns, to prevent any surprise or treachery, I fell asleep and dreamt of a paradise much after that pictured by Mohammed, where beautiful houris tended to my every want and lulled me to sleep with their sweet music.

My watch was to be the last, and when I was roused, a feeling of disappointment came over me when I realized that the paradise was but a dream.

I spent the two hours in thought. Why had we been so favored? Who was this *He*, whse power was so great?

I wondered whether it was not all *diablerie* or witchcraft.

CHAPTER XII.

WE GET MARRIED.

THE sun was high in the heavens before our cave was entered by the "Father."

I had carefully examined it and could find no way to escape if we were so minded. We were prisoners, securely incarcerated in the cave.

When the "Father" entered, and he seemed to glide through the solid wall, he bade us welcome, and hoped we had slept soundly and well.

A meal, consisting of fish and fruit, with bread made of yams, was served, and we began to wonder whether we were to be allowed to see daylight.

The giant "Father" said something in Spanish which was welcome to us, although we did not understand the meaning. But all our party spoke Spanish, and, therefore, it was better than having to interpret every word to my companions.

I told the "Father" so, and then in that language he explained to us that *He* always spoke in Hebrew, but that his household used Spanish as the general language. The natives and all outside spoke a dialect or language which was a strange compound of Chinese, Spanish and Polynesian.

"Were you born here?" I asked, my curiosity getting the better of my discretion.

"No; I came from Montu-Kaokao when I was two years old, and was trained by, and under the direction of, *He*."

"And you never saw *He*?"

"Many times, but never saw his face; that is always

covered, except when any one is to be killed for wrong done, and then——".

The man paused, evidently wondering whether he was doing right in telling us. I waited anxiously for him to continue. After reflection, he thought it well to tell us, and so continued:

"When any one is to be killed, he is taken before *He the Mighty*; all withdraw, leaving the culprit alone with *He*. The moment the veil is removed, one flash of the eye strikes sudden death to the culprit."

"That is lively!" I remarked.

"It is true; the great Tabu gave the power to *He* before the city was destroyed."

"What city?" I asked, incredulously.

"The great city of Akahauga, where dwelt people, as many as the sand on the seashore or the hair of thy head, oh, paleface!"

"What was the city like, and how destroyed?" asked Fjord, growing intensely interested.

The old man paused, and seemed to be reflecting.

"I cannot give dates that you would understand, but the wise king, Solomon, ruled in Jerusalem."

"You mean to tell me that this mighty *He* has lived here thousands of years?"

"He lived here before this cave was made, before these images were cut."

"Who told you so?" asked Fjord, rudely.

"Every one knows it; and I have seen a writing graven on wood, and with the superscription of Khung-fu-tsze, Chief of Loo, commending his people to the care of the mighty *He*."

The sailors crossed themselves and muttered some prayers, and Fjord and I began to think we had got among some strange people, who were evidently *non compos mentis*.

"But come!" and the "Father" beckoned us to the wall, which instantly opened, and led us to the rocks over-looking the garden and the lake we had seen the night before.

We were not sorry to breathe again the pure air of the garden, and to our joy we saw that our boat was safely moored. There were the five of us and the "Father," standing beside the lake, when the thought occurred to me that this was a most democratic island, for the seamen were treated as our equals.

I ventured to put a question bearing upon that subject to the "Father," and he answered:

"All guests of the great Tabu and his mighty *He* are equal; when they are not equal their flesh is given to the dogs."

Our conversation was stopped by the entrance of a number of girls, who, evidently, had come out of true feminine curiosity, for they walked boldly up to us, looked us in the face, examined our clothes, marched round us, and then retired a distance to consult.

They were all fine, handsomely-proportioned girls, varying, I should say, from sixteen to twenty years of age.

They wore a kind of gown, which hung in graceful folds from the shoulders. Their faces were light as a Mongolian's, but the lips and nose approached nearer to the Polynesian. Their hair was curly, but light-brown in color. They certainly differed from any tribe or race I had seen or read about.

This was also the opinion of Captain Fjord and my skipper, both of whom had traveled largely in the South Seas.

Wondering what the girls were talking about, I turned to look at them, when one, certainly the handsomest in the crowd, came running toward me.

She seized my legs and threw me to the ground. I was angry, and felt inclined to strike her; but no sooner had I fallen than she began kissing and hugging me.

I struggled to my feet, the girl clinging to me, and then the "Father" came and declared us to be wed.

I had been chosen by the girl, and to refuse her would have meant banishment, perhaps death.

My wife—for so I suppose I must call her—looked at her companions with a satisfied expression of face, and her example was quickly followed; Fjord and the seamen each getting a wife the morning after they landed on this strange island.

I questioned the "Father" about this strange custom, and he told me that the girls were from the inner circle of *He*, and had been sent by *He* to choose a husband from among us.

The "Father" further informed us that our new wives would guide us about the place, show us all worth seeing, and that, unless we accepted the girls as our wives, we should never have a chance of seeing the power and majesty of *He the Mighty*.

I arranged with Fjord and the seamen a series of calls and cries in case of any emergency, and cautioned them always to keep together, so that in need we could unite our forces.

I found my new wife—who answered to the name of Rapa Tepithe—very intelligent. She spoke Spanish very well, and had picked up a few words of Hebrew. The dialect of the natives, I learned from her, was partly Polynesian, and contained a smattering of French and Tahitian.

I questioned her about the island, and all she could tell me was that it was generally called Teppithe Hemma, or Rapa Nui, but that the great people ruled over by Tabu and *He* had no connection with the savage barbarians across the hills.

As she told me this, her head was raised in lofty disdain, and the pride of race showed itself clearly.

I had time to examine the rocks, and found that the lake was the crater of a huge volcano; the rocks were covered with lava, and presented a most brilliant and many-hued picture as the sun shone on them.

CHAPTER XIII.
TAKING HOME THE BRIDE.

RAPA TEPITHE led me through a secret opening which she found in the side of the lava-covered rock, and into a long passage. We were followed by Captain Fjord and his bride, but the seamen could not be induced to go into the cave.

The passage was very dark, and I kept stumbling over the loose rocks. Rapa kept hold of my hand and dragged me forward.

After traversing the narrow *crevasse* for several minutes we saw a streak of daylight before us. This was welcome, for I had a great dislike to the darkness. The light got nearer, and a moment later we emerged into the open air.

We had passed through the mountain and stood at an elevation of some hundreds of feet overlooking the island.

In the valley beneath I could see the ruins of a city. Houses and large buildings had evidently, at some remote period, stood where now desolation reigned.

Wherever the streets intersected—and their lines were clearly marked—stood a great platform on which we could see a group of statues.

These, Rapa told me, were the idols worshiped by the people in the days that were gone.

"Do you not worship them now?" I asked.

She shook her head, and then made reply in a whisper:

"No, not since the mighty *He* found the great white god which he keeps in his own residence."

"Tell me of that great white god," I said, and with a lover's rapture I clasped my arm round the dusky girl's waist.

"Oh, but she is lovely! Her great eyes haunt you when they are seen, her lips look as though they would speak; but oh! she is so cold; the stone is nothing to it."

"Whom are you speaking of?" I inquired.

"The great white god in *He the Mighty's* palace."

"Is this god stone, then?"

"Yes, to all but *He*. When he wills it she becomes warm and full of life, and they say loves him, oh, so much!"

"Where are we going to next?" I said, getting rather giddy with standing on a narrow ledge of rock so many feet above the valley.

I suddenly remembered Fjord, and wondered what had become of him.

My companion divined my thoughts, and put me somewhat at ease, as she chanted:

> "He hath been led captive by love;
> Love the eternal; love the grand;
> The sun shines and gives life.
> Love is to man the sun of his life.
> Oh, my love, sweet art thou, and fair;
> Thou art my own, and none can part us;
> *He* has willed it, and in solitude
> Thy friend woos his love, and tastes its sweets." *

This is as near a translation as I can give of the weird chant which was borne upon the morning air from Rapa's sweet voice.

I was further told that Captain Fjord had been taken by his bride to her own residence, as I was about to be taken to mine.

It appeared to be the custom of this strange people for the females to provide a home to which they took their husbands. I further learned that after a man had been married two years, his wife could, if she so desired, present him with a new wife. If she did so, the tribe rewarded her by raising her to a higher rank. At the end of five years more the man could choose another wife for himself, but the first wife bore the title of the great mother, and was specially honored.

Rapa took my hand, and in a kind of chanting or intoning voice said:

---

* The Dutch admiral, Raggewein, brought back from the South Sea Islands, in 1722, a love-chant very similar to that intoned by Rapa Tepithe. Perhaps it had been chanted to him by some loving Tabitian.

"Come, my beloved—we will hie us to our home—
 The home where love is, where the great spirit Tabu shall bless my
  beloved——"

"We have to go down there," said Rapa, stopping her chant suddenly, and pointing to the ruined town beneath us.

"But how shall we reach it?" I asked, a cold, shivering sensation passing over me.

"That is very easy. Come."

She laid herself down on the ledge of rock, and looked over its almost perpendicular sides, and then turned her face up to me, and said:

"It is quite safe, but don't look down, do just as I do."

She then gathered herself together almost like a ball, and shot her legs out over the cliff, hanging on to the rocks by her hands.

I grew sick at the thought, for, to my inexperienced eye, there was nothing to prevent us meeting certain death.

I called on her to come back, but she laughed.

"Come, my beloved, to thy bride and her home."

She loosened her hold on the rock and dropped. A sickening sensation crept over me, and I was certain my bride of an hour was a mangled corpse.

"Come!" she shouted; "it is quite safe. I await you."

I have ever been of a daring disposition, and I did not like to feel that I could not do the same feat I had seen performed by a woman.

I slowly and cautiously lowered myself over the side of the rock, not daring to do it as she had done; and then, when I felt my whole weight hanging on my hands, she called out:

"Drop!"

With a muttered prayer for safety, I did so. The moment she gave the command, I felt her seize me by the clothing, and as I dropped she pulled me toward the rock, and I found myself in a cave some ten or twelve feet square.

She was sitting there laughing, and then she kindly pointed out the danger I had escaped. About nine feet from the top there was a narrow ledge about twelve inches wide. This was the flooring of the cave.

The feat of dexterity she performed was swinging her body toward the cave as she fell, and so landing inside the cavern. Had she not seized me by the legs and pulled me toward her, I should have struck the ledge, and gone bounding down to the ruins beneath, a distance of some hundreds of feet.

"Is this the way you always go home?" I asked, nervously.

"No."

"Is the other way easier?"

"Yes, my beloved."

"Then why did you bring me this way and endanger my life?"

She looked at me, her eyes flashing with the love-light, and made reply:

"Oh, my beloved, I wanted to know if trust was in you. I said you were safe, and you risked your life by trusting to my word. You are brave, oh, my beloved."

If any young wives read this true history of my adventures, I earnestly entreat of them not to put their husbands to such a terrible test of faithfulness and trust as I had to undergo.

After sitting in the cave a short time, she rose and motioned me to follow.

At the opposite side some rude steps had been carved or hollowed out of the stone, and down these she led me.

Another cavern was reached, and here Rapa suggested we should sit and rest.

She seated herself and asked me to join her, when, to my horror, I saw that her seat was composed of a pile of skulls.

The sight was horrible, and I shrunk from it, holding my hand over my eyes.

"Oh, you poor pale-face!" she lisped. "see, there is no harm;" and she took up one of the skulls, and commenced throwing it up and catching it, as one might a rubber ball. I was horrified; and not wishing to scare me too much, she rose and continued her journey down the steps.

At the bottom—and it seemed that we must have passed down hundreds of steps—we came to a pool of water about ten feet wide.

There was no way round it, for the entire space was covered with the water.

"We have to cross it," she said.

"But how?"

"Jump it."

I looked across. Ten feet was not much; I had often leaped a greater space than that; but here I must make a standing jump, and if I missed—what then?

"Is it deep?" I asked.

"Listen!" And then Rapa took a heavy stone and dropped it into the water. Several seconds passed before I heard it strike the bottom. I knew the water must be at least a hundred feet in depth.

"If the pale-face lover is afraid, Rapa will carry him."

It sounded like a taunt, and so I prepared to jump.

Rapa cleared it as easily as if it had only been a foot across, and then I braced myself for the leap.

I struck my foot on the opposite side, and slipped into the water.

Rapa seized me by the collar, and, with the strength of a giantess, lifted me up out of the pond or well, and shook me free from the slime and green stuff as she placed me on the bank.

CHAPTER XIV.

MY NEW HOME, AND A DISCOVERY.

I BECAME wearied of married life before I had been a benedict six hours.

I do not think many would wish to undertake its cares and responsibilities if they had to drop over a perpendicular rock, with only about twelve inches of foothold to save them from a fall through space on pointed and jagged rocks five hundred feet below.

Then, saved from one calamity, to have to leap a wellnigh bottomless pond, and get pulled out by the bride, would be sufficient to dampen the ardor of the most passionate lover. Yet this was my predicament, and I wished my bride at—— Well, anywhere so long as she was powerless to test my trust further than she had already done.

My troubles were nearly at an end, for we now found ourselves amid the ruins of the city.

Rapa traversed the old streets, and then suddenly disappeared.

She had been several paces in advance of me, and I was mystified.

A deep hole in the ground, however, was just in my path, and Rapa's voice, bidding me jump down, assured me of her place of hiding.

I was desperate, and obeyed her command.

The cellar into which I jumped was only three or four feet deep, but had the appearance from the surface of being three times that depth.

I landed safely on my feet and was told to stoop down and descend some steps.

With lover-like obedience I obeyed and soon found myself clasped, with iron-like grip, in the arms of Rapa, who sang, with a sweet voice:

"My own, my beloved,
The sun is in the east,
And my beloved
Is in my chamber.
He is in my chamber;
He treads in my footsteps, and comes to me."*

The bridal-chamber and residence of Rapa was a cave or cellar, hewn out of the solid rock, and, evidently, dated back to the time when Akahauga was a great city.

On one side a shelf or projection from the wall was used for couch or bed; some thick fur skins laid upon it, and it looked comfortable enough but for one thing. Instead of a pillow, a large thigh-bone, evidently that of a giant, was laid across the slab, and one of the fur skins thrown over it, making a slight elevation for the head.

On a large slab in the center of the cave a light was burning, but, oh, horror! the lamp was composed of a skull resting on a tripod formed of three leg bones.

Some linen strips served as wicks, and they projected from the eye-sockets of the skull.

The part formerly occupied by the brain was filled with some kind of fat, which furnished the volatile oil for the wick.

Everywhere bones were used; seats were made of them, bones crossed made ornaments on the walls. while from every corner a skull grinned at the inmates of the dwelling.

I found that Rapa would sooner go without food than lose these ghastly reminders of the future of all.

A steaming pot of soup was soon made, and I was able to do good justice to it; plenty of fruit and a cup of *meta* followed, and although I was not waited on by a troop of pretty damsels as on the previous night, I thoroughly enjoyed the first meal prepared for me by my new wife.

While I was partaking of the supper, Rapa had prostrated herself before a small wooden image in one corner, and before I could induce her to join in the repast, she moved the image to the table.

It was our family god. Not very handsome, but Rapa told me that no other resident of the island except the great *He* had one half so handsome.

---

* This song of Rapa's is almost identical with the Confucian ode contained in the "She King," part I., book 8, ode 4, generally attributed to Confucius himself. It is certainly strange that such a similarity of idea and language should be found in a South Sea island, unless the tradition is true that the island was peopled by Chinese sent thither by Confucius.
—EDITOR.

I made a sketch of it, so that if opportunity offered I could compare it with others.

This family god was made of a dark yellow toroiniro wood, and seemed to have been carved centuries ago.

Rapa told me that Tabu himself had specially blessed this god, and that *He the Mighty* had uncovered before it. This was a great honor.

To me the idol did not possess much beauty. The ears were too large, the eyebrows too heavy, and the head disproportionately long, but Rapa told me, when I dared to offer my criticisms, that the pale-faces from the East were no judges of beauty.

The night passed pleasantly enough, although I had a conscious feeling of being buried alive, and I felt as though I should suffocate. What had become of Captain Fjord? Where had the seamen got to? These things worried me a great deal, for I had not too much confidence in this strange people.

The morning dawned, but not a ray of light pierced the darkness of the cave.

A loud blast on some horn roused me from my slumber.

"Come, my beloved!" said Rapa, holding out her hand.

She was now standing near the lamp, which cast a glimmer over the room.

I proceeded to dress, but she stopped me and half dragged me across the cave. Wondering what her movement could mean, I ventured to ask if that was a part of wifely duty in Rapa Nui.

She laughed, and told me it was the custom to take a bath before breakfast. This suited me exactly, for I felt in need of a refreshing dip into the clear, cold water; but I could not see why I was not allowed to dress.

Some more superstitions—for my wife told me that misfortune would come if I put on garments without first taking a bath.

I noticed she was in a state of nudity, and had wondered why she did not dress, though her garment only consisted of a single loose gown.

It was necessary to humor her, and so, grasping her hand, I, Theodosius Aristophano, a collegiate from an aristocratic college, who had been considered somewhat of a dandy in the ballrooms of fashionable society, might have been seen running across a dry, parched plain, with a young woman, both habited in the garb worn by Adam and Eve before female ingenuity devised a fig-leaf apron.

Arrived at a beautiful sheet of water, I was joyfully surprised, though my blushes told of my shame at being seen naked. I saw Captain Fjord and all the seamen similarly unadorned.

We plunged into the water, which was far from cold, and enjoyed the bath immensely.

After dressing we breakfasted, and then we all wandered forth to look at these strange people's manner of cultivating the soil.

Everything seemed done under the direction of a "Father," and each who received such designation was a giant in stature.

The spade used by the agriculturalists was made like a spear-head, and seemed to be fashioned from flint.

Although small, it was surprising how rapidly the soil was turned over, and the fruits, vegetables, and corn grown testified to the perfect system adopted.

Fjord told me he was heartily tired, and suggested we should find a way to reach the mysterious ruler—god or king—who was known as *He*.

Failing to find him, he desired to leave the island and travel to some country where there would be a wider field for research.

When I told him of the ruins of the great city, he changed his mind, and was willing to live his entire life on the island if he could be allowed to explore its ruins.

We made an excuse to our wives, who kept as close to us

as shadows, and started off to see if we could discover anything worth preserving in our records.

We entered a cave, and found by the accumulated evidences, that it had been used for the purposes of burial.

I had no liking for bones, whether animal or human, but I verily believe Fjord would have been happy if he were allowed to open the graves and examine the bodies of those who had been dead for years.

This cave delighted him. It was amusing and yet horrible to see the way he would take up a bone, smell it, examine it, take out a measure and note its proportions, and then throw it on one side, as if it had never had the slightest interest for him.

"Whew!" he whistled, after a long silence, during which I was vainly trying to read some hieroglyphics scratched on one of the walls.

These hieroglyphics interested me very much, but the more I puzzled over them, the more obscure their meaning seemed to be.

"Copy them, old boy, and at your leisure puzzle over them," Fjord suggested.

"A good idea; that is just what I will do," I answered, and then I made a copy of the one which had so interested me. It was like this:

"Come here when you have made your copy," he called out from a recess in the cave which he had entered.

I followed that voice, and saw him holding in his hand a beautiful model in white stone of a female arm.

"By Jupiter! but that is lovely!" I exclaimed, for it was the most perfect piece of modeling I had ever seen.

"Lovely! I should say so; I would like to find the whole body."

"I believe you Fjord; you would then have something equal to the far-famed Venus."

"Yes; as superior as nature is always to art."

"I don't follow you; what is superior to art?"

"Why, nature, Theo."

"Of course; but we are talking of this arm."

"So am I. Can you tell me what substance this is?"

"Is it not marble?" I asked in reply.

"If this is marble, it is a kind I cannot classify. I don't believe this is stone at all. See the veins, and even the pores of the skin. I think it is an instance of metamorphism."

"You do? But I don't think I quite understand you yet."

"Then to explain to you, each and every organism in undergoing metamorphosis follows the composition of the earth where it is placed. There was a Florentine of the last century, I think his name was Legato, who found a way of transforming vegetables and animals into jasper; and I have seen most beautiful polished slabs for tabletops made out of matter which originally was organic, both animal and vegetable. I am even now searching for this secret, which I believe the ancients possessed."

"Very learned, Fjord, I dare say; but what has that theory to do with this marble arm?"

"To be very plain with you, Theo., I believe this arm was really and truly once a portion of a living human being."

"You are mad."

"Not quite; but I am going to test it."

He drew a small vial from his pocket, and, loosening the glass stopper, allowed a drop of the liquid to fall on the arm. Instantly the stone began to bubble like lime under the action of the acid.

"It is not marble, you see," said he; "and now for another test."

He raised a heavy stone and tried to chip off a portion of the arm. It was so hard that it resisted all his efforts for a time. When he succeeded, he held the fragment in his hand and examined it closely.

"See," he said, "every vein, every muscle, each fibre can be traced through the arm. It is not marble; it is a perfect petrifaction of a lovely female arm. Oh, how I wish I could find the whole body!"

Rapa's voice was heard calling me, and I was so recently married that I left the cave to rejoin her.

Captain Fjord followed, bearing with him his precious relic of a lost art.

When Rapa saw it she called to Fjord's wife, who bore the name of Milo, and, laughing, declared that she should be jealous if I carried about other girl's arms.

CHAPTER XV.

ACROSS THE MOUNTAIN.

A WEEK passed without any event of importance transpiring.

I was beginning to get impatient, for we seemed to be as far off as ever from reaching the presence of *He the Mighty*.

The "Father," who told me his name was Tanoa, came to the ruins, and, with many a bow and salaam, desired an interview with me.

I sent for Fjord, and then desired Tanoa to make known his wishes.

"The sons of the East who have married the daughters of the South are honored," said the old man in tolerable Spanish.

"Most reverend 'Father,' we thank thee," I responded.

"The sun shines!" said he, whereupon Fjord nudged me in the ribs, but I kept my gravity, and profited by the lessons I had learned from my wife, so I replied:

"And the moon reflects the light."

"Good! good!" he ejaculated, well pleased to find me falling into the metaphors and imagery of his people.

"What does the great Father Tanoa wish of his eastern sons?"

"The sun has shone on the moon. The great and mighty *He* has decreed that his unworthy servant, Tanoa, shall invite his people to a trial of skill, and that the sons of the East should deign to be present."

This was a long speech for the giant, and he uttered it as though his responsibility was greater than he could bear.

"The pale sons of the East will be there," I answered; and then asked: "Will the Sun, the mighty *He*, be present?"

"He will; but take care, or a glance at his bright majesty may kill you."

"I am not afraid," I answered. My heart was beating with tumultuous joy. The long looked-for time had come at last. We should see *He*, this mysterious man, angel or fiend, to discover whom we had traveled many thousand miles.

Fjord's joy was even greater than my own. Rapa was nervous. She declared that the presence of *He* always meant the death of some, and generally strangers were put to death by the lightning flash of his eye.

Milo tried to prevent Fjord from going; but he, cunning man that he was, suggested that the danger would be greater in staying away.

Early next morning Tanoa gathered together all his followers, and bade us prepare for a long journey.

We traveled across the valley in which were the ruins of Akahauga, on the outskirts of which we were met with a cloud of driving dust. When we had crossed the valley we commenced the ascent of a steep hill.

I looked up and found that smoke was pouring from the summit.

This I pointed out to Fjord, who recalled the writing which spoke of the fires at the top of the mountains.

We found the first part of the ascent easy.

Rapa kept close to me, her devotion was commendable, and I am pleased to be able to chronicle it.

Let me here digress long enough to say, that though I had accepted the conditions of life on the island, and had adopted Rapa as my wife, my heart was still with my darling in Philadelphia, and I only bowed to the inevitable, for had I refused to take a wife, my life would have been forfeited; therefore, gentle reader, do not blame me for inconstancy, for even a savage wife is better than death.

We climbed up the side of the hill until we reached a huge crater or gap, blown out of the side, and large enough to put a good-sized building within it.

Fjord called to me and asked if I had noticed some bright, greenish-yellow flowers.

I had not seen them, and so we stepped back to look, when, to our amazement, we found the fancied flowers to be a stream of burning sulphur flowing down the mountain side.

Tanoa called to us to keep to the left, and Rapa became so fearful that I should get into danger that she seized my arm, and held it in an iron grip.

The hill now became very steep and difficult to ascend, the lava ash lying loose and slipping under the feet with every step. After climbing about a hundred feet or so, we found a long rope lying directly down the slope; this was a great help to us, for, by its means, we were enabled to climb with rapidity about four hundred yards.*

At the upper end the rope was attached to a big rock, and after reaching that the ascent was easy.

The mountain is an awful sight. In the center of a top that must have been more or less level, there is a long crater with scoria on its sides, and as far as I could see, on the bottom also. The edges are fringed with yellow and red burning sulphur. All around huge stones of lava were lying.

I was told the mountain bore the name of Anaquandoa, and was situated in nearly the center of the island.

The mountain where I stood presented an appearance of

* The Maoris of New Zealand for many generations have had ropes made of grass and hemp down the sides of their volcanos. The rope at Mount Tarawera, near the Maori town of Ohinamuter, is nearly five hundred feet long.—EDITOR.

some huge rock torn and rent by fires and earthquakes, and I could not help thinking how insignificant man was amid such wonders.

We were ordered to descend. Tanoa and his giant council or guard going first, Fjord and Milo next, while Rapa and I followed as closely as was safe.

A body of natives divided us from the skipper and his men, who had managed already to quarrel with their wives.

When about half way down the hillside, orders were given to camp for the night. We were considerably astonished to find how rapidly the day had passed.

An impromptu feast was served, consisting of bread and fruit, and for drink a plentiful supply of milk from the cow-tree. This was carried in bags made out of the tanned stomachs of goats.

Never in the whole of my travels since, and there are few parts of the world unvisited by me, have I seen anything grander than night on that mountain side.

The sky was clear and the stars glittered like so many millions of gems set in an azure ground.

The summit of the hill had the appearance of a gigantic flower garden, the beds being illuminated with various colored fires.

In one patch the greenish yellow of the burning sulphur would present a gorgeous array of varied forms; then the dark-red of molten lava merging into the bright-green of some liquid copper ore. It was a sight which needs the painter's brush rather than the pen to depict. As soon as the sun rose we continued our journey.

Everywhere we came across ruins of houses and palaces, in some cases gigantic pillars of granite, inlaid with ivory and gems, stood erect as so many finger-posts telling of a civilization further back than any records of history.

Platforms of stone, some highly polished and as smooth as any table could be, were constantly met with, and Rapa delighted me with the legends of the past.

Then we came to a huge camping-ground, in the center of which large blocks of stone stood in order forming a circle, similar to the Druidic ruins of Stonehenge in England.

I ventured to ask Tanoa the meaning of this circle.

He told me that in this enclosure a council of gods took place in the early ages of the world. That then the small island on which we stood was the only land created. It was a subject of discussion whether any additional land should be ordered to rise out of the sea, or the island to remain as the only resting-place for the gods.

Xinhtecuhtlitletl, the god of fire, who presided, threatened all manner of catastrophies unless other land was created, and to show his power he blew his horn, whereupon a multitude of eruptions took place; the atmosphere was charged with sulphurous vapors, and the sun and every object became yellow

Chalchicueye, the god of the water, became so alarmed that he gave orders for the waters to divide, and from their midst rose the islands of Rapa Ita and Montu-Kaokao.*

"It was here," continued Tanoa, "where the great god Tabu flying through the air deposited the great and mighty *He*, and clothed him with god-like and imperial power."

Rapa added to the information later by telling me that on the camping-ground to which we were hastening, a similar group of stones would be found.

Fjord and I had taken care to bring our guns and pistols with us, so as to be prepared for any emergency which might arise.

As we were going down the hill-side a strange-looking animal, which was neither goat nor deer, but seemed to partake of the peculiarities of both animals, crossed our path at a distance of some eighty or a hundred yards.

Without waiting to think, I raised my gun, took quick aim and fired.

The animal leaped into the air and fell back dead.

The effect on Tanoa and the natives was surprising, for they fell flat on their faces, and commenced a dirge in a low, monotonous tone of voice, which caused the strangest sensations to pass over me.

I looked round, and saw that out of the hundreds who accompanied us, only the five of our party were standing. All the rest—women and men—were lying prostrate.

"By thunder, you have done for us now!" exclaimed Fjord, as he stepped over a number of prostrate natives, and took his place by my side.

The seamen followed his example, for the idea seemed to have seized upon all that my life would pay the forfeit for my daring deed.

When the chant was finished, Tanoa raised his voice and commanded all to stand. Then a confused babel of sounds broke on our ears.

The gibberish was unintelligible, for nearly every dialect and language, from Spanish and French to Chinese, Tahitian and Polynesian, was heard mingled together in confusion.

Orders were given—but what they were I did not understand—but instantly a litter composed of long poles and fur skins was made, and I was lifted on it.

* In the Aztec hieroglyphics we have a similar legend or tradition, and the names of the gods have a very similar spelling.—EDITOR.

My shot had the effect of saving me from any further walking; for the remainder of the day I was carried shoulder high; and whenever my bearers grew tired, there seemed to be almost an angry contention as to who should have the honor of bearing my weight.

We camped again that night, and before the sun had risen three hours the next day, we had arrived at the great camping-ground where we were to see *He the Mighty*.

CHAPTER XVI.
A TRIAL OF SKILL.

WE were now in the midst of a great plain. On every hand the mountains rose, forming a natural barrier, and shielding the plain from the searching winds and breaking the force of the scorching sun.

There were but few trees, but what there were grew tall and erect, though of very small diameter.

The vegetation was but meager, and contrasted unfavorably with our first glimpse of fairyland on the banks of the warm lake.

Near to the highest hill stood a monster stone platform, which, originally, Tanoa told me, was used for the sacrifice of human beings before the god Tabu came to reign over the island.

On the hill there were plainly seen traces of terraced forts and earthworks, very similar to those made by more modern people for the purposes of defense in wartime.

A great body of people, some thousands in number, had gathered on the plain.

Some were as black as Africans, while others were more nearly allied to the Caucasian races.

It was a strange sight, and one which I shall remember.

Tanoa was evidently the favored "Father," for all made way for his giant band and large family to take their places in front of the great platform.

I was still carried in the litter, and was not allowed even to stand a moment until the platform was reached, when I was thankful to be allowed to exercise my legs by a little healthy walking.

I was heartily tired of the cramped position I had been compelled to endure in the litter.

Fjord was gloomy, for he fully expected, as did I, that instead of honor, degradation and most likely death were in store for me.

I could now plainly see that numerous caves and passages opened out from the hill, and I argued that some of these subterranean roads led to the residence of *He* himself.

I turned round, with my back to the platform, and saw the vast concourse ready for the sports.

A number of armed men, arranged in companies, drew up in front of the platform.

They wore a breast-plate looking more like a large tin saucepan lid than a coat of mail, or shield, and their arms consisted of rude battle-axes and spears.

The battle-axes were made of some kind of metal, but what kind it was difficult to say, as they were unpolished, and looked, in the distance, far from sharp. Below is a sketch of a battle-ax, one fifth of the size of the original:

While I was examining and noting the armed men, I heard a loud blast from a trumpet, and instantly every one, soldiers included, fell flat on their faces.

I say every one, but that is wrong, for our party of five stood erect, like the sole remaining soldiers on the field of corpses after a battle.

Then, 'mid the blare of horns with their harsh and discordant sounds, a procession emerged from the cave.

First came two torch-bearers, the torch consisting of a human skull, from the eyes of which the wick and flame protruded; then followed a score of girls, shapely and beautiful, their long hair hanging gracefully down their bare backs; a girdle of many colored grasses and leaves encircled their waists, and on their chests hung as a pendant an ovula shell.

These girls, an advance guard evidently, took their places in front of the stone platform.

As soon as they were in position. a gigantic man, who must have stood over eight feet in height, hideous in feature, and having huge rings in his ears and dependent from his nose. emerged from the cave, bearing a human skeleton which had been fixed to a pole, and from whose shoulder-joints, and between each rib, a sickly flare of light was seen.

It presented a most horrible appearance.

This was followed by a stretcher or litter, borne on the shoulders of four young girls. On the litter lay another skeleton, which was also utilized as a torch.

I examined one of these human lamps later, and found that under the bones jars filled with fat or tallow were placed, and from these came the light.

Then another procession of girls, arrayed in gowns hanging loosely from the shoulder, and swaying far from gracefully as their wearers walked.

More skeleton torches preceded a statue of the god Tabu, which was followed by another bevy of girls, decked out in feathers and skin aprons.

The horns sent forth a loud, shrill blast, and a magnificent litter, and yet one which was awe-inspiring, emerged from the cave.

A gorgeous canopy, made of beaten and polished gold, was upheld at each of its corners by grinning skeletons.

In the center of the litter, seated on a chair composed entirely of skulls, sat the great and mighty *He*.

He was enveloped in long, filmy, muslin robes. hanging so full that while he was able to see through them, no one, a yard away, could distinguish his features.

His head turned round, as though gazing on the assembled multitude, and then seeing us standing, he called for Tanoa.

That worthy "Father" wriggled like a huge snake on his body until he reached the platform, and then, with his back turned to *He*, ascended it.

Again he fell on his face and wriggled forward until *He* placed his foot on Tanao's head and bade him rise.

That was the end of the ceremony, for Tanoa conversed freely with his great master and made neither obeisance nor salaam afterward.

Tanoa descended the platform and came across to our group.

"The great and mighty *He*, who lives forever and knoweth all things, hath ordered the palefaced sons of the East to stand upon the platform made sacred by the holy foot of Tabu and the mighty *He*."

We were then lifted bodily, as easily as though we were but children, to the platform, and placed. Fjord on the right and myself on the left of *He*.

The seamen stood at the back of the throne of skulls.

The horns blew another blast, and all scrambled up from their ungraceful position, and stood with arms folded, waiting for the sports to commence.

A space was cleared, and two young natives stepped forward, making a low bow to *He*.

A thin mast or pole, thirty feet long and about two inches in diameter, was then stuck in the ground at a distance of one hundred feet from the men.

Tanoa clapped his hands, and one of the young warriors stepped forward and received a spear handed him by Tanoa.

Seizing it by the middle of the staff, he raised it above his head and flung it with a sharp jerk.

A whiz and whir, and the flagstaff or post was split down the center.

The other warrior then seized a spear, and at a signal a pole was flung into the air a hundred feet away.

The spear whizzed through the air, and cleft the pole in two before it fell to the ground.

The native spears I found were made of rods with sharp pieces of thin obsidean firmly attached to the end fashioned in this way:

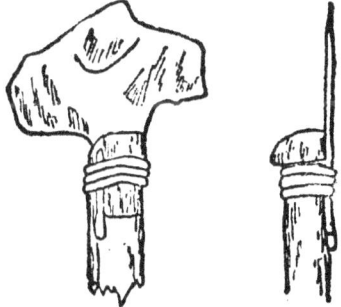

Fjord and the seamen cheered these deeds of skill in hearty fashion, and a song of praise was chanted by the people.

Tanoa was in deep conversation with *He*, and then suddenly walked away, making a low salaam as he did so.

Approaching where I stood, he bowed low, and said:

"Oh, most mighty pale-face—lord of life and death—the great and mighty *He* hath been told of thy deeds of skill, where by means of a stick the death-dealing smoke is sent, and by the aid of the mighty one his enemies are subdued."

By this wonderful speech I understood that my shot at the animal had been noised abroad as something beyond the human. and I was evidently invited to give an exhibition of my skill.

I clearly perceived that I was to be the recipient of honor instead of degradation. and the thought came to me that my comrades should share in the glory.

Obtaining permission to converse with Fjord, I suggested to him that as he was the best marksman he should first exhibit his skill.

I accordingly left the platform and walked about a hundred feet away. I then took the shattered flagstaff and affixed my pocket handkerchief to the top.

All the natives saw was a puff of smoke, all they heard was the report of the gun, but the handkerchief had a hole torn clean through it.

He stood up and bowed his head to Fjord.

A skull was then fixed on the top of the post and I was bidden to fire at it.

I was successful and knocked it clean off.

We were great men, almost as great in the estimation of the people as *He* himself.

After several other exhibitions of skill the space was cleared. and the three troops of girls marched into the center of the circle. A strange wild dance was executed. The dancers whirled round, turned somersaults, clasped hands, leaped over each other, and all seemed the wildest confusion. yet there was a grace about it which was surprising. A number of men took their places in a circle round the dancers, each holding in his hand a skull.

As the girls whirled round the skulls were thrown to and caught by them, they throwing them back to the men, the dance continuing all the time.

For several minutes a shower of skulls filled the air.

When would the gyrations stop?

Endurance could not last much longer.

Then commenced a scene of brutality—one by one the girls dropped utterly exhausted; their companions continued their dance, trampling on their fallen sisters until they must have been bruised and bleeding.

The dance continued until every dancer dropped from fatigue, and the day's sports were ended.

He gave orders for the procession to reform, and the warriors, torchbearers and litter-carriers returned to the cave, the pretty dancers being left on the ground to recover the best way they could.

Tanoa told me afterward that some of the girls were sure to die from the over-exertion and the bruises, but that was of no account, as Tabu would reward them by giving them good husbands in the happy hunting-ground to which they would go.

CHAPTER XVII.

IN THE SACRED CAVES.

AFTER all had retired, Tanoa came to me and said it was the command of *He* that Fjord and I should stay in the sacred caves, and await his pleasure.

The seamen were to return, as were also our wives Rapa and Milo.

I am ready to confess that while I was very desirous to penetrate the secrets of this wonderful *He*, who, in my mind, was but a common juggler, who worked his magic for his own ends, yet I was loath to lose Rapa, who was so useful to me in explaining the ways and manners of the people, and besides seemed to be a sort of protection. Still I felt resistance would be useless, and so allowed myself to be conducted into the sacred cave, closely followed by Fjord.

I intended insisting that we should share the same apartment, for I had no desire to endure solitary confinement.

This, however, was just what was intended, until Tanoa, seeing how obstinate I could be, and also, perhaps, fearing the effect of my gunpowder, which to him savored of the supernatural, at last consented that Fjord and I should both occupy the same cave.

We were led into a spacious cave hewn by man out of the solid rock, which we were told was to be our dwelling-place until *He* ordered differently.

Over the entrance hung a mat or rug made of palm-leaves and grass, and a lamp, formed out of the inevitable skull, hung down from the archway in the center of the cave.

Fjord was not long examining the walls, and came to the conclusion that we were in an ancient sepulcher or burial place.

On the walls were numerous inscriptions, many of which

were utterly unintelligible to us. Others we were able to read, and, as we anticipated, they referred to the departed inhabitants of the ancient city, whose dust mingled with that of the cave.

One inscription was in Chinese, and told the legend of Tabu and *He*.

It stated that in the early days (no date was given) *He*, a priest of the most ancient Isis, had gone to Lybia (Africa), and had there learned the secret of perpetual life from a great and mighty woman, who alone with the gods possessed the knowledge.

He loved another, and *She* was jealous, whereupon she tried to kill *He* by her magic. *She* would have succeeded had not the great and powerful god Tabu desired to wreak his vengeance upon *She*, and so stole away the body of *He*, slaying and leaving in its place *He's* double. *She* was blinded, so the change was never discovered, but to the end of time, or until *She* loved a mortal, her weary life would be spent by the body of the double of the man she loved.*

The inscription was very verbose, but I have condensed it and given in English a free and fair translation.

This origin of *He* accorded with several other records we had come across, and I jubilantly expressed my opinion to Fjord that we were on the verge of a great discovery.

A bounteous repast was brought to us by a girl who did not speak; this was so strange that we questioned her on her silence, but either she was well trained or was a mute, for not a sound could we obtain.

After refreshing ourselves with the food, and washing in some of the natural basins which were filled with water, I suggested we should do a little exploring on our own account.

To this Fjord readily assented, and so we journeyed forth, taking care to note the way, so that there would be no mishap in returning.

Taking one of our skull lamps, we crept quietly down the passage, past several openings, each covered by a heavy curtain.

When we had arrived at the end of the narrow passage, not daring to pull aside the curtains of any of the rooms for fear of disturbing some of the inmates, and so, perhaps, meet with our death, I was on the point of returning when Fjord seized my arm.

"Look!" he said, in a whisper, "here are steps, and a ray of light is beyond. Come!"

---

* These early inhabitants of Rapa Nui seem to have had a similar superstition to the German *doppelganger*, or double.

We crept noiselessly up the steps; the walls, which we touched on either side, the way being so narrow, were wet and slimy; snakes riggled under our feet and hissed as we stepped over them.

I began to wish we had not attempted the journey, but was too much ashamed to confess it, so followed close on Fjord's footsteps.

The light seemed no nearer after half an hour's walking.

I nearly stumbled over a skull which had been dislodged by Fjord and rolled under my feet. Regaining my equilibrium, I discovered an opening covered by a palm-leaf curtain, which had escaped Fjord's attention.

I called to him to return. The passage was so narrow that he could not turn, so had to make his way backward to where I was standing.

The cave we had discovered was evidently a tomb, but an air of warmth and comfort seemed to pervade it; this we soon discovered was a fact, for a fire was burning and several lamps suffused a mellow light over the dark cave.

The walls were covered with skins, and the place looked more wholesome than any we had yet seen.

But the moment we entered, we both—as Fjord afterward confessed—felt a strange feeling of oppression. A something hard to describe. We felt that we should suffocate—our breath came fast and heavy, and a fear like a horrible nightmare hung over us.

I laughed at the feeling, and said jestingly that it was because we were naughty boys, looking into what we had no business to examine.

Fjord tried to laugh at my boyish folly, but it seemed impossible. A moment later he had felt his way round the cave and found that the rugs or skins hung close to the wall except in one place.

Desirous of knowing the reason of this one hanging loosely, he drew it aside and, mute with terror, he sank back, nearly falling over me.

In his fright he had pulled down the rug, and as I looked I found myself face to face with a motionless, white female figure. Its eyes were fixed on me with a penetrating stare, and I recoiled, trembling with fear. I tried to get out of the cave, but in my excitement I failed to find the entrance. Fjord had fallen in abject terror on the ground. Closing my eyes to see the figure no longer, and striving to recall my reason and senses, I at length resolved to brave the apparition by boldly approaching it.

How I cursed my stupidity, how I laughed at Fjord and myself! The object of our senseless terror was a statue, life-size, enveloped in a graceful drapery of marble.

I rallied Fjord and jested with him until he looked again at the statue.

He felt it—icy coldness responded to his touch; he struck it with his signet ring, and the stony substance was apparent. He raised his head and looked into the face, when we both noticed a strange thing.

When we looked at the figure first, its eyes were wide open, staring at us, now they were closed.

That we were both very certain about. Could we have imagined it? No: the thing was too palpable.

Fjord said it was the sad human expression of the eye which had so frightened him. I felt the same, and yet the eyes were closed.

The mystery grew deeper.

We gazed long on the figure which was so admirably modeled. It was of a remarkable type. The face was partly Grecian, of the type seen in ancient statues, and more perfect than that of the modern native of the classic land. The nose was small and delicate, the upper lip short and full, the mouth small and well shaped. We had noted these particulars down when Fjord quoted:

"A perfect woman nobly planned."

"But hang it," he continued, "I wish I could see those eyes, they are too beautiful to be hidden."

I seized his arm and pointed, for I was too horrified to speak, for we both beheld the eyes wide open; they looked so natural that I could have sworn they were human.

"You see what imagination will do," said Fjord, "for I could have sworn the eyes were closed."

I looked up.

"They are closed," I gasped.

It was true; the eyes were once again shut with their marble eyelids.

Fjord laughed heartily. "All imagination," he said again, and we both tried to think so.

We continued to examine the wonderful piece of marble, the statue perhaps of some goddess.

The head inclined slightly to the right, and the right hand supported the drapery which covered the left shoulder and fell under the right arm in heavy folds.

As a statue it was perfect. Every part of the skin could be seen, the blue veins on the temple stood out just as naturally as in life; the hand was delicately molded, and through the clear skin the veins and tendons were plainly discernible.

"Come away; we have seen enough," said Fjord, trying to drag me away; for I was fascinated and spellbound.

I took one last look, and, oh, Heaven! I could swear I saw the eyes look at me and then close.

I was about leaving the cave, when a strange feeling came over me. I thought I was being pursued by the statue.

My blood seemed to turn to ice in my veins, my brain swam, and I should have fallen had not Fjord caught me in his arms.

He dragged me out into the passage, when I revived sufficiently to reach our cave. Once there our courage returned. I say our, for I am convinced that Fjord was as greatly frightened as I was.

We laughed at the adventure, but I could not really believe it was all imagination, more especially when Fjord told me that just as I was falling in the way in our cave, he fancied he saw the statue lean forward as if to see That was just the feeling I had the instant I sank into my comrade's arms.

A few more such adventures and I fear I should

We tried to sleep, but though Fjord was soon in the land of dreams, sleep would not visit my eyes that night.

CHAPTER XVIII.

HE.

BEFORE Fjord awoke the next morning the mute—if such she was—brought us a good breakfast and replenished our lamps.

We were full of the night's adventure, but neither cared to begin the conversation.

Fjord would commence. What do you think——" and then stop as though at a loss for words.

"Was it imagination?" I would urge, but like him pause as though fearful of even discussing our escapade and strange discovery.

We were relieved when Tanoa entered and bade us prepare to visit *He the Mighty*.

He gave so many cautions that it would be next to impossible to remember one half of them.

We followed one giant "Father" down the long passage some little distance, when we were met by two warriors armed with battle-axes.

Tonoa gave the password and they separated and allowed us to pass under the curtain into a large cavern.

We crossed this, and a challenge was given by our guide which brought out two more warriors armed with a kind of mace, made of hard wood, ending in a knob of large size and of the same material.

Another password was given, and we entered the second chamber.

As we approached the inner room, Tanoa bade us take off our boots, and crawl on our hands and knees.

We were about to refuse, when the stern looks of two more armed men convinced us that it would be better—this time at least—to carry out the instructions given.

The curtains parted, and we entered on all fours.

Many a laugh I have had since at the quaint figure we must have cut as we passed under those curtains.

"Rise!"

The word was uttered in Hebrew, in a voice sweet but loud.

We stood up, and found we were in the presence of *He*.

The cave was no better than the one we had slept in. It had evidently been a tomb.

In each corner stood a grinning skeleton, and everywhere skulls were seen.

He, closely veiled as we had seen him on the camp-ground, was seated on his throne, or chair of skulls.

While we were looking round, Tanoa had stood, his head bent waiting commands.

"Go!" and *He* pointed to the entrance, through which Tanoa passed.

"Now, strangers, pale-faced residents of a world I have long since left, what is your mission here?"

"Travel and knowledge," I replied, boldly.

"Is that all?"

"What more is there, or can there be? Is not knowledge all powerful?"

"Yes, and no."

"Teach us, most great and mighty *He*."

"For centuries, no one has looked upon my face and lived, yet I am tempted to withhold my power and unveil to you. Will you accept the risk?"

"We will!" answered Fjord, boldly.

"Take care, oh! rash stranger, for the lightning of my eye has slain stronger men than you."

"I am not afraid of thy magic, still I, with humility, acknowledge thy power."

"Magic!" said *He*; "and what is magic? When the traveler sees the work of past ages, the natives tell him the palaces and monuments were the work of magicians. The artist demands mastery over the past, a conception of the future—that is magic. Science discovers, art creates, therefore art is greater than science."

There was a charm about the few words uttered by *He* which we had never experienced before.

"But will not science tell us of a way to baffle death itself?" I asked, growing bold.

"You always babble about life and death. If you would live forever would you do so?"

"I would."

"So would I," added Fjord.

"Is there a pleasure in outliving all you love, to see every human tie broken, to witness the decay of nature and the destruction of cities? Is it sweet to live to be forgotten, to find the utter corruption of everything earthly? No; there are some who would wish for death rather than such an existence."

He had risen and shaken from him the loose veil-like shroud which encircled his person. As the veil fell to the floor, it seemed as though a shock of thunder had burst on the cave. He looked at Fjord, and as their eyes met my comrade raised his hands with an expression and fell back startled and unmanned.

"Save me, I doubt no more!" he cried.

"There are then forces in nature more powerful than any Norse Fjord has yet encountered?" *He* asked.

"How know you my name?" asked Fjord.

"By the exercise of my will. I read the secret thoughts and know all that actuates men, else how did I know you were going to visit me?"

"Did you know it?"

"Was not everything prepared? Did not your boat ascend the stream when, by every law of nature you know anything about, it should have gone in an opposite direction?"

"True, oh, mighty *He!* But will you deign to explain the mystery?"

"I willed it."

"You believe, then, that matter is subject to mind?" I asked, feeling greatly interested in the conversation.

"I know it. See, I say to yon chair of skulls, come, and it obeys."

Sure enough, for the chair passed rapidly across the cave.

He waved his hand over the chair, when instantly every skull separated from its fellows, and a heap of skulls took the place of a well-fashioned chair.

We stood and marveled greatly at this strange exercise of power, but our astonishment was greater when he gave another wave with his hand over the heap of skulls, and instantly, as though by unseen spirit hands, the chair was again built.

"It was by this power that I guided your boat up the hill."

He sat down; the chair was solid and substantial; we remained standing, not from choice, but simply because there were no seats for us.

I began to weary of standing, when *He*, reading my thoughts, beckoned with his finger, and instantly two chairs glided in and placed themselves imperceptibly near us.

Oh, that there were some way to describe the appearance of this remarkable person—I dare not say man.

He was dressed in the costume of an Egyptian priest of about the time of Moses.

His face was a study; it was handsome and pleasing, yet there was a something about it which savored more of the marble statue than the human being. The eye was large and full, and possessed a power which would make the strongest quail. His age seemed to be the perfection of manhood—certainly to all appearance he had not reached the time when the physical powers decline.

The marvelous exercise of power which we had seen, was sufficient to convince us that, whatever may have been his origin, *He* certainly was possessed of such gifts as would give him dominion over savages. Nay, even in more civilized countries his power would cause him to be respected.

"I have taken a fancy to you both, pale-faces from the East, but say, whence comest thou?"

Fjord spoke up:

"Surely the same power which gave you my name would tell you my residence?"

"Not so! See!" And *He* was not at all displeased at the bold answer.

When *He* uttered the word "see," the curtains gradually were drawn back by some unseen power, and in a recess stood a large ball of pure crystal.

It stood on a tripod of hard wood, and was so nicely balanced that, though firm, it looked as though a breath would disturb it.

"Approach and explain what you see."

Fjord and I stepped forward and looked into the crystal ball, when, upon its smooth surface there appeared an excellent representation of old Independence Hall, in Philadelphia. Before we could utter our surprise, the unmistakable features of Captain Fjord were visible on the globe, and under the superscription, "Norse Fjord."

"Do you now understand how I knew your name?" *He* asked.

"I see my picture and name, but I don't understand," answered Fjord.

"What building was that?" asked *He.*

"Independence Hall, in Philadelphia," answered the American, proudly.

"I never heard of it. In what country and whereabouts?"

Captain Fjord grew eloquent in his description of the scenes enacted in the old hall, and of the birth of a nation.

"Is this country you speak of greater than Egypt?"

"Egypt—a poor, miserable, one-horse place like that!"

"Stay, Fjord, or I may slay thee. Look thou in the crystal, and behold the place thou revilest."

Passing in panoramic order across the crystal, we saw Thebes, not in ruins, but in all its grandeur and glory. We witnessed the pageantry at the crowning of Pharoah, and saw the glories of Philœ.

"All that has gone," said Fjord.

"Gone?"

"Yes. Egypt is but a name, a memory, a poor dependency now."

"Alas, my poor Egypt!" For a moment *He* was sad and silent, and then rousing, turned to me.

"And thy country, stranger? See!"

I looked, and before me passed scenes of England, then Greece, with Athens in all its power and magnificence, and then a female figure was thrown in relief on the crystal.

"'Tis she!" exclaimed Fjord.

"Who?" angrily asked *He,* his face distorted and disfigured with the blackness of passion.

"No one. I only fancied I traced a resemblance to a friend."

"Oh! take care! But, boy, what seest thou? Who art thou? Tell me, or I will slay thee."

"My name," I said tremblingly, "is John Theodosius Aristophano."

He thought for a few moments, and then gathering up his discarded mantle of secrecy, pointed to the entrance.

"Go!" *He* said; and we were scarcely sorry to escape his evident anger.

"We shall have to be careful," Fjord said, when we had returned to our cave.

"Yes, I wish we were a thousand miles away from the accursed place."

A noise of thunder shook the hills, and caused our lamps to vibrate.

"Old *He* has dropped his mantle again, I guess," and

Fjord laughed, utterly forgetful of the great power which this mysterious being possessed.

CHAPTER XIX.
DELIRIUM OR REALITY—WHICH?

THE day passed away wearily. We found plenty to talk about, but every moment increased our anxiety as to our future.

That we had angered *He* in some way was certain, but how?

That was beyond our comprehension.

"What did you mean by your ejaculation, when you saw the face?" I asked.

"Why, it was the statue itself we saw."

"It looked like it to me, but the old boy evidently did not relish it. To-night I shall go and see the Marble Venus again."

"So shall I."

"What think you of *He* ?"

"Now, that's a poser," and Fjord rubbed his chin—a habit he had when in deep thought. "On the whole. I am inclined to think he does possess some remarkable power."

Night came, and when we felt assured that all had retired to sleep in the caves of this strange old city—a city of the dead—we started on our journey.

We were better prepared than on the previous night, and did not start or utter an exclamation when we felt some writhing snake beneath our feet.

Along the passage we walked slowly and deliberately.

It was a dangerous proceeding, and one that might cost us dear.

If *He* should get to know—and did he not possess the power to find out?—that we were searching into his secrets, would not death be our lot?

There was no doubt of it. The anger would be too great and the temptation too strong for him to resist.

Another fear now took possession of us.

What if any one should go to our cave and find it empty? That would in itself look bad.

Fjord suggested that I should turn back whilst he visited the strange statue. To this I would not agree, though I saw the necessity of some one remaining in the cave.

We cast lots, and it was decided by that primitive way of settling matters that Fjord was to be the watchman, whilst I went forward to the secret cave alone.

When he had left, a nervous dread came over me, and I began to wish I was well through with the night.

Once I thought of turning back. What business was it of mine to search into the mysteries of *He* or his statues? It was a piece of impertinence. Was I not his guest? Yes, I would go back, but then what did I come to the island at all for? Was not the very object impertinent? Then I feared the sneering laughter of Fjord, who would declare it was fear which kept me back.

I kept walking along while I thought. Perhaps I was the only living thing in that part of the mountain caves. It was horrible, and the very thought made my flesh creep and my blood turn cold.

"Oh, father," I murmured, "what would you advise if you were here?"

And then I thought I heard the answer:

"Go on, my son, and the secret will be yours."

I would persevere, even though it cost me my life.

The cave was reached. The curtains had been recently parted, or, at least they had that appearance to me.

The fire sent up a sickly glare, illumining the cave with its strange furnishings.

But the statue! There it stood—not in the alcove, where we had seen it the previous night, but in the center of the cave.

It stood there looking enchanting, beautiful, and fascinating.

It roused my feelings, and sent the hot blood coursing through my veins in a way nothing had ever done before.

I felt I could fall down and worship that piece of marble.

I entered the cave, and gazed with fascinated eyes on the statue.

A sort of vapor seemed to be rising from it. I took my handkerchief to wipe the moisture from my face, when I found—— Great Heaven! was I mad, or was it reality? The marble was warm and soft. I touched the hand which held up the drapery, and found it warm and pliable. I looked up, and behold! the eyes bright and gleaming were fixed upon me.

Did I faint, or was it sleep?

The events of the next few minutes were either delirium or reality. Which were they?

As Heaven is my judge, I cannot decide. So real is the remembrance to me, that I dare not assert that what took place was a phantasy, a dream.

I tell it as I believe it to be, a great and mysterious reality.

The eyes of the statue were bent on me, and one arm encircled my neck.

I felt myself drawn close to the marble—but marble no longer.

"My dear," said the statue, in a voice more melodious than any music I ever heard, "why will you not know me? Have you forgotten me? Oh, how can you be so cruel? It is not possible that you have ceased to love me; no, that I dare not think. Ever faithful to you, I recognized you the moment you entered. Why have you been so long coming? Through all the ages I have waited for you, my own, my love, my adored one! Why did you come here if not to call me back to life? I hate him! Beware his power! *He* is mighty, and can subdue everything but me. For twenty centuries I have defied him, because I am yours, and yours only. Oh, my beloved, let us flee from this horrid place! But first get *He* into your power, learn his secret, and put on the immortal, and then together we will live through the ages loving as we did twenty centuries ago."

I was puzzled and perplexed. I could not call to mind any love episode with any one in a pre-existence, but here was the statue, which I believed to be marble, declaring she was still true to me, still waiting for me.

I mumbled some sort of a reply, when my marble love continued:

"Oh, Tisisthenes, my beloved, my own, why did your father wrong you by stealing me away from you. It was cruel. It broke my heart, it killed me, but I live again and I am thy own."

My name was not Tisisthenes, but it sounded familiar. My father had, then, loved this statue; he never told me about it.

The more I thought about it the greater the mystery; I felt I was going mad.

"My dearest, my love, see I give thee the sweet kisses. Do you doubt me now?"

I certainly felt burning kisses and tears on my face. Every kiss seemed like a flaming coal. I could stand it no longer, I jumped to my feet, and rushed out of the cave; along the passage I went more rapidly than I had thought possible, and when I reached our own dwelling-place I stumbled and fell into the arms of my comrade.

The perspiration stood in great drops on my face and hands, and Fjord declared that I must have seen the devil himself, for nothing else could have so unmanned me.

It was some hours before I could summon up courage to tell him the events of the night. And then he consoled me by saying that fear had turned my brain, and imagination had done the rest.

Heaven knows. To me it was a great reality.

CHAPTER XX.

THE MYSTERIOUS CRYSTAL.

"FLEE! Flee for your life!"

These were pleasant words to hear on awakening, and yet they were the first to fall on my ears the morning after my interview with the Marble Goddess.

Who spoke? I was bewildered, but then I was half asleep.

As soon as I could arouse myself, I saw Rapa by my side.

How did she get there, and where was Fjord?

"Flee! oh, my love, for my sake flee!"

"What meanest thou, Rapa?"

"They will kill thee."

"Who? There's a good girl; come, now, tell me. Be calm, and let me know your story."

Instead of calmness she started off into a fit of hysterics, which reminded one more of a society belle than a child of nature in a South Sea island.

I tried everything I knew to calm her, but without avail. There was but one thing to do—let the fit run its course.

"Have I not loved you? Did I not choose you for mine own? Oh, my darling! why will they part us? Flee! for the evil power pursues thee. Even now the teeth are sharpened to devour thee."

I could not help thinking that Rapa was mad. But perhaps the insanity was on the other side. She might be sane and I the sufferer.

"For pity sake, Rapa, dear one, speak plainly; tell me the worst."

She seized me by the arm and pulled my head close to hers. In a harsh, grating whisper, she said:

"Then listen! The pale-faces who came with thee, my beloved, from the East, they who were rough and rude——"

"Yes—the seamen," I interjected.

"The same—they tried to reach the ground on which they came over the shining waters. Then loved ones they beat and did cruelly treat——"

"The scoundrels!" I muttered.

"So they were taken and their garments stripped from them, and a great feast prepared, and—and——"

"What!"

"They are gone."

"Where?"

I could scarcely repress a laugh when, like a child, she opened wide her mouth and pointed.

The whole truth burst upon me. My skipper and his men had been eaten by the cannibals.

"Do you mean that they were eaten?"

"Yes, after the manner of the country, their flesh was cut from their bones, and a big fire roasted them in "the waters of the lake.""

"I will see *He the Mighty*."

"He knew it. Oh, flee, my beloved, or they will kill thee!"

"Where is my friend?"

"Alas, I know not. I found thee here alone."

I was maddened at the thought of my poor servitors meeting such a sad fate. The truth of the story I never doubted, for what object could Rapa have in deceiving me? I pushed the brave girl aside—rudely, I am afraid—and rushed from my sleeping-cave.

I hurried along the passages I had been in the day before, until I reached the entrance to the outer chamber of *He's* apartments. Here the sentries tried to bar my progress.

"Take me, then," said I, "into the presence of your master."

The men evidently did not understand me. I had spoken in Spanish. I reiterated my demand in Hebrew, but no response. To push past them would be impossible, for I should certainly fall beneath their battle axes.

I then addressed them in Tahitian, but still they were dumb, and looked from one to the other in mute astonishment.

I tried another expedient. Shouting as loud as I could, I demanded an interview with *He the Mighty*.

The curtains behind the sentries opened as though by invisible hands, and the signal was understood, for I was allowed to pass unmolested. The second guardian of the great man's apartments offered no resistance. I entered the council chamber, where, to my great astonishment, I saw Fjord closeted in close conversation with *He*, and smoking some kind of very mild tobacco with a rose-perfumed smoke.

Fjord looked up as though rather annoyed.

"Why, Theo., I thought you were asleep."

"Great and mighty *He*," I said, "is it by your authority

that my servants, the white seamen, have been killed and eaten?"

He was unveiled, and a shadow seemed to pass over his face.

"Why will my people do such things? Verily, for ten centuries I have tried to improve their taste."

"Great Scott!" exclaimed Fjord, jumping to his feet. "what do you mean?"

"Only that while you have been basking in the sunshine of the presence of the mighty ruler of this country, our skipper and his men have been roasted and eaten."

Fjord's face turned pale. He seemed to realize the danger we were in, and turning to *He*, begged him to contradict the statement.

Instead of replying, *He* turned to me and asked, "Who brought you this word, and how knowest thou it is true? By what magic canst thou read the events transpiring so far away?"

"By no magic, most mighty one; but by the word of her, a daughter of the people, to whom, according to the custom, I was married."

"Knowest thou not that by the same custom Rapa must die?" asked *He*, darting a quick glance at me which caused me to stagger.

"Why, most mighty one?"

"It hath been declared that if any one shall reveal the doings of the family to one who is not a member thereof, the one must die."

"Spare her, oh mighty *He*. It was love of me—so unworthy—that prompted her."

"No harm shall come to her. I know the power of love. For twenty centuries I have loved, and though my knowledge hath not yet brought her I love to life, but for a brief time it will—it shall—yes, oh, great Tabu, it must."

He spoke in a low tone of voice as if talking to himself or thinking aloud, rather than addressing me.

He called to me to follow him into the inner room where we had looked into the crystal.

Drawing aside the curtains, I staggered back, for the large ball of glass looked like molten fire.

He waved his hand over the surface of the ball, and instantly it resumed its natural color.

"Look!" he said, "and tell me what you see."

Fjord and I stood gazing into the clear surface of the crystal.

Our skipper and his men were being dragged into the center of about a hundred natives.

Men we had not seen before. Naked savages without one redeeming feature.

Their hair was long, and hung in tangled masses on their shoulders. Their noses flat and repulsive-looking, while their mouths were hideous from the thick and projecting lips.

One, who appeared to be a chief, inasmuch as he wore an apron, while the others were nude, stepped into the circle and commenced a dance of wild delirium; this finished, two others brought long poles and stuck them in the ground in the shape of a triangle. The tops were bound together by means of a chain, and a monstrous pot was suspended in the center.

A fire was lighted and water put into the pot.

With various grimaces and incantations the chief stepped aside, and three men carried the pinioned Antonio to the fire.

The brave fellow struggled and kicked, but it was of no avail.

A knife was plunged into his side, and his life-blood flowed in a stream, but not a drop was allowed to go on the ground, for it was caught in a large basin.

His body was then cut up into smallish pieces and flung into the pot.

The bowl of blood was handed to the chief, who drank a portion of it and then passed it round to the others, all of whom partook of our seaman's blood.

I turned away from the crystal sick at heart.

The scene of murder was revolting, and I regretted I was not there to level some of the inhuman fiends in the dust.

"Look further," said *He*, who had not looked at the crystal, but seemed to understand exactly what was being shown by this miraculous ball of glass.

I again turned my eyes to the hideous sight.

The scene had changed, for now I saw a cave, deep and dark, and in this cavern-dungeon the skipper and one of the seamen were sitting.

Their lives had been spared. It must be our duty to rescue them.

"Come, Fjord," I exclaimed, "we will save them or die like true comrades."

"Why hurriest thou?" exclaimed *He*, in a tone of voice which savored more of a command to stay than a question.

"To save our comrades from those fiends," I answered, savagely.

"Look again before you go."

Across the surface of the crystal globe, I saw Milo and two other native women, who I at once recognized as being the wives of the seamen.

They were weeping bitterly, at the thought that the

men to whom they had given themselves were doomed to a cruel death.

The three women drew close together, and sobbed on each other's shoulders.

The scene was so realistic, that Fjord declared he heard the sobs.

When their sorrow was at its zenith, and they appeared utterly exhausted, we were both astonished to find a fourth person, a shadowy form which gradually grew more distinct, until *He*, himself, stood in the midst of the weeping women.

"You were not there." I said, turning to this mysterious personage, and pointing to the scene on the glass ball.

"No, that he was not, for we were with him yesterday, and I know he has not left here during the night," answered Fjord.

"It matters not, your minds are not strong enough to understand the mysterious powers of nature yet," was the only statement *He* condescended to make.

We turned our eyes again to the crystal, and once more the scene had changed.

The women were near the dungeon in which our comrades were imprisoned.

Access was obtained, and we saw the white men and their dark-skinned saviors leave the cave and cross the plain.

"They are saved!" I shouted, and then I turned to the great mystery embodied in the personage before us, and fell on my face after the manner of his people, and thanked him with a fervor which astonished Fjord.

"O ye of small faith. Could ye not trust me? I knew not in time to save Antonio, but it was not my people which did the cruel deed."

"Who told you?" I asked.

He made no answer, but pointed to the crystal.

We looked, but it merely reflected back the light of the lamps, and no pictures brightened its surface.

"Most mighty one!" I cried, "impart thy great power to me, that I also may use it to save and benefit my people."

"Nay, nay! Thy will is good, but thy strength is weak."

"Tell me, I beg of thee, most mighty one, the secret of thy power."

"Love hath made me what I am."

"Love!"

"Yes: and it is the most powerful agency there is. Did not Rapa risk and forfeit her life to save thine, because she loved thee? Did not the other women incur dangers you wot not of, to rescue the men from the cave? That was love. I loved, centuries ago, and I love the same object still. For her sake I learned the way to live for countless ages — for her sake I stay here, until she shall bid me take her to myself, as mine own. Mine—all mine! Great Tabu, can Heaven be better than that? But, alas! she still loves another—one who for ages has been in the grave, and who will never return. Oh! will she ever be mine? Great Tabu, answer!"

We knew not what to make of his strange rhapsody, which was addressed to some invisible power, of which we had no cognizance.

We withdrew quietly and apparently unobserved.

His agony seemed to be intense and more than human. The appeal to Tabu, and the expression of the hopelessness of his love seemed to rend his frame. Sighs broke from him, and such grief we felt should not be witnessed by others.

"Had we not witnessed such a manifestation of his power, I should say he was mad," said Fjord, as we left the cave.

"So should I, but if it costs me my life, I am determined to solve this mystery."

"I am with you."

Great was our joy when, a few hours later, Rapa came running to meet us, and to assure us of the safety of the sailors, and tell of the wonderful way in which they had been rescued.

The scenes were described by the excited women, and Fjord and I were still further perplexed as to the mighty *He*, when we found the stories coincide exactly with what we had witnessed in the crystal. There were powers in nature, or beyond nature, evidently, which we did not comprehend.

CHAPTER XXI.

A GLIMPSE BEYOND.

"TABU! Tabu! appear—appear!"

It was the heartrending cry and command of the all-powerful mystery to the still stranger, invisible, presiding spirit of the island. And in the lonely, cold cave which was the residence of *He* there emerged from the shadow of fantastic rocks a strange cloud, dense yet luminous, glittering and shifting.

It resembled the shining and misty spray of water

thrown up by a fountain when the clear moonlight and pale stars shed their luster over it.

The air seemed perfumed with incense swung by unseen hands from equally invisible censers.

The radiance of the shadowy column lit up the caves, and brought into relief the colored grasses of the mats and curtains as they hung on the somber walls.

A pale, tremulous light fell on the face of *He*.

"Great Tabu! Eternal art thou, the light of wisdom!" said *He*, the invoker.

"Thou to whose knowledge, grade after grade, age after age, I attained at last; thou from whom I have drawn so largely of the unutterable knowledge that has given me power over the decaying forces of nature; thou who didst rescue me from the power of *She*, and give me equal life and equal power, aid and counsel me!"

I stood at the entrance to the apartment, at first an unwitting eavesdropper. I had returned to ask a boon and crave indulgence from *He*. For the first time no guards or sentries kept the doors, and I found my way without any obstruction.

The invocation to Tabu had fascinated me, and I stood spell-bound.

The shadowy column of light attracted me more than anything I had ever before seen. What was it? Was I on the threshhold of some great mystery? Was I about to probe into the Hereafter—that strange and awful realm to which the spirits went when separated from the mortal.

I tried to leave, but my feet seemed, like my mind, fastened to the spot.

Honor bade me leave; curiosity insisted on my staying. Which was strongest? Alas! I am bound to admit that honor had to become subservient to curiosity. I looked and listened, and as my eyes, dry and hot, were riveted on the shadow, I saw emerge therefrom a shape of spiritualized glory. It was the face of a man, young but solemn-looking. The countenance seemed flushed with the consciousness of eternity and the tranquillity of pure wisdom; instead of blood flowing in the veins, which showed through the transparent skin, it appeared as if the fluid was of some phosphorescent nature. The hair was of dazzling brilliancy, and the light seemed to play upon it, emitting reflected light as from most perfect prisms.

There was nothing but a face visible; but the column of light extended from above the face to the floor.

My breath came and went rapidly. I felt that I should strangle. A chill passed through my body, especially, as it were, freezing my spinal marrow; my hair stood on end, for I was frightened.

The face was not human; it was a materialized spirit; something transcendantly beautiful, and far beyond the conception of artist or sculptor.

Gazing spell-bound on the face, I was still more fascinated by the voice, for it was the very perfection of music.

It seemed to float through the air, no harsh, vibratory sounds, but a smooth ripple, and a sweetness that cannot be described.

A new feeling came over me. I wanted to fall on my knees and worship this face and form.

"My aid shall ever be yours, when you need it; my advice was sweet to thee once; there was a time when thou couldst and didst send thy spirit into the realms of the eternal, and bask in the sunshine of the infinite. Now the dream of the past is upon thee, and thy power will leave thy grasp unless thou riddest thy soul of the mortal."

"Alas, great Tabu," answered *He*, sorrowfully, "I know too well the conditions necessary for the fulfillment of the perfection of power. I know that our wisdom comes from the separation of the spirit from earthly matters, but I love, and love is greater than all."

"Love is for mortals! It is not for us. What but a mockery must be thy love if even thou hadst thy wish gratified? If she turned her heart to thee, and resumed the mortal, as thou desirest, what then?"

"Oh, what joy! Great Tabu, let me but have my desire!"

"Thou canst not love like a mortal, for they have death and the grave before them. A short time—what is it but a day in thy life of centuries—and then thou wouldst mourn over her moldering dust. Never again couldst thou recall her, and she would enter into a new cycle of existence, leaving thee to battle with the ages alone."

"And yet mortals love and are happy."

"Ay, but they go hand in hand, each with each to the tomb; together they ascend into new spheres of existence; death, which thou cannot now understand, would not part them, for beyond the tomb is the great infinite; those who loved on earth are reunited and enjoy eternity together."

"Yet, if but for a day, I would have her in my arms. Great Tabu! I have waited for twenty centuries, and I love more than ever."

The glorified face, without seeming to notice *He* and his last speech, continued:

"Through what gradations of glory and light she would have passed before thou, the mighty but solitary one, leavest the vapor of earth for the sunlight of the eternal."

"I knew it! I feel it! thou great Tabu, who knowest all

things, canst read my soul, and know that I would only be happy with her and her love. Could I not take her through the gates of light, and initiate her into the conditions of life which I have entered?"

"Rash mortal! thy dreams might never become realities. She might grow faint-hearted before the gates. The valley might, with its terrors, be more than she could bear, and then thy grief at what thou hadst lost would be greater than thy sorrow now."

"Thou great and splendid Tabu, who forever basks in the sunshine of a pure existence, whose home is the haven of perfection, and whose every attribute is sublime; thou by the distance which separates, by the greatness of thy soul, canst not, save by sympathetic tenderness, know of the ambitions and loves of mortals."

"Alas, poor mortal!"

"I have lived here alone with her. I have watched the breathing forth into life, and have in my ecstasy clasped her perfect form in my embrace, only to hear the mocking laugh and feel the coldness of the marble. Yet I have watched and waited; I have seen cities rise and decay; I have heard of new people coming on the earth and passing away. The waters have dried up, and new lands have risen, only to be submerged again; and I have still stood alone, but one hope bearing me up, the thought that she would be mine, that love would break down every barrier, and I should clasp her in my arms and feel that even Heaven itself was the more glorious because of the love of her soul, and that the stars shone brighter when the brilliancy of her love-lit eyes was directed to them. I sought for consolation in science, in knowledge; I tried to find forgetfulness in wresting from nature her secrets, but my heart turned ever to her. She is mine, won by the devotion of the many ages. Great Tabu, aid me, or my power is a mockery, my length of days a curse."

The strong and mighty one bent his head, and grief shook his frame. I noticed, however, that no tears came to his relief.

"Thou art blind. Canst thou not see that if the life and love thou desirest were given thee, thy power would cease. Once again thou wouldst become human, and love would be thy only pleasure——"

"Grant it, and I will be happy."

"Thou mistakest. Thou wouldst be human in thy love, but the loved one would die, and thy soul would be heavy throughout the countless ages thou wouldst have to travel alone."

"Even then I would endure it. Great Tabu, give me

but this bliss of her reciprocated love, and an eternity of torture will I willingly endure as the price."

"Thy love is great, but thy darkest enemy is even now near thee. Humanity may conquer the spiritual, but I cannot aid thee—at present——"

"Say not so!"

"Where is the Egyptian—thy wife?"

A shade passed over the face of *He* as the question was asked.

"She was as but a star compared to the Sun," he answered.

"Even so, but she gave up her home, her kindred, her all for thee, and thou lovest another."

"I know it."

"The one thou lovedst was not thine, but had been given to another. By cruel arts thou stolest her away, and when she was obdurate, chained her spirit to the clay, that at any time thou mightest recall her to thy side."

"It is true, great Tabu! But he cared not, he sought another mate, while the ages have borne testimony to my love."

A smile came over the glorified face of Tabu, as he answered:

"Win thy way. Initiate those who desire to enter the gates of light, and the reward for thy zeal will make life a paradise, and heaven but a dream to be realized later."

The face vanished, the column of light left the cave, and *He* was alone.

Was it a dream, or had I been permitted to see beyond the veil, and penetrate some of the secrets of that world where matter is unknown, and where all is spirit, ethereal and pure.

Alas! I know not, but a painful throbbing in my head warned me that without more care, my feeble frame would fall a victim to the fell power of disease.

Fearful of the consequences of being found near the apartments of *He*, I staggered away, and as I entered my own cave, reeled like a drunken man.

Kapa made a decoction of some herbs and lulled me to sleep, as if I were a child. When I woke the fever had left me.

CHAPTER XXII.

SAVAGE JUSTICE.

For the next two days I had no time for either conjecture or speculation.

Fjord had been stricken down with fever, and was tossing about on the mats in wild delirium.

His pulse beat rapidly and his skin was hard, dry, and like a burning coal.

I never left his side, for though the seamen who were now with us, wanted to share my watch, I felt that the poor fellow would like to see me by his side when he regained consciousness.

Milo was an excellent nurse, but she was only a woman; she needed rest, and I was only too glad to let her take what she required.

One peculiarity struck me forcibly as to the customs of this strange people.

Rapa would not render any assistance in nursing. I questioned her, and all the answer I could extract from her for a long time was that she followed the custom.

I am sorry to say that anger got the better of my judgment, and I felt displeased at Rapa.

When Milo was by my side making cooling drinks for Fjord, or soothing his burning head by applying cool leaves to his forehead, I asked her the cause of Rapa's uncomprehensible conduct.

She laughed, and said it was the custom.

Yielding to my persuasion she explained to me, and I thought that many heartburnings might be avoided in so-called civilized society, if the same precautions were adopted as custom had taught these poor heathen.

When a man was taken sick, no one had a right to nurse him but his wife, if she were well enough to undertake the duty.

No other female was allowed to assist, for said Milo:

"Suppose my husband were to open his eyes and see a strange woman, he might think I cared not for him, or he might like her better, her hand might be cooler on his burning head, the drinks she made more refreshing, the food more tempting. And then"—Milo looked down at the form of Fjord, and raising her eyes coquettishly to me, continued—"he might get weary of me, and think he liked her best."

There was logic in the argument, and I found that femininity was the same the world over, and even the savages had learnt the lesson of woman's coquettish ways and man's fickleness.

I questioned Rapa no more, but accepted all her attentions to me as evidences of her satisfaction with her white husband chosen so strangely.

Milo had made up her mind that Fjord would die. Only *He* could save him, she declared, and *He* would not do so, for he had no love for the white captain.

I resolved I would get *He* to come and see my friend, and, if possible, save his life.

While I stood gazing at the flushed and feverish face of my companion, Tanoa entered the cave.

He looked long and, as I thought, tenderly at Fjord, and then turning to Milo, asked in a kind of chant:

"Hast thou the burial garment ready? for thy love, thy life will chase the eagles on the rocks by morning light."

By this imagery I knew that Tanoa expected Fjord to bid adieu to earth before the rising of the next day's sun.

"My son of the East, the pale-face who hast won favor from the mighty *He*, arise, gird on thy magic wand," by which he meant my gun, "and come with me into the presence of *He the Mighty One*."

"Does *He* want me?"

"*He the Mighty* commands thy presence. *He* hath mounted the platform of law, and will give judgment on those who didst ill-treat thy white traveler over the waters."

I had heard nothing of all this. I supposed from Tanoa's words that the cannibals had been taken and were to be punished.

"Come, quickly come, thou brave son of the East!"

Tanoa seized my arm and dragged me away, leaving Fjord alone, with Milo to care for him.

We reached the great plain on which the sports had taken place, and found a large number of the natives gathered there. The guards or soldiers were drawn up on all sides of the platform in military order. The people stood in dense throng, attired in the various garbs I have previously described. The only difference being that in addition to the apron worn by the men and the girdle by the women, each had now a head-dress made of some kind of leaf fastened on the top of the hair.

Tanoa told me that was a symbol of justice. That when *He* gave judgment all were expected to wear that covering for the head. *He* told me later that it had its origin in the idea that the whole people ought to suffer for the wrongs done by some of their number, but that Tabu was satisfied with the punishment of the guilty so long as the people showed their contrition by covering their heads, and so losing the benefit of the sun's rays, which they believed to be the smiles of god.

On the platform was a monster chair made of thigh bones and skulls, and over it the weapons of the country, a battle-ax, spear and knobstick crossed.

The guard at the mouth of the cave blew a blast on his horn, and instantly all, save the warriors, prostrated themselves on the ground.

The procession of girls—who seemed to so miraculously disappear save on state occasions—came in, and then *He* himself, covered with his veil, entered the plain and ascended the platform.

He called me to his side, and in Hebrew said:

"I desire thee to see the way I educate my people's sense of right and justice."

I sat down on the platform and then *He* gave the signal for all to rise.

"Bring hither the men," he commanded.

The warrior captain retired with four others, each bearing a battle-ax, and silence reigned in all that crowd.

From another cave lights were seen to emerge, and then the captain was seen, followed by eight of the men who had been the ringleaders in the murder and eating of my servant Antonio.

Never had I seen such horrid faces.

I have read somewhere that there is beauty in everything nature has designed or produced, but if this is so, then the beauty of these cannibals must have been in their extreme ugliness, for the mind of man could not conceive anything more repulsive than these creatures.

It was evident terror filled their souls. Men who could butcher and devour their fellows, who looked with savage glee on the murder of another, could not endure the thought of death.

The contortions of their features were frightful, and, I believe, would have frightened a herd of the wildest animals.

Each of them cringed with fear as they took their stand before the platform.

He looked at me, and then, in a voice which echoed among the hills in the distance, said:

"Pale-faced chief of the East, who art my honored guest, tell me: has the oracle in my chamber told thee of the crime of these men?"

"It has, most mighty one," I replied.

"Then tell me: and this people—what was revealed to thee in the oracle"

Thus commanded, I, as briefly as I could, related what I had seen in the crystal. Not a word was uttered by any save the interpreters, who, by order of *He*, translated into the language of the natives my story.

As the interpreter did so, I saw the scowl of anger on the faces of the cannibals, and my life would not have been worth much if they could have got near me.

Then my skipper was called, and he, wondering at the story I had told, for to him it seemed a miracle, after crossing himself as became a devout Catholic, confirmed my recital in every particular, and was about to tell how he escaped, but was quickly stopped by the command of *He.*

"What have ye to say?" *He* thundered forth to the condemned in their own language. "What have ye to say for so disobeying my word?"

For a long time there was no answer, and then a well-formed but immensely ugly black, without any pretense of clothing on his person, stepped forth from his fellows, and with quavering voice pleaded for mercy.

"We knew," said the fellow, "that the great pale faces, the chickens of the land across the waters"—this epithet was used to express our diminutive stature compared with theirs—"were thy guests, most mighty of rulers. But, when thy greatness sent back three of them and kept two for thy great pleasure, we thought that thou hadst given the pale faces as a present to thy faithful children, and, according to the ancient and honorable custom of our fathers, we made soup of one, but the others escaped."

This excuse occupied a long time in telling. I have only given the substance of it, stripped of all the imagery and idioms with which it was garnished by the speaker.

For a few minutes silence followed the speech of the cannibal, and then *He* raised his voice, and asked:

"What is it thy desire I should do to thee?"

The man spake again, and asked that they be pardoned, or taken over the great mountain of Akahauga and left to starve or perish, if the gods did not save them.

He thought a moment, and then gave utterance to his **judgment.**

"Unruly and wicked beasts of the grave, ye hath broken my commands, and done that which ye knew would offend me. Now, therefore, I order that ye be taken to the cave of death, and there be torn in pieces by the animals, nobler than ye, which have been gathered for my royal will. Your bodies will then be taken, and from them stew will be made, which your households must eat."

An audible groan went up from that vast assemblage. This was the greatest punishment which could be awarded, for while this tribe of savages would eat with gusto and relish the flesh of a white man or that of another tribe, it was considered a punishment to eat that of their own family or race.

Here then, not only were the ringleaders punished by death, but their families, who applauded and assisted in **the murder of Antonio,** were condemned to eat the flesh **of the savages.**

I pleaded for them, to try and save them from so terrible a death, and also tried to prevent the act of cannibalism being ordered, but *He* was obdurate.

"I have nothing to gain by vengeance," *He* said, "but I can only rule by such lessons as these."

Turning to Tanoa, *He* said:

"See that the animals have no food until to-morrow's sun has gone down, and then let them meet the goolahs (wretches)."

He walked back to his cave, escorted as on entering by the procession of girls and warriors.

CHAPTER XXIII.

A VISION OF THE NIGHT.

Fjord was in a deep and calm sleep when I returned to his sleeping-cave.

The danger had passed and I felt he would recover.

I asked the skipper to sit up and watch that night, so that I might take a much needed rest.

Rapa was delighted, for she, poor soul, was anxious for me, and declared I would die if I did not take greater care of myself.

She would wait by Fjord's cave, and if he became worse or asked for me, she would be ready to rouse me.

Hers was a devotion beautiful in its simplicity and yet grand in its ardor.

She needed rest but I was selfish enough to let her have her way.

I retired to my own cave, which since the arrival of the remainder of our party I had occupied alone, and which was in the long passage leading to the cave of the mysterious statue.

I had scarcely fallen asleep when I heard myself called. I awoke, thinking it was Rapa, and that Fjord perhaps was worse.

The lamp which I had kept constantly burning had flickered out. It had been neglected. The cave was as dark as a grave, and as cold and miserable as one.

I raised my head and asked:

"Who is there?"

A cold, soft, moist hand pressed my head, and gently laid it again on the hard pillow.

"Rapa, is it you?" I asked.

A woman's soft, loving arms were clasped round my neck, and her breath, fragrant with the sweetest and rarest perfumes, fanned my cheeks,

The arms were not those of Rapa, they were too soft and pliable.

"Who is it?" I again asked.

"It is I," answered some one. "I am here! Listen to my story."

"But what is your name?" I asked—"for I do not know you."

She unwound her arms, and stepped, as I thought, in anger away. In a moment a pale light shone out in the darkness, and to my surprise and horror I saw the outlines of the beautiful statue.

I was on the point of screaming out in my terror, but the statue waved its right hand, and looked at me with its beautiful eyes, and I was powerless. All my strength had gone, and I was chained as if by magic, or nightmare, to my couch.

"Listen to my story!" she said, approaching me, and, keeling on the cold floor, she laid her lovely head, marble, as I believed it to be, yet warm and redolent with life, by the side of mine on the pillow of rugs.

"Am I not the one who loves you, and whom you must yet love? You swore to me an eternal love. On this bronze you inscribed it," and the figure seemed to press something to her lips, and then place it in my hand. It felt like a piece of metal rounded and about two inches in diameter.

"You believed me false, but it was cruel, for I was true to you, and am still.

"Thy father stole me, and sent me to sleep, chaining my soul to my body, and then to keep me near him, turned me to marble.

"I was true to you; but you married another——"

"Poor Rapa!" I exclaimed, involuntarily.

"I talk not of the present, but of that time when, in Athens, we wandered to the Areopaga and drank in the words of wisdom, when Agrippina came between us, and at the first suggestion that I was unfaithful to you, she became your wife and the mother of your children."

"I don't remember the circumstance," I said.

"I returned many times to life, lured by promises he made, but when he promised to restore me to you, I found it but a ruse; he wanted me for himself, but that could not be. He can summon me to life, but he cannot get my love, that is for you alone. Oh, my beloved, how, through the ages, I have loved you."

"I really don't understand you at all," I exclaimed, rather displeased at what, I felt, was some trick being played upon me, and yet by whom I could not imagine.

There was a softness about the face and arms which did not seem to belong to any of the females I had seen on the island, and the voice was so sweet that no music ever produced so pleasing a sensation on my ear.

"Oh, my dearest!" continued the voice, "do not turn from me. I am thine own. If you knew how weary I have been through all the ages waiting for you. Have I not the highest, best, and most precious claim upon you? Two thousand years, as men count time, have I waited for you."

I could not resist the temptation. Such warm expressions of love were too much for me. I drew the figure to me and clasped it tightly in my embrace. She kissed me, and at every pressure of the lips a strange feeling, the like of which I had never before experienced, came over me. The love saddened me. I couldn't tell why, even though I knew that such ardor and warmth could not be purchased or obtained in the cold world.

A faint light again suffused the cave, and I saw the bright gleam of her eyes. I felt the perfect form, and saw the matchless beauty which I had admired in the statue.

I loosed her from my close embrace and looked into the azure depths of those eyes, which were as far beyond compare with human orbs as the sun is superior to the flickering of a candle.

"Be thou statue or woman!" I exclaimed, "leave me or my brain will be on fire!"

"And you too, oh my beloved, why will you not accept the devotion of my life?"

"But, Rapa——" I commenced, but was quickly interrupted:

"She is not thy wife. Thy troth was pledged to me before the race from which she sprung came into existence. Save me! Twice you have repulsed me. Remember, I will be none but yours. Even though I have to wait another decade of hundreds of years—though twice ten hundred years pass down the abyss of ages before you again come and find me—I shall still await thee, for I am thine! I have sworn it, and the gods are witnesses of our oaths. My dearest, my best beloved, I am thine!"

"Away, and let me think," I exclaimed.

The light died away, and I felt alone. That peculiar feeling came over me which is experienced in a house where death hath been and stolen the most beloved inmate. I could have screamed in my terror, and yet dared not.

The minutes passed by, each one appearing to me like the rolling along of ages. I felt I should go mad if I stayed there longer.

My body was covered with a cold perspiration, my eyes burned in their sockets and my head throbbed and ached as I never believed it possible.

If I called no one would hear me. I must get up and find Rapa.

But I dare not. Like a child, I covered my head, and, with fright, shook like one down with the palsy.

How I longed for company, and yet none came. I was alone.

I prayed earnestly for relief from my fears, but they only seemed the greater.

Would deliverance never come?

The tortures of a goblin damned were nothing to what I endured.

I dare not raise the covering from my face, for fear I saw the marble statue suddenly and mysteriously endowed with life.

And yet, why should I be afraid? Nothing ever left sculptor's chisel more beautiful or perfect than this figure, and yet I dare not meet the enamel of its eyes.

To meet such a one in life would be like heaven on earth; but a marble statue—great Heaven! I was going mad.

"'Twas but a dream," I soliloquized; but it was no use; I could not bring myself to such a belief.

When Rapa came some hour or so later, and lighted the lamp, I looked round and found we were alone.

I jumped to my feet and hugged and kissed Rapa in a way which must have astonished that devoted female, and yet, in the midst of the embrace I heard a voice, which was not that of my companion, say:

"Beware!"

"Did you speak?" I asked Rapa.

"No, my beloved; why?"

"Have you been here while I slept?"

"No; forgive me, my sun, my light."

Rapa thought I was cross with her for not leaving her watch as messenger in Fjord's cave, and this child of nature threw herself on her knees and wept hysterically. I soothed and comforted her, and when her eyes were dry, I forgot in the light of day the nightmare of the dark, until feeling a strange substance in my pocket, I drew therefrom a disc of copper, which I remembered had been given to me by my strange visitant of the night.

For some hours I had led myself to believe that I had **suffered from** a nightmare during sleep; but now, what could I think? No dream could place a copper disc in my pocket.

Some one must have entered my room, but who could it be? Rapa denied all participation in the events of the night, and I honestly believed her.

Would the mystery ever be solved? I was ill at ease,

and dreaded the return of night. I would seek the presence of *He*, and see if he could offer any solution to my problem. Yet, there was a delicacy which prevented me doing so. I wished, however, to attain to the same mastery over nature which he possessed, and therefore sought admission into his private apartment.

CHAPTER XXIV.
INITIATION.

"So you desire to wring from Nature her secrets, to pass through death's fire and yet live?" was the question put to me by *He*, when I told him my wish.

"I would," I answered, gravely.

"The first thing you have to do, is to separate yourself from the world, to live in the solitude of the mountain there, until your soul grows accustomed to the spot. You must drink in all the beauties of surrounding nature, for Nature is the source of all inspiration."

"And you can tell me the secret by which I can baffle death?"

"No! death comes to all. All we can do is to find out the secrets of the human frame, and to apply continual preventives to the effects of time."

"If you have this knowledge, and your great age proves it, why not make it known to mankind?"

"In yonder cave there lies one who but yesterday I condemned to die a death from wild, half-starved beasts! Would mankind be benefitted if he were to carry his brutal lusts and cannibal taste for centuries. Think what it would be if universally known. The bad would live for centuries and work immeasurable evil."

"Yes, most mighty *He*, but the good would live also."

"Not necessarily. I live for the attainment of one end only. That accomplished, and I would gladly share the fate of humanity."

"And that object?" I asked diffidently.

"To gain the love of one who for twenty centuries has repulsed me. Let her but give herself to me, and then when she goes to the grave, I shall not want to outlive her."

"But she lives, and——"

I noticed the frame of *He* tremble as I suggested the fact that others beside himself must be possessed of the secrets. He made no answer, but turned to me.

"You would solve the mystery, would penetrate the veil. Have you courage?"

"Ay; test me, and you will find that neither death nor life has any terrors for me."

"Well said. Come."

He seemed to glide across the vast cave; walking would have given a different motion to the body.

Through innumerable passages we walked, down many steps roughly hewn out of the rocks, neither speaking a word until *He* stopped at the bottom of a shaft whose perpendicular walls rose hundreds of feet above them, revealing a faint glimmer of sky overhead.

"Hast thou courage?"

"Proceed!" was my answer.

A huge bowlder stood at the entrance to what appeared to be another cave.

This was moved by an unseen agency, for no one touched it.

I trembled with a secret fear. What if I never again was allowed to retrace my steps?

Into this passage we entered. The stone closed again the entrance, and we were prisoners in a dark, cold cave, hundreds of yards from human aid.

Who can wonder that a shrinking terror should come over me? But never for an instant did I dream of returning, if such a thing had been possible.

The darkness was so great that I had to grope my way, guided by a mysterious light which at intervals came from the fingers of *He* as he waved his hand, beckoning me to follow.

A moment—which seemed like an age—of silence enjoined by *He*, and I found myself in a fog or vapor of strong fragrance.

It appeared like a mist or dew, thickening the air so that I could scarcely breathe.

The cave began to get lighter, until I was able to look around.

I was alone.

No sign of my strange guide, but all round me this mist, rolling in great clouds like waves of the sea.

I stood rooted to the spot. I tried to call out, but my tongue seemed to cleave to the roof of my mouth. My blood froze in my veins.

I strained my eyes into the misty vapor, and saw, or fancied I saw—— Great Heaven, I dare not think of all that passed before my startled eyes.

Gigantic forms floated on the billows of the mist. Scenes of horror were enacted before my eyes.

There I saw a mother take her new born infant and tear

it limb from limb; there I saw old age brutally ill-treating innocent youth.

Again I saw foul murder stalk forth and come with knife dripping with human blood close to where I stood, until the knife seemed about to enter my very throat. Every conceivable shape of horror; lions with human heads, and men with heads like monkeys—all that could harrow up the soul was there.

The fiends of Hades could not have brought to the mind anything more awful.

These living furies coiled and floated through the mist, getting nearer and nearer, until I felt their hot breath on my cheeks.

Then slimy, noisome snakes hissed and wriggled through the vapor, and began to encompass me round. I felt one great snake crawl up my legs, encircle my body; its head was near my face. I saw its forked tongue dart out and nearly strike my cheek; the hiss which accompanied it, together with the fast tightening coil round my body, told me my end was nigh.

I could bear it no longer.

I shrieked aloud for help, and fell to the floor utterly exhausted.

When I recovered from my swoon I was on the mountain side, lying on a bed of lava, ruddy in color, and by my side was the mysterious *He*.

"Young and daring pale-face of the East," he said, "another moment there and you would have been dead. Do you still wish to penetrate the dread secrets of nature?"

"I do. I am prepared for the ordeal. Worse than what I have experienced could not happen."

"Worse! Thou talkest of what thou hast no knowledge. What thine experience has been is but the initial, the opening. Wilt thou still persevere?"

"Most mighty one. I care not what the terrors are, teach me the wonders and secrets of nature."

"Thou art a worthy pupil. A week must elapse before I can take thee further than thou hast gone. We will return."

I followed my guide down the mountain side until we came to a declivity on the brink of which *He* halted.

The rock rose perpendicularly from the plain to where we were standing, a height of at least a hundred yards.

There appeared no way down, that I could perceive, and I saw that to climb back again would be equally dangerous.

He looked round. Had he forgotten the way?

"It is centuries since I climbed these rocks," he said "and things have changed."

About fifteen feet from us across the deep abyss was another mountainous rock.

If we could reach that, descent would be easy.

But it seemed an impossibility.

"There should be a rope here," said *He*, perplexedly. "Ah, here it is. I will go first, and throw the rope back to you."

The rope lay in a coil on the rock. How was that going to help us to cross the chasm?

My question, although mentally asked, was quickly answered, for *He* uncoiled the rope, made a running noose, and then flung it, lasso-fashion, across the gulf.

With a correct aim, the noose fell over a jutting rock. *He* pulled the rope, and finding it secure, grasped it tightly with his hands, and leaped into the air.

I shuddered at the thought of the leap I should have to take, for an inch missed without the rope meant certain death.

He cleared the abyss easily, and threw the rope to me. In doing so, however, it became loosened from its hold on the stone, and its entire length went whizzing down into the gulf.

"You must jump!" *He* cried, while a sickening sensation came over me.

I felt dizzy and faint, and expected every minute to fall. I murmured a prayer, never expecting to live another day, when a rushing sound behind me attracted my attention.

I looked round, and saw—oh, horror!—a mass of liquid, boiling, burning lava rushing down the hill.

Another moment, and I should be in its midst, and with it go over the precipice.

I closed my eyes, and with a madness of desperation, jumped.

My foot caught the edge of the opposite rock, and I felt myself bounding off, when by great presence of mind I threw myself forward and caught hold of the rock with my left hand.

I hung there suspended in space for hours I thought—it was only twenty or thirty seconds in reality. The heat from the burning lava opposite scorched my hair and blistered my cheeks.

I was about to drop, preferring death to the terrible torture I was enduring, when I found myself drawn up on the rock by the firm grasp and strong hand of the mighty *He*.

Never shall I forget the horror of those few minutes. Nothing can ever efface it from my memory.

The scar on my cheek is a constant reminder of the scorching heat of that liquid metal, and will never allow me to banish from my mind, even if memory failed to recall, that terrible leap through space.

The agony of suspense, while I clung to the rock, the certain death which awaited me if my fingers loosed their hold, the intense heat of the lava, and the whistling of the furious winds, formed a chapter in my life, the memory of which even now causes me to shudder and start with fear.

From the moment we commenced the descent to the time we reached the caves in which we had our dwelling, my companion was silent.

For this I was glad, for my nerves had been strung to such a high pitch, that if the stillness had been broken I felt I should have screamed.

CHAPTER XXV.

ANOTHER MYSTERY.

I LOST no time in visiting Captain Fjord, and to my great surprise I found him sitting at the entrance of the cave, apparently in good health.

He had been stricken down quite suddenly, and it seemed that his recovery was equally rapid.

Milo was fanning him and looked exuberant in spirits at the convalescence of her husband.

"Why, old boy," he said, jovially, "I thought you were lost! But where have you been, and what means that scar?"

"Ask me no questions if you love me," I replied rather dramatically, but with no intention of being tragic. "I have suffered horrors which words cannot describe."

"Did you get lost?"

"Not exactly, but ask me no more."

"All right, my boy; but yes, I must ask you one other question—were you alone?"

"No."

"Oh!" Fjord drawled out this little exclamation until it appeared to be a whole sentence instead of only two letters.

What did the insinuation mean? I failed to understand it, so added to my answer the assertion that *He* was with me.

"Theo., Theo., how can you?" and Fjord laughed in that peculiar manner which irritated me terribly. At all times the laugh, sarcastic and caustic, annoyed, but now I felt inclined to throw something at the man who under cover of his weakness could laugh in the way he did. However, a peculiar feeling of chumminess prevented me, the thought that we were in the power of savages and at any hour might be attacked and perhaps slain, drew me nearer in friendship to the sarcastic citizen of the Great Republic.

"What mean your strange insinuations?" I asked as calmly as possible.

"Nothing, my boy, only you got caught this time."

"For mercy sake, Fjord, tell me what you mean!"

"Well, my boy, you said *He* had been with you, whereas he has been here, and by his magic dispelled the fever, or I would have turned up my toes before this."

I looked at Fjord. Was he joking, or had he been dreaming? He looked soberly enough, and as I saw his earnest conviction that he was speaking the truth, my face paled.

"Never mind, Theo.," he said, entirely misunderstanding my agitation; "I ought not to have pressed you."

"Fjord, stop your sarcasm; I can't stand it, even from you. I tell you—I swear it, if you will not believe my word—that *He* has been with me, and only left my company when I came on here to see you."

"Forgive me, Theo.; but while I do not doubt you, there is a mystery to be explained. Milo," he called, and the faithful girl quickly responded.

"Tell my friend here what occurred while he was away."

Though it had the appearance of doubting Fjord's veracity, I did not attempt to stop the girl's story.

It was a full and complete corroboration of my friend's assertion.

"When the son of the East went his way through the hidden passages," she commenced, evidently referring to my departure from Fjord's side, "I let the eyes of my unworthy and poor self fall on him whom I love with the warmth the gods have given me. Your poor creature had tried all the things she knew, but the gods wanted to take the white-faced son to the beautiful city of light.

"Milo wanted him, for Milo never had anything to love before. But Milo saw that the gods would not let him stay, and she cried.

"Tanoa, the 'Father,' came and said white-face son of the East must be put in the caves of death, for he could not live. Rapa, she looked and shook her head, and I felt so bad just here"—and the faithful girl pressed her hand on the region of her heart.

"The place grew black, like as though no lamps were there, and I breathed not, for the gods had come for him I loved.

"I, poor Milo, put my head so," leaning it on her hands and hiding her face, "when the place became light and I saw *He the Mighty*, the son of the morning, the friend of the great God Tabu, standing looking at my brave hero. *He* waved his hand over the couch, and then the fever went, and my own loved one stood up well and strong as he is now."

The story, from which I have stripped much of the verbiage, was circumstantial and striking; besides, what object could either Fjord or Milo have in a misrepresentation?

"About what time was *He* with you?" I asked.

The time was given, and, as far as I was able to conjecture, it must have been the very time when, in the cavern, I was enduring the tortures of the waves and billows of goblins and spirits, and so nearly lost my life from the serpent's fangs.

But how could this strange character transport himself so quickly to and from Fjord's bedside?

What power did he possess by which he could conquer space and overcome the difficulties of the passage of time?

If he possessed such powers, why was it that he should have been so agitated, when for an instant he could not find the rope by which to cross the chasm?

All these things passed rapidly through my mind, and made me think that not only was *He* powerful, but incomprehensible also.

While my mind was occupied with these thoughts and perplexities, it seemed to me as though a veil was thrown over me, and instantly my brain started off on a new line of thought.

Where was that wonderful phosphorescent lake we had seen on our first landing?

Why was it we had not found it since? Was it near to us, or across the island? Was our boat safe?

Then came one of those singular day dreams which have upset all the theories of scientists and laughed to scorn their learned rules and explanations.

Before my mental vision I saw again the lake, and on its bosom riding placidly was our stanch and trim boat.

I longed to be in her, and take a sail round the island. Was it my imagination, or reality? I distinctly saw my two sailors go down to the lake side, draw in the rope, drag the boat to the side, jump in, and sail away.

"The traitors," I thought, "they have stolen the boat and left us here perhaps to perish."

I looked round and behold I was on the mountain side, and the whole vision was but a dream.

I felt more at ease; my gratification, however, was of short duration for *He* stood by my side, from whence he came or how he got there I could not understand, but there he stood, and into my ear asked the question:

"Did you see them go?"

"Who?"

"The white faces who ride over the water as men go over the land."

"I imagined it."

"There is no imagination. What the sons of men call so, is but the pictures of events past, present, or to come, mirrored on the mind."

"Am I to believe then that my men have gone away with the boat?"

"They have."

"And we are alone?"

"Just so—in my power. Do you fear?"

"No, most mighty one; for I fain would stay till the secrets of life are in my keeping."

"So let it be."

I looked round to face the speaker, when I found I was alone.

He had vanished. Not a trace of him could be seen. The disappearance had been as mysterious as his coming.

On every side my vision took in hundreds of yards of mountains and plain, but nowhere could the figure of this remarkable being be found.

It was possible some cave or opening in the ground concealed him, but that was a matter of mere conjecture.

I felt uneasy, this weird power was getting troublesome, for no one likes to feel that his every thought is known, and actions seen by a stranger.

I resolved to search for the secret recesses of the island, to master all its caves and passages, and find my way to the sea, so that when I wished to leave, I should know my bearings and be certain of the way.

Should I take Rapa with me? Prudence said yes, but my curiosity and desire for research replied in the negative, and this overmastered my reason, so bidding her farewell for a time, I started on my tour of discovery.

CHAPTER XXVI.

IN THE REALMS OF THE DEAD.

THE plain I reached after crossing the hill, as I thought, was but a huge basin or crater of a volcano, which centuries ago must have been of formidable size.

The basin must have been over a mile in diameter, and looked as though it had never been trodden by man.

Soil, thin but rich, had gathered there, and a thick brush or scrub grew over the entire surface.

I could not see beyond the towering walls of the hills, and not a tree over four feet high was visible.

I resolved to cross the plain and ascend the hill on the opposite side, which seemed the highest point, and not difficult to climb.

I wanted to have a bird's-eye view of the island, before I went beneath its surface. I had but one regret: Fjord was a good archæologist, and his knowledge would have been of great service, but he was too weak to undertake the journey.

Determined not to lose my way, I drew a map of my tour, and carefully noted the route I took by marking thereon the bearings of the pocket-compass I carried.

On the lookout for venomous snakes, which I imagined must be prolific thereabouts, I walked on quietly and observantly.

Not a sign of life crossed my vision, and I was about giving up all thought of adventure until I reached the mountain side, when I felt the soil give way beneath me.

I sunk down until my head was level with the plain.

I imagined the hole into which I had fallen must be some orifice which the water from the last rain-storm must have made.

But I was perfectly dry, and there was no appearance of mud about my boots.

I pulled myself up to the surface, and then looked down into the hole which had been so effectually concealed by the brush.

Clearing away the scrub, I saw a hole about three feet in diameter and nearly six feet deep.

Examining more closely, I saw, or thought I did, the outline of some steps.

Here, then, was to be the scene of my first discovery. Noting the bearings carefully on my improvised map, I lowered myself into the hole.

I was compelled to unstrap my gun and leave it on the bank until I examined the bottom of the cavity and the apparent steps.

I found my conjecture was right: the stone I saw was the first of a series of steps leading down; where to, of course, I could not even imagine.

Carrying my gun in a perpendicular position in front of me, I managed to get down about a dozen steps.

Here a new difficulty presented itself. The steps were continued, but the lapse of ages had caused the rock and soil to sink, so that the passageway was only about three feet high.

I must either crawl on all fours or give up my exploration. This I could never consent to do, and so down on my knees I went, and felt my way cautiously down twenty or so more steps. I dragged my gun after me, and was heartily glad that the jolting had not caused it to go off.

I was now able to stand upright. I was in a small cave almost circular in form and having a diameter of about six or seven feet.

The silence was awful. For the first time a tremor of fear came over me. What if I never got back alive? Suppose the rock, so long undisturbed, should suddenly give way and bury me alive? I was almost tempted to turn back, but I felt I could not brave the sneering laugh of Fjord, so I nerved myself for the worst, and began to think what was the next step to take.

A sharp, hissing sound fell on my ears. I looked round, expecting to see a snake, and stood ready to deal it a death-blow. The sybillations grew louder, but no snake could I find.

It was getting monotonous, and I felt like a fool, standing, with gun in my hand, ready to club the snake, and not finding one.

The hissing increased in volume, and I began to imagine that not one, but a score of the reptiles, had blended their voices into one discordant sound.

But from whence came the sound? I looked everywhere but to the arched roof. To this I turned my eyes, and only just in time, for, hanging down from the rocks overhead was a monster snake; its body was swaying to and fro as it gradually lowered itself. Its head was now on a level with mine; and I perceived it was increasing its swaying motion, so that, in a moment, it would strike my face.

Another instant and the monster lay dead at my feet.

On the opposite side of this small cave I saw a stone which appeared to be merely lodged against the projecting rocks. I conjectured rightly that this was the entrance to some other passageway.

I pushed and pulled at the stone, until by sheer force of muscle I dislodged it from the place where it had lain perhaps for centuries.

A narrow passage opened to my view, and my lamp cast a sickly glare on the cold and dark rocks.

On either wall of this passage strange devices and carvings reached from the rocks, which formed the roof, to the very floor. I was not the first human being who had been there evidently. This pleased me, for I wished to know something of the wonderful people which had formerly inhabited this island of volcanoes.

The passage was about eight or ten yards long, and at its end a rude archway had been made. This was the work of man, and not of nature. On either side of the archway stood a figure which I took to represent the ancient gods of the country. These idols, or images, were made of trachyte, the only relief being the eyes, which were of some blue enamel, giving a very life-like, and in the solitude of that chamber, a startling appearance to the face.

The heads were covered with a cap or crown of stone which bore evidence of having once been painted red, but now had, by the lapse of ages, resumed the natural color of the stone.

The faces of the statues were well formed, the noses large and regular, the eyebrows raised and very marked. The ears, especially the lobes, were of huge size and showed the custom of the time to be similar to that of the Polynesians in later years, who distended the ears by the insertion of blocks of round wood or ivory. The upper lip was cleanly shaved, but each image had a chin beard pointed like a goatee. The hair was represented as long and thick over the forehead, and passing behind the ears.

The general contour of the face was round. The arms were not distinct from the body, but simply raised above the rest of the surface.

There were no inscriptions to show whom these images represented, or whether they were idols to be worshiped or statues of the great men of the tribe.

I forgot all my fear as I gazed on these emblems of a bygone age, and when I had carefully noted all the peculiarities of the images, I entered through the arch, and found myself in a large chamber.

Upon the walls of this spacious chamber were rudely carved *bas-reliefs* of men and warriors fighting and feasting. The history of a nation might perhaps be enshrined there on walls of imperishable stone.

But my eyes glanced down from the walls to some stone benches which projected from the wall on one side of the cave.

On these benches I saw—and the realism was so intense that I felt my hair standing on end, and a shiver pass over me, as I looked on the recumbent figures stretched out in their last sleep.

Were they dead or only sleeping? If dead, they had been so carefully embalmed that they retained not only the form of the living, but much of the natural color.

I was entranced and appalled, and for several minutes stood trying to still the loud beating of my heart.

Gaining courage, I approached the figures, and found them cold as marble. They had lain there undisturbed, for who can say how long?

My lamp cast only a dim light on the shadowy atmosphere, and I wished I had the means to illuminate the cave more thoroughly.

Six men were lying on the stone biers in this room. The bodies were highly perfumed by embalming spices, the linen which was wrapped about them was so old that, as I touched it, I found it crumble into dust.

Man could embalm his fellows, but could not make the linen fiber immortal!

A slight breeze passed through the chamber, perhaps the first which had entered there for centuries.

It blew over the bodies, and in an instant every vestige of linen wrappings, exposed to the draught of air, had moldered into dust, leaving six human figures, like so many marble statues, on the slabs.

It seemed more feasible to believe that I gazed on recumbent stone figures rather than on what had been once living, breathing, thinking, fighting men.

The bodies showed that the race there represented had been a fine one.

By actual measurement each body stretched from crown of head to bottom of feet over six feet six inches. Allowing for the natural shrinkage caused by the embalming and the waste of ages, these men must have been nearly seven feet high.

On the wall immediately above each body inscriptions and *bas-reliefs* told, in language which all ages might read, the story of the life of each man. The inscriptions were partly in Hebrew—which greatly astonished me—and partly in a barbarous jargon which seemed to have been formulated at Babel's tower by some one trying to write down the conglomeration of sounds which fell upon his ear. Some of the characters looked like Chaldaic, others like Persian, while several were of such peculiar form that I could not classify them.

One inscription was made up of characters like this:

I copied many of the inscriptions, and tried afterward to translate them by finding a key. Some were to me utterly unintelligible.

CHAPTER XXVII.
TRANSMIGRATION.

BEYOND the chamber, with its strange inscriptions and mummified bodies, I found another one, which gave evidence of a refinement of taste which I had never expected to find in so strange a quarter.

The walls seemed to have been hung with tapestry or linen, on which many designs in brilliant colors had been painted.

Vases of stone and metal stood about in admirable disorder, and urns of bronze were placed on stone brackets projected at intervals from the walls.

I was so delighted with the ancient curtains and hangings, that I boldly resolved to take them away with me. I therefore did not attempt to make any copy of either the paintings, hieroglyphics, or inscriptions. Ten bodies were ranged round the chamber on slabs of polished trachyte.

The slabs were full of crystals, and a blue stone capable of a very high polish, and when I swept away some of the dust, the accretion of centuries, I could not withhold my admiration of the labor bestowed on the polished stones.

These bodies were arrayed in linen, and various designs were painted on the shroud. They were the bodies of females, hence the superiority of the last resting-place, and the garments.

In my thoughts I contrasted the bodies lying there with the natives I had seen alive.

The evolution seemed to go back toward a high civilization, instead of, as is usually the case, commencing with barbarism and reaching a higher perfection.

The bodies were clothed from head to foot in tunics similar to those of ancient Greece.

The natives I had met were savages, who clothed neither themselves nor their dead.

Even the guard of *He the Mighty* wore but scanty raiment, and the girls who were the especial favorites of *He* who made any pretense of dressing other than the fringed girdle, wore only a linen or grass garment without any more shape than a sack, with holes for head and arms.

But in the cave, the bodies were tastefully dressed, and evidently varied colors had been employed.

Unfortunately, the action of the air only gave me a few moments' inspection of the drapery, for it crumbled to dust, leaving the nude bodies as monuments of the embalming skill of preceding ages.

The same action of the air destroyed all the tapestry hangings which I had, in my egotism, prided myself would create a great sensation in Europe.

It was gone, and I had no proof to offer of my visit to the caves of the dead, and their beautiful draperies.

Either the embalmer had produced a whiteness of flesh not natural to the living, or the race which had left its representatives there, was whiter than any I had seen on the island.

As to beauty, I can say that having visited the art galleries of Florence and Rome, of Paris and Munich, I never saw greater perfection of form and figure than I did in those actual bodies so beautifully preserved.

The female forms were lovely, the faces as clear cut as a Grecian, the limbs modeled as beautifully as ever came from sculptor's chisel. Several of the figures would have made excellent models for the highest conception of Venus, so perfect and without blemish were they. I could have gazed for hours—nay, the hours could have lengthened into days, and the days into weeks, before I should have wearied of looking on so much perfection.

I had provided myself with provisions to last several days, and I had sufficient fat for my lamp to last for at least a weeks' continuous burning.

I began to feel hungry, and amid the dust of countless ages I ate a hearty meal.

Wearied with my tramp over the mountains, I fell asleep, and only awoke just in time to replenish my lamp, whose flame was fast flickering out.

This gave me cause for alarm. I had no means of relighting my lamp should it go out, for I had used up my last match—brought from the realms of civilization—the day before, and I had failed to provide myself with the kindling sticks which the natives used to get a light or fire.

These sticks were peculiar to the island, and up to that time no one would tell me the name of the wood. By rubbing the sticks together, the friction produced a flame from which the grass or linen wick of the lamp was lighted.

Only one kind of wood yielded so readily to the friction, and the natives ascribed the fire to the gods, declaring that the rubbing together was the prayer to the god of fire. These sticks were used but seldom, as the inhabitants considered it an ill omen if the lamp went out.

I quickly added fat to my lamp, and so kept my light. The tallow used was made from the melted fat of the goat or any other animal killed, and cocoanut oil—the oil was extracted by roasting the nut and allowing the greasy matter to fall into a pan. This was mixed with the other tallow, and afforded an excellent ingredient for the lamps.

I felt refreshed by my long sleep, and after having a good meal, searched round me for new discoveries.

When I look back to that night spent in a cave with twenty or more white figures, which I knew had once been living human beings, I wonder that fear did not rob me of repose, but I can honestly declare that I never spent a more peaceful night than among those mummies.

Some of the urns were of elaborate design, but very weighty. I tried to lift one from its bracket for closer inspection, but it was too heavy for me.

On the urn I tried to move, bunches of grapes and cups were engraved. The artistic work was very fine, and a few of the vases and urns would have made the fortune of an enterprising dealer in articles of virtu.

By the side of each female figure lay a necklace and several rings.

The necklace was made of the teeth of some animal, highly polished, and strung together on fine gold wire. The rings consisted of a bronze or gold band holding a large stone, on which was carved some hieroglyphic or portrait. I brought away several of the rings, and antiquarians have told me they must date back to a period antecedent to the Christian era by at least two thousand years.

Had I been the first to explore these caves? The crumbling into dust of the linen swathing clothes, robes and hangings would lead one to think so.

These tombs, if such were the case, would have been there undiscovered by Mongolian and Spaniard, by European and Polynesian alike. How strange that *He* had never visited them. Surely his knowledge would lead him, in all the centuries he claimed to have lived, to search amid the tombs and caves of an age prior to his landing on the island.

The mysteries of the place seemed to increase the longer I stayed.

Did these ancient dames occupy the inner chamber, or was there another beyond? I tried the walls; they seemed solid. I pushed, but there was no evidence of any doorway or chamber beyond.

How well guarded were these dead! The idea was touching and beautiful. There in an inner chamber reposed the women of the family, while their natural protectors and guards lay outside. The unities were preserved even in grim death.

A new feature caught my eye and riveted my attention.

There were holes, evidently cut by a sharp instrument, at regular intervals reaching up to the roof.

They must have been cut for some purpose; what could it have been?

Were they steps?

That seemed the most probable solution, but if so, where did they lead to?

"Nothing venture, nothing have," was always a favorite maxim of mine, so I started my perilous journey up the steps.

It was like climbing the side of a house, with nothing but niches scarcely two inches deep for finger-holds and steps.

The ascent was slow, but gradually I went higher and higher, until my head reached the arched rocks which formed the roof.

All my journey for no account. I was about to descend, vexed with myself for having risked my limbs, when a painting on one of the rocks attracted my attention. I mounted a step higher to examine it, and in doing so struck my head against the rocks.

I was nearly stunned, and for a moment the place seemed to swim round, and I grew dizzy. If I fell I stood a chance of breaking my limbs, or at least destroying my fragile lamp, and I did not care to be left in the dark to grope my way through the long passages. This thought roused me, and I reached my hand up to try and get a more secure hold. The rock above me seemed to lift up, and I drew myself up into another chamber. Resting myself on one of the stone biers, on which reposed some old warrior, I examined this new apartment. The same strange, fantastic paintings on the walls—earthenware jars and vases were placed in irregular order on the floor, and on the biers were the bodies of men, with spears and battle-axes by their side.

The drapery had long since moldered into dust, and some of the bodies less carefully embalmed showed signs of decay.

A foot had fallen from the leg of one of the warriors and looked ghastly as it lay on the floor by the side of his last bed; near by, a hand grasping the haft of a spear had fallen, evidently broken off by the weight of the weapon and the action of centuries of time.

Why were these bodies decaying? Had they not been so carefully embalmed, or did they belong to a later age when the process was not so well understood?

There was but little to interest me in this chamber; if I must study the dead, let it be among the perfect specimens of the preservative art rather than here, where the moldering hand of nature had triumphed over the science and skill of man.

I was about to descend into the chamber beneath, when I perceived still another passage beyond. Into this I went and found it full of little children all well preserved and perfectly formed.

The inscriptions on the walls were here plainly carved, and by means of the sculptured designs I was able to learn that this people of the far past believed that it took several centuries for a soul to grow.

A human soul was created—ran the idea as far as I was able to translate and understand the inscriptions--and had to pass through several stages of existence before it became perfect. In some cases the soul only dwelt long enough in human form to gain its right to immortality. In these cases the child died, and the spirit or soul would enter some sacred animal, either the dog or the pig—for on this island I learned that the pig was sacred, and although the natives would kill and eat the boar, they would first offer a portion of the flesh as a burnt sacrifice to their gods. On the death of the animal the soul would enter a bird—this was to give it ambition, a desire to soar above the world. After passing from the bird the human spirit would seek an habitation in some other animal, or it might be in another child. Often—according to these legends—one spirit had dwelt in a dozen human forms in a score of years. During the ages required for perfection it would dwell in human bodies, each one more developed or more intelligent until perfection was reached. Then came the most wonderful theory in connection with this transmigration. The spirit perfected would search back through the ages of its existence and try to find the body which had the greatest physical beauty.

If the body had been preserved, the spirit took possession of it; if it had moldered in the dust, a perfect child was born and the purified spirit dwelt in its frame, and during life manifested its perfection by rising superior to any other living person.

Such was the strange and yet beautiful idea these ancient people—to whatever nation they originally belonged—had concerning the human soul. It was easy to see now why the art of embalming had been so carefully practiced, and this doctrine also accounted for the fact I had noticed in the caves of the dead, that the forms there preserved were all beautiful, the figure perfect, and the limbs exquisitely moulded. These bodies were waiting the appearance of the revivifying soul.

Would their hope ever be realized? Who can say!

Nature is too full of mysteries for me to set up my poor judgment against the unknowable.

CHAPTER XXVIII.

A NEW EXPERIENCE.

I FELT I was in a strange city—one peopled by those whose last breaths had been drawn, it may be, thousands of years before.

Who were these warriors—these men and women and little children? Their skins were fair, their faces classical, and their bodies perfect. I could not help exclaiming:

> " The footsteps of an elder race are here,
> And memories of an heroic time,
> And shadows of an old, mysterious faith;
> So that the isle seems haunted, and strange sounds
> Float on the wind through all its ruin'd depths.
> Ages have gone, and creeds and dynasties,
> And a new order reigns o'er all the earth;
> Yet still the mighty presence keeps the isle—
> Awful and serene, and grandly tranquil."

I enjoyed the grand sublimity of the scene, and only regretted that the cold commonplace world would perhaps drive all the imagery and poetry of the reflections away from my mind, even as the wind will scatter the early morning's haze.

To whosoever it is given to dwell in an ideal world, or to realize the immensity of creation's plan, the world of men and women seems but a poor thing, and I was fast beginning to long more for the ideal and——

Could it be that *He* would give me an eternity of life if I so wished it?

There must be some way to baffle death. History has proved it. Did not some live a hundred years, others a hundred and fifty? If so, why not a thousand?

I would master these secrets, and then would use my age and power to restore to the world these hidden and lost arts.

These ideas flitted across my brain, as I sat contemplating the bodies of the children.

There was a silence, a solitude, a sense of ownership that made these subterranean sepulchers beautiful to my mind. I was the first, perhaps, for centuries to step within their walls.

I sat speculating, when a strange sensation passed over me.

My head began to swim, the scene around me vanished, and I felt as though I was about to faint, and yet I was in full possession of my faculties.

I saw nothing but the blank wall on the opposite side of the chamber of death. A shivering took possession of my frame. It seemed that everything was shaking and trembling also. The silence which I had so much enjoyed became awful in its intensity, and in that silence I felt a presence—invisible, 'tis true, but still tangible.

It touched me on the forehead as gently as a woman's fair hand could do.

I raised my head and peered into the darkness beyond.

Nothing could be seen, but the figures of the children wrapt in a mantle of eternal sleep.

The touch was renewed.

It filled me with ineffable pleasure. A thrill passed through my body, and I sighed for a renewal of the delicious sensation.

I was filled with overwhelming joy when a second time and yet a third time it came.

Pleasure the most exquisite thrilled every nerve in my body.

The hand rested for a moment on my forehead, then a gentle pressure drew my head down and it seemed to rest on some fair one's shoulder.

The pleasure was intense. The perfumes wafted from the movement of the invisible clothes which garbed the fair spirit lulled my senses. The breath which fanned my cheek was sweeter than the perfume of roses borne upon the zephyr breeze.

I could feel the gentle rising and falling of a bosom 'neath my head, and yet I saw no form, and could not touch it with my outstretched hand.

My blood coursed rapidly through my veins, my brain was on fire with frenzied delight, and I wanted but one thing to perfect my happiness—a sight of her who had so thrilled and fascinated me.

I prayed, that the fair one would materialize and manifest herself to my mortal eyes, but that boon was denied.

I felt a kiss, warm and passionate, pressed on my forehead, and later our lips met. It was the very ecstasy of bliss.

I put out my arms to clasp the presence.

For one moment I was able to do so, or rather, for one moment I was embraced. I felt the arms encircle me, and on my lips another kiss was imprinted.

Then the presence left me. The old state returned. I was alone in a cold vault, with no companions but the dead. The touch of the lips seemed to linger still with me, the clasp of the arms pressed me and melted away. I was alone!

Had it been a dream?

No! Of that I was confident. It had been a vision of another world, and arms had embraced me and lips kissed me, which were not the chimeras of imagination, but were actual realities.

For the first time I now felt afraid, and even the very air seemed so oppressive, and the stillness so awful, that I wanted to scream out in my affright.

I rose from my seat, and determined to leave.

Should I return the way I had come, or seek some further chamber which might contain still greater beauties and reveal other kingdoms of the dead, over whom some king reigned whose name and power had vanished, as the stars are paled by the effulgence of the sun?

Fear overcame my curiosity, and I had but one desire, and that was to get into the open air.

I retraced my steps into the chamber, where reposed the warriors. I knew I had to descend some steps into the apartment occupied by the ancient ladies; but, although I searched for half an hour, not a trace of any movable stone in the floor could I find.

I was trapped. If there were no passages in the vaults by which I could reach the open, save that through which I had entered, it looked as though my life would wear itself away amid the dead, and that when my spirit left the body, I know all that was mortal would exist but for a moment in comparison with the companions in death, whose vault it would share.

I had no desire to face death under such conditions, and so proceeded to search for a means of exit. I retraced my steps into the children's room, and found an archway which evidently led to still further caves.

Here a new difficulty presented itself. Was I not going further away from freedom? What if I got into the very center of the mountain, and had to retrace my steps without food or light?

The very thought froze my blood.

At Fjord's advice I had brought with me a ball of twine. This I fastened at one end to a stone bier, and then, as I walked along, gradually allowed it to unwind.

In my return I had only to follow the twine, and I should reach—not liberty, for I had been unable to find an exit, but should at least die amid beauty.

The passage in which I now entered was long and narrow, and I found my twine giving out very rapidly.

Was there no end to the corridor, or should I be compelled to return along its dreary length? I was getting weary and longed for rest.

A glimmer of light in the dim distance gave me courage and hope. It was evident there was a means of reaching the mountain side. I hurried forward, sometimes stumbling over bones and skulls, or loose pieces of rock which lie scattered in the pathway,

The light seemed as distant as when I started, and I began to feel weary with the walk. A new fear almost overpowered me—I needed rest. To lie down in the passage was loathsome to me, and possibly dangerous; to proceed only added to my fatigue, while I even doubted whether I possessed sufficient strength to return. My troubles and perplexities were not at an end, for my twine had given out, and I was obliged to trust to my good luck to find my way back. I still hoped another exit would be found. My brain began to swim, my temples throbbed, and my forehead seemed on fire.

If I could but get a breath of fresh air, I thought; and scarcely had the idea found a place in my mind than I experienced a gentle fanning sensation. The cool air passed over me, and I felt refreshed; but whence came it? That is to me an unexplained mystery.

It was real and tangible, but I saw no way for accounting for it.

I began to grow alarmed, for the fanning was producing a somnolent effect on me, and I feared I would fall asleep.

To exert myself and go forward toward the gleam of light was what I felt essential, but my limbs refused to support me, and I fell to the floor of the passage.

My body was weak, but beyond a sleepiness, my mental faculties were clear and bright. Distinctly I remember everything which passed, for this manuscript was not written until months had elapsed.

As I lay on the floor, which was cold and wet, I seemed to see a procession of the dead, whose forms I had beheld in the caverns beyond.

The men passed before me, looking ghastly in their whiteness; then the women, whose forms were never excelled in beauty by the brush of painter or the chisel of sculptor. As they passed, it seemed to me that they chanted a kind of hymn, the burden of which, as far as I could understand, being one of thanks to me for waking them from their slumber. What surprised me was that a brilliancy of light seemed to so encircle each figure that every detail of face and form could be seen.

It was beautiful. My senses were thrilled with delight, and I wished my father had been alive to have enjoyed the vision of the past, or that Fjord had been strong enough to have joined me in my explorations.

As each form passed me by, it seemed that I was gently fanned by a zephyr breeze redolent with perfume.

I closed my eyes, dazzled by the flashes of light emitted from each of the processionists, and gradually lost consciousness. My mind was sufficiently awake to know that I should soon have to succumb; but with a desperate resolve I calmed myself, and resigned myself to death, for that I felt to be my fate.

The last thing I remember was the flickering of my lamp, and the sudden flare with which it announced its last gasp of light. I was in the dark. Ahead of me tauntingly appeared the little glimmer of light, but all else was as black as Erebus. I was alone and dying. Yet no fear came to me. I was resigned and content. The sensation was pleasant; and if this was death, I felt it could have no terrors for me.

CHAPTER XXIX.

CAPTAIN FJORD'S STORY.

My friend and comrade Theodosius Aristophano has asked me to write an account of what took place after he started on his tour of explorations.

I am not so good with a pen as he is, but, perhaps, I think just as much, and, it may be, form as clear a conception of general happenings, but I dislike writing.

The story of our adventures would not be complete, however, if I didn't tell of those things which befell me when I had to act on my own hook.

It can readily be understood that I was impressed with the strange power possessed by our curious and mysterious host, more especially when I found myself so rapidly getting better from what all have told me was a fatal sickness, the recovery being brought about by the waving of his hands.

Milo was a good, faithful nurse, but unlike Theo.'s wife who was intelligent, she was more of the animal than the mental. Her knowledge of the legends was but slight, and very few places of interest on the island had she visited.

As I neared convalescence, I tried to learn from her some of the history of the people, and to find out why there were so many races apparently living there.

To all she would answer that there were but two people, those of the household of *He* and the savage natives.

On one subject she was very eloquent, and it was the only one on which she would ever talk coherently.

Milo insisted that this was the fourth time she had lived on the earth.

The first time, she said, in her own quaint, idiomatic speech, she was a pig.

I laughed, but then she became quite angry and declared she would not tell me any more. I explained away my laugh by saying that was the way the pale-faces expressed pleasure at any statement.

This mollified her a little, and she continued her story. The pig died, and its spirit entered into one of the savage babies, but very soon the young barbarian offended *He*, and was ordered to die. "But," said Milo, with charming *naivete*, "my spirit went to *He* and found him when asleep, so he did not kill me, but only the black body I was in."

I tried to grasp her meaning, and could perceive that her spirit, according to her, retained all its individuality throughout each stage of existence.

"When the black body was dead, I looked round for a white one, and *He* sent me into the cave of Thaloc, and there a little white child was born. I was its spirit, but it got killed in the wars, and I then was strong and good enough to be a female."

By repeated questionings, I learned that this strange people held to the idea that woman was to be the absolute perfection of creation.

That after many generations, or it might be thousands of years, all born would be girl children, and that would be the proof of Nature's perfection. Even now, Milo informed me women were better than men. I was too gallant to contradict a statement which my readers may, perhaps, hold to as strongly as did my Milo.

I think Theo. has somewhere written that each of *He's* household or family had a special god. Milo's favorite deity was one whose name she did not know. It was star-shaped, and had a large hole in its center, so that it could be worn as an amulet, if she preferred that way of keeping herself constantly in the presence of the god.

Unlike most of the idols I had seen, which were made of wood and stone, this one was of metal, roughly engraved and bearing the marks of great age upon it.

I questioned her as to her story of prior existence, but the only answers I could obtain were that she knew it to be so, and had not *He* himself—the mighty one, known her in all those states of existence?.

On asking her where she got the idol from, she told me it was in the cave of Thaloc.

"Who was Thaloc?" I asked, but she was unable to answer me.

Tanoa, the giant "Father," paid me a visit just at the time when I had asked this question, and so I repeated it to him.

Thaloc, I learned, was the god of water, and lived in a large cave, whose mouth went right up to the stars, so at least Tanoa told me.

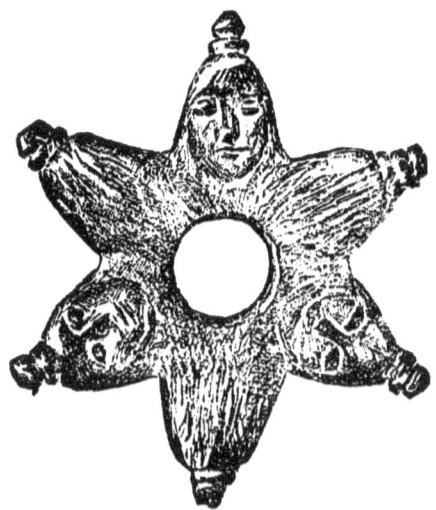

MILO'S IDOL.

"This god of water," Tanoa explained, "was on the island before *He* arrived there, and had a magnificent palace standing on each side of a great square. In the courtyard in the center there were four great holes of water, one of which was for the good rains, two for the bad rains, and another for white rain."

I was much amused at Tanoa's story, every word of which he devoutly believed. The scientists who read this chapter may learn something, when I tell them that Tanoa declared that Thaloc made a number of great bags which he called *thaloques*, and these bags he hung up in the sky by means of great strings. The *thaloques* had large

* Evidently these *thaloques* were clouds.

pitchers at the ends of poles and by these pitchers the water out of the holes was drawn up into the bags. When Thaloc wished for rain, he gave orders for the *thaloques* to empty themselves by means of the pitchers. Sometimes Tonacuto, another god, got angry and beat the *thaloques* with rods and the noise was so great that the people beneath were frightened. Occasionally some of the pitchers got broken and as the pieces fell a ray of light was seen.*

I noticed whenever Tanoa mentioned Thaloc, Milo took her metal god or talisman in her right hand, and with gentle pressure pressed it to her heart. I fully resolved to visit the cave of the water god, convinced that I should meet with many curiosities and antiquities. Milo consented to show me the way, but positively refused to enter the cave, although a blessing would be hers every time she visited the residence of her patron idol.

Theo.'s continued absence alarmed me. I knew he had taken with him provision for two or three days, but when the third morning broke and Rapa had not received any intelligence from him, I began to be alarmed.

I was now strong enough to start out on an exploring expedition, and had I known which way to go, should have tried to find my friend, for whom I felt a warmer feeling than I had ever before experienced for mortal, either male or female. He had not been near me since the strange time when he had restored me to health.

While I was wishing to see him, and resolving on seeking an interview, I suddenly raised my head and *He* was standing in front of me.

I had not seen him approach, although my eyes had but a moment before glanced round hoping to see Theo. I started up as if I had received an electric shock, and the next instant felt annoyed to think that any mortal's presence should so unman me.

He was always veiled, and that irritated me. It looked like the act of a charlatan.

"So you wonder what has become of your friend," said *He*, in an insinuating voice.

"I do."

"What if he be dead, as you call it."

"Dead?" I repeated, trying to penetrate the veil and catch a glimpse of the face.

"That is what I said, but mayhap you do not believe in death, but only look upon it as merely a long sleep, in which we are undergoing a preparation for a new and different existence."

"I have had such thoughts," I said, "but just now I

* This was Tanoa's explanation of thunder and lightning.

would like to know what mischance has befallen my comrade."

He turned away as though in thought, and then facing me, asked:

"Do you love your friend?"

"I do: better than I ever loved mortal!"

"Tush, tush! what idiocy is this? You would not give up the slightest thing for your so-called friendship."

"Try me!" I exclaimed: "for I swear——"

"The great Tabu forbid! Don't swear. I have seen mortals take an oath of fealty to a ruler, and then plot to kill him. I have known men swear and perjure their souls for a woman's smiles, and then when gained have flung her aside as carrion. I have heard—— But what matters it; human nature is ever the same, and you would swear you loved your boyish friend, and before the winter's darkness came would be ready to sell him if you could find a buyer."

"You wrong me!" I exclaimed indignantly, starting to my feet, and in my rage, assuming an attitude of defiance.

He laughed with the tremulousness of a hyena's laugh; and then, as I felt constrained to throw myself upon him and wrestle with him, utterly regardless of any real or supposed supernatural power, *He* shot out his dexter finger until it pointed straight into my face, and I fell to the ground stunned and stupefied.

He had not touched me, yet I felt bruised, and could not have endured greater punishment if I had been struck by Hercules on the forehead.

"So, my brave fellow," sneered the mysterious one, "you thought your poor strength was sufficient against me. I could wither you with a look. Nay, if I so desired, I could drain every drop of blood from your veins, dry up the flesh until life became a burden, and then, with a wave of my hand, could crumble what remained into dust."

"I do not doubt your strength," I gasped; "but taunt me not; tell me where my friend has gone."

"Take this," he said, seizing a crystal cup which savored of antiquity, "and fill it with water."

I did so, and *He* then made several wavy motions of his hand over it, and said:

"Now look!"

I gazed into the water, which assumed the varied tints of the opal, and a singularly beautiful spectacle was unfolded.

I saw a room or cave in which a number of dead were lying in graceful attitudes on polished marble tables.

On one reclined a body whose form possessed a familiar look, but whose face was hidden by the long tresses of a most beautifully proportioned girl who bent over it.

Her garments were different to any I had seen on the island; they seemed to be made of some filmy gauze which was so transparent that the olive-tinted skin could be plainly seen.

Was she weeping over some loved one whose spirit had taken flight?

"Look longer!" exclaimed *He*.

I continued my gaze, and the female rose and moved away, leaving the face of the reclining person distinctly visible.

I shrunk back aghast, for the face was that of Theo. Where was he, and who mourned over him? That was still a mystery.

"Is he dead?" I asked.

"Dead! What a word. Why, pale-faced and effeminate being, knowest thou not that death is but a phantom of ignorance, it has no existence at all; the body is only the outer garb of the spirit; the flesh is not the man, but only the covering of the man; whenever the body gets worn out, the spirit quits its frail tenement and moves into new and, perhaps, better quarters."

"That may be so, but still, when the body dies the spirit, as you call it, loses its individuality."

"Sometimes, but not always. I never lost my individuality, though I have changed my outward garment many times."

"Tell me, most mighty one, shall I ever see my friend again?"

"Friend!" *He* sneered. "Always friend; why, Fjord, I tell thee that your friendship would not last till next moon unless it suited you."

"My friendship is everlasting."

A low, mocking laugh was the only answer, and I got so mad that again I jumped to my feet, only to find that I was alone.

Was it all a dream or a fearful reality? I almost cursed myself for ever coming to this place; there was something in its very atmosphere which acted like opium, for I seemed to be in a constant delirium and dream.

CHAPTER XXX.
GO SLAY THY FRIEND!

MILO found me lying on my back asleep or in a swoon. When I awoke from a troubled nightmare, she was fanning me and singing a plaintive song, which might almost serve as a lullaby for a fond mother to sing by the cradle side.

The sight of my dusky bride recalled me to my senses, and I asked how long I had been asleep.

This she could not tell me, but said that as soon as *He the Mighty* allowed her to come to me she did so.

Had *He* prevented her? I asked her several times, but she did not comprehend my question. When she fairly understood me, she replied that she had not seen this powerful *He*, but that she had felt his influence keeping her back. And she was also sure that death would be her lot had she dared to contend against such influence.

It was yet broad day, and I entreated her to show me the way to the cave or dwelling of Thaloc.

After considerable hesitation she consented, and a few minutes later we were crossing the valley and were within a short distance of the, to me, enchanted ground.

When we neared one of the extinct volcanoes, Milo pointed to the summit where, to my surprise, I saw *He* standing in an attitude of rapt meditation.

Milo was afraid to approach the rocks until I assured her that there was no danger which could possibly befall her.

I felt her shudder, but her confidence was so great that she overcame her fear and pressed me to the rocky entrance to the cave of Thaloc.

How can I describe the entrance? It is almost impossible for words to convey to the mind an idea of that gateway to the realms of the god of the waters.

Imagine an immense rock standing at least a hundred feet high, and with a diameter of say thirty feet, a solid mass of stone whose every side was incrusted with lava of various colors and tints; then glance down and find that this gigantic bowlder was balanced on a sort of pedestal of less than six feet in diameter, and this pedestal again resting on a smaller rock, and you have some idea of the peculiar "rock in the road." It was a balanced rock with a vengeance, and though I am possessed of considerable strength of nerve, I trembled as I went on all fours to crawl by the side of the pedestal, and under the hundreds of ton of stone above me.

I raised my head rather too soon and struck it with great force on the rock, when I imagined I detected a movement of the mass above me.

I quickened my speed and was very glad when I stood again in an upright position.

I told Milo that I thought the rock had moved.

She laughed, and, as she showed a perfect set of ivories, I could not help wondering why this child of nature had such perfect teeth, when the daughters of civilization so often had irregular and imperfect ones.

Milo laughed, and calling on me to look, she went close up to the rock and pushed it. To my surprise it began to rock with a gentle, undulating motion, as easily as a cradle responds to the action of the nurse.

"Come away!" I cried, but Milo only laughed the more, and again pushed the rock.

In her own primitive fashion she told me that she had often been rocked to sleep on its top, the wind swaying the bowlder. We stood in a deep ravine, the stone walls, lava-covered, standing almost perpendicularly some hundreds of feet above us. The passage was narrow.

Along this we walked in single file for fifty or sixty yards, when we found the way get so narrow that it was with difficulty I could squeeze through.

Our trouble was well repaid, for a plateau or basin was now reached, and as I stood looking at its lofty walls, so beautifully bedecked with many-tinted streams of cold lava, I felt I was in one of nature's temples, and a feeling of reverential awe came over me.

This was the site of the palace of the god Thaloc: so said Milo; and I readily understood that, at some time, a temple or dwelling had really stood there.

Many huge blocks of stone lay scattered about, and several inevitable idol platforms were to be found.

On one was a tall column, octagonal in shape, with its sides covered with hieroglyphics very similar to those I had once seen in Egypt taken from the temple of Heliopolus, and known in modern ages as Cleopatra's Needle.

On one side was a figure of the god Thaloc; the carving was very clear, every line showing as if it had only just left the sculptor's chisel, whereas it had doubtless stood there a thousand years.

Under the platform on which stood this obelisk was a small passage-way, by which an underground vault could be reached.

Milo shuddered when she knew that it was my intention to go down into its depths, and with many speeches and supplications urged me to stay with her. Promising that my journey would be a short one, I left her to await my return, and slowly descended the steps. The descent was difficult, the passage very narrow; the little light which glinted through the rocks only seemed to make the way more perilous by its uncertain reflection. I thrust myself forward, bruising myself at every step. After fully ten minutes of such scrambling and stumbling I reached the bottom, and stood in a small chamber hewn by nature's hand in the hard gray rock. On one side was a shaft or opening which admitted a faint streak of light. On the opposite side a monster pile of bones showed that the cave had been used as a burial-place. Skulls were seen everywhere, and I could scarcely step without kicking some with my feet.

THE GOD THALOC.

I stooped to pick one up, when out of its eye-sockets wriggled a viper. I quickly dropped the skull, and killed the reptile with a stick which I carried. A sensation of sickness came over me. It was horrible to contemplate that in the skull of some one who had once breathed and lived as I did a poisonous reptile should hide itself.

"Not at all pleasing, is it?" exclaimed a voice over my shoulder.

I turned and beheld the veiled prophet or fiend who rejoiced in the cognomen of *Hé*.

"How came you here?" I asked, but no answer was vouchsafed.

"Are you man or devil?" I inquired.

"Neither. I am just what I am, the representative of Will."

"You are a mystery."

"Perhaps so, but what I am you can be also."

"How?"

"By doing as I did."

"You are immortal?" I asserted, but at the same time gave it as a suggestion of a question.

"No, and yes. If by immortal you mean I can never die, that my will, myself, will always live, then I am; but if you mean that this body will always exist, why that is absurd. I am tired of it now, and would like to exchange it for another."

"Very likely, but that is impossible."

"Not at all. I have even thought I should like your friend's body."

"Spare him," I pleaded.

"That is as it may be, but if I had his body she would love me."

"She?"

"Yes, the one who for twenty long centuries I have waited for, my only love."

Thinking to unravel some of the mystery, I fell into his way of speaking, and so said:

"But is any one woman worth loving so long?"

"Yes, she is, and though I have to live for thousands of years longer, I shall do so, until she places her head on my shoulder and says in my ear, 'I am thine.'"

"And then," I said, "you would soon tire of her, and regret the waste of so many years."

"Very probable, for I know that the words 'I love you' from the same lips must soon weary the same ear."

What a contradiction was this veiled ruler! Loving one object, according to his own account, for centuries, and then admitting he would soon tire of her love if it was once his.

I could not understand his philosophy, so sought to change the subject by asking:

"What made you follow me here?"

"I never follow any. I go where it pleaseth me."

"Do you often, oh, mighty one, come here?"

"Who art thou, to question me, whose power is greater than all the kings of the outer world, whose majesty is so mighty that did I but say the word, all nations would bow before me? By what right, I ask thee, dost thou try to find out my doings?"

"Nay, oh, mighty one, I am not curious, and yet, if there be a power by which the thoughts of others can be read, and the doings of the people known, I fain would find it out."

"Hast thou the courage?"

"I have."

"What wouldst thou give for this power?"

"Canst thou, great ruler, give it to me?"

"I might, if you refuse not the conditions."

"Tell me what they are, for whatever they are I consent to them, even if my soul pays the forfeit!"

"Tush! Who wants thy soul, even if it be of value? You possess no power over thy soul. But what else wouldst thou give?"

"All, everything! I will sign any compact, will do anything for this power."

"There is no compact. I know more about the human body, and its interior consciousness, which you call soul, than you do, that is all. But thou sayest that all wouldst thou give to know the secrets of life?"

"All, yes, there is nothing I would not give."

"I will put you to the test. Go, slay thy friend."

I started, a sudden fear came over me.

The cave was dark, not a solitary ray of light now pierced its gloom, and I was alone.

The words kept ringing in my ears.

"Go, slay thy friend."

Did *He* utter them or was it only a dream, a thought conjured up by the weird associations of the burial-place?

With my brain on fire I groped my way up the stairs and found Milo keeping faithful watch at the entrance.

I was pleased to see her. It was a comfort to have even her company and presence.

"Is there any other way to the cave?" I asked.

"Which cave?"

"The one I have been in."

"No!"

"Have you seen the mighty *He* enter the cave?"

"No; I have waited alone for you, my own, my beloved."

I was now convinced it must have been imagination, but ringing in my ears was the constant repetition of the command:

"Go, slay thy friend!"

I suggested that we return, and Milo was nothing loath.

We passed under the balanced rock, not without some nervous dread on my part, and reached our dwelling-place without further adventure.

"Go, slay thy friend!" What did it mean? Was I

going mad? To slay Theo., whom I had learned to warmly love, was impossible. Still the words seemed like fire burning into my brain, and I remembered I had said I would do everything or anything to possess the power which *He* alone seemed to enjoy.

What if that were the condition? Could I do it? No—a thousand times no, and yet, what was one life compared to the eternity I should win?

"Great Heaven!" I thought, "has it come to this, that I should even entertain the thought of purchasing a lease of life by the murder of the youth committed to my care?"

I fell asleep that night with the haunting words searing my brain, "Go, slay thy friend."

CHAPTER XXXI.
PARTLY AUTOBIOGRAPHICAL.

"IF we could be but always young," was my first thought on awakening the following morning. It had been the dream of my life to find that secret elixir which would perpetuate youth. I had pored over the writings of the Pythagoreans; I had studied mysteries in Hindoostan, and vainly sought in the works of the Alchemists and Rosicrucians for the great secret.

This had been the work of my life, for I had one great horror, and that was—I dreaded old age.

Once when walking along the streets of my native city, I was accosted by an old rheum eyed man. He was shrunken and wrinkled, his body was bent with the weight of years, and his voice was shrill and feeble. He presented to my young mind a horrid fear-like specter. I dreaded to become old. I was but young, but my resolve was made, that if the opportunity ever came I would search for the elixir, and failing to find it, I would seek repose in the grave before old age palled upon me. I was early left with an ample fortune, and no one had power to curb my desires or control my movements. Then passing for an enthusiastic antiquarian, I traveled everywhere, stored my mind with the stories of the Middle Ages, drunk deep of the love which inspired the legend of Faust, came to believe in the truth of Ahasuerus, and never doubted that a tree of life did flourish in some part of the world.

This was my state of mind when, passing through Madre-di-Dios, I fell in with the Aristophanos, father and son.

In them I saw seekers after the same idea, and the conjunction was pleasant to me.

I had sacrificed all human ties, denied myself home associations, everything so that I could devote my whole attention to this one thing.

I had bowed to the custom of Rapa Nui, and accepted Milo as my wife, because I found I had no means of escaping the vengeance of the great chief and his people unless I conformed to their customs.

Did I love Milo? That I can scarcely answer. She was as amiable as a young lady of a fashionable city, she was affectionate and attentive, would do all in her power for me, her life seemed bound up in my welfare, but I cannot conscientiously say that I loved her as a wife deserves to be loved.

She was necessary and convenient. I had one love, and that was the secret I was trying to find.

Oh, to be always young. Once let me find out that secret, and then mine it should be to enjoy life, to love, to revel!

"Go, slay thy friend!"

Why that haunting thought? Would *He* show me, when next I saw him, that this great mystery can be attained; but will he forbid me attaining it unless I slay my friend? What would *He* benefit by Theo.'s death? That was a perplexing question, and its very strangeness made me feel that I was not free from fever's delirium, but that its heated frenzy still flowed in burning torrents through my veins.

I took a bath, hoping that would cool my blood and refresh me, but while my body was invigorated, it seemed as if before me was the ever horrible thought, "Slay thy friend."

Turn which way I would, the haunting demon whispered in my ears: "Slay thy friend." The wind caused the grass to rustle, and its every sound murmured the same words.

I could bear it no longer; I would seek the presence of *He the Mighty*, and demand from him the meaning of this perpetual, insinuating, haunting thought.

To his apartments I went, and was welcomed with a warmth greater than I had before experienced.

"Come, Fjord, my pale faced Eastern disciple, thou art in time to witness the dance, the merry revels of my faithful girls."

I stood by the side of the chair of skulls upon which *He* sat, when turning to me he commanded me to be seated.

A chair, which came I know not where from, glided up behind me, and I sat down, entirely regardless of the fact that every part of the seat had once been clothed with human flesh.

Tanoa, who appeared to be a grand high chamberlain, clapped his hands.

The moment the signal was given, the curtains parted, and a dozen young girls entered.

They were habited differently to what I had heretofore seen them.

Their shoulders were bare, their bosoms covered with a kind of cuirass made of shells, linked together with very fine thread or wire; this cuirass, which clearly defined the outlines of their figures, did not reach quite to the waist.

About four or five inches below was bare as the shoulders; then a fine muslin or linen scarf was fastened round the waist, and its transparent folds acted as a transition between the clear nudity of the upper part and the drapery which hid the hips and fell round the lower extremities in voluminous folds as low as the ankles.

The effect of this dress was peculiar, but not graceful. I thought it would have been better to have equalized the drapery by putting more on the upper parts and still leaving plenty to cover the lower limbs.

The twelve girls made a deep salaam before their ruler, who sat motionless as a statue, and then at another signal from Tanoa, they commenced a weird dance.

I could not conceive how they were prevented from falling, the drapery seemed so redundant, and clung to their limbs; but as the steps grew quicker, I saw that the lower garments were double, for the girls raised the upper skirt, if it could be called by such a name, and raising it above their heads, whirled round rapidly. Their appearance being very much like some giant shell, with a vision of loveliness in the person of a girl in the center.

As this dance proceeded, getting noisier, wilder, and gayer, the girls seemed to most thoroughly abandon themselves to the excitement, and it looked as if their resolve was to dance or die.

The drapery, by a simultaneous movement, was unfastened and thrown into a corner of the room, and then the girls continued the dance in all the fury of the wildest of tarantulas, their clothing consisting of the Ireeree fringe and the cuirass.

It was a beautiful sight, and would have charmed any who beheld it.

The movements continued until one by one the girls sank exhausted, and then *He* rose and motioned me to follow him to another apartment. The dancers were left on the floor until tired nature had recuperated itself.

"A pretty sight," said *He*, when we were alone. "What thinkest thou of it?"

"A pretty sight indeed," I repeated.

"Old age cannot dance; youth can have all the pleasures. Who would grow old—to feel the stiffness of the joints, to have the will to dance, but lose the power; to feel the eyes getting dim, the sight fading, the brain failing, the hold upon the world weakening—who would be old?"

He looked through his veil at me, and then seeing my paleness, for I was unduly excited by his words, he continued:

"Make the best of youth, Fjord, for with youth there is light when the maidens smile, a dimness when the rosy blush suffuses her cheek, and darkness when a frown wrinkles her brow. Oh, youth is the time for love, for joy, for the revel, but age hath its pleasures. Yes, the old man can be wheeled about by the young, to watch the rout he would like to join. You are getting old, my Fjord."

"Torment me not. I cannot stand it. Wilt thou tell me how to attain perpetual youth?"

"Of what use? Thou wouldst never attain it, fear and scruples would hold you back."

"Never."

"First penetrate the barrier, by intense enthusiasm, purified from all that is carnal. Remove every obstruction from your path, even if it be thy friend—ah, you start! But listen and don't interrupt.

"He who would establish intercourse with the spirits of the atmosphere, some of surpassing wisdom, others hostile as fiends, is a traveler in an unknown land. He is exposed to strange dangers and unconjectured terrors. The deadliest foes beset his path, and I would not stir to protect him. Pass through this period bravely and unscathed, and Tabu, the eternal, the mighty, the great presence, will give thee that which thou cravest. Dost thy courage falter?"

"Nay, I but desire it the more."

"Then thou shalt be tested."

"What of my friend?"

"Still thy friend. He may be safe, or he may be with the dead—what is that to thee? Go, seek repose and await my summons."

I was about to question further, but *He* waved his hand, and I was forced by an unseen power to leave his presence.

CHAPTER XXXII.

FJORD'S VISION OF THE INFERNO.

THAT night I could not sleep. I tossed on my couch almost delirious. Poor Milo feared that the fever was returning to me.

I had passed a couple of hours in this wild unrest, when my mind was still further disturbed by the entrance of Rapa, who seemed distracted with grief.

"My beloved has gone," she chanted, her voice husky with emotion. "The great spirits of the grave have taken him from me, and Rapa will see him no more."

"What do you mean?" I asked.

"In the darkness of night, when the god closed my eyes, and the shadow of the dark was on me, I saw my own, my dear one, caressed and loved by those whose bodies are in the caves of the dead. I shall never see him more."

A wild, wailing sound broke from the girl who had learned to love my handsome young comrade, and neither Milo nor I could console her.

She had a fixed and irrevocable opinion that Theo. was dead.

Then occurred to me what *He* had insinuated, and the horrible thought passed through my mind that when I did not seek and slay my friend, *He* had perhaps done the deed himself.

Milo wept with Rapa, and the grief of the two women was more than I could stand, so I bade Rapa be of good cheer, that on the morrow I would seek my friend, and we should all be reunited and happy.

Leaving them together, I went out, and my curiosity led me along the passage, and to the vault or cave in which we had seen the perfect statue.

I was desirous of again examining it, and, as I could not sleep, the present was as good as any other time. To the dwellers in the caves, night was no different to day; we gloried in the darkness, and many of the household beheld the light of day but seldom.

Guided by the little stream of light, I readily found my way to the cave in which the lovely marble stood.

The curtains looked as if they had been quite recently drawn aside, and I felt rather curious to know who visited the stone woman.

That a fire was kept in the cave was sufficient of itself to arouse my curiosity. Then the stories I had read of the wonderful woman loved by *He*, whose form turned to stone when others were near, so excited my imagination, that, as they recurred to my mind, I fancied I heard voices beyond the curtain.

My heart beat violently, my blood rushed madly through my veins, and the very delirium of joy and pleasure possessed me.

But it was no fancy. I distinctly heard some one speaking.

One was a voice of heavenly sweetness, mingled with a sadness which was unnatural in so lovely a voice.

The other was harder, and masculine. I drew near, moving cautiously for very fear that my approach might be discovered. A light was flickering through the curtains, and, oh, great Heaven! I could see into the cave beyond.

The fire burned with a blue flame, casting a weird light over the strange apartment. In the center stood the marble statue, calm and unruffled as I had seen it before, but either my imagination was very vivid, or I had been mistaken on the previous inspection, for now the lovely female had a different attitude. Her head was bent, and her left hand was extended, pointing toward—— Great Heaven! The sight appalled me, and I felt the blood freeze in my veins, for the figure kneeling in front of the statue was the mysterious *He*.

The veil had been removed, and *He* was habited in a tunic of pure white, edged and broidered with gold. His hair seemed as long as a woman's, and hung on his shoulders in graceful profusion.

There was a sadness on his face which I could never have imagined he could show.

His face fascinated me, and yet it was the fascination of terror. The eye was not so bright, and the mien less haughty, but there was something which even then bespoke the majesty of the man.

My head began to swim, and I had to lean my weight against the wall to save me from falling.

The whole scene was weird, and savored of the supernatural.

The hand of the statue fell to its side—of that I feel sure —and then in a voice of plaintive sadness, but divinely sweet, it said: "Rise, thou who conquered the secrets of the grave, and by the mastery of nature performs such wonders, let thy power be thy love——"

"Oh hear me!" implored the recumbent man, "hear me; for all the ages I have loved thee, for thy sake I forsook all, and having learnt as thou sayest the secrets of the tomb, the mystery of life and death, I have lived but for one object, thy love. Turn not from me, or my grief will be greater than I can bear. Lovely angel of the ages, thy soul has been chained to the marble, only to become purer and more noble; let not the ages pass without thy love."

The agony was terrible to witness, and as I saw his features distorted with the hopelessness of his passion, I began to think of myself. But even if I had known that I should never leave those curtains alive, I could not move. I was fixed and rooted to the spot, for I was spell-bound and fascinated. Still I knew my danger. I was fully conscious that should *He* by his magic or other power discover my presence, my fate was sealed, and I should instantly meet a doom from which there would be no appeal on earth.

"Rise, thou Egyptian; my love was given to thy son, who has again inhabited human form——"

"My son alive!" he gasped.

"Alive, yes! I have seen him, and for over two thousand years I have waited, and endured the coldness of the marble; for two decades of centuries my passion has sustained me, for I loved him then—I love him now—and though he believes me not, and passes again into the realms of the grave, he will come again, and I shall in his arms breathe out my love into his ear and be at rest."

"Never! Hark to my words. I chained thee to the marble, and transported thee hither. For thy sake I have lived amid scenes of savagery, and made a dwelling-place of a tomb. Thinkest thou not that I would have achieved marvels in that old world of ours? Would not Isis have rewarded her servant and priest?

"But, for thy sake, I forsook all. Be my love, and together we will return, and thou shalt be queen of the fairest realms, and shalt make the nations of Asia and Africa thy footstool, as from dear old Athens thy word shall rule the world. Wilt thou give heed to my prayer?"

"Never; though ten thousand times as many years roll by, my answer will still be the same. I love another, and my love is strong and unquenchable, and all the waters of the universe could never wash it away. My beloved shall bask in that love, none other."

"Then," *He* exclaimed, standing erect, "by that same power which chained thee to the marble, I shall destroy thee, and banish thy soul to that death from which there is no return."

"That, most mighty one, is beyond thy power, for I, too, have learned of the ages, and dwelt in a realm where the secrets of nature are reflected as in a mirror, and my power is greater than thine. My beloved shall be mine!"

"Curse him!" he hissed, through his teeth. "Curse him, and curse the mother who bore him!

"Let his name be forever accursed!

"If the gods decree that he again visit the realms of earth-life, may the blighting curse of Tabu and all the gods rest upon him!"

His anger was terrible to behold, and his voice curdled my blood. The energy was frightful, and at every curse the echo through the cave sounded like a thunder shock.

"Wouldst thou curse thine own son, the son of the priestess who left a throne to live with thee?"

"Curse her and curse him! I would curse all for thy sake. For one glance of love from thine eye, I would spend eternities of torture; for one word of love from thy pure lips, all the fiends of the nether regions might tear me to pieces, and drag my lacerated body writhing with pain through the countless ages.

"For thy sake I would steep my hands in blood, and slay those who trusted me most. I sinned, perhaps, in my unholy passion two thousand years ago, but the ages have atoned for that, and our love shall make life bright. Say that thou lovest me a little."

"I love thee not, and my only regret is that thou hast the power to reanimate this marble, for my life is one of expectant love till thou art by my side.

"One word! one look! Oh, my darling, my love! It is no use; the vital spark has gone—I talk to nothing but the cold marble."

He flung himself on the ground. His agony was greater than I thought a human being could endure and live.

I saw the necessity of leaving before I was discovered.

I tried to move, but my legs refused to support me, and I fell to the ground.

I had to creep along the passage, trembling and shaking with fear at every step. I stumbled and fell on my face many times. Now I placed my hand on a snake, which hissed with fear as it wriggled from beneath my weight; again an obstacle was in my path, and, pushing it away, I found it was a human skull.

A rat of a large and ferocious kind attacked me, and before I could beat it away it had inserted its teeth several times in my flesh, drawing streams of blood.

It was a night of horror. A vision of hell with its damned and tortured spirits. My curiosity had given me a glimpse beyond the veil, and I saw that stronger than life or death, firmer than the tomb, and greater than the myriad hosts of heaven and earth, was love.

Unhallowed it may be, but a fierce passion which time could never quench and nothing kill.

I arrived back faint and exhausted, and under the

gentle, lulling influence of Milo, sought forgetfulness in sleep.*

CHAPTER XXXIII.

THEO. RESUMES HIS STORY.

THE sensations experienced by me when fanned by the unseen hands, were more delicious than any I had before known.

If that was death, I hailed it as a blessing rather than a terror.

The dreams of that sleep were of fascinating pleasure. It seemed to me that I soared away through the clouds into the pure azure of the sky, until I reached a palace on which was seated the Queen of Beauty.

She waved her scepter, and motioned me to approach: I fell on my knees before her, not daring to look into her face.

"Rise, mortal," she said, "and share my throne with me, for it has been reserved for you for ages."

Astonished at such a speech, I raised my eyes and beheld the most lovely woman I had ever seen. Her face shone like the sun, and the radiance which proceeded from the halo of glory which encircled her head was of dazzling brilliancy.

Her face was slightly averted, and so I was able to take a longer look at her. There was something about the form and figure which appeared familiar; she turned, and as she did so, a ray of light seemed to flash like lightning from each eye.

Gradually she lowered them and looked at me, when to my surprise I saw it was the wonderful statue.

"Come, my beloved," she said, "and through the ages we will live, hand in hand, showing that love is eternal."

Then there arose through the perfume-laden air sounds of music wafted from unseen instruments, beautiful, delicious and absorbing.

Never did I so enjoy the dreams of night. I wished they might be eternal, could it be that I was in the land of spirits? No, for I felt my visions gradually fading, my hot blood began to course again through my veins, and I felt that I had but taken a glimpse of the wonderland in the visions of sleep.

When I awoke I was lying on a fur skin in a cave which seemed strange to me. It was some time before I could

---

* The numerous erasures in Fjord's MSS., and the similarity of style, tells me that Theo. must have written from Fjord's dictation.—ED.

realize that I was awake; when I did so, I raised my head and saw by my side a young woman, or girl, for she could not have been more than sixteen years old.

Her complexion was scarcely so dark as a Thitian, and approached more nearly to that of a Mongolian.

She possessed wonderful regularity of features, and her large, full eyes were of a most seraphic blue. Her shoulders were bare and only a thin scarf crossed her bosom. The lower part of her body was draped with white muslin arranged in almost Grecian manner; its folds left the development of the hips, so admirably shaped, to the imagination to realize.

She fanned me gently, and as every breath of air passed over me it was laden with perfume.

I fancied this was but a continuation of my dream, and again closed my eyes, so that the illusion might not be dispelled.

The fanning ceased, and instead of the rose-scented breeze a more appetizing, if not so æsthetic, perfume ascended my nostrils. It was that of warm soup, and to a hungry man it possessed a charm which transcended all else.

I felt the gentle pressure of a hand on my arm, and opening my eyes, I saw that I was expected to rise and eat.

A very few minutes sufficed for the emptying of the basin of soup, it was so good and savory.

When every drop had disappeared, the lovely blue-eyed gazelle glided across the rock-hewn cave, and returned bearing vegetables and fruits of the most luscious kind.

I endeavored to find who my beautiful attendant was, or how I got to such excellent quarters, but not a word could I get from her.

I tried Spanish, but she was silent; Hebrew, but not a ray of intelligence crossed her face; then I spoke Arabic, but silence was my answer. Mongolian and Tahitian, at least, as much as I understood, all met with responsive silence, until I began to feel that either she had been commanded not to speak, or that she was a mute.

When I had finished my repast, she motioned for me to again lie down and then commenced the fanning.

I was lulled to sleep, and soon dreamed fair dreams of joy and love and happiness. When wrapped in the deepest slumber, it seemed as if a hot breath passed across my face, and that a burning kiss was impressed upon my lips.

The effect produced by this dream was so violent, that I could not for a long time afterward decide in my own mind whether it was a dream or reality.

A strange thing occurred to me; by degrees and under the influence of the perpetual fanning, my memory of the past faded away, just as we lose sight of a landscape in the surrounding mists as we gradually leave it in the distance; then it entirely disappeared from my mind, and all my efforts to recall it were ineffectual.

It seemed to me that I had always lived there, that the strange girl had been my constant companion. I lay on my rugs looking in fixed contemplation on her, absorbed in the happiness of her presence. Yet I did not love her. The feeling was a peculiar one, which it is powerless to describe.

Was it her lips that imprinted the warm kiss, or was that only a dream?

How I wished she would speak, but though I questioned her often, not a syllable would she utter.

I longed to clasp her in my arms, but dare not attempt it.

Whenever she looked at me, and her blue eyes pierced into my very soul, it seemed that she, too, would like the passionate kisses which I had felt in my sleep.

But she made no motion, and kept a reserve as cold as though no fire of passion's tempest passed over her frame or burning lava flowed through her veins. Slowly I seemed to realize that I had not always been there, but what the past had been, or who were my companions and comrades I had not the faintest remembrance.

The constant attendance of the lovely girl seemed to create in me a strong desire to tell her I loved her.

I was young in age, but experience had placed many more years to my credit.

Had I forgotten Rapa? No, there was a faint remembrance of her, but only as if she had been a resident of another world, or that I had met her, as Fjord would say, in a prior existence. The faintness of memory only made me the more desirous to clasp this beauteous being in my arms.

"Dear one, beautiful as the morning star," I cried. "I love you; do not leave me in solitude."

Either she did not understand me or purposely turned a deaf ear to my love entreaty, for she made no sign, never spoke a word, but went around with the same undeviating precision as before. Not a flutter in her bosom, not a blush was called to her cheek. Was she mortal, for surely if my language was not understood the accents of love appeal to the heart as much as the ear.

I grew bolder, and leaping to my feet with the intention of addressing her, I found that I was weak and helpless, and fell to the floor. I could not rise without assistance, and when my attendant had helped me to regain my couch, I seized her by the waist and drawing her down kissed her ruby lips many times. I was more than ever perplexed, for while she made no resistance there was no reciprocation; she submitted to the kisses as a matter of course, but not a tremor passed through her, the color of her cheeks was not heightened, and as she withdrew from my grasp, she went around as unconcernedly as though nothing unusual had happened.

Was she mortal? Her form was that of a beauteous girl, her skin was soft and velvety, her lips were luscious and warm, but it seemed, when I clasped her in my arms, it was more like a piece of animated statuary than a living being.

The wonders of these caves seemed to be endless, and I was beginning to think that life would be but one long exploration, and when death came the research would not be ended.

The moment the idea of death shaped itself to my mind, it appeared to me as if a chorus of spirits was singing. "There is no death. The past is a mere idle phantom, the future a vision. Let flesh and blood enjoy the present, for love renders its recipient the monarch of the world."

The words were sounded in my ears quite distinctly, and even now as I write, they recur to me as if it were only a moment ago since I heard them.

I slept, and when I awoke I saw, to my dismay, that my fair attendant had given place to another.

My love paroxysm perhaps had offended her, but there was no fear of its return with my present assistant, for she was the very antithesis of the other.

The first one was fair skinned, this one was as dark as a negress; the other delicately formed, the one now present stout and of bad figure. She, too, refused to speak, but patiently waited on me and helped me toward convalescence.

With her by my side memory returned to me, and I regained my individuality. I wondered what had become of Fjord, and whether Rapa mourned for me as one lost. Where was *He* that his power was not great enough to find me?

So I pondered and wondered, until the lamp which lighted the cave flickered and died out.

I called for a light. No response. The very darkness seemed dense and palpable, and I realized what that plague of Egyptian darkness really was.

I felt for the stone on which my black nurse had sat; it was there, but unoccupied. I realized I was alone.

CHAPTER XXXIV.

THE MYSTERIOUS STATUE.

How long I remained alone I know not, but I suddenly felt a presence enter the cavern.

I say felt, for it was impossible to see any one. The feeling was a strange one, but I could detect every movement of the visitor, and could tell just when he or she halted, and when moving forward.

A stifling, choking feeling seemed to overpower me, and I raised my hand to ward off the hands of a strangler, for I verily believed I was being strangled by some unseen but palpable body.

I failed to feel any one, but the strangling sensation continued. I felt I should soon succumb, my tongue seemed swelling, my eyes were starting from their sockets. I tried to scream out but could not; the words died in my throat.

In an instant the sensation left me, and, with the exception of a slight weakness, no ill results remained.

Oh! if there had been a light, I thought; but my wish was not gratified.

Again I felt some one approaching, and, instinctively, I raised my hands to my throat, as a protection.

I closed my eyes, and awaited my doom. The presence halted near me, and, as I was uninjured, I opened my eyes, and there, standing in a brilliant light which surrounded her, I beheld the Marble Statue. I passed my hand over my eyes in an endeavor to find whether I was dreaming or awake.

Everything was so real, and has been so indelibly stamped on my mind, that I am inclined to think it was reality, and not a chimera of the imagination. The Statue drew near, and sank with gentle grace upon the stone seat near my couch.

I had seen so many marvels that I was not surprised at this seeming impossibility.

"Come!" she said sweetly, beckoning me to rise.

Fascinated by her radiant beauty, and impelled by some mysterious power, I rose from my couch, and, to my astonishment, was able to walk.

A few hours ago, or so it seemed to me, my limbs were powerless; now I felt strong and hearty.

My lovely guide moved over the surface of the cave with a gentle undulation, and seemed like a column of light pointing and guiding the way.

She spoke not until we passed into a larger cavern,

where I saw the girl whose form I had so passionately clasped in my arms.

She saw me, and I imagined a deepened tint was on her face.

Her head was bent down, and she seemed only intent in gazing on a skull which lay at her feet.

I was about to ask my guide about this lovely girl, when my thoughts were read, and the statuesque Venus turned her carven but piercing eyes on me and said:

"You awakened a soul. That lovely body"—pointing to the girl—"was soulless. It came into the world before any spirit was ready to inhabit it. No passion or feeling stirred the child as it grew up. Everything which could be performed automatically, or by instinct or imitation, it could do, but there was no thought, no soul. To arouse the animal nature, I ordered that she should wait upon you. You became struck with her beauty, dazzled by her simplicity, and made love to her. She was soulless, and therefore gave no response. You kissed her lips and drew her form to your own. That was animal, and it stirred the pulses of her heart, and she thought she liked you. In solitude she began to think. Love had kindled the spark of intelligence, and only now a soul has entered the beautiful body."

"Is it possible," I asked, "for a human being to enter the world unpossessed of a soul?"

"Why not? The animal is distinct from the mental. The one is subject to decay, the other is eternal; the one suffers, the other is free from pain. A perfect man or woman consists of two distinct organisms, each of which can exist independent of the other."

"I never thought of that," I said.

"Likely not; but hast thou not met, oh, my dear one, with men and women who have no brain power, who never think, who walk only because they are made to do it by the necessities of their nature, who eat and drink and die, and that is all."

"Thou sayest truly," was my response.

"Then are the gods to blame if these creatures possess an immortal soul which is so stunted that thought is impossible?"

"No more," I answered, boldly, "than parents are to blame if they bring into the world children with stunted frames or undeveloped bodies."

"That is true. Then are the gods to blame because nature is perfect, and every deformed child at birth, every stunted frame, every wine-bibing, gluttonous, rapacious child only entered with those propensities or deformities because of their parents' neglect of physical laws?"

"I cannot argue with you," I said, feeling that the philosophy of my youth was being overturned.

"Come, then, and I will show thee where lie those who were with me when I came to this island of caves. Look at this cave. Hast thou ever seen its equal? and yet it was hewn by the mighty race which dwelt here in times past."

I looked at the walls of this mammoth cave, and found them covered with inscriptions, of which I had time to copy only this one:

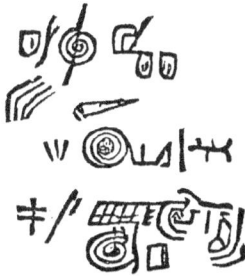

Before a stone slab which had the appearance of having been carefully smoothed and polished, my guide stopped, and bade me read the long inscription.

This I was unable to do. The characters seemed like the Chinese—but of this language I had but a poor knowledge—so I confessed my ignorance.

Thereupon she read it for me, and translated it, as near as I can remember, as follows:

"In the year of the most august and mighty Khung-fu-tsze was this cave finished by order of Haya, the great king, to be a resting-place for his children and the great men of Ana Quena who might come after him, and seeing that Ana Quena had been ruled over by Haya and his fathers before him for three thousand seven hundred and seventy-three epochs, it was therefore enacted that three thousand seven hundred and seventy-three slaves should be gathered together from the lands which bowed not before Tabu, and made to carve out the caves for the people. May the blessing of Tabu and all the myriads of gods rest upon those who shall sleep herein, until the man whose face shall shine as the sun bids them arise.

"Thou seest, then, that these caves," she continued, "were made nearly four thousand years after the country was inhabited, but when I was brought here, two thousand years ago, they were like they are now."

I was mystified; it seemed as though I had lost the power of speech. My guide passed along into another cavern where I saw a carving of a man and woman clasped in each other's arms. Over their heads was an inscription in Greek, which read: "They loved with the love the waters cannot quench, and in each other's arms await the signal from the man whose face shines as the sun."*

"Believest thou in such love?" she asked.

"Oh, most incomprehensible one," I replied, "I am but an infant in knowledge, and every hour seems to unfold to my frail mind new ideas."

"Wouldst thou be satisfied to wait in the grave for centuries for the rising with the one thou lovest, or wouldst thou rather that both should possess the art and power of prolonging life, so that for them there shouldst be no death?"

"Mysterious one, is it possible to live forever?"

"No, but *He* possesses the power to retain perpetual youth, and as the ages roll by *He* knows no change, other than that when first I saw him he looked older than now."

"How old is *He*?" I inquired.

"Knowest thou not?"

"No, how should I?"

"When the sun shines again on winter's snows, *He* will have been here two thousand years. Then he had but counted seventy winters."

"And yet he looks young," I exclaimed.

"Woe is me! yes," and she heaved a sigh which seemed to betoken deep anguish of mind.

"What name may I call thee by, oh, most mysterious one?" I asked.

"When a girl in mine own home they called me Alethea, which signified Truth. Wouldst thou like to hear my story?"

"Divine Alethea, thou readest my thoughts as a book."

"Then come, and I will tell thee of my woes and my triumphs."

CHAPTER XXXV.

THE STATUE'S STORY.

ALETHEA, or the statue, led the way to an inner cavern, which seemed warmer than the one I had just left.

---

* This and many other inscriptions, copied in the MSS., showed a belief in a savior who should call the dead to life again.—ED.

Here she motioned me to a seat, and then began a story which, if true, is one of the most remarkable ever told by mortal to mortals, and which I give in my life history just as I heard it from the lovely Alethea.

' I was born, I have been told, the year after Alexander of Macedon married the fair Persian Stateira, at Susa.*

"My father was a Greek, who had followed the fortunes of Philip of Macedon, and afterward of his son Alexander. My mother was a Persian, named Phillina, and died soon after I was born.

"At Opis, on the Tigris, a mutiny broke out, and as my father was active in putting down the rebellious ones, the mutineers thought the best way they could have their revenge was to steal his only child.

"When, therefore, I was a year old, I was carried by rough soldiers to Ecbatana and given to the care of a Hebrew family. By them I was brought up until, by diligent search, my father recovered me and took me to Athens, when I had reached the age of sixteen.

"On the first of June, Tisneo was on horseback, and saluted my father as he passed the house in which we dwelt.

"I inquired who the gallant young man was, and my father told me that Tisneo was the bravest youth and the most valiant hunter in all Greece. I well remember how well Tisneo looked as he rode on his jet-black steed, a collar of gold encircling his neck, proclaiming the high rank he had already attained.

"Behind Tisneo rode his attendant, the brave youth Orestes.

"At the baths later I met Tisneo, and my heart went out to him and I loved him.

"Orestes reproved his master, and bade him not to give himself up to thoughts of love, for there were to be stirring times; that Aridaeus, by the advice of his guardian Perdiccas, to whom Alexander had on his death-bed delivered his ring, had ordered all soldiers to be ready for a march and consequent war.

"Tisneo declared himself ready for the wars, but laughingly declared that he worshiped at the shrine of Eros as well as Mars.

"My father smiled on my lover, and asked no questions, he only cared for my happiness.

"Well would it have been had he done so, for much trouble would have been saved, and I should have been happier.

"In front of the altar of Eros we plighted our troth, and

* This must have been about the year B. C. 324.—EDITOR.

we were to have been married when Tisneo returned from the wars.

"There was another link between us; both were motherless. Tisneo's mother had been a princess of the house of Egypt and was a priestess of Isis. I was afterward told that Tisneo's father was a celibate priest of Isis, who broke his vows and perjured himself in marrying. He had to flee from Egypt, driven therefrom by Nectanebo, who sought his life. This I did not learn until long afterward.

"The day arrived when Tisneo should leave for the wars, and I gave him a scarf which I had worn, and which had been bathed in the holy waters of the Temple of Eros, and bade him wear it always. Return to me,' I said, 'a conqueror; but never a defeated warrior, for I should not wish to marry one who thought more of his life than of his honor.'

"Aridæus had not gone to the wars, but his guardian, Perdiccas, took command in person. Aridæus had sunk into low habits of dissipation, and had formed a friendship with a strange philosopher, who had just begun to discourse on Mars' Hill.

"My father, who had joined Perdiccas, had given me in the keeping of Eudora, his favorite sister. My aunt Eudora was much averse to my marrying Tisneo, and began to hint that, if I was wise, if I would do as she wished, I could marry the king.

"My answer was ever the same, I would never marry any one but Tisneo; at least, not until he returned my Eros-consecrated scarf.

"The old philosopher began to call and talk sagely to Eudora, and we looked for his coming on all occasions when it was proper for a lady of high degree to receive male visitors.

"How shall I describe this philosopher, who called himself Isistheno? He must have been old, for he knew everything and had been everywhere. He had studied in Egypt, and had fought in Libya, he knew Babylon, and had traveled in Gaul. No wonder that King Aridœus liked him, for he could tell a good story and work miracles.

"Thou openest thine eyes, but it is a verity I am telling. Isistheno would at times sit in my aunt's room and raise his finger, when the table, on which were the fruits of the garden, would glide over to him.

"When Eudora was more than usually interested, he would tell her that he had that wonderful elixir by the use of which he could live forever.

"Eudora sent me from the room when Isistheno spoke of such things.

"Soon, however, Eudora would praise him to me, and say what a happy woman his wife would be, for to her he would give eternal youth and together they would live always.

"I suggested that she herself—who was fair and comely, ripe in age, and a virgin—should marry him, but she laughed and said she would make way for me.

"Isistheno found means to meet me, to follow me, and then asked me to go to the Temple of Eros and become his betrothed.

"I told him of my betrothal, but he grew angry and said I must break my vows.

"That I would never do.

"Eudora came to me, crying, the next day, and declared that we were all ruined, for Aridæus had sent for us to the palace.

"We journeyed to the place appointed, and then the king, who was weak-minded but fair to look upon, commanded my betrothal to Isistheno.

"I fell on my knees and prayed him to rescind his command. I told him of Tisneo, the brave man who was fighting for his king: I said I could not be false to him.

"I fell on my face, and kissed the hem of his garment; but Aridæus was obdurate and commanded that unless in one month I was betrothed to Isistheno I must become a virgin of the temple, and remain unmarried all my life.

"Better death than such a fate," I thought.

"Eudora coaxed and pleaded, and tried to persuade me. Then, when all failed and the time for decision had come, I went alone to the king's palace, and fell on my knees before Aridæus, and asked him to let me be true to Tisneo.

"My tears watered the floor, my heart was breaking, and the king was obdurate.

"'Marry Isistheno,' he said, 'or join the virgins of the temple.'

"Again and again I knelt to him, and for a moment I thought his heart softened. He looked down to me, and in a lascivious voice said: 'Alethea, thou fairest of Grecians, thou art rightly named, for thou art truth itself. I wish I had thee for a wife, but I have vowed before the altar of Pallas Athenæ that I would give thee only to Isisthenes; but give me one kiss with thy fair lips, and who knows but that may wash away my oath and bestow thee on the gallant Tisneo?'

"My maiden cheeks were scarlet with blushes, but what would I not do for the sake of my true love? I raised my face near that of Aridæus, but for very shame could not kiss him; whereupon he drew me to him, pressed me to his bosom, and burnt my lips with his lascivious kisses.

"A noise disturbed him, and I tore myself away, my face and throat burning like living fire, and was about to rush from the room to seek death—for I could not outlive my shame—when I was confronted by Tisneo.

"'Away, false woman!' he cried. 'Take thy Eros-watered scarf and stay with thy paramour!'

"Hear me, Tisneo, my beloved, before I die——"

"There is no need of excuses; I have seen all," he exclaimed, as he rushed from the room.

"I swooned away, and when I recovered Eudora was bathing my cheeks with the fair perfumes of Arabia.

"Then for many weeks I lay in delirium's chains, and Eudora watched over me, so that I loved her more than before.

"Oh, that I could become a Virgin of the Temple!" I cried, day and night; but that was an impossibility, as a man's kisses had been showered on my lips.

"I wanted to die, but found no chance to escape. Isistheno renewed his suit, but I hated him. He it was who had planned all; he had arranged for Tisneo to see my ravished face scorching from the kisses of a false king.

"He knew that the sight would cause my lover, my adored one, to leave me, and then he hoped to gain his suit.

"I refused to listen to him. A swift messenger was Orestes, who had been left behind with the army, and he brought tidings that my father had fallen, thrust through with a spear.

"I was alone, for Eudora pleaded so much for me to marry Isistheno that I refused to see her.

"What could I do? I hated Isistheno, though all men praised him. He healed the sick, and when the son of the great Hypastia was dead, he breathed on the boy's face, and life returned to him.

"All these things were constantly brought before my mind, and even force was used to coerce me.

"At length I could endure the torture no longer, and I left the house, and proceeded to the Temple of Minerva, where I was about to sacrifice my life, when I felt some one near me. I raised my head, and Isistheno stood before me."

Alethea looked at me, and saw how deeply interested I was. The story which she had told possessed for me a strange reality. There were times when the realism was so intense that I fancied myself a participant in the events mentioned. Was it possible that I had really been there? could it be that I had previously existed? Fjord's ideas flashed through my bewildered brain, and I wished he were with me, and yet the story seemed destined by

Alethea for my ears alone. It was given in sacred confidence, and but for after events would never have been put on paper for others to read.

Alethea looked at me, and I was tempted to place my arm round her perfect waist. The hand was raised, and I placed my lips upon it.

It was as cold as marble. Not one drop of life-blood seemed to tingle through the veins. Was it fancy or reality, did a faint tinge relieve the marble whiteness of her statuesque face? I know not.

My thoughts began to wander, and I remembered to have read legends which told how spirits of the departed had spoken through trumpets and statues. Was this wonder being performed now? No, that would not solve the problem; for this statue really walked and led the way for me into the room where the narrative was told.

The more I thought over the matter the greater became my perplexity.

Alethea having turned her eyes away from me, I ventured to look up, and saw that a tear had fallen on her marble cheek.

"Don't continue your story if it recalls painful remembrances," I said, but I confess I was desirous of hearing the conclusion.

"Thy thoughts belie thy words, oh, thou fickle one," she said, and a smile passed over her face.

"Why callest thou me fickle?" I asked. No sooner had I asked the question than I regretted it, for the query had sharpened my memory.

"Fickle and false both," she answered; "didst thou not pledge thy troth to a fair maid who dwelleth in the cold climes of the North! Where is thy memory if thou hast forgotten Rapa Tepithe who was so devoted to thee, oh, thou fickle Tisneo, why were thy burning kisses on the lips of the soulless maiden who tended thee?"

As Alethea proceeded with her questions I felt the hot blood suffusing my face, and I hung my head with very shame.

Like a silly boy I began to make excuse:

"She kissed me whilst I slept," I said.

"Thou art mistaken, that maiden never kissed mortal or she should not have been thy attendant."

"Didst thou not call me Tisneo?"

"What if I did? my fancy roveth free."

"Do with me as thou pleasest!" I exclaimed, my whole soul going out to the marble beauty.

Her bosom swelled with emotion, her eyelids drooped and the pearly tears fell on her raiment. She wept. I was inclined to join her also, but when I approached her, she waved me away and bade me listen to the conclusion of her story.

"Isistheno," she said, "was by me at the Temple of Minerva and upbraided me with desiring to take that life which I had not the power to regain. 'The grave is dark,' he said, 'and the spirits to be encountered many, who would rend thee to pieces. Be my wife and I will give thee centuries of life.' 'I would rather die than dwell with thee!' I exclaimed. 'Then hear my vow,' said Isistheno; 'I swear that thou shalt never leave my presence, that I will claim thee one week from to-day, and that throughout all ages, when this temple becomes a heap of ruins, when the cities of Babylon, and Athens, and Corinth have passed from the memory of man, still thou shalt be with me!'"

"'I defy thy power!' I exclaimed; but Isistheno continued: 'Seek thy solace in death. I will restore thee to life from which thou canst not escape. Through all the ages thou art and shall be mine.' 'Never, monster, fiend, or evil spirit, whatever thou art; if thy art can give me eternity of days, it will give me eternity of hate.' And I hate him yet," said Alethea, breaking off from her narrative, and looking round as though she would like to wreak her vengeance on Isistheno.

I thought it more judicious to remain silent, and so waited for her to resume.

In a few moments she did so.

"A week later," said Alethea, "and I had not seen Isistheno, when my chamber window opened. I went to see the reason, when I was seized and borne out of the window and placed in a litter. A strange feeling of faintness came over me, and I lost all remembrance. When I awoke I was in a large boat, and by my side stood Isistheno. 'Monster!' I cried, 'whither art thou taking me?' 'Where Tisneo can never find thee!' was his answer. I was powerless, but while I retained my faculties I could repel all his advances, and if he attempted force I swore to kill myself. We landed on this island, a strange magnetic current bearing us into a lovely lake of fire.

"For years I repulsed him, and for all those years I conquered. At last, to break away from him, I resolved to seek the first white man who came to the island, and beg him to take me for wife. When Isistheno read my resolve, he swore I should be turned to stone, and only given the power to return to consciousness for a few hours each day, but that the instant I left the caves I should become stone again.

"I laughed at his threats, and then one day, galled into bitterness of spirit, he struck me, and by the god Tabu ordered my flesh to become stone, never to return to life for more than a few hours, until Tisneo claimed me.

"For two thousand years," continued Alethea, "I have loved Tisneo, and for all those ages I have hated Isistheno."

The last sentence was murmured softly. I raised my head and found I was alone in the passage, grasping the end of the ball of twine which I had used to mark my passage.

Had I dreamed it all, or was the story actually told me by the mysterious statue?

CHAPTER XXXVI.

IN THE CITY OF THE DEAD.

IT was some minutes before I realized that I was awake. The events which came to my mind so realistically could not have been the effect of imagination or the result of dreams.

Yet how did I get back to the passage, and possession of the twine? How gradual is the return to consciousness after a long and troubled sleep, and how difficult it is for some time to realize which of our thoughts and remembrances refer to dreams and phantasms of the night and which to the sober and stern realities of the day.

I had been asleep, that I was ready to admit, but had I not also been awake and in the marvelous caves of the dead?

Little by little my memory came back to me, and I remembered the time when I fell asleep, or died, as at that time I thought.

I knew now that my ball of twine had long since been exhausted, therefore, either in my sleep I had wandered back and found the twine, or it had been removed from its fastening, but if so, by whom?

How came it in my hand? That was my first puzzle. Then across the dimness of my brain and mental vision came the phantasmagoric remembrance that my lamp had gone out for lack of fat. Now it was burning brightly at my side. If, then, I had dreamt all which I have described, I must also in my dream have trimmed my lamp, but from whence the oil?

I began to feel hungry and wished I was clear out of the caves, for there was no way to replenish my haversack in which I carried my food.

Seizing it, I found it full of food, and near by a bowl of

soup fast getting cold. This was a convincing proof that some one had been near me, and had looked after my inner man as well as the outside.

I started back with the intention of finding Fjord, and with him returning at some future day.

Following the twine, I soon reached the caves where reposed the perfect forms of the dead.

I had no difficulty in finding my way through them, and in a very short space of time I again stood in the open air, and looked around for the familiar landmarks by which I should be able to find my friend.

The effect of the free, pure air was like an intoxicant. I had so long breathed the close, dense atmosphere of the caves that, when my lungs were inflated with the pure oxygen, I reeled and staggered like a drunken man.

Resting myself awhile, I thought over the mysteries which I had seen, and resolved that now I would be more determined to quaff the elixir and overcome the weakness of nature, if such a thing were possible.

Near the entrance to our dwelling caverns I met Rapa, who fell on her face and prayed for mercy. She had taken me for a specter, and it was only after considerable hugging that I could make her believe it was veritable flesh and blood, and not a spirit, which had returned to her.

Then she commenced a chant of welcome, which, while far from poetical, sounded quite musical as it came from her naturally good voice. It ran, as far as I could catch the words, somewhat as follows:

" He has come, my own, my sweet.
　The grave has given him back.
　In every pulse I feel the scorching fire,
　As my warm life-blood rushes to and fro
　When I see his brave face. My beloved, thou art very beautiful.
　I have waited for thee and wept. I did desire thee.
　Who hath a face so fair as thine, or who hath a heart so good?
　Thine eyes are like the stars—they glitter and shine with love.
　Press me, beloved, to thine heart, for I am all thy own, my love, my sweet."

How much longer the chant would have continued, it is impossible to say, for it was evidently improvised for the occasion, but was cut short by Milo catching sight of Rapa singing and dancing. She, in turn, set up a song of joy in unison, and then fetched Fjord, who was so delighted at finding me alive and well that he clasped me around the neck, and kissed me many times.

My welcome was a warm one, and, when pressed to tell my adventures, I begged for time, saying I had slept so long that I could not at once recall my thoughts.

"We thought you dead," said Fjord.

"I thought so myself, once," was my rejoinder; "but tell me, how long have I been away?"

"Eight days."

"Nonsense, man! don't fool with me, but tell me."

"Sober truth; but you must be starved, for you only took away food for three days."

"I have had plenty, and have some still left."

"Tell me later, my boy," said Fjord, "all your adventures."

"I will, but I reckon you will either say I have been dreaming or gone mad."

While we were talking, He sent Tanoa to say that the mighty one would like us to visit him.

Fjord and I went at once to his audience cavern, and then fixing his eyes on me, He asked:

"Didst thou enjoy thy exploration?"

"I did, and many marvels have I seen."

"If thou wouldst see all the wonders of this place I will be thy guide."

Was this a courtesy, or only to convey to our minds that if we wandered away alone we should displease our host.

"Thy offer is gratefully accepted." Fjord answered for both.

"What thinkst thou of the caverns of the dead?" asked He.

"They seem to show that the island is very old," was my cautious reply.

"Old, yes indeed it is, but how old is the world? Nations existed, built mighty cities, and passed away, even the very ruins of the cities disappearing; they were succeeded by other nations who in their turn succumbed to the inevitable decay of the ages. This island was once inhabited with a race of people who were more perfect than any which existed elsewhere. An infant child, imperfectly formed or with blemish, was not allowed to live. Then, as time passed away, the maidens were not allowed to marry unless they were physically perfect, and their husbands equally free from spot, blemish or deformity. My arts are not sufficient to tell thee when they lived or the other means they used to attain perfection, but they lived many thousands of years ago. When Tabu transported me hither, things in the caves were much as they are now. Thousands of years before that the black man lived here, and he left behind a record of the marvelous white race which had preceded him. Wouldst thou like to examine the ancient caves of Anaquaudoa and Akabauga?"

"We should, most mighty one."

"Come then, and I will show thee marvels which thine eyes shall never witness again."

Although I would have preferred a rest after my long adventure, I was ready to seize the opportunity, and still further penetrate the mysteries of this wonderful island.

Accordingly we followed him to a side passage opening out of the corridor in which his apartments were placed. Here we were joined by four girls, who acted as torch-bearers, carrying on the end of a long pole a skull from which protruded three wicks, one from each eye and one from the mouth. These skull torches gave a very good light, and we were better able to see the wonders of the caves. We descended many steps, which looked as if they were hewn out of the solid rock. At the bottom a circular tunnel was seen; this work of a bygone age and long forgotten people was a wonderful specimen of engineering skill. It was bored through the rock, its surface being smooth and well polished, it had a diameter of about fifteen feet. The air was pure and refreshing. The ventilation coming from shafts or borings that ran upward at distances of about every six yards. I was unable to find out where the air came from, for no light was visible, so that the borings could not have gone in a straight course to the surface.

When we had traversed this tunnel for about a hundred yards, we descended some more steps, and then entered a huge cave, larger than any I had ever before seen. It must have had a diameter of a hundred yards at least.

The girls held aloft their torches and we witnessed a strange sight when our eyes got accustomed to the gloom.

The pit was one vast charnel-house. There was something appalling in this sepulcher of the dead.

I had noticed that in the other caves I had visited, the bodies were carefully embalmed; here there was nothing but the bones and skeletons. No attempt at preservation had been made. But some one with ghastly ideas had tried to arrange weird devices out of the bones of the departed.

In the center of the cave stood a group of six skeletons, so arranged as to represent a terpsichorean tableau.

The skeletons were hanging on wires, and we perceived that they could be worked very much as marionettes are in a puppet show. Another group was made to represent a convivial party. One skeleton held in its bony clutch a goblet, another a jug from which he was about to pour the fiery compound.

I started back and almost shrieked with fear as the torch-light was directed to a corner in which was a pyramid of skulls, the faces all being outward. What startled me was, that in the eye-sockets of each skull colored glass had been inserted, and as the light from the torches fell upon the pyramid the glistening of the eyes in a thousand skulls presented a most horrible effect.

One of the torchbearers, who evidently knew no fear, picked up a skull and flung it at the dancers. Instantly there was a rattling of the bones, and for several minutes the arms and legs of the skeletons executed various movements which were weird and horrible to look upon.

"Who were these people?" I asked.

"That I am unable to answer," *He* replied, thoughtfully, "the people of Haya embalmed their dead, and the Anaquenians before that cremated the bodies of their departed ones. Prior to that people, dwelt a race of blacks who worshiped a black divinity, called *Hujapanj*. He was represented with broad nose and thick lips, characteristic of the African. Come, I will show you this black god." He opened the door of a passage at the end of which was a monster head resting on a stand which looked like ivory.

HEAD OF HUJAPANJ.

It was white and highly polished, but as its measurements were about six feet long, an equal number broad, and several inches thick, the slab could not have been ivory.

The head was far from pleasant to look upon. It seemed to be made from some kind of black lava; harder than granite, but still stone. The only attempt at coloring or ornamentation was in the eyes and lips, and on those some pigment had been used, probably by a more recent people.

"These blacks," continued our guide, "either destroyed or followed a race of most perfect people, who held that if the bodies were perfect, without blemish and absolutely beautiful, they should be preserved, so that when the spirit had passed through all the stages of its existence, which might take many thousands of years, these bodies would be ready for their return.

"Do you mean us to understand that the spirit would, after the lapse of thousands of years, return and take possession of its original body?" I asked.

"Of the first human body it inhabited, which was perfect," He answered.

"I don't quite understand you," I said, and my mind instantly recurred to the lovely forms I had seen in the caverns I had explored.

"A spirit," He said, "originates in a germ; at least so said the ancient philosophers, who lived ten thousand years ago on this island. That germ might be in a grain of sand, or in a weed of the field; from there it, having gained more strength, would try a loftier existence and become a flower, or perhaps some fruit, for wherever there is life there is spirit. From the flower or fruit, the germ or spirit would doubtless get more ambitious, and desire intelligence as well as life. It would, therefore, animate some insect, which would breathe away its short life when the sun went down. The morrow would see the spirit in a butterfly, and then, by various gradations, as it would gain strength and ambition, it would join its intelligence to the animal nature of a bird; perhaps it would confine itself to the feathered kingdom, and keep expanding until it was the animating guiding power of an eagle, if warlike and fond of power; or a dove, if gentle and tame; a peacock, if vain; a seagull, if fond of water; and so on, according to its likes and dislikes. Having reached the perfection of the animal or bird kingdom, this spirit would assimilate with the human organism of a new-born babe, and grow with it. The child might grow into an undeveloped, badly-formed, or ill-conditioned man or woman; the spirit, then, would have to enter another baby form, and continue through the ages until perfection was reached."

He paused.

"Do you believe this?" asked Fjord, who was deeply interested in the philosophy of the ancients.

"I form no opinion. I told thee what these islanders believed and taught ten thousand years ago."

"What did they believe about the origin of the first germ?" I inquired.

"The first germ, said these philosophers, was fashioned and made by a God of gods, who made the first of everything, but who had never been seen by mortal, because he was too perfect, and his brightness too dazzling for human eyes to behold."

His philosophy was interesting, and I wondered whether *He* was only evolving the ideas from his inner consciousness, or whether they were recorded anywhere.

My thoughts were easily read, for *He* turned away from the black god, and pointed in the direction of the entrance.

We preceded him from the cave, but as soon as he emerged we awaited his directions.

"Come," he said, "and I will show thee the inscriptions which I translated for thee but just now."

Following him, we arrived at a square cavern whose walls were like polished ivory, and covered with many inscriptions deeply cut into the white substance.

We were unable to read them, but had no reason to doubt the ability of our mysterious guide to translate them for our benefit.

"We have had enough for to-day," *He* said, leading the way into the cave of skulls. Here he paused, and soliloquized, or thought aloud.

"Behold the end of us all," he said, "life for a span and then the tomb. We can trace by our philosophy the germ until it reaches the perfection of manhood, but at the gate of the tomb we have to stop. Even I, who have withstood the decay of two thousand years, must some day be kicked about by a succeeding race even as these," and the veiled mystic kicked a pile of bones, sending them rolling about the floor of the cave. "When I die, what will be the awakening? Shall I have eternal forgetfulness, or will the memory of the past be ever with me? What will it matter, then, that I have lived a few more years than others? What is a span of two or five or even twenty thousand years of life compared to the millions upon millions of a never-ending existence beyond the tomb? Ay, they were right—we shall awake, shall live again, and play our little parts in a succession of bodies till the sun can give no more light, the moon be worn by the friction and revolution of ages to a shadow, till the world itself is dead. What is life? 'tis but the day; and the darkness, with its sleep and dreams, typifies death—ah, yes, death is but life's night; and the dreams? What are they? Glimpses of what? That I cannot answer. Come!"

He led the way back, and we all remained silent until the weird and mysterious presence had left us, and Fjord and I returned to our dwelling impressed with the awful and yet instructive grandeur which we had seen.

CHAPTER XXXVII.
IXCOZAUHQUI.

I CONVERSED with Rapa about the cave of Thaloc to which Milo had guided Captain Fjord, and from Rapa I heard that there were caves beyond which contained most sparkling stones. She showed me one, which I recognized as a diamond of the first water.

There were plenty of them, she told me, but it was very hazardous to get them.

We resolved to make a party to get the diamonds and explore the other caves.

Milo could not be persuaded to go with us, so, with Rapa for our guide, Fjord and I, with several days' provisions, started on our quest.

We proceeded in a northerly direction, passing the mountain on the other side of which, we believed, lay the enchanted lake, on whose phosphorescent waters we had gazed the day we landed.

Gradually the last vestiges of cultivation disappeared, the stunted trees which broke the monotony of the valley were succeeded by mountains and rocks strange in shape and varied in height. On close examination these freaks of nature were composed of lava, which had been belched forth at some period from some of the volcanoes, and had fallen in pyramidic shape, cooling as it fell. One rock was so good a resemblance of some of the idols we had seen, that until we examined it closely we were under the impression that it was the work of man. Another looked like a gigantic cathedral, lifting its lofty towers and pinnacles high up into the clouds.

In the middle of a basin, formed by the crater of some extinct volcano, stood a gigantic pyramid of rock, towering high above the ground. Its base seemed to rest upon piles of lava, cinders, fragments of basalt and scoria.

Before this rock Rapa rested, and told us that the caves she wished us to see were under the rock. We began to clear away a portion of the *debris*, and soon discovered the steps down which we had to descend. At the bottom of about a dozen steps we stopped in admiration at the sight which so unexpectedly met our gaze.

We were in a cavern vaulted like a cathedral, the roof supported on pillars as perfect in form as if they had been fashioned by the hand of man and the chisel of mason. On the walls were tablets on which inscriptions in various languages were written.

One inscription was engraved on the most beautiful stone I had ever seen. It was iridescent, every color seemed reflected from it, and whichever way we gazed on it, the light flashed as from myriads of diamonds. Rapa said there were many such to be found in the caves to which we were going. Fjord was enchanted, and declared he would go no further. He had sufficient to occupy his attention for weeks. We persuaded him, however, to come with us, promising that on our return he should stay as long as he pleased in that particular cave.

We left by a narrow passage which scarcely gave us room to squeeze our bodies through, but when we had succeeded we found ourselves in another cave which seemed like a temple. On a large platform stood a large image or idol.

Before it Rapa prostrated herself, and rising, told us that it was the custom of the country to offer a sacrifice to the sun god before continuing the journey.

Bidding her be as quick as possible, Fjord and I watched Rapa at her devotions, which were intended for our good as well as her own.

She gathered a few leaves and dried grasses which had been left by preceding worshipers, and then tore a piece off her already scanty garment. Fjord and I had to give something to help build the fire. When the pile was as complete as she could make it, she fell flat on her face and implored the clemency of the god.

Taking the kindling sticks she produced a fire, and as the flames ascended, shedding a strangely weird light over the cave, she commenced a chant in slow and monotonous rhythm.

"Mighty god of the glorious sun," she said, "thou whose breath is a tempest, and whose every sigh sends forth flames as high as the clouds above the mountain tops, thou pure spirit, have pity on us, thy children

"I weep: let my tears be less bitter.

"I am the dove, which lives only for its mate, whose kisses are sweeter than honey.

"The flower I offer thee is fair as the face of him I love. Genius of the mountain, god of the fire, I offer thee my life. Take it, but spare those who are with me. Let the dark-skinned dove die, if by that death the pale-faced sons of the East may live."

There was something solemn in the young girl's devotion and willingness to give her life, if need be, for her chosen one.

The somber beauty of the surroundings, the accessories of the picture, the fantastic beauty of Rapa herself, who, as the dying light of the fire shone upon her, seemed like a

IXCOZAUHQUI, THE SUN GOD.

priestess of the night, the trembling tones of her voice as she chanted her anthem to the idol, all impressed the imagination, and caused a new sentiment to come over us both. We wondered what there could be in the idol to call forth such a spirit of devotion.

When Rapa had finished she scattered the fire with her bare foot, not noticing the heat of the dying embers.

"Who is this god?" I asked, reverently.

"He is Ixcozauhqui, the god of the sun," answered Rapa.

Bidding Rapa enlighten us on the history of this god, she commenced:

"In the caves of the dead, there is no heat. all is coldness and darkness, but that the mansions may not be quite joyless, the sun which has been giving light and heat all day, spends his solitude in the dark time with the lord of the dead. The sun is the fire which gives heat, and without it we could not live, his color is ruby in the day and yellow when about retiring, therefore our fathers gave him the name of Ixcozauhqui, which means, as I have heard said, the god of the fire of the sun."*

I have stripped Rapa's description of all the flowery metaphors and the strange mixture of languages in which she told it, and have reduced it as much as consistent.

I was nearer loving Rapa than I had ever before been, and, when I heard her supplication to the fire spirit, I felt such devotion was worthy of my love. An untutored child of the desert, a poor South Sea Islander, whose parentage was lost in obscurity, possessed a spirit of love and self-sacrifice but seldom found in civilized society.

We continued our journey and entered another cave, which was built of human bones piled up in various fantastic designs, making a weird architectural structure, the like of which we had never before seen.

Leading from that, Rapa led us into a cavern in which stood several nude figures. They were as perfectly formed as though they were human instead of stone.

Rapa informed us that they were not marble, but that they were really men and women who had once lived there. I told Fjord I had seen many such. His curiosity was aroused, and he closely examined the figures. He darted at the statues, and felt the substance, squeezed the fingers, and then struck the solid stone with his fist.

"I tell you, Theo.," he exclaimed; "I am going to take one of these home with me. Just fancy a veritable human being. Our discovery is the greatest and most profound of modern times."

"Touch one and you shall die." We looked round and

* The ancient Nahoans had a similar god. The Nahoans said that the fire of the sun went at night to give light to the mansions of the dead. And that, unless the fire of the sun went there, no resurrection could take place. The sun kept together the germs of life.—ED.

was confronted by the ruler of the island, the man-fiend—*He*.

"How came you here?" Fjord gasped.

"The spirit of the air directed me. Look at what pleaseth thee, but if one piece is broken or one missing thou shalt surely die."

"Explain, most mighty one, this great mystery," I said.

"There is a plant growing—I say not where—for its use would be a curse rather than a blessing—the leaves of which if boiled will turn flesh into stone. The root of the plant if smoked will restore the stone to flesh."

"Pardon me for doubting, most mighty one, the last statement you made."

"It is man's province to doubt. I blame thee not. Nay, I commend thee for it and urge thee and thy kin to prove everything before believing it."

While *He* was thus praising Fjord's doubt he had taken from some receptacle a piece of wood or root about the size of a large pea, and then taking the lamp away from Rapa, he dropped the wooden pea into the flame.

Relieved of the lamp, Rapa had fallen prostrate before the mighty one.

The cavern was soon filled with a vapor having a strange perfume. I could never have imagined that so small a piece of wood could have made so much smoke. Soon the white figures became indistinct; we could only see them through the mist. "Look!" *He* exclaimed, and as we did so the statues seemed to move. One raised his arm in the attitude of defense, another commenced dancing, then all marched up and down the cavern, until both Fjord and myself got frightened at the sight and hid our faces. As the smoke cleared away we looked up, and behold! every statue was as we had at first seen it. Seeing our surprise, *He* looked intently at us for a few moments and then said, "Destiny is less inexorable than it appears. The resources of the great architect of the universe are not so scanty and so weak as men are apt to declare. The tree of knowledge is known, but the tree of life flourishes, if science would but acknowledge it. And yet I have often asked myself through the ages whether there is not a crime in eating of that forbidden fruit which makes men even as gods. It is true the higher we ascend the more hateful seem to us the vices of the little insects called men. But how many virtues lie dead in those who live in the world of death and refuse to die. Is not this state one of sublime and yet rash egotism—the state of abstraction and reverie—a resignation of that nobility which alone makes men great? To live on in no dread of foes, undegraded by infirmity, secure through the cares of life, free from diseases, is a spectacle which has charms for some until they enjoy it, and then they would resign it if they could."

"Nay, but we would both like to be initiated into the mysteries of perpetual existence," said Fjord.

"And I would exchange places with you, if I could, but for one thing——"

"And that is?" I asked.

"Love! Love is the real treasure; it is the only one which can last throughout eternity. We may carry that one thing to the grave, and love is the only thing which makes us happy in immortality. It transports my whole frame, its happiness fills the heart and soul. If the one I loved did but reciprocate my love, I would gladly resign my length of life, and lie with her side by side in the silent tomb."

This was always the burden of the cry of this strange personage. Fjord had not the key, and so what appeared to him to be but the ravings of a diseased and disordered mind, had a different meaning and significance to me; for had not Alethea told me her wonderful story, and did not the speech we had just heard harmonize entirely with it? Alas! I felt I was only on the threshold of knowledge. Would I ever attain an insight into the realm beyond?

We followed our supernatural guide through the caverns; but though his descriptions were knowledge instead of tradition, facts rather than legends, our minds were so preoccupied with the thoughts of the marvels we had witnessed, that we paid but little heed to what was being said.

With the best of guides our journey was not so pleasing as it would have been if Rapa had been our only companion.

CHAPTER XXXVIII.

FJORD'S PASSION.

THEO. has asked me to again take the pen and write down an account of a dream, a vision, a nightmare, a reality—I cannot tell which. It occurred to me on the night after our visit to the cave, or temple, of the sun god.

We were both glad to get back to our dwelling. I questioned *He* very closely about his history, but beyond learning that his name was Isistheno, or at least that was his chosen cognomen, I could not get anything satisfactory.

"Various names have I had, oh, pale-face questioner!" he said. "The gentle Greeks called me Kallikrates and Isistheno, but of all the names I have been called by Isistheno pleaseth me best."

I was struck by the names, for had not one of them been mentioned in the parchment and on the tablet? Was not Kallikrates the husband of Amenartas and father of Tisisthenes, and was it not he who was loved by the marvelous woman of Africa, the great *She*, who thought she had killed him? Yes, my memory was not at fault, so here was a further corroboration of the truth of the records which prompted Theo.'s search.

That night, when sleep came to the eyelids of all save myself, when Theo. was taking a rest. of which his body stood greatly in need, and Rapa and Milo rested from the cares of their duties. I felt prompted in my wakefulness to again visit the statue, whose name. Theo. told me, was Alethea.

I groped my way silently and cautiously along the passage, and when I neared the cavern, I saw the curtains drawn aside and a ray of light come from the inner recess.

A voice as sweet as the seraphim's song, and as clear as that of the nightingale, bade me welcome.

I entered the room, and found the fair Alethea, no longer standing on a pedestal in statuesque form, but seated near the fire.

"Welcome, O Fjord! for thy manners pleaseth me, and I would fain know somewhat of that world which thou hast seen, but of which I know not. Think, O man, that, for centuries, I have had none but slaves to talk with, except *He*, whom I hate. Marvel not when I tell thee that, though I have been clothed in marble, my mind has been free, and the thoughts of my brain have led me to wisdom. Thy coming to the land of caves has given me greater freedom. I can return to flesh at will. Why is it, O mighty philosopher?"

"Nay, I know not, divine Alethea," I answered.

"Callest thou me Alethea? That is sweet, for I have heard it but from few for all these ages. As you callest me that, I will unburden myself to thee; we will talk of thy friend, for he is comely."

"Yes, he is fair to look upon, and as good as he is fair."

"Where did his mother rear him?"

"In England."

"England—and where is that? I know it not."

I explained, as well as I could, its location, and then Alethea said:

"I had a grand-uncle who used to trade with the Cassiterides,* and bring back tin. Is it near there?"

"Yes, most lovely Alethea. Albion——"

* The Phœnicians gave this name to the Scilly Isles and the Cornwall tin district. B. C. 1000.

"I thought thou saidst England. Albion I know."

I explained to her that England was the modern name, and told her how the name got to be applied. She laughed at the legend, and then appeared to be in deep thought.

"But is thy friend, whom thou callest Theo., English?"

"No; his father's family were Greeks, and descended from a most honorable family."

"I know it. Kallikrates was the founder."

"How dost thou know that?"

Alethea remained silent for a moment, and then looked me straight in the face, and asked, coquettishly:

"Thinkest thou me beautiful?"

"Never since the sun shone on woman has thy equal been seen."

She looked pleased, and then clapped her hands.

"Dost thou mean it? Tell me truly, look at me, examine me—see my hair," and Alethea took the long tresses and threw them over her head, for the nonce completely obscuring the beauty of that wonderful, clear-cut face. With a toss of her head the tresses went back to their place, and she continued: "Look at my neck, my bust, my arms, examine the pearly tint of my skin; tell me what thinkest thou of my form; see my ankles," and she raised the drapery of her dress, "and my feet. Now tell me hast thou seen one more perfect?"

I was intoxicated with rapture. Never had I seen greater beauty, never more infinite perfection. Every feature, every detail was absolutely perfect. I stood overwhelmed, not able to express my thoughts.

"See!" she continued. "Am I not well-proportioned?" and she let the drapery fall from her wrist, baring the arm to the shoulder. "Touch me, and see if my skin is not as soft as velvet. I am old, remember; two thousand years old; do I look it? Speak to me, oh, Fjord! thou who art impervious to woman and above temptation—see, press thy hand on my heart—so," and she took my hand in hers and placed it over the throbbing organ of life. "I breathe, I live, I feel; see the blushes on my face."

I was going mad, for never had man endured such temptation before. She raised her arms, and the drapery fell from the upper part of the body, baring the glorious perfection of her bosom.

I could endure no more. I fell on my knees and hid my face in my hands.

I should have been more than human had I remained unmoved. I was dazed and subdued. How often I had declared that no woman could ever hold me in thralldom, and now I was powerless. My mind gave way, and I felt

I could deify her, and worship forever at the shrine of Alethea.

I pleaded with her; I expressed a wish to marry her. She only laughed, and told me she was not for me. I vowed I would sacrifice all I held dear but for one look, one glance of love.

"Alethea, divine yet dearest love, words cannot express my feelings, my love, my adoration for thee. Could I give my soul to eternal perdition for one kiss from thy lips, I would do it!"

"Oh, Fjord, rise; I was wrong. I have been from the world so long that I forgot the frailty of man. These lips have not been kissed by man since they were ravished by the passionate stolen kisses of Aridæus--kisses which burned into my soul and lost me my love. Rise, and be a man. I love one with all the passionate fervor thou hast expressed. I would, as thou sayest, forfeit all for that love; but it is the one who for two thousand years has been my idol, my brave Tisneo, who died false to me and his vows, because he believed me unfaithful, but who, in the land of vernal pastures, has learned that I was true to him. He lives; oh Fjord, thinkest thou he would love me as thou dost?"

My spirit was broken. I felt all the hopelessness of my passion, and in humility I declared:

"Man does not live who could gaze on thy charms and fail to worship thee."

"Thou hast made me happy, but say again, thinkest thou he can love me?"

I repeated my assurance, and then pleaded:

"If, oh, divine Alethea, he fails thee, then wilt thou bestow thy glances on me?"

"If he does not love! Oh, great powers above! I know not what then! But he shall, he must love!"

"Thou sayest this Tisneo lives now?"

"Man, art thou blind? art thou mad? Knowest thou not that he whom thou callest Theo. is, of a verity, my Tisneo returned again to earth?"

I was thunderstruck. I never imagined that this wonderful woman—statue or deity—believed that Theo. was the re-incarnation of the Græco-Egyptian Tisneo.

"Tell me," I said, my pulse on fire, "tell me, how knowest thou that Tisneo lives again?"

"There is that within me which tells me—that which since I was transformed to stone has never deceived me—has never failed. It warned me that Tisneo, my beloved, my own, was coming, and when my eyes were fixed upon him, my pulses thrilled as they had never done before."

"Explain, my divinity, how it is that *He* exercises such power for all the ages."

"That I know not. But the end is near; canst thou not see it?"

I confessed I did not understand, and then Alethea continued:

"*He*, as thou callest him, is Isistheno, the father of Tisneo. Hast thou not felt that *He* hated thy friend, my beloved?"

Instantly the thought crossed my mind that once *He* had hinted to me, and the hint haunted me, that I must slay my friend. Was that jealousy?

"*He* hateth him, for he knoweth that Tisneo hath power to call me back to life, and that once in Tisneo's arms, Isistheno's power is gone. He only has endured to win my love, and for two thousand years or more has kept me near him, though he was powerless to get one look of love, or one word of kindness."

"It is worth a million years of torture to see thee but for a minute daily," I said; and in my ecstasy I believed it.

"Flatterer! go tell thy friend that I await him."

"But he loves another," I hinted.

"Loves another! He has never loved."

"But, indeed, thou art, O beauteous Alethea, mistaken."

"Dost thou refer to the girl Rapa?"

"No!"

"To the pale-faced daughter of the cold north, whose pulses never beat quicker at his approach, and who has long since forgotten him?"

"I suppose you refer to the same."

"That is not love. He has loved many such. Did he not tell Rapa he loved her, and yet the very next day he was wasting his kisses on one of my attendants, clasping her in his arms, and bartering his very soul for a kiss. Oh, such is not love."

"I know it, most glorious one, but the girl of the north is ever in his mind."

"He loves not, I tell thee. That passion has yet to be roused. He has yet to feel that love is the reduction of the universe to a single being, that it is the exaltation of the one being above friends, philosophy, honor, demons, angels, and up to God himself. Love is that power which subdues all things to itself. It is the most mighty power in the universe. It is the salutation of the angels to the stars. The love I bear and which Tisneo must bear toward me, must be a portion of the soul itself. It is the divine spark, and like it, it is incompatible, indivisible, imperishable.

"Love, O Fjord, is the spark of fire within us which is

immortal, is infinite, which never changes, which nothing diminishes and nothing extinguishes. We feel it burning in the marrow of our bones, and see it flashing in the depths of the azure sky. God is the fullness of creation, but even so, love is the fullness of man. The soul which truly loves, soars above the world with its follies, falsehoods, treacheries, hatreds, vanities, and lives in the pure azure sky of truth and wisdom. Nothing can add to its strength or its happiness, the greatest god is but love—the grandest heaven is but the abode of love. The gods Jupiter, Minerva or Tabu cannot add to its intensity. It is soul absorbing, and that love Tisneo has not yet felt. When he does, it will be a whirlwind of passion sweeping all before it. Understandest thou me?"

Alethea had talked like a whirlwind. I had listened, and felt all she said. It was the whirlwind of passion which I felt for her, born instantaneously, but I felt that I even hated Theo. if he stood in the way of my love.

"I understand, alas! too well," I sighed.

"Then teach Tisneo, him thou callest Theo.—tell him of the passion I feel—tell him I have waited all the ages for him, for his love, and that, if it is denied me now, I shall continue and wait until the cycles go round and he returns again."

"Tell me, Alethea, thou mystery of mysteries, why didst thou tempt me?"

"'Twas woman's fault. I would that thou shouldst tell me if I had the power to attract love, and thou hadst boasted of thy power to withstand temptation."

"I know it; but now my life is ruined, my hopes withered, and, though the ages pass, the memory of that blissful moment when my hand was on thy heart will live forever in my remembrance."

"I am sorry, but it was thine own fault. In the future, when thou thinkest of me, let it be as a piece of marble."

"Grant me but one favor."

"What is it, Fjord?"

"Let me but kiss thy cheek, so that in the dark days which will be before me, I may have the pleasant remembrance of that glimpse of heaven. I know, I realize that thou art not for me, that thy perfection which is like that of the sun is as far above me as is that orb of light, yet I would crave the one small favor."

"Thou knowest not what thou askest, but if thou likest to take the risk and if the kiss will be a solace to you, for I know that I have tempted thee, then thou mayst take one."

The feeling which came over me at that time is difficult to describe. Had an alternative been offered—had some superior power said, "Fjord, take the kiss but if thou dost, death will be thy portion," I should have accepted death. Nay, so strong was my passion that I would have given my life, my soul, all, everything present or to come. I would have staked my eternal happiness for that one kiss. The burning lava flowed through my veins; my throat was choked with phlegm; my eyes were like coals of fire, burning me to the very soul; my body trembled so that I could scarcely support myself. I leaned forward, my head rested on Alethea's bosom. I could feel the heart beat; I heard the throbbing; I looked up into her face; her eyes were turned away as though she was submitting to a desecration. I gently raised my head. What would I not have given to pillow it there forever! my lips were close to her cheek. I could feel myself fanned with her perfumed breath. My lips met her flesh in one long, long kiss, with all the passion of my soul concentrating like rays into one focus. I felt, oh, horror! the cheek getting cold and rigid, I withdrew my lips and beheld nothing but the marble statue of Alethea, as I had seen it first. Not a pulsation disturbed its serenity, nothing to tell that it had ever been endowed with life. It was stone—hard, cold marble.

Great Heavens! the thought caused the perspiration to start from every pore of my body, my hair stood on end, and I rushed from the place like a madman.

I know not whether it was an illusion. I don't think it was, but even if it were, I would still declare that that moment of bliss, the intoxication of that passion, the blinding beauty of the form of Alethea, the hurried words, the invited kiss, were to me a better glimpse of Heaven than any I had before or since—and for a repetition, I say in cold blood, I would even now give my life and barter my eternal soul. Such is the power of a love which seemed to me beyond the human.

I learned the power of love, and knew that love was stronger than death, and would outlive all things created.

CHAPTER XXXIX.

A FATAT PRESENTIMENT.

THE events narrated by Fjord in the preceding chapter had such effect upon him, that he was again delirious with the fever. I began to fear that the stifling air in the caves, added to the sulphurous fumes which were often wafted from the volcanoes, would altogether destroy his health. I stood the climate far better than he did.

There was no chance to escape. We were kept virtually prisoners; for, wherever we went, if we exceeded a certain distance, we were sure to encounter Isistheno, and *He* would at once, in his suave manner, lead us back to our caverns.

We had no desire to escape just then, for we were both anxious to test the power of *He* to confer prolongation of life upon us.

Whenever we approached him on the subject, *He* would always find some excuse for delay.

To add to our difficulties, we had no boat. The seamen, tiring of life on land, had stolen away from the island, having found a way to leave the phosphorescent lake. They fared badly, for, as Tanoa informed us, they had not reached the sea before the boat was dashed to pieces on the rocks, and the dead bodies of the two men were washed ashore.

Five had landed, and now only two survived. One had been eaten, and had formed a toothsome repast to the cannibal islanders; two had been drowned, and their bodies, most likely, had also served to allay the appetite of the naked blacks.

I feared for Fjord; as for myself, I was lulled into such a feeling of apathy or ease, that I was almost content to stay in the caves for the remainder of my life.

There was a fascination about the life, which, for the present, suited me. I loved mystery, and so long as all the mysteries added to my comfort I did not care. I would have liked to have gone beyond the mountain, for I felt sure there would be opportunity for hunting and other sport. I had the idea, which I afterward proved to be correct, that we lived in the crater of an extinct volcano, and that all the caves, passages, vaults and tunnels, were in and about the sides of the crater, and under in the bowels of the mountain.

That we constituted a world by ourselves, beyond which was land occupied by savages, who had not learned the first principles of civilization. Was there no way of getting over the mountain? There must be, for had not the savages crossed to us to participate in and witness the sports?

Rapa should aid me, and her love should be the key to unlock this closed problem.

The girl loved me as much as her innocent nature could, but I confess I had not the same feeling for her. I admired her devotion; I accepted her attentions; no cross word did I address to her, and I knew she would give her life for my sake, therefore I respected her, but beyond that I had no feeling.

I lived in a peculiar frame of mind. There were times

when I was almost inclined to view the whole thing as a great and long dream. Especially was this so when Fjord told me of his adventures with Alethea. But, on the other hand, was it possible we should both dream the same thing at different times? Could it be that Alethea was a myth, the creature of our imagination?

But then what is imagination? Is it possible to imagine that which does not or cannot exist? Is not that very thing we call imagination rather a clearer sight, is it not the effect of that certain ecstatical or transporting power which, when excited or stirred up by an ardent desire, is able to conduct the spirit or mind even to some distant object in this or other worlds? What are dreams? Are they not rather the very commencement of knowledge, are they not bridges across the great abyss which separates the finite from the infinite? There was one thing which destroyed the idea of our adventures being the result of a dream. I had been away eight days, and only took food for three, yet I was not hungry when I returned, neither had I an empty haversack.

These things perplexed me and were beyond my capability of explanation. While I might account for the mystery surrounding *He*, by rating him as a charlatan, what could I do about the statue and the dwellers in the caves? Mythological legend told of talking marbles and of statues returning to life, but hitherto I had accepted such statements only as legendary, teaching, under that fascinating garb, lessons of moral ethics.

But this statue—this Alethea—what of it? Its beauty was dazzling, the fair skin and lovely hair made it look like a divinity of a superior order. Alethea was like a perfume of the earth, an emanation of the essences of perfection, which nothing could make more beautiful or holy.

The more I reflected the greater became the mystery, and in the very madness of despair I resolved that I would reason no more but follow instinct until the end was found—the end—what would it be? Madness or a prolonged life? "Rapa, I want to go over the mountain!" I said to the devoted girl, a little later.

"Go—over—the—mountain?" she repeated, pausing between each word.

"Is there anything strange in that?" I asked, looking rather amused at the terror-stricken face of Rapa.

"The one who ventures there must surely die," was her answer, given in a hoarse whisper.

"Who says so?"

She leaned her head close to mine, and whispered in my ear the one word—"*He.*" And then the tears filled her eyes and she gasped out, her voice broken with sobs, "Oh, be careful! *He* will kill thee. Thy life will be blasted! Already he hath wished thee dead."

"Nonsense, Rapa, *He* would rather I lived and stayed here always."

"Do not be deceived, I have warned thee."

"Rapa, my good girl, will you show me the way over the mountains?"

"If thou desirest, but, oh! my beloved, thy Rapa will never return. The vengeance of *He the Mighty One* will smite me."

"Not so," I answered, selfishly. "Come."

Like a willing slave she obeyed, but I almost broke my resolve when I saw her tearful leave-taking of all she possessed.

The idol was placed on the table, and with many tears she bedewed its head.

Her agony was so great that, at last, I could stand it no longer, and I exclaimed, almost angrily:

"If you are so much afraid, stay behind. I can get other guides."

"Nay, my beloved, what is Rapa that she should fear? what is her life in comparison with thy wishes? Oh, my beloved, my own, I have given thee the love of my whole heart, and thou hast been mine, but the gods have said: 'Rapa thy heart must break, for he thou lovest will belong to another. In the midst of thy love thou shalt be cut off and his love shall bless a whiter and fairer one!'"

"What nonsense is all this, Rapa; I shall soon think you are indeed afraid."

"I am thy slave and thou my master. I know no fear. Come!"

I said not a word to Fjord, for I anticipated I should be back again the next day, and as he was so delirious and easily excited, I was sure it was better to let him think I was near by. And then the very dangers—bah! I was getting as superstitious as Rapa.

We started and began to climb up the mountain. The loose cinders and lava made its ascent extremely difficult; our pace was slow, and often when we thought we had made good progress, the lava and scoria would slip from under our feet, and we would fall perhaps twenty yards or so, only with difficulty saving ourselves. I seized Rapa's hand; it was dry and burning to the touch; a nervous trembling agitated her whole frame. It seemed we had been walking for hours, and yet were no nearer the top.

The further we got away from the caverns of Ana Quena the more resigned appeared Rapa. Her apprehension and terror grew less, and with feverish anxiety she bade me hurry.

"Come! Come!" was her constant cry.

Occasionally she seized my hand, pressed her lips passionately to it, and then would place it against her bosom, which heaved with the tumultuous pulsations of her heart. She leaned toward me when we rested and laid her head on my breast. She was delirious with the warmth of love's passion, I equally so; but mine was with the strong desire to see beyond the realms ruled over by the great mystery. I thought of nothing but the one thing. I was feverish with excitement, and when a plateau was reached and Rapa suggested we should rest there for the night, I became almost angry. We halted to partake of food, and then I expressed a desire that we should go further, as the night was pleasant.

"See! Look! O my beloved, look!" and Rapa pointed to a column of smoke, bright and luminous, passing over the crater we had just left.

"That is nothing," I remarked.

"Nothing! Oh, my beloved, go no further. It is *He the Mighty* coming to wreak vengeance on us."

"To show you how absurd your fears are, I command you to come!" I said, sternly.

The girl stood erect, and with her body shaking with emotion, yet with voice firm and steady, said:

"Rapa cannot and will not lead thee over the mountain."

"You shall!" I answered, sternly.

"Rapa will not!"

"Wretch, slave!" and I raised my hand as though I would strike; and then, feeling ashamed of myself, said softly, "Is this your love, your boundless love for me? Didst thou not say life was of no value except to serve me, and now the first request and thou mockest me?"

Rapa threw herself on my breast, and sobbed as though her heart would break.

"Strike me to thy feet, my beloved, if thou seest well, but never doubt my love. I will go."

Happening to glance on the ground I saw a little stream of blood flowing from Rapa's feet. She was barefoot and climbing up the loose cinders and sharp rocks, while even I found the ascent difficult, although well shod.

I was now thoroughly ashamed of myself and insisted on halting for the night.

The stars shone brightly, the southern cross resplendently lit the heavens, and I sat looking at all the glories of the firmament.

Rapa was asleep, when suddenly she started to her feet and uttered a hoarse cry, as if an invisible hand had seized her by the throat, as if some fiendish vision had suddenly appeared before her.

Her body trembled convulsively, her breathing grew hard and difficult, and her eyes, red and burning, were fixed on a spot higher up the mountain.

I looked and saw a column of smoke or fire, apparently the same we had seen before—halting just beyond us.

"It is nothing." I said.

"No. nothing." she sighed. "Rapa will prove her love; her life shall testify her devotion. Oh, my beloved, thou art safe, and thy years shall be many; but Rapa will seek rest in the grave, where troubles never come."

Attributing her excitement and emotion to fear, I tried to comfort her. I told her of the great world beyond the seas, and of the home I had left. I promised that when I returned she should go with me.

She became calm and placid; but I could see it was only the calmness of resignation, and not of courage.

"It is my destiny," she crooned, "and I will fulfill it; but, oh. my beloved, in the after days, keep a memory of Rapa in thy heart of hearts!"

An hour later we resumed our journey. Rapa appeared more cheerful, and went forward, singing and laughing.

I was pleased at the change, and often praised her for it. She expressed her pleasure that I was gratified, but I could see her heart was still haunted with a vague fear.

The smoke column seemed stationary, and I was almost afraid. My stay with this superstitious people was making me as bad as Rapa.

When the summit of the rock had been gained, I was able to see that between us and the rock beyond was a deep *crevasse* or ravine. The lofty peak on the other side was the one we should have to climb, and I now understood that the difficulties of escape from the island were greater that I had imagined. The column of smoke had disappeared, and all was dark. "We must wait here," said Rapa, "for daylight."

A weird sound like the moan of the dying was made by the wind as it rushed among the rocks.

Rapa was trembling, and I drew her to me, pressing her in my arms.

"Say thou lovest me, my own, my sweet," she said in a tremulous voice.

"I do love you, Rapa; and we will go back."

"No. Rapa will prove her love, and will lead her beloved over the abyss of death."

An hour or so passed away, and then, between the two black lines of the gigantic rocks, through the opening they thus formed, I perceived a bright line of light, from which issued rays of rose-colored flame, illumining the deep, dark abyss. It was the rising sun.

"Must we cross that?" I said, pointing to the ravine.

"The way is dark, but safe, to all but Rapa."

"Why is it not safe to you?"

"Destiny forbids it."

"Then let us go back," I said, in a half-hearted way.

"No, no, no, Rapa will lead her love to the world beyond."

As the light got brighter and clearer, I perceived the two rocks were united by a bridge, a frail-looking structure, which, on close inspection, I found to be a canoe.

This was the only way of getting across. My curiosity and love of adventure were so great that even though death was before me, I intended to risk it.

"Kiss me, beloved, thy kisses are sweet, and will comfort thy Rapa in the tomb to which she is going."

I was beginning to feel annoyed at this unusual expression of fear. It was the first time I had seen any manifestation of such a feeling from either male or female since I left civilization.

"Don't be so stupid, Rapa, take my hand and we can cross easily."

"No, no, you go first."

To show how easy it was to cross, I walked the canoe and stood safe on the other side.

"Come, Rapa, or shall I fetch you?"

She laughed, and then stepped gracefully on the narrow bridge. I watched her for a moment, and then turned my head, thinking perhaps my gaze might unnerve her.

I heard a scream, and turned. There was nothing to be seen but a column of smoke in the center of the bridge. Had she fallen? No; for I saw her, as though she had been lifted, by an invisible power, at least two feet above the bridge, and then, snap! crash! the bridge broke, and Rapa was precipitated to the bottom.

There remained, motionless, the column of smoke, luminous and weird, a moment, and a laugh, horrid and supernatural, broke upon my ears; the mist rose, the column disappeared, and only the two shattered ends of the frail bridge remained to testify of the catastrophe and terrible accident.

CHAPTER XL.

THE DEATH OF RAPA.

How I cursed my fatal curiosity; how I blamed myself for not giving heed to Rapa's warnings. I was filled with remorse, for had I listened to Rapa, her life would have been saved. I was in danger, the hill I had still to climb seemed inaccessible, and I had not power to leap across the abyss. My breathing became difficult, my brain grew confused, and it seemed as if a thousand streams of fire were coursing through my veins. My brain was pierced with inconceivable agony.

"My own, my beloved," fell upon my ear like a vague confused sound.

Was it possible that Rapa was alive.

The thought restored my equilibrium, and I listened intently. Yes, again it came in accents feeble but loving. My name was called. Rapa was still alive.

How could I reach her? I crawled along the rocks. I dare not stand upright, for I feared the giddiness would cause me to lose my balance.

I would reach her, even if it was as a mangled corpse; we would be united in death, for I owed her my life, seeing she had given hers for me.

I found a place where I thought I could descend. A few yards was managed without difficulty and then I grew dizzy and confused; to save myself from falling I laid down on the brink of the precipice. It seemed to me the rocks were moving. But I lost consciousness, and the next I knew I was at the bottom of the ravine with my head resting on Rapa's knees.

"Saved, my beloved, saved!" she gasped.

"Yes, but canst thou forgive me, Rapa, my love? I ought to have heeded thy warning."

"Death will be sweet now, my own."

"Talk not of death. You must not die—you shall not."

"Yes, my own, my choice, thy Rapa in a few moments will have passed to join her ancestors. Rapa felt it when she bade farewell to all, and to die in your arms will be like a beautiful dream.

"The gods will take care of Rapa, and her spirit, which loves you, will watch over and guard you, my own, my dear."

"Rapa, tell me the way out of this terrible valley, and I will carry thee to where thy life will be spared."

"Too late—too late! Go, or darkness will prevent."

"I will not leave thee, Rapa."

"I am happy. Love is forever, and to die in thy arms will win me the lasting ages of love. Oh, go! my beloved, go!"

"Never, without thee! Let me carry you."

I lifted her in my arms, but she gave utterance to most heart-rending shrieks, and I knew her spine was broken.

Gently I laid her down, and sat by her side fanning her, as she had so often fanned me.

"Kiss me," she gasped.

I kissed her over and over again. I saw the death-dew on her brow, the rattle was in her throat, and a moment later she threw up her arms and grasped me round the neck, and, with her lips pressed to mine, Rapa the devoted breathed away her soul on the morning air.

I was almost beside myself with grief, and cursed my curiosity for having been the means of leading her to her death. I sat beside the rapidly stiffening corpse, and would have given all I possessed could I have brought back life to it.

What should I do with it? I could not carry it down the mountain, even if I found the way. I was in a fix, worse than any I had yet encountered. My own safety demanded that I should seek a way of exit from the ravine. The light would not last long, for it was only while the sun was over the *crevasse* that any light penetrated its depths.

I kissed the cold face of Rapa, and then began to make her as good a grave as I could. I built up the loose rocks round her and then tried to arch them over the top. I think I succeeded fairly well, but if I failed, her pure spirit, if it retains its individual consciousness, will know that I did my best, and that my soul was nearer loving her than it had ever been. She died in serving me, and for my curiosity, all that was left was the mangled corpse of as good a girl as ever drew the breath of life.

How came the bridge to break, and whence that strange appearance of the cloud or pillar of luminous smoke? Rapa had called it Destiny, had imagined it was *He the Mighty*, warning us of our danger and trying to prevent our journey. But that was all imagination, and absurd, I thought, when scarcely had the idea been formulated than an answer came borne on the wind:

"Knowest thou all in nature, that thou art ready to call everything strange, absurd?"

I turned in the direction of the voice, but saw no one.

"Another freak of imagination," I said, mad at myself for being duped.

"What is imagination, thou pale-faced son of the East!" came again to mine ear.

I looked round, and just above me, seated on a crag of rock, I saw Isistheno, the mysterious *He*.

"Man or devil!" I exclaimed; "is this thy work?" And I pointed to the place where lay the body of Rapa.

Instead of answering, he questioned me: "And dost thou regret her death?"

"Heaven knows I do

"And yet thou wouldst pierce the veil and live forever, so that thou mightst see all thy loved ones die and rot, that thy affection might be fixed on one for a brief span, which in thy life would then be but as a day, and when night came, consign her to the tomb. Thou art not fit for the life of ages."

"Thou art a devil!" I exclaimed, angrily.

"And what is a devil?" *He* asked, in the same tone as one would ask the commonest act of civility.

"Why didst thou kill her?" I asked.

"Kill! I kill? Thou didst not see me kill her. Why, thou poor pale-face, what should I take her puny life for? Of what value was it to me?"

"Trifle not with me; but tell me, why did she die?"

"She told thee that one of thy men who journeyed over the big waters had gone into the stew-pot. I told thee her life was forfeit. Rapa knew that it was death for her to show thee the way to the beyond, but for love of you she did it. I did not kill her. If thou hadst listened to her voice, she might have comforted thee for years. Ask thyself who killed her."

"Leave me, fiend, for I hate thee!"

"Yet thou wouldst have me guide thy feet through the fire of life, so thou couldst live for the ages and epochs of all time."

It was true, and now more than ever was I determined to wrest the secret from him.

"Instruct me, most mighty one. I will be thy pupil, thy slave; only let me see into the mysteries of the great Beyond."

"First thou must rid thyself of human emotion; thou must learn to look upon suffering and death without a throb; nay, thy heart must be so hardened that thou couldst strike down the one who was dearest to thee without a pang"

"Is not that inhuman?" I tremblingly asked.

"Human! Death is human; suffering and pain are human; if a snake bites, it is human to die; the puma growls and fixes its teeth in its prey—it is human to endure torture and perish. Thou askest to rise above that, to feel no pain, to submit to torture which does not affect, to be able to laugh at the beasts of the forest, to handle vipers without fear, and when the specter of death comes, to be able with a wave of thy hand to bid it begone. And yet thou quailest before a word. Inhuman, indeed! Go think of what thou askest before my commands are questioned."

The last words seemed to die away on the air, and I knew, without raising my head, that I was alone.

Alone! There was a strange meaning in that word to me just then. Alone with my dead.

Alone! A few hours and my body may be stiff and stark, like poor Rapa's, for I was in a valley, the outlet of which I was entirely ignorant of.

A false step, and death was before me. What if I never found my way out—a slow death from starvation and exposure would be the result.

I was wretched. Death had new fears and new terrors for me, and, rising up and baring my head, I registered a vow that I should never cease my researches until old age dimmed my eyes or I found that magic elixir, which to quaff signified victory over death.

CHAPTER XLI.

A FRIGHTFUL TERROR.

I STUMBLED and fell many times in my journey through the valley. Sometimes in the dark I would find some obstacle in my path, and as my foot struck it there would fall on my ears the rattling of bones, which told me too plainly that a corpse, whitened by age, had lain across the narrow way. Tired and worn out with fatigue and suffering, both mental and physical, I leaned against a projecting rock, only to find it give way, and fall with a heavy, crashing sound in the abyss beneath, for the road was now skirting the mountain side, and while the rocks were mountains high on one side, a deep chasm yawned on the other.

It seemed that there was to be no rest for me, that I must wander on, and find neither peace nor repose. I dare not lie down, for on every hand hissing, writhing, wriggling snakes, poisonous reptiles, and animals fearful to look upon crossed my path.

If ever a man knew fear, I did then, for all my ingenuity was taxed to ward off the attacks of the serpents and strange animals.

On I went slowly, cautiously, and with stumbling footsteps, heedless of all, save my own safety. Where was I going? That I had no means of ascertaining. If my foot slipped I should go to the tomb, that I knew. A screech from some bird startled me, and I nearly fell. It seemed as though all the demons of sheol were pursuing me and making my life miserable. I had foolishly left my gun behind, or I might have woke the echoes and attracted attention. The sound as of water fell on my ear. I had not seen a river or stream on the island. Where could I have got to, and whence came the water?

The air seemed heavy and thick, and I commenced to cough; my throat filled with the sulphur vapor. I hurried forward as rapidly as I dare move, when, as I turned round a sharp angle in the road, I saw what caused the rushing sound as of waters.

Great Father in heaven! Right down the mountainside, across the very path I was traveling, a mighty stream was rushing. A stream superbly grand, but intensely awful.

A stream not of water, that pure, refreshing distillation, fresh from the Creator's own hand! No! but of liquid, boiling, bubbling sulphur.

I looked up to the mountain summit and saw a column of fire and smoke ascending high up into the clouds and then falling like a shower of rain-fire on the sides of the hill. The molten lava poured down, carrying everything before it. The few stunted trees were torn up by the roots, the rocks were dislodged from the anchorage which had held them bound for millions of years, and, with a thunderous crash, went dashing madly down into the valley beneath.

The birds of the rocks screeched with very agony, the snakes seemed to find fresh hiding-places, and all nature stood aghast at the sight of the mighty upheaval.

Five hundred feet above the valley, a thousand feet from the mountain-top, I stood, solitary amid the poisonous vapors and burning lava.

I was spell-bound and fascinated. I looked and saw the stream getting wider every minute, the river of fire with its cascades of burning metal was within a few yards of where I stood. I felt it blistering my face and scorching my hair. I pushed my hands in my pockets to save them from the heat, and stood gazing on the magnificently grand spectacle.

A rock was dislodged just above me, and came dashing and crashing past me, so close that it grazed my legs as it was whirled across the narrow path. I stood with my face looking up the mountain, every minute expecting to be ingulfed in the stream of fire. I could not move. There was a fascination which was greater than had ever before been exercised over me. If my life—if the lives of those I loved most—if heaven itself depended on my moving, I could not have done so. I was roused to consciousness by the movement of the stones under my feet.

Everything seemed to be swinging and swaying. I roused myself and walked back, up the valley. I reached the entrance to the narrow ravine, in which the body of my faithful Rapa was laid, when I saw a sight which froze the blood in my veins.

I jumped to a ledge of rock a foot or so above the floor of the ravine, just in time to escape a stream of the liquid lava, which poured down the path.

With the courage of desperation I held on to the rock, determined that I would avert death as long as possible. The lava rushed down with a sound of many waters.

I thought of Rapa. Poor girl, her body must have been destroyed by the devouring element before now. Great Heaven, what is that? Something met my gaze which nearly cost me my life, for I had difficulty in retaining my hold on the rock.

Floating down on the stream of fire was the body of Rapa, as calm and placid as if borne upon water instead of metal melted to white heat.

The face was upturned, and one hand raised as I had seen it when she put it round my neck in her death-struggle. She floated past me, looking at me, it seemed, as she went on her fearful journey. Now my eyes were riveted on her.

I saw the arm fall into the liquid fire, then the head was separated from the body; and oh, horror! I could not endure it longer—I imagined the head turned round, and the large eyes stared into mine!

"Heaven save me!" I cried; but the cry of a screech-owl was the only answer. My fingers were getting stiff. Another moment and I must loose my hold, and follow Rapa to her fiery grave.

My head began to swim; my legs refused to hold my body; and, with a prayer to the Almighty for my soul, I let go of the rock and closed my eyes.

I did not fall.

For at that very instant a strong hand grasped me and drew me up the mountain side. I was saved. Nothing but a miracle could have done it. Who was my deliverer, to whom could I give my thanks!—there was but one able to do it, and *He* it was. Up the mountain-side he carried me until I was able to breathe the purer air and look at the sulphurous lake in the distance.

"Thou thought the way was easy," he said, tauntingly.

"Slay me if thou wilt, oh, great Isistheno, but spare me thy taunts."

"Slay thee! I would rather give thee life, nay, I have proved thee, and if thou art still desirous of testing the power of the column of eternal fire and living for the ages, I will lead thee to the goal thou desirest."

"Great and mighty one, grant but that, and my gratitude will be thine."

"Dost thou love any on earth?"

I made no reply, and then I thought a shudder passed over him as he said:

"Swear thou dost not love her!"

"Whom dost thou refer to?"

"Swear, I say. Swear that thou wilt never love her!"

I was getting impatient, and wondered whether I had to deal with a madman.

"Seeing that she is dead"—I thought he referred to Rapa—"of what use would be my oath?"

"I refer not to the woman of my household, but to her, the divine Alethea."

I started. Had he discovered my knowledge of the statue's story? I would feign surprise and test his power.

"Alethea!" I repeated.

"Ay, Alethea, who for two thousand years I have loved."

"I want not thy ancient love," I answered. "Give me the fresh hot blood of youth rather than an ancient dame."

Love is proverbially blind, and my answer satisfied him.

In silence we went down the mountain side, the way he showed me was easy of descent, and I wondered why Rapa had not known it.

I had noticed that whenever *He* was directing the way or acting as guide he was unusually silent.

We reached the city of caves again safely, but the fright had so unnerved me, and the death of Rapa had been so great a shock, that I followed the example of Fjord and fell sick. During a tedious illness lasting—so Fjord tells me—many days, I had some strange dreams, but as my friend was a victim to the same illusions I let him write about them, only observing, that I had a distinct remembance of seeing many things and hearing various conversations to which he testifies. The whole narrative is so marvelous that I have begun to believe that it is the impossible that always happens.

I make no attempt to explain the mystery, but only give it as Fjord has written it.

CHAPTER XLII.

FJORD'S STORY OF THEO.'S SICKNESS.

Rapa Nui was not a healthy place; at least it did not agree with my constitution, for I was always getting an attack of some kind of fever. One kind would seize me quite suddenly, and stay as a sort of warm, uncomfortable companion for four-and-twenty hours, and then leave me without so much as apologizing for its intrusion. I was just recovering from one of these spasmodic attacks when Theo. returned from the mountain.

He seemed heart-broken and dejected, and it pained me to see him like that. The death of Rapa was enough to upset any one, and the tragic end of this devoted girl almost unnerved me as the story was pathetically told by Theo.

I was convinced that my young comrade had the spell put on him, and that he would try a taste of fever before he explored any further. I was right in my conjecture, for the next morning I went to look at him, as he did not rise as early as usual, and found him tossing about feverish and heavy. He took my hand in his, and looked at me steadily for a time, and then said:

"Fjord, old boy, I'm going. Get away from here as fast as you can."

"Nonsense, Theo.; I'll have you all right in a day or two," I responded, but at the same time my hopes were very small.

He was soon delirious and dangerous. It required all our exertions to hold him down. Sometimes he would seize me by the throat and try to strangle me. Then poor Milo, who assisted me to nurse him now that he was wifeless, would get thrown away from the stone couch in his paroxysms.

I sent for Tanoa, who was medicine-man of the household as well as chamberlain, and he made a decoction of various dried herbs which we poured down the poor young fellow's throat.

It had but little effect, and I determined to seek the presence of *He*, and get him to do something for his neophyte.

I found *He* engaged in some chemical experiment in a very fine laboratory which he had fitted up in one of the caves.

I told him my errand, but, instead of answering me, he began a discussion on the properties of the atmosphere.

"It occurs to me," he said, "that all the constituents of the human body can be found in the air we breathe. If that be the case, then what need is there for food? I am trying now to extract certain properties from the atmosphere which I call life essentials, and then I will solidify them. If I succeed, then my people will never need food."

I listened, and wondered how any one having a grain of intelligence could talk such nonsense.

"You think me a fool," he said, bluntly; "well, perhaps I am; but, tell me, do you eat everything which the body requires?"

"I do not follow you," I replied.

"You need great quantities of lime; how do you get it? Not by eating it, but by taking into the system those things which produces the gases which generate lime—just so, the same with iron and other things. Now every thing in nature derives its life from the oxygen and gases in the atmosphere. If I can solidify or capture and hold these gases in control, then by their use we need not partake of food."

"The idea is chimerical."

"Not so much as you think. Different atmospheres produce different results. In some nations the people sing; they cannot help doing it any more than birds can help flying, or dogs barking. Why is that? It can only be accounted for by the difference of the atmosphere. I would solidify that atmosphere and give it to any who desired to become singers."

"The ideas are good," I said, at length, anxious to close the discussion; "but will you not come and see my comrade, who is dying."

"Dying?" he asked.

"Yes, dying."

"Oh, there is plenty of time; come and watch me."

"But, thou mighty one, leave it not too late, for I love my friend and he is sick unto death."

"He won't die."

"I trust not. Will you come?"

"Thou art anxious. I will come."

I returned to find Theo. in a deep sleep; it was a good sign, I thought, but Tanoa came in and when he saw him wrung his hands and declared that the morning sun would not find him alive.

"It is the sleep that sleeps," Tanoa quaintly said, signifying that there would no awakening from that sleep.

I began to fear so likewise, for the heart began to beat in a very uncertain manner, the breath came spasmodically instead of in regular inhalations and exhalation, and a hectic flush dyed his cheeks. Why did not Isistheno come? A moment later *He* entered the cavern, walked up to the couch and placed his hand on Theo.'s forehead.

After allowing it to remain there for some time he removed it and placed it over the heart. That was all. A minute later he had gone, and I was alone with my friend.

I now resigned all hope, for if *He* would not help us, there was no chance of life.

Had *He* gone to prepare some compound?

No, or he would have so intimated. It was the very quintessence of cruelty to serve me so.

The night came and still Theo. slept.

It seemed to me that the breathing was more regular, and the heart pulsations natural.

Could it be that without the administration of any drug *He* had calmed the fevered blood and produced a crisis with a turn for the better? I fell asleep while I watched; I do not want to excuse myself, but let it be remembered that I had scarcely recovered my strength after the last attack of fever myself.

I slept soundly, and when my senses seemed awakening a gentle zephyr-like breeze lulled me back to sleep. I could not rouse.

Later when I awoke I felt ashamed of myself for having slept, I looked up and saw Theo. lying asleep, just as I had left him, but a cloth was on his brow, that I am positive was not there when I fell asleep. Peering through the darkness of the large cavern I saw a dim form in the far corner which I mistook for Milo.

"Milo," I called, but there came no response.

"Milo, why didst thou let me sleep?"

I rose and walked across the cavern, but the figure vanished.

I felt annoyed, for why did not Milo answer me? I left the cavern in search of her, and she declared that she had not been in once since the dread presence of *He* drove her therefrom.

Thinking over this new mystery I returned and saw Alethea standing by the couch side fanning Theo. At every wave of the fan, a delightful perfume was generated.

She glanced up as I entered, and then without a word continued the fanning.

"He is sick, canst thou save him?" I asked.

"He is saved, he will live. I will send my maiden to watch. She sleeps not."

Though kindly spoken there was a rebuke in the words which I knew I merited. Alethea divined my thoughts, for she instantly said:

"Blame not thyself, I sent thee to sleep, for thy tired body needed it. But I will send some one to watch with thee."

Alethea looked sorrowful as she glided from the cavern, and presently there entered the girl which, from the description I had received from Theo., was the one whose soul had been awakened by his embrace. The day passed and still Theo. slept, watched over by Alethea and the young girl, with myself. Not a word would the girl speak, and I should have thought her a mute, had I not heard her voice speaking to Alethea as they passed away from the cavern.

I was watching the sleep of my hero, for to me he was a hero, when *He* again entered.

The same movements, a pressure of the hand on the forehead and over the heart, and then he turned to me.

"He will live. When he wakes give him this," and Isistheno held out a small vial containing about two drops of a bright ruby liquid.

For several hours Alethea—who returned the instant *He* had gone—fanned the face and form of the one she loved, her Tisneo, as she persisted in calling him.

Theo. opened his eyes, and saw the radiant beauty of his nurse. Overcome by the sight, he hid his face, only to raise it again, and then Alethea sat down on the couch, and drew his head on her bosom.

A change came over the beautiful statue.

The marble whiteness of the cheeks disappeared, and in its place the rosy tint of health and life came like the blush of summer sunshine after the winter's snows.

Her bosom heaved with emotion; her whole frame seemed animated as I had never seen it before, and as she bent her head and pressed those charmingly perfect lips upon those of Theo., a pang of jealousy passed through me.

I would have given my soul for such a kiss. A kiss which was richer than the richest nectar or ambrosial dews.

I bethought me of the vial, and suggested that I give its contents to Theo.

Without a word she took it from me, examined it closely, and then let the two drops fall into the mouth of him who rested calmly on her perfect breast.

It was an anxious time. For fully five minutes we did not know whether Theo. would live or die, then the turn came. Alethea trembled so that she was compelled to put the loved head again on the pillow; her emotion was beyond description. She could see that Time was holding the balance—a breath might stir it on either side. The looked-for moment came, and Alethea clasped her lovely hands and cried: "He is saved! My love is alive! He will live, and the kisses of his mouth shall be mine. Through the ages we will go hand in hand, and no power shall part us more. Oh, Tisneo, my beloved, speak to me, and call me thine own!"

"Rapa, is that you?" These were the first words spoken by Theo. when he roused from his long sleep.

Alethea was grieved, but her womanly tact came to the

rescue, and she left the cavern, fearful that her presence might retard recovery.

Theo. began to improve that very hour, and the magic liquid given to he seemed to work wonders. The rosy hue of health returned to his cheeks, and, with the rapidity of the lightning's flash, he regained his health.

I ventured to leave him alone so that I might for a time escape the closeness of the atmosphere and breathe the purer air of the plain.

I was but gone an hour, and when I returned I found the cavern empty. Theo. had gone, and no trace of him could be found.

I went to Alethea's cavern, but it was empty; she also had disappeared.

I was afraid to question Isistheno. All I could do was to watch and wait, feeling that Theo. was a favorite of the gods, and that no harm would come to him.

Yet a sadness overshadowed me, and I had a presentiment that the end was near. I cared not for myself: I had one wish—the wish of my life—to learn the mystery believed in by Paralelsus, Hermes and Albert, to grasp the secret of the Rosicrucians, and, by finding the key of life, be able to ward off disease and its concomitant, death, at will. Yet, though I had sought this knowledge long and studied deeply, I would give up the ambition and return to civilized life, if by that means I could benefit Theo.

Whenever I made such a resolve, it appeared as though the spirit of Theo.'s father was hovering near me and imparting a calm peace to my troubled soul.

"There is no death," was breathed upon the tablet of my mind; "and though the bodies moldered in the dust, or stood in statuesque form as they came from the embalmer's hands, though the incinerated bodies could be grasped in a human hand, yet it was pleasing to feel that it was only the outward casket which perished; that the immortal, the precious gem, the jewel beyond all price, that breath of God which lives in and quickens man, would live forever, and though unseen, was ever alert, guiding our destinies and shaping our lives."

These thoughts seemed breathed into my ear as I thought of Theo.'s father, and the trust I had accepted from him, in the guardianship and friendship of his son. But where was Theo.? That mystery was not solved when the sun went down and the southern cross blazed in the heavens.

CHAPTER XLIII.

A CAPTIVE OF LOVE.

Fjord has told of the careful nursing I received during my strange sickness, but with the most charming modesty he has not told of his own devotion. He makes the fact of his sleep very prominent, but he does not say, as I learned from Milo, that he never once closed his eyes for nearly sixty hours, that his devotion was almost beyond human comprehension.

There is an advantage in being sick. Despite all the pain, the agonizing torture, the weariness, there is a joy which cannot be experienced in any other way.

In sickness the devotion of friends proves that, amid all the cares of life, in every man's heart there is an angel spot still; the wife, forgetful of all the fretfulness and impatience of the husband, soothes him as no other can; her soft, delicate hand being like an angel's healing touch, and the fragrance of her breath like the gentle fanning of an angel cooling the fevered brow.

In sickness the lusciousness of the grapes, the stimulation of the food, the kindly words and acts of all round the sick-bed, are as welcome as the oasis in the desert. All this I experienced; but far and away above all was the ministration of her, who was as far above me in goodness and beauty as the sun is above the earth.

Sweet, divine Alethea, let me record thy praises; never shall mortal look upon thy like again. If ever angel's kiss was pressed upon perfect brow it was on thine; if, since Creation's plan was conceived, a perfect woman, perfect in feature and form, absolutely spotless in mind and body, dwelt upon this planet, it was thee.

Patient and gentle as a nurse, loving as a friend, oh, if it had been our lot to have met in other worlds, or other places—but why conjecture. Thy perfection was far above me, I can only lay this tribute at thy feet, that if beyond the grave there is a life of knowledge of love, that I may lie at thy feet and breathe thy breath, I shall be happy as archangels are happy, for thou didst teach me that even as God is love, so love is the divine passion, the perfection of mankind.

When I was able to walk, Alethea beckoned me to follow. I had no power to resist even if I had so desired. She led me through a door which I had not before seen, and which seemed to open automatically and close again noiselessly. Along a narrow passage we went until I was surprised to find myself in the chamber where reposed the bodies of the petrified or preserved females. Through that cavern into another, warm and comfortable, was I led, and here she bade me be seated.

"Look on me, my dear one—gaze on me, and tell me dost thou love me?"

"Nay, Alethea, thou knowest!"

"Then listen! Thy love in the north was good and pure, but not one responsive throb passed through her veins; she did not know what love was, neither dost thou."

"Thou wrongest me, oh, divine one!"

"Nay! I know thee! I know that never has that divine afflatus filled thy soul. I have waited for thee two thousand years."

"For me?" I asked, in astonishment.

"Yes, even so, for thou art my own Tisneo, who left me at the Palace of Aridæus, and cast me off because of the desecration. I submitted to it for thy sake. Thou art my love, my bethrothed; dost thou not feel it? Nay, speak not till I have finished. Thy spirit has passed through the ages, and at last thou wast sent to me, to reach me and restore me to life, so that together we might fulfill our destiny. Is it not so?"

"'Tis true, most lovely one, that I started out with my father, to search for him who hath length of days, because the ancient records of our house did command it, and did say that Kallikrates was not killed by the wonderful woman of Libya, but escaped by miracle, and was to be found here."

"Of a verity 'tis so, and *He the Mighty* is Kallikrates or Isistheno thy ancestor, the father of my Tisneo, the man who stole me away from his son and by his accursed power chained me to the marble."

"Then I am the descendant of *He ?*"

"Thou art, and I am thy love who has retained her virgin purity for two thousand years for thy sake."

"I am bewildered. I do not love thee," I said.

"But thou wilt. See!" And Alethea loosened the tresses of her hair and let them fall as a veil over her face and bosom, at the same time letting her garments fall to her waist, exposing through the veil of hair the beautiful perfection of her form.

She threw back her hair, and as she stood there, more perfect than any conception of sculpture, the warm blood tinged the fair flesh, and her face became suffused with rosy blushes.

Never had I seen such beauty, never had poet described so fair a figure. The artist never lived who could have done justice to it, and as I gazed upon the vision of loveliness, I could have fallen down and worshiped.

She held out her arms, and even though I had died I could not resist, and in a moment I was pressed to her bosom, and our lips met in a long, ecstatic kiss—a kiss of such burning that fire would feel cold beside it.

Then she chanted a weird but beautiful chant—a love-song unequaled for its beauty; the words I have often tried to recall, but have failed, except in a few of the lines, which run:

" Love is pure—it is like the sweet waters in the sandy desert.
Love is the star that guides the wanderer.
It is the sun of the universe, the angel of truth.
It is the flower that blooms and then dies, because love is pure and lasts forever.
The angels love, the gods bow before Eros, and love is lord of all."

Then she pressed me tighter to her embrace, and kissed me many times, taking up her chant again.

" At Eros' temple did I plight my troth—
The priestess sang the chant of love, and I
Vowed my truth should e'er be thine.
Tisneo, I have waited twice a thousand years.
Come to me, beloved, for I am thine own, my sweet."

The chant had a peculiar effect upon me; it was musical in its rhythm, but untranslatable. She ceased, and releasing me from her arms, hid her face in her hands and wept. That was more than I could endure. I clasped her in my arms, and pledged to her eternal love.

"Seek Isistheno," she said, "and learn from him the secret thou wouldst have, and then together through the ages Tisneo and Alethea shall clasp each other's hands and prove to the gods that love is eternal."

I longed to fold her in my arms again, but she was gone. In her place stood the attendant who had once been embraced by me, and she, speechless, motioned for me to follow her.

I did so, and at the entrance to my own cavern she left me.

"Where have you been?" exclaimed Fjord. "Thy face shines like the sun."

I answered in what must have appeared a strange manner to him:

"I have been in heaven, and the light of beauty is reflected from my face."

"Have pleasant dreams come to thee?" Fjord asked, as I thought, with a sneer.

"And even if they have, what are dreams?" I replied; "when at night the body sleeps, matter subsides into a state of torpor, and the spirit, freed from its earthly trammels, wings its flight toward the highest heaven, which is its home, its resting place. It towers on high, it soars upward, and is able to see clearer, to meet angels face to face, and to feel the glow which emanates from the great Architect of the Universe, the Light of the World."

"True, oh, Theo.," he answered; "but then you admit you have been dreaming."

"No, except so far as this—that I never believed so much grace, loveliness, and truth could exist on earth."

"Thou hast been with Alethea."

"I have, and, as I pillowed my head on her bosom, I had but one wish——"

"And that?"

"To die there."

"Better live there, I should fancy," said Fjord; but there was an expression on his face which was new to me. Was it possible that he, too, was in love with Alethea?

Why not? Was he mortal? If so, he must love her, for nothing human could withstand her grace, her beauty, and the fascinating beams from her lovely eyes. I turned away, for I was not in a humor to talk, especially if Fjord also loved the same object, for side by side with my love was a dark hate, the passion of murder, and I could have killed any who dared to look with eyes of love on my Alethea. Why is it that murder and hatred go together in the same breast as such ineffable love as I felt for Alethea?

I grew impatient, *He* must now fulfill his promise and initiate me into the mysteries of the Beyond. I would wrest from him the secret of life, for Alethea's sake I must get equal power with Isistheno.

Such was my resolve, such my ambition.

Would I be able to accomplish it? Time alone would tell.

Fjord was also equally determined, and with him I sought the presence of this mighty master of the great secrets.

CHAPTER XLIV.

THE MYSTERY OF THE CRYSTAL.

"THOU wert expected," was the salutation bestowed on us when we entered the dwelling-chamber of the mysterious one.

"Thou knowest all things," I replied.

"No, only such as the great Tabu desires I should have knowledge of."

"How know you these things?" Fjord asked.

"Look, examine yonder crystal," and *He* pointed to the glass-ball into which we had previously looked.

As we gazed on its polished surface, it appeared as though huge waves were foaming and dashing on land; not a ship or boat was in sight, fortunately, for it would be impossible for any save the stanchest to weather such a gale. The thunder roared, at least so realistic was the picture that it required but a very slight stretch of the imagination to hear the thunders of Heaven's artillery, especially as the lightning flashed across the crystal striking into the water with its deadly balls of fire.

Then on the top of the wave, we saw a small boat tossed to and fro like a cork on the angry waters.

Fjord and I stood spellbound and fascinated, we could not take our eyes away from the picture so vividly portrayed on the crystal.

Our excitement was great, and it increased as we watched the wild despair of the men in the boat.

They fell on their knees and prayed for mercy, prayed to the God of the storm to save them. It was useless, their prayers were unanswered.

A huge wave, mountain high, struck the boat and swamped it. The scene changed, the waters became calm and unruffled as a fresh-water lake.

The change was so sudden that we started back aghast at such a rapid transformation. Could it be the same water? Yes, for there was the boat floating keel uppermost. Where were the men? Our question was quickly answered, for we saw two white faces floating on the bosom of the waters and being borne toward land.

"Look at them," I said, and Fjord ejaculated, "Great Heaven! they are our seamen."

It was true; we had seen in the magic crystal a representation of the wreck of our whaleboat and the drowning of the seamen who had left us, thinking more of their own safety.

"Now thou seest how Tabu, the great and mighty lord of the earth and sea, tells me the mysteries of the world," *He* said, as he drew the curtain and hid the crystal from view.

"But thou hast supernatural power," I said.

"Not so; there is nothing outside of nature. Man is arrogant in proportion to his ignorance, and attributes to the Supreme that which he does not understand. Man is but in the infancy of knowledge, and yet thinks that the whole creation was formed for him. Yet man is but one grade in the order of life, just as the caterpillar is superior to the insects on which it feeds.

"Man saw in times past the countless worlds that hang

and sparkle in space, like the bubbles on the shoreless ocean, and thought they were so many jewels set in the sky for his pleasure, so many flashing gems to break the monotony of the darkness, and make night more agreeable. Yet such is not the case, for each of them is a world, and the people who live there look down upon the puny creatures of this planet as man in his egotism looks upon the monkey tribe."

"Dost thou tell us that the planets are the residences of a superior people?"

"They must be, for life is everywhere. In the small as well as the vast, all nature teems with life. Each drop of water in the pool, the lake, the mighty ocean is an orb more populous than the earth itself. Every blade of grass, every leaf of a tree is a world peopled by as great a variety of life as is this world; then why doubt that the stars are the dwelling-place of beings as superior to man as the planets are superior to the earth?"

He paused, and then walked away from the crystal alcove, before which he had been standing. "Tell us, most mighty one, how the lake was lighted on the night of our first entrance here."

"That was nothing. In the waters there is a certain compound which men call phosphor. All that has been done, was to bring that to the surface, and light was generated."

"But would not such an invention be of value to the world?" asked Fjord.

"Of value? Verily so; but if thou wilt chain the lightning so that it can be used to scatter an army and kill thy fellows—if thou discoverest means to destroy life—nations will reward thee. Discover that which will triumph over disease, will give health and knowledge to the people, and the same nations will starve thee. Ay, teach men how to get rich, and keep their brethren poor—so that the rich will get richer and the poor poorer—and poets will chant thy praises, and nations will build monuments to perpetuate thy fame; but turn thy attention to the means to equalize wealth, to give to all comfort, to bring happiness to all who toil honestly, and the poets will denounce thee, and the nations will throw thy body into the dungeon vault. Is it not so?"

"It is too true," asserted Fjord.

"See, here is a means of making the lightning the servant of man." And *He* touched a small wire, when immediately the cavern was lighted with a brightness far superior to any artificial light ever produced.* "This same light-

* This MS. was evidently written by Aristophano before the utilization of electricity for illuminating purposes.—EDITOR.

ning," said *He*, "will rend rocks and destroy mountains, making the way straight and smooth."

"We would learn these secrets."

"The journey is risky, the dangers are many, thou wilt have to encounter fiends hostile to humanity, others as gentle as the messengers of the truth. I can gain thee admission to the temple, but intercourse once gained, I cannot guard thee against the dangers and chances to which thou wilt be exposed. But if thou art so desirous of life, so enamored of its varied cares, as only to wish to live on, and with the purification of fire, have also the life-renewing elixir, then I can serve thee."

"But why not give the elixir now?" asked Fjord, who was growing impatient.

"Because thy frame could not endure it. The elixir once taken makes manifest to thee the sound of the larvæ on the leaves, and the animalculæ in the water; thou art admitted into the presence of a multitude of unseen but manifest powers, and, unless thy frame is hardened by toil and travel, by danger and fear, and at last purified by the fire which lies at the center of the earth, thou couldst not endure the life thou cravest. Some I have known, who have started on the journey, and have been so affrighted at the phantoms met on the way, that they have fallen on their knees, and called on the rocks to cover them. When thou reachest the fire, thou shalt see the eyes of one glaring at thee, one who surpasseth all the malignity of the fiends, but thou wilt have to pass by. The power of that malignant fiend increases in the same proportion as thy fear. Dost thou still desire to take the journey?"

"I will follow thee, though perdition sends all its fiends to harrow up my very soul!" I exclaimed.

Fjord was silent. Could it be that fear had taken possession of him? No; I would not so wrong him. Yet why the strange silence? I spoke to him, but he made no reply. I shook him, and with a yawn he started up, and looked round bewildered.

"Fjord, you have been asleep."

"No, that I deny," he answered seriously.

"But, man, did I not just wake thee?"

"Of that I know not, but I have seen them all."

"Seen what?"

"The spirits of the air, who make or mar the bliss of man," he replied, absently.

"You have been dreaming."

"'Pon my honor, I have never slept."

Isistheno seized Fjord by the shoulder and dragged him across the room.

Instantly Fjord renewed his normal condition, and

seemed surprised at finding his surroundings so different to his dreams.

"Explain!" I said, looking at *He*, who had again veiled his face.

"Fjord, thy friend," he said, "was reduced to that condition by a careless glance of mine eye. Had I not veiled, he would have died."*

Fjord looked like one just arisen from a profound slumber, and as he rubbed his eyes, he had a far-away look which told that his mind had been greatly affected by what he had experienced in the trance to which a glance of the eye of the magician had consigned him.

"If thou still desirest to penetrate the secrets, be ready at an hour before midnight to journey with me."

"Desire! ay, we will follow thee," answered Fjord.

As we returned to our dwelling-cave, our minds were filled with an exaltation the like of which I had not before known. We were on the threshold; what would be the result? The doubts flocked to our minds, and our reason told us that no man possessed the secrets claimed by Isistheno, yet whence came his power?

I paid a visit to the boudoir—if I may use such a word—of Alethea. Nothing was changed since the first visit.

A fire burned on the hearth, the walls were hung with grass mats, and in the alcove stood the beautiful statue.

I approached it, gazed into its eyes, felt the beautifully modeled arms, pressed the cheeks—but no response answered to my touch. It was marble, cold and hard. I was overcome. I had expected to have a warm loverlike greeting. I wanted to tell Alethea that for her sake I was about to brave the dangers of the threshold; but not one word to cheer me, not one glance to bid me be of good courage, not an embrace, the memory of which would have nerved me to face all and every danger.

I clasped the statue in my arms; it was but a cold, lifeless stone. I sank on the floor and wept.

The tears flowed from my eyes, and fell on the floor like rain, and I felt most miserable. I realized that I must go on the journey alone; that no companion could face its dangers for me. Without a look of love, or word of comfort, I left the alcove, crossed the cavern, and, with heart heavy as lead, returned to Fjord, whose lot I almost envied, for he had Milo to cheer and comfort him.

It was with a sad heart that I began my preparations for the eventful journey.

---

* Was this mesmerism?

CHAPTER XLV.

THE ORDEAL.

THE hour of departure arrived. We took a good supply of provisions, and strapped our guns to our backs. I had suggested that our guns should be left behind, but Fjord insisted that we might need them; so, although heavy and cumbersome, we—as it afterward proved—wisely submitted to the burden.

The watch I carried spoke the time to be one hour before midnight. Fjord envied me my timekeeper, for his had not been able to withstand the climatic influences; and when I was not near he was compelled to time himself by the sun, as the natives did.

We were proceeding to the dwelling place of *He*, when we were met by that personage, veiled as usual, and looking more like a statuesque column draped in muslin than a human being.

He was accompanied by **Tanoa** and the giant band.

Out of the caves, on the plain, I was surprised to find the whole household gathered.

There were male torch-bearers, and girls bearing the skulls, from which a sickly glare of light emanated.

The lovely attendants who had waited on us the first time we partook of food on the island, were there also, with their sashes of grape-vines and bunches of luscious fruit hanging in clusters over their bosom.

I could never find where these grapes were obtained, for I had not seen a vine on the island, yet there seemed a plentiful supply of nature's most delicious food.

The dancing girls were also in the crowd, and to judge from appearances, a great merry-making was to take place instead of so serious a journey.

All had fallen on their faces when *He* and his giant guard emerged from the cave, but when Tanoa clapped his hands, every one stood erect, and with a stiffness which was astonishing awaited further orders.

In a few minutes we formed ourselves in a weird procession, the torches throwing a sickly glare over the mountain-side, and yet giving the processionists a most picturesque appearance.

We crossed the plain or basin of the huge crater, and then descended some steps into a lower basin, in which stood the ruins of the city, whose deserted streets I had traversed with Rapa on our wedding-day.

Many of the ruins were in good preservation, and as the light shone on them, their strange carvings stood out like visions of spirits in the gloom of night.

We entered what appeared to have been the main thoroughfare of the city, and I turned to Isistheno and remarked that the builders of the city were good designers.

"Verily they were," *He* said; "for the city hath endured many thousand years. When the great Tabu transported me hither two thousand years ago, everything was as thou seest it to-day. The city was a ruin, and the generation then living could only say that the mind of the oldest ancestor never conceived the time of its destruction."

There was a regularity in the laying out of the streets which I had not previously noticed. Trees had evidently grown between the houses, and at intervals of every hundred yards or so, would be found a hole, which Isistheno said was the ruin of an ancient well.

The procession wound itself through the streets until the opposite hill was reached, and then *He* turned, facing the household, and bade them return to their dwellings.

With one accord they turned, and we watched them as they walked through the ruins carrying their torches high above their heads.

When the last torch had disappeared, *He* showed Fjord and me how to carry our lamps. We slung them in front of us, and at an angle so that the light was thrown on our path instead of to the roof of the passage we now entered

In this cave, or passage, we halted for the remainder of the night, and we—at least I can answer for Fjord as well as myself—were heartily glad to get a rest, though neither cared to sleep in such close proximity to the deathless one.

The morning dawned, though its sun's rays did not penetrate the cavern, and we proceeded on our journey. It seemed that we were making a gradual descent into the bowels of the mountain.

Again we entered a mammoth cavern, the walls of which were carved in relief.

One figure, that of a woman weaving (in appearance like this), occupied the entire side, and must have measured

fifty feet long, yet it was admirably proportioned.

By the side of the woman was a small hole, through which we had to crawl, and then our way led down a number of rudely-cut steps.

At the foot of these steps we stood for a moment, gazing in silent awe on the immensity around us. We had reached the open air, and must have been many hundred feet below the level of the plain on which stood the ruins of the city.

The steps ended on a jutting piece of rock, shaped almost like a cathedral spire. The apex forming a platform of about six feet square. On this platform we stood and looked round. Below us was a vast depth, at the bottom of which we could see a stream of water, the first we had seen on the island. Round us were nothing but bleak, perpendicular rocks. Opposite was a similar platform to the one on which we were standing, but separated from us by about ten feet.

He sprung over the gulf, as though it were of no account, but though fearless generally, a tremor passed over my body at the thought of the consequences of a misstep.

However, I summoned up courage and jumped, landing safely on the other side, as also did Fjord.

We entered another passage, and descended more steps until we came to a circular cavern.

Here we were left alone. Isistheno declaring that he must leave us to commune with the dwellers on the threshold. On no account were we to leave until he returned, and, even though we were in fear, it would be useless to call out, as he would be beyond hearing.

Scarcely had he left us, when a sickening vapor filled the chamber, and was as thick as a suncloud, or, better still, a London fog. Now, on our astonished eyes burst a sight which, for a moment, unnerved us. Myriads of stars seemed to break through the mist, these stars, as we looked upon them, evolved into shapes of human form, but headless. Their bodies were transparent and beautiful. I leaned forward to clasp one in my arms when, suddenly, it changed into a hideous, laughing, grinning fiend. Slowly they glided round the chamber, and then disappeared. The darkness was now intense, the air suffocating, and it was with difficulty that we could breathe.

We became conscious of a presence undefined and undefinable. We tried to pierce the gloom, and for a moment nothing but the painful darkness met our vision. Out of the darkness gradually emerged a cloud like a column of light, fleecy smoke. Crowning the column was a human head, covered with a thick veil, through which glared with demoniac fire eyes that froze our blood and turned to ice the marrow in our bones. All fancies of poets, all conceptions of artists, paled before the hideousness of this vision. The eyes glared and burnt into our very souls.

I put my hand over my eyes, but the burning glare was still there. All else was dark, our lamps had been extinguished, and the only light in the chamber was the horrid flame of fire which proceeded from those eyes. I could endure no more. I seized hold of a projecting rock to save me from falling; I felt my brain on fire; my eyes were glazed and rigid and my hair stood erect. The form spoke. Its voice was as horrible as its appearance.

"Who are ye who would contend with death?" it said. "I am the dweller in the cave of death, and thou wouldst woo me as thine own. Come to my arms, Aristophano. Clasp me to thy bosom, O Fjord, for together we will dwell."

The horrible figure or Presence approached nearer. I could feel its breath upon my cheek; and in an agony so great that the blood burst through the pores of my skin I fell to the ground, shrieking like a maniac.

The Presence neared Fjord, and his courage vanished likewise, and as he fell in a heap on the ground he tried to reach my hand, so that in our terror we might have at least the consolation of companionship.

We laid there I cannot tell how long, but the air got clearer, and we were able to breathe more freely, but neither dared look up.

The sulphurous atmosphere gave place to one of rare perfume, and I felt myself touched on the shoulder. The pressure was gentle and soft, and gave me courage to raise my head, when, to my joy and surprise, I beheld the loved form of Alethea.

I never questioned as to how she got there. It did not seem to me a greater mystery than others I had experienced since first I had seen the animated statue. My joy was so great that I threw myself in her arms and felt her sweet kisses of rapture on my lips, my cheeks, my forehead.

"Behold I kiss thee," she said, "for the last time, before thou puttest on length of life. And yet there is a sadness where there should be but joy. It seems to me that after waiting all these centuries, that something will snatch thee from me. It cannot be *He*, no, that can never be; even if *He* slay thee, yet will I be true to thee, my own, my Tisneo. Oh for the rapture of that time, when we shall both be purified, and thou shalt go with me hand in hand through the ages. Thy friend, my Fjord, as I shall call him, will know that I am for thee, and in our happiness he will seek his own."

Alethea paused and crossed to where Fjord was standing. She coquettishly put up her face to him, and in the sweetest of voices said:

"Thou wilt need all thy courage, so thou canst kiss my cheek if it pleaseth thee so to do."

I was not jealous, yet a thrill did pass through every nerve of my body, as I saw the lips of my friend press the pure alabaster of her cheek.

The mist again gathered, and Alethea vanished. We were alone.

CHAPTER XLVI.

THE COLUMN OF FIRE.

Scarcely had we realized that the beautiful vision had left us, before a glimmer of light appeared in the distance, and we saw Isistheno approach.

"Come, all is ready! Thy courage hath withstood the test. Now shalt thou go into the very center of the earth and bathe in the eternal fire, which is the mainspring of the world, and which, when once inhaled in thy system, will live and last until thou desirest death."

"But the elixir?" I asked.

"The elixir shall be quaffed when thou hast passed through the fire, and returned therefrom rejuvenated."

Isistheno led the way down an incline, until we reached another cavern, dark and grewsome. Here we rested, as *He* told us that we should need all our strength for the descent down thousands of steps. An hour passed away. *He* stood staring vacantly at the entrance to the cavern, and soliloquized. Evidently he had no thought that his words would be overheard.

"Tabu, thou mighty one, am I doing wrong in initiating these into thy mysteries? I comprehend the great law which binds man to man, and I would not be longer alone. Vain was my thought that happiness could be found in solitude. O great Tabu, let the initiation of these neophytes be the opening of the gates of Alethea's love!"

I started; what if it should be so? What if the passing through the fire, and the quaffing of the elixir, should give Alethea life in the arms of my great rival?

No; it could not be.

Isistheno continued:

"What thou warnedst me of has come to pass; the love of two thousand years has become so strong that it absorbs all things to itself. For Alethea's sake I have submitted,

Let her love reward me. Tabu, give me her love, or let me perish; give me Alethea as mine own, or let me die the death."

The soliloquy was cut short by a terrific crash of thunder, which seemed to shake the mountain to its base.

"Come! the time hath arrived!"

We followed him down some steps, which were so many in number that our knees began to tremble and our bodies grew faint.

"Seest thou that light?" he asked. Peering into the abyss we distinguished flash after flash of a bright ruby light.

"That is the flame of life," he said.

The thought gave us renewed courage and we descended the few remaining steps without feeling fatigue.

At the bottom was a mammoth cave, evidently the work of volcanic action.

"Thou art now in the earth's center. At the place from whence proceedeth every germ which originates life," *He* said. "See yon flame." We looked and saw what man but seldom had opportunity to witness.

A column of fire, tall and smooth as though carved in stone, glided toward us. Yet glided is scarcely a fair description of its movement, for it seemed to revolve, each revolution bringing it nearer.

"That is the column of the fire of life," *He* said. "To him that hath inhaled its fire, and quaffed the elixir, neither pain, nor sorrow, nor death can come. Hast thou power to test it to the last?"

"Ay, even though it consumes me to ashes," I replied.

"And so will I," exclaimed Fjord.

He stood in rapt contemplation, and then raising his right hand, invoked the spirit of the great Tabu.

The thunders rolled, the mountain seemed to rock, and I trembled at the nearness of death.

"Tabu, I implore thee! By the mystic power thou conferred upon me! By the length of life thou endowedst me with, let this moment give me Alethea, that together our love may live always."

"I will never be thine," exclaimed the well-known voice of Alethea.

Isistheno turned and recoiled as he stood confronting the statue.

"Thou slandered my name, thou stolest from me my love, and then to win thy purpose chained me to the marble from which thou vowedst I should never get free till Tisneo appeared. Behold, though the centuries have rolled on, my love has returned, and in Theo. behold my lost love, thy so:. I am his through the ages, and if death seek us together we go to the tomb and enter the land of spirits faithful even in death. Take this heed! A million years could never atone for a woman's slandered name."

Isistheno turned savagely. His face was dark as a thunder cloud, and looking at Alethea, who was entrancing, more so than usual, he exclaimed:

"My love hath turned to hate; but in its hate it can prevent thee from having thy wish. I have lived the centuries for thee, and if I am not to possess thee, neither shall another."

He struck Alethea a fearful blow, and broke the statue into a hundred pieces.

A fearful crash of thunder rent the air, and the cave grew dark.

A moment later the cloudiness disappeared and we looked round. Not a vestige of the marble appeared. Alethea had effectually vanished. The thought was impressed on our mind that it must have been a dream or a freak of imagination.

The column of fire returned, and as it did so, *He* exclaimed:

"Follow my example and inhale the mighty, mysterious fire of life."

He entered the flame. For a moment he was encompassed as with a garment.

Then his face shone through the fiery halo, resplendent in its beauty; but while we watched, the face changed, the eyes grew smaller, the face became more pointed. From the head proceeded a pair of horns, and the great Isistheno became transformed into a goat of such hideousness that we hid our faces with very fear.

Out of the cloud it came, rushing and butting. There was no semblance of humanity, but the voice was left.

"I have sinned," it said. "The ages have not atoned for the slander of Alethea's fair name. Old age, terrible in its hideousness, has come upon me, and in this frightful shape I must work out the destiny of the ages. Seek not to penetrate the Hereafter, but accept death as the fulfillment of life."

The lightning flashed, and the thunder rolled louder than ten thousand guns, and then we saw the rocks shake to their very foundation.

We rushed from the spot, fear lending speed to our footsteps, and when we reached the first great plateau in the open air, we looked at each other. Our hair was white as driven snow, our cheeks furrowed as if by the weight of years, and our backs were bent as though age had left its impress upon them.

Scarcely had we left the mountain-side before a terrific

explosion rent the air, and the mountain was shattered by volcanic power into millions of fragments, falling and burying beneath it the marvelous caves of the dead and their inmates.

Not a vestige was left to mark the spot, and nature had swallowed up and engulfed the many mysteries we had seen. Mankind lost much; but what we saw, we tell to the world.

CHAPTER XLVII.
L'ENVOI.

My story is ended. We found our way easily to the sea coast, on the opposite side of the island to that where stood the gigantic image of Tabu.

We lived for a week on what fruits we could gather, and the birds we shot, and then to our great joy we saw a vessel in the distance. By dint of signaling, firing our guns, and making a fire, we attracted attention, and the next day we were taken on board the good ship Labrador, bound for Australia.

We were glad to escape so well, but never, if we live until the sun has gone its course a thousand years, shall we forget the terrible experiences on the island of Rapa Nui.

Fjord continues his researches, and will not allow any one to throw doubt on the narrative of the long life of Isistheno, or the miracle of the animated statue. I will not express an opinion, save that only he who has mastered all the secrets of Nature, is able to decide whether the spirit of Tisneo is not reincarnated in my body, and whether there be not some way by which life may be preserved beyond the period usually allotted to man.

The whitened hair, the furrowed cheeks, and bent bodies of Fjord and myself tell of the agonies and tortures we endured, and bear witness to the truth of my story.

As I write, the fair spirit of Alethea seems with me, and directs my hand; and oftentimes when the stars twinkle like so many diamonds in the azure sky, I feel her presence and hear the chanting of her songs of love; of that love which neither time, nor space, age, nor eternity could alter; a love, which, like its great parent, God, is eternal, and while it makes a paradise on earth to those who possess it, gives a greater glory and a brighter radiance to the Heaven of heavens.

[THE END.]

MUNRO'S LIBRARY.

Vol. 50. No. 726.   April 15, 1887.

Entered at the Post Office, N. Y., as Second Class Matter.
Munro's Library is issued Tri-Weekly.

"IT."

A Wild, Weird History of Marvelous, Miraculous, Phantasmagorial Adventures in Search of

HE, SHE, and JESS,

And Leading to the Finding of

"IT."

A HAGGARD CONCLUSION.

[John De Morgan]

Entered according to Act of Congress, in the year 1887, by Norman L. Munro, in the office of the Librarian of Congress, at Washington, D. C.

NEW YORK:
NORMAN L. MUNRO, PUBLISHER,
24 AND 26 VANDEWATER ST.

"IT."

A Haggard Conclusion

INTRODUCTION.

On a miserable evening in January I was seated in my library toasting my feet in front of a cheerful grate fire, and congratulating myself that I could not conceive of anything which would cause me to leave the house that evening.

The wind whistled down the streets, and at every corner played strange havoc with the hats and umbrellas of foot-passengers. The rain came down in torrents, and every drop as it fell seemed to rebound with savage glee from the pavement. Not a star could be seen, and although it was supposed to be moonlight, the dark and heavy clouds so obscured the "queen of night" that her radiant beauty was invisible. It was, as the Scotch would say, "an uncanny night."

I lighted my pipe—when I am alone I always prefer a meerschaum to a cigar, though my wife objects to a pipe, as being low and vulgar—and took up the evening paper for a quiet read. For I was alone in the house, keeping bachelor hall for a few days while my wife enjoyed herself with her relatives.

I was restless and ill at ease, that strange feeling of unrest came over me, which is so hard to account for; my ears burned, caused so, my wife would say, by the fact that some one was talking of me. I shivered, and a cold chill sought my spinal marrow; so, taking it altogether, I was uncomfortable. A presentiment haunted me that something strange and startling was to take place. What it was I could not imagine, but so strong was its hold on me, that when a double rat-tat came to the door a moment later, I nearly jumped from my chair and shouted.

The reaction came, and I resumed my normal calm, just as my servant entered the room, bearing in her hand a package.

"Please, sir, a boy brought this, and there was no answer."

"Thank, you, Jane," I responded, taking it from her.

I saw that the bulky parcel was addressed in strange writing. A letter accompanied it, sealed in a square envelope, slightly soiled, I suppose, by the boy's dirty hands.

What did the package contain? Was it an infernal machine, and was my grave presentiment coming true? Ah, I remembered then that my wife, who was learned in omens and folk-lore, had told me that a chill down the spine meant that some one was walking over my grave. I trembled with very fear. I, who, as reporter for the *Daily Thunderer*, had gone into the lowest haunts of Wapping, had encountered the fishwives of Billingsgate, had spent a night as an amateur casual in a workhouse, and consorted (for the purposes of my profession) with thieves—I was really frightened. I would not touch the parcel, but there could be no harm in the letter, so I broke the seal, which, strangely enough, was a skull, and read as follows:

" —— Hotel, London, Jan., 188–.

"MY DEAR SIR,—Some time since I sent you the MS. of my adventures in Rapa Nui, which you published for me under the title of '*He*.' Since that was written I have passed through many adventures, which were far more terrible than those recorded in my previous work. Besides, I venture to think that my discoveries will be of value to the scientific world and deeply interesting to the general public. I therefore have written them out and with this letter send the MS. to you, asking you to be my editor.

"Should there be any profit, you can use it as you think best, should any loss accrue you can draw on my bankers—whose card I enclose—for whatever deficiency there may be. I would add that the narrative is a true one, the facts just as I have stated them, and I can give undoubted proof that I, with my friends, visited races of people which had never seen a white man before; traveled over territory unmarked on any map, and explored kingdoms of which the world was entirely ignorant. The finding of '*It*' alone is an achievement which will be of absorbing interest to all future generations. With every expression of esteem

"I am your friend and admirer,
"J. THEODOSIUS ARISTOPHANO."

I read the letter over carefully a second time, and then let it fall on my knee while the clouds of smoke curled in fantastic columns to the ceiling. I looked into the smoke to find an answer there to my strange friend's letter. What should I do? I had been interested in "He," and why should not the public have the benefit of later discoveries by the same writer?

I determined to read the manuscript. Turning up the gas to get a better light, I cut the string and opened out the parcel. On the top lay a crisp Bank of England note for one hundred pounds, and pinned to it a tag, on which was written: "For preliminary expenses incurred in the publication of 'It.' Old Aristophano was very thoughtful. I drew my chair to the table, and began to read. The night passed rapidly away, but I still read on; the fire flickered out, but I felt not the cold, so entranced was I with the story. At times my hair would stand on end, and I would shiver with fear; at others my blood would course madly through my veins as some daring adventure was recorded. I read on, until the girl came in to sweep up the room and light the fire in the morning, for I was so fascinated and interested that I could not rise from the manuscript until the end was reached. The great mystery of life was being solved, and the name of Aristophano would shine brightly in the ranks of the immortals. I tied up the parcel, and carried it with my own hands to the publisher.

I have only this to say in addition. I have taken no liberties with the copy, but have allowed Aristophano to tell his story in his own way. My hope is that its million readers will be as greatly fascinated by the thrilling romance of actual adventures as I have been.

THE EDITOR.

CHATER I.
PRESENTIMENT.

WHEN I returned from my last journey of adventure I determined to spend the remainder of my days in the quiet of home life.

As I stood on the deck of the steamer, homeward bound, my heart beat with happy exultation at the thought of the calm which was to be mine. For when one has traveled very nearly all over the world, been blinded by the hot, burning sand of an Egyptian desert, frozen in the artic regions, and sweltered in the tropics; when one's life has been at the mercy of South Sea Island cannibals, and had for companions the Hottentots of Africa; when for years the lion and tiger, the elephant and rhinoceros have been hunted, and many hairbreadth escapes experienced, there is a pleasure in retiring to the quiet calm of civilization, such as I knew awaited me in my pretty ivy-clad cottage, surrounded by trees from whose branches the sweet feathered songsters of England would warble so delightfully.

Such were my thoughts as the good ship neared the white cliffs of Albion. One month afterward and I was dissatisfied, and was again longing for adventure.

And yet I, John Theodosius Aristophano, had everything that heart could wish. Wealth not exactly that of the Rothschilds, but enough and to spare, a pretty cottage picturesquely situated on the banks of the river Avon, not far from the place where Shakespeare saw the light of day, wooed sweet Anne Hathaway, and stole the deer from the neighboring forest. As I looked from my garden gate in the opposite direction I saw the ivy-mantled towers of Kenilworth Castle, and often thought of the gay revels which took place therein when Leicester entertained Queen Elizabeth, and then my mind would wander to the cruel murder of sweet Amy Robsart. Old Warwick Castle frowned down on me, and near by was the far-famed city of Coventry, with its quaint legend of Lady Godiva and Peeping Tom.

In all England no prettier place could be found; the cottage was old, dating back to the Elizabethan period, but was stanch and trim, old-fashioned but comfortable. In front, and extending down to the river bank, was the garden and pretty lawn. A few trees helped to ward off the hottest rays of the sun, and give shelter to the nightingale and other sweet singers of the air.

If any man had reason for contentment, surely I had. I was in every way independent; I had neither chick nor child, and no one to trouble me but a housekeeper who ruled despotically. I entertained but few visitors, for I had long since ceased to care for friends who only put their feet under your table and drink your wine so that they may listen to your adventures and go away laughing at the garrulous old man.

For I am old—that is, if experience counts for anything. I have grown so accustomed to measure age by events that I often wonder whether my span of life must not be reckoned by centuries instead of years. If I am old, I am active. I can fire a rifle and bring down a lion as well as I could thirty years ago. I have not met the man who could grapple with me successfully, and although my hair is white and my beard grizzled, yet my muscles are like iron and my heart beats with the glowing pulsations of health.

Yet I felt, at the time of which I am writing, uneasy. It was a weariness of life. The monotony was growing unbearable. I—who had slept with no other cover but the canopy of heaven's blue vault, without bed or bedding, a rifle for bedfellow and a stone for pillow for years—could not get accustomed to the softness of feathers and the luxury of a home.

I sat in my rocking-chair smoking a pipe which had traveled thousands of miles with me, and as I watched the clouds of smoke curl upward and grow dense, then light, until they eddied away in the dim mistland, I fell to thinking.

In the clouds I saw again the wild despair which seized on me when I was pursued by a lion. I had exhausted all my ammunition save one cartridge. Inserting it quickly in my rifle. I took aim, but, as ill luck would have it, my foot slipped, and my bullet only grazed the monarch's shoulder, making him furious and mad. On he charged, and I ran with all the speed I could command away from him.

He—noble beast that he was—gained upon me. I was out of breath, but staggered rather than ran forward. I felt the animal close to me, I heard its deep breathing and I murmured a prayer for safety. Another step and my brain grew dizzy, my knees shook like aspen leaves, my legs refused to support me, and I fell.

I felt the hot breath of my conqueror on my cheek; my time had come. The noble animal was weak from loss of blood, and breathless from his long run. With his heavy paws on my chest crushing out my last gasping breath, he stood like a victorious gladiator, his foe beneath him.

I closed my eyes, and then like a lightning flash the thought of my heavy hunting-knife occurred to me. I let my hand glide softly to my belt, and with equal steadiness drew the knife from the sheath. The slightest movement, if perceived by the lion, would have been the signal for my death. The knife was drawn, and it appeared as though ages passed in the few seconds it took me to raise the weapon and with a sudden movement drive it home though the brute's heart.

He fell over and a moment later was dead. Now I come to think of it, the skin of that very lion was thrown over the chair on which I was sitting and smoking.

Did that cause me to think of it? Perhaps so, for who can tell what magnetism there is still in the skin of a dead animal?

We are but on the threshold of knowledge and the dawn of a new world is opening up to us. But I was troubled. My hands itched for the hunt, my brain was all on fire. I must be off again, and though I die on some mountain side, with no friend but my rifle, better that than a tame, monotonous existence in a quiet riverside cottage.

What had become of my old friend, Captain Norse Fjord? He was older in years than I, and yet was still traveling in search of that marvelous elixir which would give him power over death. It was two years since I had heard from him.

He was not dead, that I knew.

How could I know that, seeing I had not heard anything from him?

Ah, curious reader, shall I gratify your curiosity?

Shall I draw the veil aside for a moment and tell you that a compact had been made between our respective spirits that whenever either of us got rid of the cumbersome body, the other should be at once made acquainted with the fact? How? Ah, there is the mystery, but in the new world which is gradually being revealed, it will not be mystery, but fact, not a chimera, but a scientific reality.

I was firmly convinced that had Fjord "shuffled off the mortal coil," I should have known of it in some way.

I wished for his presence and company, or if I knew in what part of the world he could be found I would join him.

I was roused from my reverie by a vigorous shaking, administered by my housekeeper. Let me introduce this worthy lady.

She was—well, it would be unfair to state her age, even if I knew it within a dozen or so years—but suffice it to say that her length of days was an uncertain quantity. She was tall and rather angular, and had lived in the cottage for thirty years. I sometimes thought that my coming home was an intrusion which needed an apology. True, I paid her a fair salary or allowance for looking after my property, but she had so long reigned in undisputed sovereignty that it must have been rather hard on her to have me back again.

Dame Powell—for so she liked to be called—was a good housekeeper, a good cook, and a good woman, but not handsome.

"You lazy good-for-nothing!" she began, after her vigorous shaking. "Always smoking or sleeping! One would think you would want to tidy up the garden a bit after being away so long."

"My good woman," I commenced, but was quickly stopped by Dame Powell turning on me with all the anger and fury of a lioness when robbed of its cubs.

"Don't 'good-woman' me, I won't stand it. Come in and get your tea."

I rose meekly and entered the house, Dame Powell maintaining silence all the time until the evening meal was nearly over. She, good soul, was not bad-hearted, but her ways were rather abrupt and a stranger might have taken offense at her manner of speaking.

"Do you know," she said, "that there is no wood sawn or chopped?"

"I did not know it," I answered, mildly, "but can't you get a man to do it?"

"Get a man when you are at home, indeed! but there, it's a strange world, ah me!"

"Yes, Dame, it is a strange world, and there are strange people in it, but I am thinking of going away again."

"Going away?"

"Yes."

"What for? Where to? When do you start, and how long shall you be away?" The questions were showered on me with all the vigor of a talkative woman's tongue, but I had roused her curiosity and only answered with a laugh.

It was too bad to tease the old lady, but the temptation was sometimes too great to withstand.

I spent the evening outside with my pipe and when night came I was restless and uneasy, for a strange unrest had come upon me. I wanted change and excitement. My sleep was haunted by dreams of wild adventure. I stood again on the side of that terrible, burning mountain, when the hot melted metal poured like rivers of fire all round me, and only a fragment of rock saved me from a fearful death. I saw in my mental vision the torrent of fire as it rushed madly down the little valley, and then, as real as though it had only just occurred, I saw the lifeless body of Rapa Tepithe, my beautiful South Sea Island wife, float past me on the burning river of sulphur. I felt again the hand of *He the Mighty One* snatching me from death and then, with his strange laugh, telling me of the secret life which he possessed.

In visions of the past, with its wild adventures and stirring situations, my night was spent, and when the first streaks of morning light pierced through the ivy-covered casements and penetrated into the room, I was surprised to find I was in civilized England instead of on the island of Rapa Nui. Yet such was the fact, and I had to prepare myself for civilized life, which was almost irksome to me.

Much as I enjoyed the warm cakes which Dame Powell

knew so well how to bake, the nicely browned slice of ham and the fresh-laid eggs, washed down with a cup of most excellent hot coffee, yet many a breakfast of half-roasted bear or buffalo steak, eaten without bread, and with no other beverage but thick, slimy or brackish water, to which I had grown accustomed, possessed for me a greater charm.

I was unfit for the life I was leading, and could only feel at home in the camp or on the hunting-ground.

The reader will perceive how thoroughly ill at ease I had become.

Before the day was out, the apathetic, uneasy fit had disappeared, and I was active, bright and happy. How the change was effected deserves another chapter.

CHAPTER II.

THE PRESENTIMENT IS VERIFIED, AND I START OUT AGAIN.

I WAS sauntering about the garden, my pipe in my mouth and my hands pushed deep into my pocket, wondering what would be my next move, when I saw the village letter-carrier trudging his weary rounds, and, to my surprise, stop at my gate.

This was an unusual episode, for letters were but seldom received at Rapa Cottage, for such I had renamed my house when I returned from Rapa Nui. Most likely it was some letter for Dame Powell, I thought, but what was my astonishment when I read in a bold hand on the envelope:

J. THEO. ARISTOPHANO, ESQ.,
Rapa Cottage,
Near Stratford-on-Avon,
WARWICKSHIRE.

Who could it be from? I was like a young girl who had received her first love-letter. For a few minutes I hesitated before breaking the seal; my heart throbbed with excitement, and I felt my temples flush.

When I summoned up the necessary courage, I read as follows:

"Brayley Hall, Yorkshire.

"MY DEAR THEO.,—I chanced to see in a society

paper that you were again in England, but how long you have been here I know not, but presume your arrival is but recent. After all your adventures I suppose you are going to seek the quiet and repose of a 'real old English gentleman.' Ever since I heard you relate the extraordinary adventures you met with in the South Sea Islands, when I was but a youngster, I have felt the keenest interest in all your doings, and have hoped our lot might be cast together at some time, but that seems more than ever improbable.

"While you have been making love to the almond-eyed beauties of China or Japan, or trying to unravel the quaint legends and traditions of the Esquimaux, I have been in Africa or India. Now we are both in England, but only for a few days, for I am about to seek fresh adventures and perhaps solve some very difficult problems. But I will tell you how it all came about. I was in London two weeks ago, and went to old Drury to see Shakespere's play of 'Othello.' It was romantic, and to a traveler parts of it very interesting. When Othello recounted how he had won the fair Desdemona by telling her 'of moving accidents, by flood and field; of hairbreadth 'scapes i' the eminent deadly breach,' I grew interested, but my fate was sealed when with becoming emphasis Othello gave utterance to the lines:

"'Wherein of antres* vast, and deserts idle,
Rough quarries, rocks, and hills whose heads touch heaven,
It was my hint to speak, such was the process;
And of the cannibals that each other eat.
The Anthropophagi, and men whose heads
Do grow beneath their shoulders.'†

"I fell into a rhapsody of thought. I remembered when returning with Allan Quartermain—a rare good fellow that—and Captain John Good from my visit to King Solomon's mines, that we fell in with some hunters who told us several yarns about a strange race of men whose heads were under the right arm instead of above the shoulders. These men, they solemnly averred, lived in Central Africa, and that they had known men who had seen them.

* Caves.
† "Othello," act i., scene iii.

"I laughed at the time at the stupidity of the idea, and Quartermain, who had hunted all through Africa, said it was a yarn only fit to be told to the marines. But when I heard the lines from the theater stage, I thought there must be something in it, so I have resolved to start for Zanzibar at once and penetrate into the center of Africa, and may perhaps visit the wonderful caves of Kor if I can find them, and see if the people have any new facts about the wonderful woman *She*, of whom you must have heard, especially as it is probable your ancestor, the great *He*, obtained his length of life from her. While I am away look upon Brayley Hall as your home; there is good shooting and excellent fishing, and my steward is told to expect you.

"When I return, if I ever do so, I may have some wonderful things to relate. I have invited Captain Good and Allan Quartermain to join me. Good-bye, old comrade, and remember me ever as,
                                    "Yours sincerely,
                                           "HENRY CURTIS.

"P. S.—If I hear of anything interesting I will make use of the first postoffice I reach to mail you full particulars, but it is hardly likely I shall be able to send you a letter for two or three years, and by that time the jackals may have picked my bones pretty clean.   H. C."

I read the letter—which occupied several sheets of paper, Curtis being a very bold writer, several times, and then, without a second thought, my mind was made up.

I went into the house, looked up my old hunting outfit, examined my rifles and revolvers, and prepared to join Sir Henry Curtis.

What if I was old? I was young enough to dodge an antelope or to grapple with a lion.

My blood flowed faster than it had done for weeks. The thought of hunting and shooting, of camping out in the desert, or exploring the caves, filled me with delight.

I went to the telegraph office and wired a message to Curtis, asking him to wait for me at Southampton, and then I took train to London. I ordered from well-known firms a good substantial outfit.

When I had got all together, I found the list to be as follows:

A good express rifle, with five hundred rounds of ammunition.

A Winchester repeating rifle, with five hundred ball cartridges.

Two revolvers, one a heavy caliber, "Smith and Wesson," and the other "Colt's improved," forty-four caliber, and a plentiful supply of cartridges for each.

Two hunter's knives, one of them being dagger-shaped at the point, that is, sharp at both edges.

A cartridge hunting belt; a portable medicine chest; and a variety of other articles which go to make up a traveler's kit in Africa.

I also got twenty pounds of beads, taking care to have some iridescent ones, and a plentiful sprinkling of gold and silver-colored ones; these would be of more value to us than all the wealth of the Bank of England; although I did not neglect to get two letters of credit for £1000 each; one on Zanzibar and the other on the Cape.

A happy thought flashed across my mind—I saw a quantity of little china dolls, about three inches in length. I bought a gross of them, and before I had been in Africa a month, I had reason to bless my purchase.

The china dolls were gods to the blacks, who had never seen anything beyond their own crude carvings.

The next day I bade Dame Powell farewell, and having arranged my affairs went to London. A slight hitch occurred and I was delayed a day, but was more annoyed when I arrived at Southampton to find the steamer gone, and Sir Henry Curtis with it. For an hour I was mad and furious. I judged Curtis harshly. In my rage I believed he had purposely gone without me, and for that reason had not answered my telegram.

A week must elapse before another steamer left for Africa, and I must drag on a weary existence the best way I could.

I strolled into a strange hotel, led thither by some uncontrollable impulse, which I could never explain. I looked round almost expecting to meet with some well-known face, but was disappointed. I walked into the billiard-room, but was ill at ease and felt no interest in the game. I stood at the bar watching the various types of character which passed in and out. Nothing seemed to interest me however, until I heard a woman say:

"What shall be done with this letter?"

"Who is it for?" asked a masculine and harsh voice.

"Sir Henry Curtis. It has been here a week."

All my lack of interest had gone, and I walked into the little bar parlor, and saw the landlady holding the letter in her hand, while her husband, a surly-looking fellow, was standing with his hands in his pockets leaning his back against the mantel-piece.

"Pardon me, madam," I said, "but Sir Henry Curtis is my friend, and he has gone to Africa."

"Indeed!" and the lady opened her eyes and looked at me with suspicion.

"Yes, madam," I continued, not noticing the unpleasant look, "and I was to have joined him. His residence is Brayley Hall, and if I mistake not, that envelope covers a telegram I sent him, and which has miscarried."

"Give the gentleman the letter," said the landlord: and I obtained possession of the envelope. I telegraphed at once to Brayley Hall, and learned within an hour that my sudden conjecture was right; my telegram had been mailed to Sir Henry Curtis, but by some mischance sent to the Royal Hotel, instead of the Royal Hants Hotel, at which Sir Henry always stopped.

I managed to pass away the week, and then with joy and almost boyish glee jumped on the deck of a good stanch steamer bound for Africa.

There were but few incidents of any moment on the voyage. What there were only paled into insignificance when compared with the startling and thrilling adventures through which I passed before I wrote this narrative—adventures; the like of which mortal had never before recorded, and which, perhaps, may never again be met with. But as it is a true history I am writing, and as the heroes of the adventures were my personal friends, whose names and characters are so well known, I will not digress longer. but continue my narrative of adventures on the dark Continent, the like of which, I believe, have never before been recorded.

I had never been through the Suez Canal, and, therefore, my first journey through that wonderful monument of engineering skill was fraught with interest. I made the acquaintance on board of a great friend of De Lesseps, and to him I unburdened myself of a scheme which had long been a hobby with me.

"Why not flood the great desert of Sahara?" I asked, "and so make a vast inland sea which would open up the dark Continent to civilization?"

The engineer looked at me as though I had suggested a railroad to the sun, with stopping places at a few of the planets.

I felt annoyed, for was not my suggestion feasible and good?

When his astonishment had somewhat subsided, he walked along the deck a few yards, returned, and putting his hands under his coat-tails, asked:

"And why should we murder perhaps millions for such a Utopian object?"

"I fail to understand you. I never suggested murder."

"My dear sir, in that so-called desert there live races of men whose number, if tabulated, would astonish you."

"Do you mean it?" I asked in surprise.

"Africa," he continued, "is an unknown land to us, and yet races of men are living there who trace back their civilization to the time of Solomon. Nations flourish of whose very existence England has never heard, and yet they can date back their nationhood to a time when England was unknown. Nay, more, I believe man had his origin in the center of that so-called desert, and if any one had the money, the strength, and power of endurance to explore Sahara I am convinced the most startling facts could be gathered together, and much of our ignorance relating to the origin of species cleared away."

My first thoughts were that my new acquaintance was a lunatic—harmless, but still *non compos mentis;* and yet Curtis was not insane, and he was going to search for men whose heads grew out of place.

"Perhaps you may have heard," I said, "of men whose heads grow beneath their shoulders."

"Yes, Aristophano, I have, and what is more, I have seen men, seen them, mark you, who could guide you to a tribe who live in the desert, every male of which has the appearance of being half horse."

This was said with a solemnity which showed the man was in earnest, and really believed the statements he had made.

What would Sir Henry Curtis say to these ideas? Who knows but our path might lie through this very country, and we might be able to clear away all the doubts about the origin of species and set at rest the misgivings of scientists.

An immortal name would be ours if successful.

The good ship emerged from the Suez Canal, and made good time through the Red Sea.

The first really stormy weather we had encountered was after we had passed through the Straits of Babel-Mandeb, and passed near the island of Socotra. The wind blew a gale, and the ship was strained to its utmost strength, but no damage was done.

To the very day announced we cast anchor at Zanzibar.

My heart beat rapidly as I stepped from the steamer, for I began to feel I was again in my element, and would soon have the greatest and grandest residence man ever slept in--the broad expanse of nature with the arched canopy of heaven for a roof.

I entered the European Hotel with the intention of examining the register, when before me I saw a man whose face once seen could never be forgotten.

He was a big, powerful, athletic fellow, with yellow hair, a big, flowing, yellow beard, clear-cut features, and large gray eyes set deep in his head.

He looked at me for a moment as though uncertain as to my identity; of course he never expected to find me at Zanzibar, but after waiting for a moment, just when he was about to turn away, I tapped him on the shoulder.

"Curtis, you were awfully mean to run away and leave me."

"Aristophano, by all that's holy!" he exclaimed.

"The same," I answered.

"What brings you here, and where are you going?"

"A ship, and to join you if you will have me for a comrade."

"You mean it?"

"On my honor!" I replied.

Whereupon he grasped me by the hand so vigorously

that it seemed as though all the bones would be reduced to pulp and a rifle trigger be of no value to me.

"Hold on, Curtis, or you will have a cripple instead of a hunter."

He laughed with that merriment which always characterized him, and then we lighted our cigars and talked over the past, present, and our future prospects.

"I should have been away yesterday," he said, "but for that fellow, Good; he has not turned up yet."

"Where is he?"

"Goodness only knows; why, by the living Jingo, there he is!"

I looked, and beheld an Englishman as prim and spry as if he were walking along Regent Street or promenading in the Zoo.

He had a new suit of large check pattern clothes, a high starched collar, his face was cleanly shaven, and in his eye the glass about which I had so often heard. Had I not known his courage and daring, I should have hesitated joining a party of which he was a member, for he appeared to be too great a swell to make a good explorer or hunter.

However, he had proved his worth, both on the battle-field and in front of noble game, so I was heartily glad to shake his soft hand.

"Deuced sorry, Curtis, but the tailor delayed me; he could not get these clothes ready in time."

That was all the excuse he made for keeping his friend waiting.

"For once," answered Sir Henry, "I am pleased with your tailor."

"So you like the style?" put in Captain John Good of her majesty's navy, as he *pirouetted* round to show off the clothes to advantage.

"Heaven save the man, no; the Kaffirs may appreciate the pattern, but I am glad, because we shall now have the company of Aristophano."

"Right you are, my boy; well, when do we start?"

"I propose that we do Zanzibar and the neighboring coast, now that you are both here," said Curtis. And to this I was nothing loth, for I felt that a few days together would make us better acquainted.

We were standing in front of the hotel, smoking some

most villainous cigars which we had purchased for "the good of the house," when I saw my strange friend of the steamer approaching. A smile passed over his open countenance and I flattered myself that he was rejoiced to meet me on land, but I was too previous, for, putting out his hand long before he reached us, he shouted:

"Why, Curtis, old boy, who would have thought of meeting you?"

"Reverse it, rather, Tresiger, my boy, and let me ask what brings you out in Africa."

"Business; shall be off back again in a month. Ah! here is my friend Aristophano. Do you know Curtis?" he asked as, after his rapture, he found time to recognize me.

We passed a glorious time together, and Tresiger retold his stories of the strange races and tribes, and Curtis was enthusiastic in his belief in the truth of the yarns.

"What say you, Theo?" he asked, "shall we go?"

"As good one way as another," was my response, with which Captain John Good heartily coincided.

If Tresiger could have arranged his business affairs I feel pretty sure he would have joined our party.

CHAPTER III.
"GOD-MAKERS."

SIR HENRY, I found, had made good use of his time in Zanzibar, for he had crossed over several times to the mainland and had got together an outfit which would serve us for many a month.

First he had secured a small boat made of very thin wood, but iron-plated to protect it from arrows and spears. This boat was similar to the ones which, some time previously, Stanley had made for the purposes of his exploration and search for Livingstone. It was so light that a Kaffir could carry it easily on his back.

Then we had a twenty-foot wagon, with iron axles and very strong, yet light. It was built entirely of seasoned stinkwood and had been well tested. It was half-tented, that is, about ten feet of it was covered in, leaving the front part open and free for whatever nonperishable stores we wished to carry. In the tent was a fixed bed large enough for two, and every article necessary for an explorer's household; racks for rifles, waterproof compartments for ammunition, and other conveniences.

Sir Henry had also purchased a team of ten oxen, but on my advice he disposed of them. I thought they were too fresh and therefore very unsuitable for the life we were expecting to lead. A day or so later we fell in with twenty-four well "salted" oxen, and as the owner would not sell part, we bought the whole team, and finer cattle I never set eyes on. They had "done" the country and become proof against the various diseases which prove so disastrous to cattle on strange "veldt."

We each possessed a private, portable medicine chest, but thought it well to take an extra supply of quinine.

Curtis had some good double-eight breech-loading elephant guns, and so with our other supplies we were well equipped.

The next matter we had to deal with was a most difficult one—namely, suitable servants and assistants.

This was a greater trouble than all else, for the men we wanted most refused to go with us except on such terms as were impossible to grant.

It was necessary to have at least five men—three servants and a driver and leader.

Good got hold of a Kaffir who was tough and well seasoned, and secured him as driver. By rare good luck I found a native who knew the route to Ujiji, and tried to persuade him to go with us, but he turned a deaf ear to all my persuasive eloquence until I had exhausted every promise I could think of, when a happy thought occurred to me. I had taken from one of my cases a few of the china dolls which I had bought in London.

I remembered I had one in my pocket; by a little sleight-of-hand I slipped one up my sleeve and then showed my empty hand to the black. He looked at it, and to his great astonishment a little white china doll appeared.

The effect of this simple trick was marvelous. He fell on his face and crawled to me, kissing my boots most liberally.

I was the most wonderful "man of magic" he had

ever seen, and he would go with us. I told him he should have the doll for himself the day we started.

Such was his great joy that before nightfall he had secured three companions—one of them a Zulu—who were in every way suitable for our work.

The native of Ujiji gave as his name Umbilla. The Zulu was a smart, intelligent savage, almost civilized, except in the matter of dress, and had discarded his native name, preferring the English one, Jack.

These two men were my favorites, and I felt that if the necessity should arise I could with safety trust them.

On a bright sunny morning in March we started from Bagamoya and commenced our journey in a northwestern direction, intending to reach Fuga before we fixed definitely on our route.

Had we intended exploring Sahara when we left England, we should have selected a different port to Zanzibar, but old hunters had told us of races of men to be found in the Kilimandjaro Mountains who possessed marvelous powers, and that alone was sufficient incentive to us to make our trip longer and see all we could.

The first day we were on tolerably good roads, and made thirty miles before camping. As the crow flies, Fuga is distant about one hundred miles from Bagamoya, but as we had to skirt the mountains and select our roads, we reckoned on one hundred and fifty miles' march.

Very few white men traveled north; most who made Bagamoya their starting-point had gone in a southeastern direction, hence we were objects of curiosity to the Zanguebars. We had a glorious expanse of fertile fields on which to camp that first night out from the civilizing influences of a good hotel. A little kraal was near by, from which tiny columns of smoke arose, but as the inhabitants had not troubled us, we saw no cause for alarm.

The sun had scarcely risen the following morning before we had our first experience of native hospitality.

Although placing great confidence in Umbilla and Zulu Jack, we thought it advisable for one of us to be on the watch all night, so we divided the night into three equal lengths of three hours each.

I was fast asleep by the side of Curtis in our tented

wagon, when Good, whose watch it was, being just before sunrise, suddenly thrust his head into the tent and shook us violently. We rubbed our eyes, wondering what piece of devilry Good had planned, for thought of treachery or hostility never occurred to us. We saw, however, that Good was alarmed, and through his eye-glass was glaring fiercely.

"Get up out of this," he said, unceremoniously, "or we shall all be murdered."

It was only the work of a minute for us to be outside, and then we found that our over-zealous servant, Umbilla, had been the unintentional cause of our being disturbed. He had told some of the tribe about the doll, and an old witch had declared that we were "godmakers," and would destroy their religion, and, what was worse, ruin their country.

Hence, about thirty of the most diabolical-looking blacks I ever saw had come out with the intention of killing us and seizing our possessions.

This did not coincide with our ideas, and we saw it would be a question of fighting. Our servants, we knew, would not fight against their comrades, so while they would remain neutral it was a force of three white men against thirty savages armed with assegais and other native weapons.

Sir Henry, who was an adept in several African dialects and languages, addressed them and asked what they wanted.

"White men come here to kill our gods," said the leader, who was prompted by the evil-eyed old witch who stood by his side.

"We will not harm your gods or your land, for we are going to leave it as soon as we can," was Sir Henry's reply.

The witch muttered something which seemed to rouse all the savagery of their nature, for instantly every spear was raised.

I had heard that the spears of the Zanguebars were poisoned, and that death would most surely ensue from even the slightest scratch. I whispered to Good and Curtis, and then Sir Henry standing erect in front of the wagon held up his right hand, a signal for a palaver.

"Brave men of Zanguebar," he said, and at once every

spear dropped, the flattering address pleasing the savages; "we are not here to injure you, but if you want to fight, we are ready. Remember we have magic on our side, and all we shall do will be to point our magic tubes at you and you will all die."

Again the spears were raised threateningly, and the savage scowl showed that nothing but a fight would satisfy them.

"Which of you desires to die first?" asked Curtis. "Step forward and the god-maker" (meaning me) "will meet him single-handed."

A tall fellow, the very picture of rude savage health, responded to the invitation, and I stepped out of the wagon and stood about twenty paces from him.

I am not a coward by any means. I never yet knew fear, but as I stood close to that savage, whose muscles were like iron, and whose sinews stood out like whipcords, I felt my time to solve the mystery of death was near at hand.

I did not want to be killed, and I was nearly as loath to take the fellow's life.

The old witch seemed delighted, for she was sure in single combat the three of us could be easily picked off.

Curtis looked at us both for a moment, and then addressing the Zanguebar said:

"The brave warrior whose father is the rising sun, will surely have his bones picked by the jackal before the sun rises again."

The warrior only laughed, and grasped his spear more firmly.

Then I tried pacific means.

"Let the brave Zanguebar, the son of the morning and the choice of the gods, beware how he strikes the white man, who can slay him with a breath," I said, assuming the most pompous manner possible.

The savage did not understand me, so Curtis translated my speech and added to it quite a flowery peroration.

"The brave man fears not thy magic," was the lofty response.

"Let the brave man witness my power. Let him hold the spear above his head, and by a breath I will strike it from his hand."

When this was translated by Sir Henry the old witch laughed, or rather crooned, over the idea, and suggested that it should be done.

Zulu Jack had told me that the natives had seen the rifle, but had no knowledge of a revolver, so I determined to use that weapon.

The savage held aloft his assegai, a defiant look on his face. He knew that if I took his life he would be avenged, and mine would quickly pay the forfeit.

I drew my "Smith & Wesson," and took steady aim. I was always a crack shot with a revolver, and felt sure I could do as I had promised.

I fired, when a howl of pain went up from the savage. I had struck the spear close to his hand; the jarring of the handle so shook him that for a moment he imagined himself seriously hurt. The spear head had fallen to the ground when the haft was shattered. I had not counted on the result; instead of satisfying the natives with my skill and magic, it only infuriated them, and the fellow snatched a spear from one of the others and flung it with such force that had it struck me I should never have written this history. Fortunately, I had dodged the spear. Trifling was no use, so I quietly sent a bullet from the Smith & Wesson straight through the heart of the black. He fell dead without a struggle or groan. Two assegais were raised aloft to pierce me to the heart, when bullets sent home by Curtis and Good caused the arms to fall powerless, and the grass was stained with the life-blood of the three warriors.

To the horde of savages it had the appearance of magic, and seeing three of their number dead, while we were uninjured, they began to feel timorous and afraid.

The witch's taunts were unheeded, the warriors, so brave and fearless, took to their heels and left us. I felt sad to think that three lives had to be sacrificed, but it was unavoidable, and self-preservation is the first law of nature; at least so I was taught when I had the good fortune to learn wisdom from my father, whose spirit is ever near me watching over and protecting me from harm.

Acting on Umbilla's advice we started on our journey at once, not even waiting to prepare breakfast.

We conjectured that before an hour had passed the

natives would have recovered from their fright and returned to the charge.

Three hours later we camped again and partook of a hearty breakfast.

The day's march found us over fifty miles from Bagamoya, which was considered good progress to make over such bad roads as we had met with on our second day.

The night passed without adventure, but when morning dawned and all three of us were taking our bearings, looking round and scanning the wide expanse of country which stretched before us, we heard a noise in the scrub which caused us to sharpen our ears.

The scrub was about eight feet high on either side of the trail, and so afforded shelter for animals of quite a respectable size.

We listened and at last located the sound, which was right ahead of us.

A moment and a heard of small antelopes known as gnus dashed across the trail.

Sir Henry could not resist the temptation, and raising his Winchester, he fired. The ball pierced the heart of a fine buck, and our servants were not long in taking from it such portions as we cared about for food.

A week passed without further adventure, and we had now got out into the mountains beyond Zanguebar, and might expect to meet with adventures at any time.

In the distance we could see the shadowy forms of the Kilimandjaro Mountains, on the northern side of which lay in calm repose Lake Nyanza. The whole country was hilly, and covered with a plentiful supply of scrub. Woods and small forests abounded, and Curtis soon discovered the "machabell" tree with its clusters of beautiful fruit. This is the favorite food of the elephant, so we were pretty certain to fall in with a herd at almost any time.

A deep growl was heard in the distance, and I was under the impression that it proceeded from a lion, but was mistaken, for Umbilla told me it was the sound of a female elephant in trouble or distress.

We got ready for some exciting hunting, and made all our arrangements as secretly as possible. The elephant possesses a keen scent, and can detect a hunter a couple of hundred yards away if the wind is favorable.

I watched the grass, and saw that the wind was blowing toward us, so if the elephants were in front we were all right.

We crawled through the bush until we could almost hear the breathing of a score of fine animals.

They were rather smaller than the Asiatic elephant, but the ivory was even better, and of course all hunters feel proud of getting the tusks, even if they have wealth enough to enable them to rise above the merchant feeling of profitable hunting.

One big fellow, a bull, raised his ponderous head and began sniffing the air.

Instantly he gave warning, and the herd started off at a quick pace away from us.

To have fired would have been madness, as it would most likely have brought the whole herd down on us, and endangered our lives unnecessarily.

At Fuga we heard that a white hunter was in the Kilimandjaro Mountains, and had sent down for supplies.

The people had forgotten his name, but from the description given, both Curtis and Good decided it must be Allan Quatermain.

We had very good reasons for so believing, inasmuch as Curtis had received a letter from Durban saying Quatermain was north in search of some caves which he believed contained the bones of an extinct species of elephant. We were rejoiced to think it might be our luck to meet with him, for he had hunted in Africa thirty years, and knew the ground well. He would be invaluable to us, both as guide and companion. So confident were we of his identity that we decided to make for the mountains before fixing on our further course.

We camped early on a little fertile oasis well protected by thick brush, through which nothing could penetrate without giving an alarm.

As we sat round the camp fire, our servants being at some little distance drinking the most abominable intoxicant ever manufactured, but which they seemed to heartily enjoy, we spent our time telling of our adventures. Curtis retold the horrible experiences he and Good, guided by Quatermain, had in finding King Solomon's mines, while I recalled many incidents of my journey to Rapa Nui.

"Theo., have you got rid of your old hobby yet?" asked Curtis.

"What hobby?" I asked. "I have so many that you ought to be more explicit."

"Why, you know well I refer to your old idea that man can live forever."

"Gracious goodness, Aristophano, you don't believe in any such nonsense?" exclaimed Good as he stared at me through that wonderful eye-glass.

"I never believed man could live forever," I said, "but I have long been convinced that old age alone should be the cause of death, and that old age should not commence until the hundreds have been reached."

"But it is natural to die," responded Good.

"Yes, I admit it, but what I contend for is that man should live at least one hundred and twenty years, and that he should be able, by strict adherence to the laws of life, to live a thousand if he wished."

"Oh, come now. Isn't seventy years the limit of man's life?" asked Curtis.

"Who says so?" I exclaimed rather testily, for I had heard the Psalmist's words quoted so often. "Tell me, did not Moses live to be one hundred and twenty; Isaac to one hundred and eighty; and Abraham to one hundred and seventy-five? Was the age of Methusaleh a myth? Do you believe Holy Writ when it says he lived to be nearly one thousand years old. Tell me, my good friends, is the Bible true or only a legend? If true, why do you doubt the power of man to live beyond one hundred years?"

"By Jove!" exclaimed Good, "our friend is eloquent. But tell me, were not those cases exceptions?"

"Not at all. We old travelers and hunters know that the normal age of any animal is five times the time it takes to arrive at maturity. If man is an animal then, and arrives at full maturity at twenty-five, his normal age ought to be one hundred and twenty-five."

"That's so. I never thought of it in that way," said Curtis. "I always looked upon the ages of Parr, who lived to be one hundred and forty years, and the seventeen hundred who reached over one hundred years, recorded by an old author,* to be either miraculous or the exceptions which we always used to say proved the rule."

"Depend upon it, Curtis, there is a way to prevent the decay of the tissues and so prevent death for many years."

"That is just what Holly told me was the opinion of *She*, the mysterious woman whose age ran into the thousands."

"Yes, my friends," I exclaimed, enthusiastically, "and I believe we shall find that means before we return to England."

My companions saw I was in earnest, and they respected my convictions, even if they did not share them.

CHAPTER IV.
ZULU JACK'S FATE.

THE discussion had made both Curtis and Good drowsy, and so, as it was my first watch, they got ready to retire.

The naval captain, Good, made the same elaborate preparations as usual, taking his artificial teeth from his mouth, and, after carefully wiping them, he put them in his trousers pocket. Curtis was fast asleep before these toilet arrangements were completed.

As I sat by the camp fire. smoking like a volcano, trying to keep off the terrible tsetse flies, which were so poisonous, my thoughts went back to the beautiful Statue, the charming Alethea, and I wondered whether I should ever again behold her loveliness, either on this earth or in the great beyond.

Although I had visited many South Sea Islands since, I had never again landed on Rapa Nui; why, I cannot conjecture, but as I sat gazing at the curling clouds of smoke, a strange longing came over me, and I almost resolved—if my life was spared—to again tread its shores and climb its mountain sides.

In happy waking dreams of my devoted Rapa, and the beautiful Alethea with her raptures of passionate endear-

* "Human Longevity," by James Easton, published in Salisbury, England, 1799.

ment, my watch passed rapidly, and Curtis relieved me of my position. A few moments later sufficed to find me seeking in sleep that natural re-invigoration for the time which I believed could be continued indefinitely. I slept soundly, and while I slumbered, Nature was busy repairing and mending, recreating and building up the temporary exhaustion of nature.

"Rouse, Theo., rouse!" were the first words I heard after what appeared to me to have only been a few minutes' sleep.

Sir Henry Curtis was fully equipped with his double-eight elephant gun, and no sooner had I stepped outside than I saw Captain Good equally ready.

"What's in the wind, now?" I asked, rubbing my eyes.

"Umbilla says the elephants are near, so I thought we would try for some ivory and get an appetite for breakfast," responded Curtis.

"All right, old fellow, I am always ready for sport."

Umbilla was correct in his surmise, and as we cautiously cleared a way through the brush, we saw five splendid bull-elephants drinking at a little stream about two hundred yards distant.

Five bulls and only three of us, for I would not trust a rifle in the hands of our servants, and I had no confidence in the assegai as a weapon for elephant-hunting.

Curtis gave me the honor of deciding on a plan of action, and I thought for a few minutes of the danger to be encountered, as I well knew that if we killed three, the other two would be so infuriated that most likely they would charge upon us and give but slight opportunity for landing a bullet in the only vulnerable part of the giant beast.

When I had fully made up my mind, I said:

"I will take the outside right-hand one. You, Curtis, aim for the middle one, and Good the extreme left."

We took aim.

The suspense for a moment was great, our very lives depended on our rifles, and we were morally certain that we should have to kill all five before we were safe. A cloud of smoke and three simultaneous reports, and through the smoke we could see three of the monster brutes rolling over on their backs; the other two stood for a moment irresolute.

Then, with a bound, they started toward us.

Three more shots and another bull lay dead.

Its companion was now furious, for it had been wounded.

As it dashed about, maddened with pain, our lives were jeopardized.

It was no good firing at random. All we could do was to wait with our rifles ready for the attack and then our lives would be spared or lost on the result.

The maddened beast dashed at us, its tread seeming to shake the very earth.

As it neared us, Zulu Jack threw himself in its path, right in front of me, and waved his assegai ready to fling it at the animal.

It was a foolhardy thing to do, but, like all Zulus, he had more confidence in his poisoned spear than in the white man's magic tubes, as the natives called our rifles.

For a moment the elephant stood irresolute and turned a broadside upon us, making it perfectly futile to attempt to shoot.

Those who have studied the elephant nature will acknowledge its great power of concentration and thought.

I was not surprised, therefore, at the strategy displayed by the wounded bull.

It turned its tail on us and started on a run; this was continued for a few yards, probably a hundred or so, then it quickly turned and charged us.

As it approached, Jack raised his assegai and flung it with such force that its whizzing through the air was like the crack of a whip.

The poisoned blade pierced the elephant's eye, and as the weight of the spear caused it to fall to the ground, we saw with a sickening sensation that the eye and a good portion of flesh came with it.

With a screech of pain, the now furious bull dashed forward, and winding its trunk round poor Jack's body, raised him above its head and dashed into the scrub beyond.

We followed as rapidly as we could, closely keeping the elephant's trail. Umbilla, whether from cowardice or anxiety, begged of us not to follow, for he was sure we could not save Jack and should only endanger our own lives.

We were desperate, and even though we knew that a similar fate awaited us, we could not have been easy until we had rescued or avenged our faithful Zulu. Never had I seen an elephant run so rapidly; it was with difficulty we could keep up with it. To shoot at its thick hide from the rear would have been useless, so we were powerless unless the brute turned.

We could see its immense form tremble with pain. The poison of the assagai was doing its work slowly but surely. We wondered why it had not slain Jack long before. We were soon to see the deep cruelty and cunning which the animal possessed.

On it tore, carrying its living burden high above its head, until some rocks were reached, and then its object was apparent. The body of the Zulu was swayed up and down swiftly for a moment, and then with tremendous force brought down on the rocks.

The one blow of course killed poor Jack; his brains were scattered in every direction, and even we were splashed with blood and brain. The bull then loosed its hold of Jack, and placing one of its ponderous feet on the lower parts of his body, wound its trunk round the poor fellow's chest, and literally tore the body apart. A grunt of joy echoed through the hills at the terrible revenge wrought by the beast, but that shout of triumph was fatal to it, for as it shouted, its head was turned, and a couple of bullets went crashing into its brain. We buried poor Jack as well as we could, and wept many tears over his untimely fate.

After securing the ivory, we continued our journey toward the mountains, meeting with no further adventure until several days later we struck the banks of a river. The water was clear and of a beautiful blue tint. What surprised us most was that it seemed to flow toward the mountain and from the sea, instead of the opposite direction.

At first Curtis declared it must be an optical illusion, but we threw various light articles into the water and saw them float in the direction of the hills.

We launched our boat, and giving directions to Umbilla and the men to follow us with the wagon, we rowed down the river. There was but little need of oars, for the current was strong.

Every mile and the mountains were more distinct, and by the end of the next day one of the hills rose almost perpendicularly above us.

We beached our boat and waited for morning light to explain for us the mystery of the course of the river.

We consulted our maps, but the river was not marked.

In the morning we stood by the river's bank looking up and down the stream.

"Well, I'm blessed!" exclaimed Good, who was a typical Englishman in the use of exclamations and expletives, often of a nature which could not be published.

The cause of his particular frame of mind was the fact that the river did not flow up the mountain, which would have been unnatural at least, neither was its channel diverted along the side of the hill, but it actually ran through the blue mass of towering rocks.

A cave or tunnel was before us.

After giving directions to Umbilla to camp and wait for our return, we launched our boat and entered the mouth of the tunnel, which appeared to be about twenty feet wide and five feet high.

We cast the lead and our sounding showed over fifteen feet of water.

This entrance formed a thread-like canal, inclosed between the natural walls of the rock, and roofed over with the same material.

Its passage for some distance was shrouded in darkness; but the further we went the more evident and clear became a peculiar twilight effect, by which we were able to discern the breadth and height of the tunnel, which was illuminated by a surprising play of colors. At first the water under the keel of the boat appeared to be of a dark blue green; then the color gradually changed to a clear blue, and at last to a pure azure which grew brighter and brighter until we came to a subterranean lake, lighted by shafts ascending through the mountain. The principal illumination seemed to come from the bottom of the water; our oars appeared silver white in the transparent blue flood, and when we threw some stones into the lake they shone like diamonds as they descended through the water.

Never before, or since, have I seen so strange a phenomenon. The whole surface of the lake, which appeared to be almost circular and of at least one hundred feet diameter, was a brilliant shimmering blue flood, from which the light shone with a softness covering everything with a strange glamour.*

We looked at each other, but uttered no word for several minutes. Had we reached fairy land? The more our eyes grew accustomed to the light, or rather semi-darkness, the more beautiful appeared the colors.

"I'm blessed!" at last ejaculated Good; but that was all. Curtis gazed round the cave, then on the surface of the lake, and as he did so the thought occurred to him to take soundings of the center of the lake. We did so, but our line was played out and no bottom reached. We dropped a stone and watched its course. The further it fell the brighter it seemed to get, until it had more the appearance of a very brilliant comet shooting through space than a stone falling in water.

We counted the seconds, but though we saw the flashing light descend, we never heard it reach the bottom.

The lake was so deep that it justified us in calling it bottomless.

"Look!" exclaimed Curtis, as he pointed toward the water.

I turned my eyes in the direction indicated, and saw what made my blood freeze in my veins.

"What is it?" I gasped, thoroughly startled by the strange appearance.

"Heaven only knows!" Curtis answered, solemnly. Good, who, when in great bodily danger, was inclined to be religious, and professed himself a Catholic, crossed himself and repeated some prayers.

As we looked—and it was impossible to withdraw our eyes—we saw, to all appearance, two human beings in the water, wrestling and struggling with each other.

They appeared to be of opposite sexes, and their skins were white. Perhaps it would be nearer the truth to say that the skins were transparent, for we saw the bones

* There is a similar effect produced in the Blue Grotto of the Island of Busi, in the Adriatic. The sea there gives forth the same peculiar light as it washes into the long cavernous grotto. —EDITOR.

shining through, and could discern the heart, liver, and other organs apparently fulfilling their work. The faces we could not see, but the one we imagined to be female had a mass of long hair, the color of which it was impossible to tell, owing to the rainbow hues reflected by every movement; the hair seemed to act as a veil, covering the face and bosom. Every movement was like the flashing of lightning, for a most brilliant radiance was given out.

The struggling ceased, and the figures disappeared, leaving no trace behind.

"Let us get out of here," exclaimed Good, when he had recovered somewhat from his nervousness.

"Do you believe in mermaids?" Curtis asked, as we began to descend the river again.

"I never did," was my reply, "but I am inclined to that belief now."

When we got out of the cave and through the tunnel, we found Umbilla and the servants dancing a funeral or death dance, for they thought we were dead. We dare not tell them what we had seen, but Umbilla, by persistent questioning got an inkling and his fears were increased. "We had seen the sea gods," he told the men, and all with one accord fell on their faces before us, for as we learned later there was a legend that no one had been known to return alive from the mysterious lake.

We camped that night by the side of the river, and in the morning, determined to ascend the hills to some caves of which we had heard, and where we hoped to find some trace of Allan Quatermain.

CHAPTER V.
AMONG THE OBODOS.

EARLY the following morning we bestirred ourselves and started from the banks of the mysterious river on our ascent up the mountains.

We carefully marked the river, however, on our map so that we could easily locate it on our return.

I have had many a journey over hills, but that was the worst I ever experienced.

All day we marched in the broiling sun, and when night came it appeared we had made but little progress.

Our camp was pitched on a table-land overlooking the river, and as far as we could ascertain, over the lake with its strange phenomena.

The sun-rise saw us ready for our journey. Our party was now a small one for we had been compelled to leave two men behind with the oxen, wagon and boat. It was our intention to return in three days at furthest.

We had reached a pass which seemed to cut through the range of hills and was as broad and even as a well-made turnpike road. If only we had been able to get our wagon and oxen up there, we should have enjoyed our trip much better.

Curtis was of the opinion that it would be better to turn back and get rid of our stores, except such as we could easily carry with us; but Good coincided with me that we would explore for a few days before returning. The majority being for the journey, Curtis withdrew his objection.

By noon that day we saw the smoke rising from a kraal a little ahead of us. It was a pleasure to get near human habitations, even if the men were savage cannibals.

Umbilla was walking in front at a distance of thirty or forty paces, when he suddenly stopped and waited for us to approach.

"Back, master," he said. "The kraal is that of the Obodos, and we shall all be eaten."

"All serene, Umbilla," I answered. "We will go and look at these people, and perhaps we shall get away safely."

The poor fellow looked so frightened that I suggested he should return and we would go on alone, but he was far too faithful for that, and said if we were determined, he would go with us, even if he got eaten for his pains.

Taking care that our revolvers—and we each carried two—were loaded, we advanced until within a hundred yards of the kraal.

Our appearance was noticed, and we were to be welcomed by all the residents, evidently, for we saw a crowd gather and come toward us.

They were led by an old man, about sixty years of age, but without any of the dignity of a chief.

His hair was gray, and was adorned in a most peculiar fashion. I learnt afterward that the wooly hair is matted and worked with thread into a flat form like a beaver's tail.

THE CHIEF OF THE OBODOS

The old fellow began playing strange antics, until I began to think he was a clown in a pantomime or circus, instead of the chief of a nation.

Apparently ignoring our presence as rational beings he gave orders for his braves to surround us and, at his word, about a hundred men formed a circle; each man held in his hand a small, cup-shaped drum, formed of hollowed wood, one end only being perforated, and this was covered with the skin of the elephant's ear tightly stretched. The chief dancer stepped out from the others and wore, suspended from his shoulders, an immense drum also covered with the elephant's ear skin.

The dance commenced by all singing, remarkably well, a wild but agreeable tune in chorus; the big drum directing the time, and the entire number of little drums being struck at regular intervals, with such admirable precision, that it sounded almost like a single instrument.

The dancing was most vigorous and far superior to anything I had seen in any other African tribe.

The figures varied continually, and ended with a grand galop at a tremendous pace, the inner ring revolving in an opposite direction to the outer.

When the dance was over the chief called out several times in a harsh voice:

"Deeang! Deeang!" (Obodo for cow.)

Neither of us understood the meaning of the word, but the old fellow made such excellent pantomimic gestures that we came to the conclusion that he meant an ox.

Curtis knew the Latooka language, so he asked in that dialect if such was what the brave man wanted.

The chief did not understand, so Umbilla pressed his hand on the middle of his back and exclaimed in another dialect, "Kittan," (a cow).

There was a hurried consultation and then the chief came forward and by means of an interpreter told Umbilla that unless we furnished the tribe with a cow our lives would be forfeited.

Umbilla answered that we had no cow to give, but that there was a mighty man of magic with him, who could produce for them a god if they so desired. When this was translated to me, I took the hint and gave the chief one of the china dolls and showed him a handful of beads.

He was enchanted, and we were drawn in triumph to the kraal.

A feast was prepared for our benefit, and most excellent it was.

The few beads and the little doll had apparently worked wonders among the Obodos.

The men wore a skin slung across their shoulders and loins; but the women were almost naked, and instead of wearing the leather apron and tail adopted by other tribes and by the Zanguebars, they were contented with a slight fringe of leather shreds, about four inches long by two broad, suspended from a belt.

I found three kinds of dress, or undress, however, among the females of this tribe.

The unmarried girls go entirely naked unless they are rich, and then they wear three or four strings of beads, about three inches in length, as a covering. The old ladies, the venerable dames of the tribe, have a peculiar dress.

It consists of a string round the waist, in which is stuck a bunch of green leaves, the stalks uppermost.

A few of the girls who could not procure the beads, and

who did not fancy an actual state of nudity, adopted this fashionable petticoat. Good, who is a typical sailor, and ready to make love to every girl he fancies, observed that all the women were pretty.

UNMARRIED GIRL OBODO.

One thing, however, appeared to him exceedingly strange, all the women were addicted to smoking.

The wife always lighted the pipe for her husband, and after several good and prolonged "draws," would hand it to her lord and master while she fetched water or performed her other work.

That evening the old chief made known to us that if we would get him a cow, and give him a quantity of beads, we could have all the wives we wished.

He possessed, so we were told, wives in twenty villages, and had one hundred and sixteen children living.

A MARRIED OBODO.

I, through Umballa, thanked him on behalf of myself and friends, and promised to consider his offer.

The next day we went out, hoping to find some game. The old chief and twenty of his men followed us, and kept so close that there was no doubt we were to be kept prisoners.

After we had walked some distance, I called the attention of my companions to some tall heads towering above the low mimosas.

"Giraffes as I'm a living sinner," exclaimed Curtis.

Good raised his Winchester and without a moment's thought fired, but fortunately did not alarm the herd.

We had to move slowly for there is no animal so easily alarmed as the giraffe.

A moment later and the giraffes had spotted us and started off at a sharp trot.

Curtis fired a shot from his express rifle and succeeded in wounding fatally one of the animals.

The giraffes ran for some distance and then suddenly turned and made toward us.

A splendid bull was crashing before me like a locomotive obelisk through the mimosas, bending the elastic boughs before him in his irresistible rush, which sprung back with a force which would have upset the strongest horse.

I fired and had the pleasure of sending a bullet through his heart.

I flattered myself on my skill, but found I had made a great mistake; the bull-giraffe was a sacred animal, and by killing it I had insured the enmity of the tribe.

Instantly every man had his spear ready to hurl it at us when the command should be given.

The chief and his men closed in, and looked angry and defiant.

Umbilla tried the effects of a palaver, but the passions of the savages were aroused, and it was plainly evident that nothing short of bloodshed would satisfy them.

The brutes formed a circle round us and therefore had every advantage.

Hastily consulting together, we formed a square, standing shoulder to shoulder. Our weakest point was that occupied by Umbilla, for he was armed only with his assegai.

Umbilla told of the effects of our magic tubes, and warned them that their deaths were certain.

With a wild whoop or howl the fellows commenced dancing round us, gradually making their circles smaller.

We now perceived their intention to be to get close to us and to pin us with their sharp spears, which were surely poisoned.

The dance continued, and a wild yell went up from their throats.

The savages were now within eight feet of us; three feet more, and the points of the spears would touch our breasts.

"Fire!" I shouted, and three shots were sent into the bosoms of the same number of Obodos. The men closed in their circle, and we had to again fire.

Three more fell before the magic of gunpowder. Again we sent the death-dealing missiles to our foes, and, to our great astonishment, a whistling bullet came whizzing past our heads, sent by some one on the hills above.

A moment later, and a white man came bounding down the hillside, and using his rifle as a club, dealt such heavy blows right and left that in a few minutes we were victors.

Neither of our party had received a scratch. We turned to our able assistant to thank him, when he rushed forward and grasped me round the neck, squeezing me in a most affectionate embrace.

"Why, Theo., my boy, who would have thought of seeing you?"

I looked at the man for a minute before I could recognize him, and then I was equally enthusiastic as I recalled the well-known features of Norse Fjord. There was this difficulty in the way, however: he was at least fifteen years older than I was, yet now I looked twenty years older than him.

How was it? Had he found the elixir? If so, our meeting was fortunate.

"Get away from here, my boy," he said, "for these fellows, the Obodos, are very devils incarnate; they may patch up a peace with you, but they will poison the water, or send some of the girls to stab you while you sleep. I know them for being varmints. I have to leave, too, for my life is forfeit if I stay."

"Where's your camp?" I asked.

"Here, and all my property is on my back, more's the pity. I had a horse, but——"

"But what?"

"I was chasing some giraffes intending to pot a cow, for the bull is sacred, when some rascally fellow shot my horse from under me." Fjord twisted up his lips in a way which told me he had a pretty good guess that it was one of our party.

"What time was it, and where?" I asked.

When Fjord told us, we turned the laugh on Captain John Good of her majesty's royal navy, for he had fired at the giraffes at that particular time and missed them.

So he had killed Fjord's Arab instead.

"It was my rascally left eye," said Good, as an apology.

"Say rather your eyeglass in your right eye," laughed Curtis.

When we told Fjord of our camp at the foot of the mountain, he offered to join us, and we were highly delighted.

"What are you doing in Africa?" I asked, as we slowly descended the hill.

"Searching for *It*."

"For what?" I asked, not understanding his answer.

"Just what I say. Perhaps, to be more explicit, I am looking for *He, She,* or *It*," he said.

"You are an inveterate humbug, Fjord, or I should say you were cracked."

"Perhaps so, but I tell you I will find *It* yet."

"For mercy sake, explain what you mean."

"Don't be in too great a hurry," he said, and at the very moment his foot slipped and he fell, rolling down twenty yards or so, and only saving himself by catching hold of a huge bowlder.

I could not resist the temptation, so I shouted:

"Fjord, have you found *It* yet?"

He laughed good-naturedly, and as he was not hurt, we took his fall as a little diversion to our day's tramp. The next night we had reached our camp, but only just in time, for the rascals we had left in charge were just preparing to take away our team and wagon with all our surplus stores. The fellows thought we were dead, and were frightened at the prospect of remaining longer by the enchanted river.

We had been several days longer than anticipated, but we felt there was no excuse for the men believing we were dead, and however much they might apologize, it was impossible to help mistrusting them.

Sir Henry Curtis had met Fjord once, but he had failed

to recognize him. Evidently the white man who had sent down to Fuga for stores was Fjord and not Quatermain. If so, where could our exploring hunter be?

As we sat round our camp fire that night we were desirous of listening to Norse Fjord's story, knowing well, as I did, that it would be lively and interesting. He was welcomed as a *bon camarade*, and we all expressed a hope he would join us.

CHATER VI.
FJORD'S STORY.

"YES, Theo., I will go with you, live in the same camp, eat out of the same plate, and at last help to fill the same grave, if only you and your comrades will help me find *It*."

"I reckon we are ready, Fjord, to join you in your search, providing always there is something tangible to search for."

In this view both Curtis and Good coincided.

"Then, comrades, I will tell you my story, and you shall see whether the adventures are worth following up."

Fjord lighted his pipe, and after taking a few strong pulls, an example, I need scarcely say, we followed, he cleared his throat and began:

"When I got back from Rapa Nui—you haven't forgot that adventure, have you, Theo.?'

"No, nor never shall."

"Neither shall I, and I often think of Alethea (now don't get angry or jealous, old boy, for you are welcome to her) and of Milo, and wonder what became of all the people after that terrible earthquake and volcanic eruption—— But to return to my story; after I left you I had one fixed idea in my head, and that was, 'It is possible to live forever.'"

"Another crank!" muttered Good, beneath his breath, and only loud enough for Curtis and myself to hear.

"If, then, it is possible," continued Fjord, not noticing the uncomplimentary interruption, "I am going to find the way, or die in the attempt."

"That's what most men do," Good put in quietly.

"So I started off to Italy, to find out something about the Rosicrucians and Alchemists. In Florence I fell in with an old man, who assured me he had lived in that city when Dante left it to go into exile; that he had seen all the changes of five hundred years. You may laugh"—Good was laughing quietly to himself—"but the old boy looked it. His skin was like parchment, and I don't think he had a pint of blood in his whole body. I became fast friends with him right away, and learned that in Athens or near by there lived an old woman who for a good round sum would sell a few drops of a liquid which would perpetuate life. 'For how long?' I asked. 'Just as long as it lasts,' was his reply. When I pressed him further, he admitted he had only been wealthy enough to buy ten drops, and he had to take one drop every hundred years; when his supply was exhausted, he must die. He had about four drops left, and his life was a misery to him, for he was always fearing that it might be stolen from him, or that his life would end in four hundred years. I got a description of the old woman, and started for Athens. I fell in with the American consul, and through his influence I was able to search the archives; and what think you, Theo.? I found out all about Isisthenes and his Egyptian wife. I also came across a record of Tisneo being cheated out of his wife, Alethea——"

"You did?" I exclaimed.

"Yes; so Alethea told us the truth, my boy, and I love her—don't be jealous—all the better. Well, I left Athens and searched for the old witch, only to learn that she had gone to Africa. An old crony—a regular witch —had known her, and had evidently taken a few drops of the magic elixir, for she said that the woman I wanted had promised to meet her in a hundred years' time.

"'What has she gone to Africa for?'" I asked. 'To find *It*,' was the reply. '*It?* What?' I asked, but nothing further could I get. I left Greece, grand old Greece once, Aristophano, but dirty, miserable Greece now, and started for this dark continent.

"When we neared Socotra the ship I was in—a merchantman whose captain I knew—encountered some heavy seas, and was wrecked. Eight of the crew and myself were in one of the ship's boats, and were driven about by the waves for several days, until our bones felt an uncommon desire to get through our skin; then a wave bigger than the preceding ones capsized the boat and we were all struggling in the water.

"I possess a pretty strong grip, as you know, Theo., so I clung tight to the boat, but could not right it. As for the other fellows, they went to Davy Jones' locker in quick time. I drifted about for a long time before I was able to climb on the top of the upturned boat. All that day I sat drying myself in the sun, but almost as soon as my clothes would get somewhat free from water, a heavy wave would wash over me again. I endured that for nearly twenty-four hours, until I got considerably riled, and, I am afraid, I began to swear.

Something, either the swearing, or my bad temper, did good, for the wind changed, and I was driven on the beach of a strange little island, which is not marked on any map I have ever seen. It lies to the southwest of Socotra.

I very soon left the boat and took a walk for the sake of exercise. I climbed up the hill which rose almost directly from the sea, so that I might get a fair view of the country.

The island was only a small one, but the people— oh, my, I never saw their equals.

The men were as black as midnight, but varied the blackness by painting long stripes of red down the body. They stood over eight feet high, every one of them. I looked quite like a dwarf among a lot of giants.

As soon as they caught sight of me, they took gigantic strides up the hillside, and seized me round the waist and carried me down to a square place surrounded by stones standing several feet high.

The men and women were entirely nude, and what appeared to me to be so remarkable was that the women were the tallest, many of them being so tall that the men were able to walk under their outstretched arms.

When I was put down on a stone in the center of the square, the men and women walked round, looking at me as though I was a great curiosity.

I counted eighty in all, and it seemed there were no others on the island, as I got a good view of the place, for it was but little more than a good-sized rock, and failed to observe any but those assembled in the square.

After the inspection had lasted for some time, I began to get weary of it, and asked what was their good pleasure.

"'He talks,' said one of the women, in a language or dialect very similar to what I had heard spoken in Abyssinia by some of the mountain tribes.

Fortunately, their language was quite familiar to me, and I was able to tell the story of my misfortune. They had but a poor idea of what it meant to be wrecked, and when I made use of all my eloquence in describing the way I had drifted about astride the bottom of the boat, they were so delighted that they began to insist I should show them how it was done. This was by no means pleasing to me, but they were resolute. I pleaded I was hungry, having partaken of food for the last time three days before.

Instantly one of the giantesses left the circle and disappeared. I could not at the time find out which way she went, but her reappearance was equally as startling.

In her hand she carried a large shell filled with small dark leaves. These she bade me eat. It looked like a cruel joke on a hungry man. Three days without food, and then to be offered merely a few dry leaves. However, I was in such a condition that I would have eaten grass, so I took the leaves and was about to fill my mouth when one of the men pulled my hand away, and taking the shell from me gave me three of the leaves. I put them in my mouth and scarcely had I swallowed them than I felt refreshed. A gentle, soothing influence passed over me, and I almost imagined I had become ethereal. Three more leaves were handed me, and when I had eaten them I lost all sense of hunger. A mild exhilaration came over me, and I felt not only refreshed in body, but very contented and happy in my mind.*

I was then requested or ordered to go down to the water edge and get astride my boat to show them how I had landed on the island.

My feelings were so elated by the stimulating properties of the leaves that I would have done far more than that to please my hosts.

However, no sooner had I got on the boat than two of

* Most probably the leaves were those of the *Erythroxylon Coca.*—ED.

the giants pushed it out into the water, walking in the surf until they were submerged up to their waists. They then gave the boat a violent push and returned to land.

The crowd of people had gathered on the beach and laughed to see how the boat was tossed about on the water, but when one monster wave capsized the frail bark, and I had to struggle with the elements of the deep, they fairly roared with delight.

As you know, Theo., I am a good swimmer, and so I had but little difficulty in reaching land, but my progress was impeded by my persistent efforts to drag the boat along. Eventually I succeeded, and when I stood erect on land the men gathered round me, stripped off my clothes, and made me run about on the beach to restore the circulation to its proper condition. I hardly liked being in a state *deshabille* before a mixed assemblage, but I was only in the same condition as my hosts, so it was no use being squeamish.

Some more of the leaves were given me, and then, about an hour later, we had a repast, the like of which I had never before eaten.

What the dishes were made of I never could ascertain, but they were good.

All the inhabitants seemed to live as one family.

I had seen no children. This was strange, so I asked about it.

"All our children are dead," said one of the men, "they died long ago, and we are too old to have any more."

I laughed at the conceit, for not one seemed to be more than forty or fifty years of age at the utmost. To my astonishment, they told me that their youngest child died fifty years ago.

I pretended that I felt no surprise, but, on the contrary, accepted the truth of the remark, and jokingly said, that as there were so many really handsome ladies, and such good-looking men, it was a pity for the race to die out.

"That it will never do," said one, "for we cannot die."

I pressed them to explain, and if you are not weary I will tell you what was the account they gave of themselves.

Fjord paused and refilled his pipe, while we remained silent a few moments, thinking over his strange adventure.

"It is really remarkable," said Curtis.

"Remarkable isn't the word! By Jove! I would like to see those people," exclaimed Good.

"Go on with your story, Fjord, for it is interesting, and I would rather hear it than sleep."

"Well, Theo., I have no objection, so here goes."

The spokesman of the giants began his story in the regular, old-fashioned way, prefacing it with the well-worn phrase, "Once upon a time."

I should weary you if I told it with all the verbosity with which he clothed his narrative, for it took me many days before I had heard it all, but I will tell it as briefly as possible.

It appeared that several centuries ago two giants, with their wives, settled on the island; they were the only inhabitants.

When they had been there two years their number had increased to six, as two young savages had been born and were thriving.

After several years had passed, and the children had married, an old woman was wrecked near the island. A monster shark pursued her through the water, and the old lady was gradually getting exhausted, when some of the young people of the island went to her rescue. They beat off the sea-monster, and rescued the woman. She was a witch, and was so thankful to the people for saving her, that she promised them immortality on certain conditions and under various restrictions.

The giant families listened to her story, and then one of the elder women asked why, if she was immortal, she feared the shark.

The witch looked at her for a time and then replied:

"There are two things only which can destroy my life; one is falling from a building, and the other an attack from an animal which lives without breathing, so the shark might have killed me, seeing it does not breathe as we do. If ye do as I direct, your children can live forever until they number eighty adults, after which no child shall live long enough to perpetuate the race."

What the old witch promised came true; the original

families died off, and their children lived and prospered. When our number had reached eighty we thought of the old woman's prophecy, but laughed at it, when a dozen children were running about, some of them ten years old. However, not one lived to reach maturity, and although children continued to come, yet the same fate awaited them; we are destined to live on.

"Happy people," I said, "who are exempt from that universal calamity of human nature, who have your minds free and disengaged, without the weight and depression of spirits caused by the apprehension of death."

The natives, however, were not so happy, for their lives had become so monotonous that they longed for change, even if it was by death.

I heard that the old woman who had conferred the length of life on these people, lived somewhere in Central Africa, and was a native of a land ruled over by a personage bearing the cognomen of *It*.

I asked my hosts if they had ever heard a description of *It*, or knew anything about the mysterious country.

To this one of the women answered that she had learned from the old witch that, as everything had an origin, so there was somewhere the personification of the origin of man. In some country there lived an eternal link between the animals—who could not speak, reason, or act with intelligence—and man, and this link, which was the original of man, was still living, and, on account of its complex nature, was known as *It*.

"I don't mean to tell you," continued Fjord, "that the giantess, whose age must have run considerably into the centuries, told me this in the words I have uttered; her story was very prolix, but I have reduced it, as I promised. I saw the likelihood of the story, for had I not seen, with you, Theo., the mighty wonder of *He*, and was not the lesson taught by his strange metamorphosis that man originated in the animal, and would return to the animal if he disobeyed the rules and laws of nature?"

"How long did you stay on the island?" asked Curtis, who had listened very intently to the story.

"About a month altogether, and heartily tired I was of the people and their primitive ways, so I, one night, got down to the beach and launched my boat, having made a rough pair of sculls. I drifted about for some time, and at last was picked up by a vessel and taken to the small port of Juba."

"Did you say the people had no houses?" inquired Good, and I thought there was a touch of sarcasm in his voice.

"They hesitated to erect any kind of dwelling, for fear they might get crushed and thus end their existence, so they dwelt in caves. I brought away a good package of the leaves, and as perhaps you have never experienced the delightful sensation, I advise you to eat two or three of them."

Norse Fjord unfastened a broad belt which we had noticed he wore round his waist, and which appeared to be larger and thicker than an ordinary one. The inside of the belt was full of pockets, and in each pocket Fjord had stored two or three ounces of the marvelous leaves.

He handed each of us two leaves, which we put at once in our mouths.

The taste was slightly bitter, but not at all unpleasant, and the sensation after eating was one which I find it difficult to describe. I was not intoxicated, yet I felt a genial glow all over me, and before my mind passed phantasmagorial shapes, pleasing and exciting. Every nerve in my body seemed thrilled with delight, and as I closed my eyes I could easily imagine myself in a most glorious paradise.

The next morning we compared notes, and both Good and Curtis declared their sensations to have been similar. The leaves, whatever tree may have produced them, were a godsend to travelers in the desert.

I slept and dreamed sweet dreams of fantastic people and strange things, and was so refreshed when I awoke that I laughingly advised Fjord to sleep with the belt for a pillow, or some of us might steal it. He only smiled at the thought, and I verily believe he was so overjoyed at meeting us, that even if we had stolen his belt he would still have been happy.

CHAPTER VII.

A SNAKE ADVENTURE.

EARLY the following morning Umbilla told us that he had unmistakable proof of elephant spoor, and that our camp must have been visited during the night by some of the noble animals.

Fjord proposed we should have a little excitement before we continued our journey, so we started out all well armed and fully determined to return with some good ivory.

Almost immediately after we started I saw two bulls with splendid tusks about a hundred yards from us, apparently the leaders of an approaching herd. The ground was exceedingly favorable, being tolerably open, and yet with sufficient bush to afford a slight cover.

Presently, several elephants appeared and joined the two leaders. There was evidently a considerable number in the herd.

Had we been mounted we should have had some rare fun, but as we were on foot, we had to watch our opportunity.

After a quarter of an hour I had got sufficiently near a fine bull to warrant a shot; so, raising my double-eight elephant rifle, I took aim and sent a bullet right into his shoulder. I could hear the crashing of the bone even at that distance. The bull set up a wild howl, and started toward where I was standing at a quick pace.

Fjord raised his rifle and landed a shot exactly behind the blade bone. With a shrill scream the elephant changed its course, and charged upon Fjord like a steam-engine. The hardy hunter doubled and the bull dashed on. Immediately we were all in pursuit over ruts and gullies, the high dry grass whistling in our ears as we ran through, forcing it to the ground.

The elephant halted. I thought he was dying as he stood with trunk drooping and ears closely pressed back upon his neck.

Curtis advised us to close up our ranks and to give the animal a finishing shot. Just at that moment I heard the rush of elephants advancing through the green bush upon the rising ground above the hollow formed by the open space of high, withered grass in which we were standing. The sound increased, and the heads of a closely packed herd of about fifteen elephants showed above the low scrub, and they broke cover, bearing down directly upon us. It was a lovely sight, and the ivory alone represented a small fortune.

We set up a big shout and yelled with all the fury we we could command. This had the desired effect; it diverted their attention, and four shots were immediately sent whizzing through the air.

Two bulls were fatally wounded, and they fell to the ground groaning and crying most piteously. The others charged wildly in all directions. One big fellow made for me, and as he turned his head a moment I fired a steady shot at his shoulder; he fell on his knees, but was quickly on his feet again and gave chase. I could not stand to fire, for I could almost feel the brute's breath fanning my cheek.

Curtis and the others had enough to do to ward off the attacks of the other elephants, so each had to look after his own safety.

We ran for a quarter of a mile, I being the fresher of the two, for the elephant was faint from loss of blood.

Steadily, however, he gained upon me, and at last was only about twelve yards or so away, when with desperation I turned and made one more attempt to shoot. Fortunately the bullet went crashing into the animal's skull, and with a savage cry of pain the noble brute fell to the ground.

I was fairly exhausted, and sat down to rest, taking care, however, to improve the occasion by reloading all my weapons.

I had just got my Winchester chamber again filled when I heard the unmistakable sound of one of the elephants charging in my direction.

I looked round and saw a fine bull dashing toward me, and holding Good in its trunk high above its head.

Here was a new danger; if I fired I might hit my friend, and if I struck the elephant I was afraid it might wreak its vengeance on its victim.

However, I must do my best, and I fired three shots in rapid succession at the animal. Its raised trunk gave me an advantage, and when the first shot struck its head, it

opened its mouth and sent up a shout of agony, receiving
the second and third bullet in its throat. The animal
dropped dead, and I stepped up to its carcase to see if
Good was alive. A few minutes elapsed before the trunk
relaxed its hold, and then Good got up from his uncomfortable position, took his eyeglass from his eye, carefully
wiped it as coolly as though he were in a room, replaced
it in position, looked at his dead enemy and then stretched
out his hand in true British fashion, and as he grasped
mine, he said quite coolly:

"Thanks, old boy, you saved my life, I'll do as much
for you some day."

We walked back to the camp, sending our servants to
get the tusks of the six bulls which testified to our
prowess on the hunting field that day. Our casualties
were very slight; Fjord had the little finger of his left
hand broken, Good was bruised and his nerves were considerably shaken, but for Curtis and myself we had nothing to complain of but excessive exhaustion.

Fjord's magic leaves acted like a charm, for after partaking of a few of them, we seemed to lose all our weariness and fatigue.

When we had secured the ivory, we arranged to explore still more the river under the mountain and trace
it to its source.

Fjord showed Umbilla the road round the hill, and
fixed on a place for a camp, which would be secluded
and at the same time convenient for us.

We took plenty of ammunition, and each carried two
guns, two revolvers, and two good sharp hunting-knives.

In addition we had about five pounds each of biltong
(dried beef) and about the same weight of crackers, our
water bottles were filled, so we knew we were good for
six days' absence from our source of supplies.

In our boat we took care to store a goodly supply of
crackers, biltong, and of course we did not forget the
ammunition.

The four of us were just ready to start, when Umbilla
pleaded so hard to be allowed to go that we consented on
his giving a solemn pledge that the others would not attempt to steal our team and wagon, or make away with
our stores.

"They will not touch them, Baas," he said, "for I have told them they are all 'tagati'" (bewitched).

We were pleased in our hearts that the black was going with us.

"What tribe do you belong to?" I asked him once, and he answered by striking a number of attitudes, which showed the custom of his nation. I judged him, therefore, to be of the Barii tribe.

He would, when at rest, stand on one leg, the foot of his raised leg resting on the inside of the other knee.

He was equally an adept with the assegai of the Zulus or his own native spear, the end of which is well smeared with the slimy juice of the euphorbia root.

The action of this juice is such that wherever it enters human flesh, whether the wound is a scratch or a deep one it matters not, the flesh will begin to corrode, it loses its fiber, and, after severe inflammation and swelling, drops away like jelly.

Generally the Barii tribe is very hostile to the whites, but Umbilla was an exception. His long residence at Bagemoya and Zanzibar had civilized him. However, before he started on the journey up the river, he took off his girdle and the scarf which he had worn across his shoulders and replaced the three cock feathers, worn by his tribe, in the little tuft of his hair.

He explained this action by saying he would be ashamed to be seen by any of his people if he was clothed.

When all was ready we jumped into our little steel-plated boat and pulled up the river.

Fjord was full of admiration of the water and its many-colored hues, and when he reached the lake, nothing would satisfy him but a bath in its peculiar water.

Fjord was almost an amphibean, he could dive and swim better than any man I had ever met with, and, therefore, I did not anticipate any harm coming to him through a bath in the clear lake.

He stripped off his clothes, and, while we held the boat steady, he took a header into the water.

When he had got below its surface we watched his descent. His flesh appeared highly luminous.

Would he ever stop? It seemed that he was diving hundreds of feet; what if he never returned? It might be that the water was impregnated with some subtle essence which would suffocate him.

We could still see him going lower and yet lower. Curtis had timed his descent, and now strained his eyes anxiously at the water.

"He cannot live," said he, "for he has been descending four minutes, and if it takes as long to get back, it will be impossible for him to survive."

Another minute passed. I was anxious; poor fellow, it was sad to think I had lured him on to destruction.

Another sixty seconds passed, we had lost sight of his body; the cave seemed to be growing dark, or, perhaps, that was only our imagination.

Seven, eight, nine minutes and no trace of our friend.

"It is useless hoping," said Good, who, being a seaman, ought to have a knowledge of the water and its dangers.

"I shall wait here all day," I said, with an air of authority, for I was not going to leave my old friend. If I did not have him as a companion, I would at least see that his dead body had a careful, honest burial.

So we waited another minute, and then I thought I heard Fjord's voice calling me.

"Listen!" I commanded.

"Theo.!" The voice was faint and indistinct.

"Fjord!" I shouted, as loudly as I possibly could.

"Ay! Row ahead!" came back the reply.

We bent ourselves to the oars and pulled through the lake, no sign of our friend was discernible. We entered another tunnel or cave and pulled with all our strength.

"Fjord!" I shouted.

"Ay! Theo!" was the response, and it sounded nearer.

We pulled, but made small headway, for the current was strongly against us. It seemed that the river on either side emptied itself into the lake, so the stream was toward the center of the hill, and against us.

Still we gained some little advantage; our oars creaked with the strain, and my back began to get stiff and painful.

Sir Henry Curtis was as strong as an elephant; in fact, wherever he went in Africa he was called "Incubu" (elephant). I am sure that we should have been carried back to the lake had it not been for the great strength of Curtis and Umbilla.

After a quarter of an hour's hard pulling we discerned the form of Fjord standing on a narrow ledge of rock right ahead of us.

The sight gave us courage and renewed our strength, so we pulled faster and with stronger strokes, until we brought our boat to Fjord's resting-place. He dropped to the seat without a word, and, without attempting to dress or explain, helped us to pull the boat.

"How came you there?" I asked, after quite a lengthy silence.

"Don't question me now, as you love me," was his reply. "I will tell you all later."

It was no use questioning Fjord, for he was so determined that whenever he made up his mind to a thing all the powers of earth could not turn him therefrom.

We pulled with redoubled vigor, and soon found ourselves in the open air. The river had tunneled the mountain through, and we were now on a great plateau some hundreds of feet above the sea-level—and this was something which I have never been able to explain, for the water had evidently been running up-hill as far as the lake.

We drew our boat out of the water, and, having beached it, looked round for a good place to camp.

Fjord had not spoken a word since the time when he had begged us not to question him as to his adventures.

On his face there was a puzzled, confused look, which with any one else I should have said betokened fright, but I never believed Captain Norse Fjord had any knowledge of timidity or fear.

Umbilla said he had never been before in the country, and had no knowledge of its people, if, indeed, it was inhabited.

We had just succeeded in making a fire, when Umbilla, who had gone out a little distance to look over the country, came running back for his spear, which he had left with us.

He threw it at some object which was hidden from our sight.

Curtis and I hurried forward, taking our revolvers, and Curtis carried a native spear in addition.

When I got close to Umbilla I saw the most horrid monster that ever crossed my vision. Curtis immediately pinned its head to the ground, while I severed it at one blow with my hunting knife, damaging the keen edge of my favorite blade upon the hard rock. It was a puff-adder of the most enormous dimensions. I took out my small measuring tape and found its length to be six feet, its girth fifteen inches. The tail, as is usual in all African poisonous snakes, was extremely blunt, and the head perfectly flat and about three inches broad. I counted eight teeth and secured five poison-fangs, the two most prominent being an inch in length.

The poison fangs were artfully contrived by some diabolic freak of nature as pointed tubes, through which the poison is injected into the base of the wound. The extreme point of one of these fangs was solid and so finely sharpened that beneath a powerful microscope which, fortunately, Fjord had with him, it looked perfectly smooth although a needle point was rough and uneven. A short distance above the solid point of the fang the surface of the tube appeared to be cut away, and it was through this aperture that the poison was ejected.

Our first encounter with a native was decided in our favor, and Umbilla thought it a good omen.

CHAPTER VIII.

"MEN WHOSE HEADS DO GROW BENEATH THEIR SHOULDERS."

WE had retired to rest, leaving Umbilla on the watch for the first half of the night, about an hour, when a tremendous clap of thunder shook the earth and echoed from rock to rock among the mountains. It roused us all, and we sprung to our feet, alarmed, and not understanding for a moment what had caused the noise.

The next instant we were enlightened, for a flash of lightning, the most vivid I had ever witnessed, lighted up the whole surrounding country, and almost simultaneously a deafening peal roared from the black clouds which obscured the stars. Down came the rain and before we could seek the shelter of our boat we were drenched to the skin. That did not affect Umbilla, seeing he had no clothes to be saturated with the rain.

It never ceased raining until morning dawned and then with the first rays of the sun came finer and clearer weather.

Leaving Curtis and Good to guard the boat and camp, Fjord and I, accompanied by Umbilla, went up into the country exploring.

We walked amid the long grass very cautiously for fear of being surprised or suddenly shot with an arrow from behind or on either side. We saw before us a beaten road which gave evidence of inhabitants.

Along this road we went for a few minutes, when we saw a strange animal dart across our path and hide in the scrub.

It was followed by another. The distance was so great that we could not discern what kind of creatures they were.

Fjord, whose eyes were focused for a long range, declared that the animals had human faces, but as to their bodies, he was not so certain.

Had he not been so positive I should have fired, but I had no desire to shoot a human being unless provoked thereto.

Umbilla offered to run forward and examine these creatures closer. If they were men, he, being a naked savage, would be less likely to meet with hostility than we should, being white.

We hid ourselves in the long grass, and awaited his return.

Ten minutes passed away before we heard his footsteps, and then we looked out from our hiding-place and saw our servant running toward us at a speed of which I had never imagined he was capable.

"Inkoosi!"* he shouted as he passed us. "Come and warn Incubu and the other white man!"

"What is it, Umbilla?"

It was no use asking, for the man ran on as though his life depended on the speed he made. Fear is infectious, and although we neither conjectured the cause of the sudden fright manifested by Umbilla, we joined in the

* Chief.

run, and all three reached the camp breathless and exhausted.

"What is the matter?" asked Curtis.

"I don't know," was my reply, when Good took his eyeglass from his eye, rubbed it clean, and having screwed it into its place, looked first at me and then at Fjord.

"Come, cap," he said, addressing Fjord, "what were you running away from?"

Fjord laughed heartily, the first laugh I had heard from him since his submersion in the lake, and so thoroughly was he given up to mirth that the tears rolled down his cheeks and his sides fairly shook.

Curtis was rather inclined to be cross about it, and spoke as I had never before heard him.

"Don't act like madmen," he said, sternly, "but tell us what is the matter, for if there is danger it would be better to prepare for it than to stand there laughing."

Although I felt rather nettled at the speech, its soundness was unquestionable, and so I openly told him that we were both entirely ignorant of the matter, and that we only followed Umbilla's example.

We commanded the man to speak, and after he had regained his breath, he commenced:

"Great Incubu"—he always addressed Curtis when speaking to us, and, on occasions like the present, he used the term elephant as being more expressive—"great Incubu, may my flesh be given to the aasvogels* if I speak not the truth. When I left the two mighty men of magic, I went forward until I saw two men standing in the grass. They were both tagati,† for neither had a head on his shoulders. I was frightened at these headless men, and stood still, not daring to move, when one of them raised his arm, and what think you, great Incubu, he had a head ander his arm! This creature who carried his head under his arm moved, and I was so afraid he was going to run after me, that I ran, and called on the two Inkoosis to follow me, which they did."

We knew of a certainty that Umbilla had not been drinking daccha, or we should certainly have said he was drunk; but Curtis maintained his solemnity and waved the man away.

* Vultures.
† Bewitched.

"Aristophano," he said, "do you remember me writing you about my visit to the theater, and the actor repeating the lines:

> " 'And of the cannibals that each other eat,
> The Anthropophagi, and men whose heads
> Do grow beneath their shoulders?' "

"I remember it well," I replied, and I must confess I was staggered by Umbilla's story, for he had not read Shakespeare, and we had not told him that we were desirous of proving that such people lived, yet here was an unlettered savage declaring that he had seen men whose heads were beneath their shoulders.

What should be done? Fjord proposed that we should abandon our camp and follow up the trail. Curtis, who was moved deeply by the statement of the savage, seemed inclined to leave the camp intact and under the care of Umbilla, while we explored the country and examined these strange people.

This course was agreed upon with but one change: Good insisted on staying by the boat and stores, for he said since the silly conduct of Umbilla he would not trust him alone.

We were sorry to leave Good, but, after all, perhaps it was the wisest plan. It would be well to know that our boat was safe, so that when occasion required it we could return.

Taking our rifles and revolvers and three days' supply of food, we started on our journey. Curtis was more animated than I had ever seen him.

We walked rapidly, but observing the greatest caution; Curtis undertaking to look ahead, while Fjord kept watch on the right, and I on the left. We maintained silence, for fear our conversation might affright the strange people or endanger our lives.

We had gone some distance when we saw a crowd gathered in front of some houses which differed from any we had before seen.

"They are going to attack us," I cried, while Curtis got his rifle ready to fire upon them if they showed any hostility.

"Put up your gun, Curtis," said Fjord, "do you not see that they have only their spears and no shields?

Would they attack us without their shields? I tell you they are coming to welcome us."

Fjord's idea seemed plausible, so, as we had a good point of vantage where we were, we agreed to wait for the attack or welcome. A huge rock shielded us very well from arrows or spears, and at the same time gave us excellent opportunity for picking off some of the savages if they came too close.

When the natives had got within two hundred yards of us they waited, and sent up a shout of "Koom! Koom!" (the king, the king). We were, therefore, to be welcomed by the ruler of the tribe.

We had not seen any of the headless men yet, but supposed either that Umbilla was mistaken or that they were monstrosities, and therefore scarce.

I called on Curtis and Fjord to follow me, and we would go to the king. If he was inclined to be an enemy, we should fare no worse for putting a bold face on it; if a friend, our meeting him half way would be considered a great honor by the monarch.

Upon my approach the crowd which surrounded the king gave way, and a mat was spread out in front of the king and immediately at his feet.

We had got within thirty yards or so, when a dozen naked warriors rushed toward us, and without asking our consent, lifted us from the ground and carried us on their shoulders to the king.

We were thrown rather than placed on the mat, and it was some minutes before we recovered from the unpleasant jolting we had experienced as we had entered the presence of royalty.

Judging from first appearance, I thought the king was a fine-looking man, but with a very peculiar expression of his eyes, and a still stranger lower lip. I found this was caused by a piece of wood shaped like a long, thin nail with a flat head being pushed through the lip, the nail-head being on the inside of the lip.

The king was seated, but as soon as we recovered from our surprise he rose up. He was the strangest looking creature I ever saw. His shoulders were very broad, so that when he was sitting down he had the appearance of being very muscular; but as he stood up we observed that his body tapered off to the hips, which were extremely narrow, and the legs were the smallest I had ever seen on a man.

His whole figure was triangular, with his shoulders as the base and his feet as the apex. His neck was long, and his head seemed as though it was too heavy. When the king sat down he had a rest specially fixed for his head, so as to relieve his neck from the burden.

"Who art thou, most noble one?" he said, as he fixed his eyes on Curtis.

I noticed that Sir Henry was always singled out when a savage wished to address us, and the reason was not far to seek.

Of commanding stature, good, broad shoulders, arms and legs like those of one of the old Roman gladiators, no wonder he should be looked upon as a monarch among men.

The language spoken was one that, fortunately, both Fjord and Curtis were familiar with.

I did not understand one word, but had to trust to their interpretations.

"Great and mighty warrior," answered Curtis; "we have come to see thy great country, and to bow ourselves before thee, bringing thee presents from afar."

Fjord turned to me and, in English, said, in an undertone:

"Get out a handful of beads, old boy, for I like not the king's looks."

"Presents! Gifts!" exclaimed Kasheebar, the king. "And who art thou that thinkest the monarch of all the earth needs thy gifts?"

"We are but thy children, come from afar to tell thee, mighty one, that thou art wise and great."

As Fjord made a running translation for my benefit, I had difficulty in refraining from laughter.

"Hast thou gifts greater than we know of?" asked Kasheebar.

"Nay, mighty one, but such as thy poor servants could command."

The old fellow raised his nose, and with a contemptuous leer on his face, called for his warriors.

"It's all up with us," whispered Fjord. "I guess Curtis will fail."

"It is a case of jealousy," I answered. "The old boy don't like to see such a handsome man."

Fjord put his fingers in his mouth and sent therefrom such a shrill, piercing whistle, that both Curtis and I were glad to get our fingers into our ears.

"Good! very good!" exclaimed the king. "Again! again!"

The whistling was something new, and had pleased Kasheebar.

Fjord whistled three times, and scarcely had the echoes of the last shrill note died away before a few drops of rain came pattering down.

"Tage! Tage!"* shouted the king.

Fjord took advantage of the idea, and with great coolness declared that he had whistled for rain to show the king that the white men from across the hills and the big water could do more than any of his magicians.

"Good, good!" he again ejaculated, and then he fixed his strange eyes on me. I was expected to do something, so I stepped forward and did a little hocus-pocus, procuring from my sleeve, but apparently from the air, a quantity of pretty beads.

Kasheebar stepped from his seat and grabbed the beads with almost brutal force. When he found they did not disappear he smiled, and oh, such a smile! The skewer or nail projected out at a right angle from his face, and his teeth, beautifully blackened and polished, looked ready to make a feast of our flesh.

I saw that my effort had pleased him, so I produced a doll in the same way. The old fellow became frantic, and hopped and danced about like a child with a new toy.

"Koro! Koro!" he shouted, and from the back of the crowd a boy of the same shape as the king stepped forward. There was no need to say it was his son. That was plain enough, but the strangest part was that he too had the triangular form.

Koro saw the doll, and instantly put it in his mouth to try and eat it. I saw the boy was hungry, so I slipped my hand quickly into Fjord's haversack, and drew therefrom a very large biscuit. Again I adopted the hocus-pocus, drawing from the back of my neck the biscuit,

* A magician or witch.

which I handed Koro, and which he devoured with amazing rapidity.

KORO DEVOURING THE BISCUIT.

Koro, as he swallowed the hard biscuit, presented a strange and ugly appearance. He was, however, the pet of the native women, and his form was greatly admired. I learned later that, although the boy inherited the peculiar shape of his father, yet art was resorted to, and he was compelled to stay more than half his time in a triangular box made of rough boards, and which was capable of being screwed tighter each day, thus pressing the organs of the stomach up into the chest. To add to the success of the torture the boy was only allowed to eat three days in each week, so starvation and the pressure of the boards would, by the time he reached manhood, produce a kingly form. I could not help slightly altering Madame Roland's famous expression, and exclaiming:

"O Fashion! how many crimes are committed in thy name."

Kasheebar told us one day that no one was worthy to be a king unless he was prepared to endure torture to bring his body into the fashionable shape.

The giving of the biscuit to Koro, on one of his banqueting-days was the last stroke.

We were now admitted to favor and taken to the village or kraal.

The streets were laid out very precisely, the rows of houses, rather different to any I had heretofore seen in Africa, were at a distance of about sixty yards, and made quite respectable streets.

The houses were built in circular shape, and thatched with long grass, which was afterward smeared over with a preparation of a tree-juice and cow-dung. This made them proof against both water and intense heat.

The door, which was the only opening, was a small hole two feet high; so to get either out or into the house, it was necessary to go on all fours, and wriggle through the hole.

When we arrived at the village we each had a house given to us.

Not that there were any empty houses, but the natives who had built them were ordered out, and told to erect others for themselves.

Food was brought us, and we made ourselves very comfortable.

When we found it safe to confer together we talked over our reception, and Fjord convinced us we had much of interest to learn from this people, so we decided to fetch our boat, and complete our party. Good and Umbilla would be useful to us, and if our stay was to be a long one, of course it was only right they should join us.

CHAPTER IX.
A LINK IN THE CHAIN.

It was late the next day before we could get audience with the king, and then we found that he was distrustful. We were evidently not to be allowed to escape, and the only way we could induce Kasheebar to allow us to fetch our companions and boat was by the promise of large quantities of beads and feathers.

He sent us mounted on oxen, and a guard of twenty picked men in war paint were to accompany us.

The escort was a fine one. Every man stood over six feet, and their muscles were like iron. They were perfectly nude, with the exception of a ring round each wrist and each ankle, from which protruded barbed spikes two inches long, and made of finely sharpened metal. These spikes were poisoned, and one could easily see what a formidable weapon they would become in hand-to-hand fighting.

A BRACELET OF POISONED BARBS.

The men carried spears, a bow and about a dozen arrows, together with a large pipe, for these people were inveterate smokers.

We had not been gone half an hour before we were overtaken by another body of men, who had been sent after us with orders to bring back Curtis and myself, to be held as hostages for the safe return of Fjord and the escort.

We did not relish this new move, and feared treachery. Curtis was inclined to resist, but after all, though he was rightly called Incubu, what could our strength avail against forty or fifty armed men?

We had to separate; there was but one alternative, and that was death through resistance.

Curtis, on our way back, tried to get into conversation with the royal messenger, but either that man was mute or had orders not to talk, for not a word could he be induced to utter.

We arrived at the village, and after Curtis and I had crawled inside my house, we found, to our dismay, that we were to be kept close prisoners, for a sentry was seated at the doorway, and his back effectually shut out every ray of light.

Curtis had difficulty in restraining himself from scratching the fellow's bare back, or performing some practical joke upon him.

We asked him to move, but he would not. Curtis pushed him so vigorously that he rolled over, only to again squat himself down on his haunches in front of the hole.

"I'll rouse him," said Curtis, with a smile.

I watched him and wondered what he was about to do.

The man had laid his pipe down by his side, and Sir Henry managed to draw it quietly away. We then loaded it well with tobacco, and inserted a nice sprinkling of gunpowder in the bowl.

The pipe was then quietly restored to its place. The next move was one well calculated to scare any savage.

Curtis scratched a small trench with his finger in the soil round the sentry. So mute did the man sit that he never appeared to notice what we were doing. This trench we filled with powder.

When we had the train complete, I lighted a match and applied it to the explosive.

The fire ran along the train and into the little trench, spluttering, hissing, and cracking round the man, until he jumped to his feet, and saw fire apparently coming out of the ground.

Such was the discipline practiced on these warriors that, though we could see the muscles of the man's thighs and legs quivering with absolute fear, he made no attempt to leave his post, changing only from a sitting to a standing posture.

As the powder burned away, the man took up his pipe, and was astonished to see it filled with "white man's glory," as they call our tobacco. The leaves smoked by the native are a species of dock or plantain, and even to old smokers make a very fair substitute for tobacco.

The pipeful of the "white man's glory" was evidently a great treat to the warrior, for he forgot his fear, and sat down to rub his fire sticks together.

He soon produced a little fire with which he lighted his tobacco. As the smoke passed into his mouth, he kept ejaculating "Good, good!"

We peeped through the hole, lying on our stomachs full length on the ground to enable us to do so, and waited the *denouement*.

"Puff, puff!" The smoke continued so long that we almost began to think some mishap had happened the powder, but in a moment more a burst of flame and tobacco, followed by a report, came from the pipe, which fell from the man's hand, shattered in a hundred pieces.

The warrior cared no longer for the penalty of disobedience, but rushed up and down the streets, crying frantically for the gods to protect him.

The men crawled from their houses in all directions to see what calamity had happened.

Our warrior was unable to tell them, but all he could make them understand was that wherever the white *taye* were, fire and smoke went with them.

The king himself heard the cry and was just as eager to know the cause as the people.

When the mystery of the pipe was spoken of the king demanded that we should show him what kind of leaf it was we smoked.

We had to get rid of his importunities by saying that the fire and explosion only took place when we exerted our magic. In proof—for these people are never satisfied without proof—we filled two pipes with our best tobacco and gave one to the king, taking care there was no powder in it, while the other containing a light charge we handed to one of the soldiers who was commanded to smoke it. Curtis and I filled our pipes and lighted them.

This gave confidence to the king who followed our example. Many words of praise did he bestow on the tobacco although he every moment feared the explosion. When the pipes were nearly exhausted without any mishap, Curtis gave me a hint to pass my hand over the pipe which was being smoked by the soldier.

Scarcely had I done so when he was nearly blinded by

the burst of flame and tobacco and the smashing of the pipe.

The king continued smoking until the last vestige of tobacco was consumed and, of course, without any unpleasant consequences.

This boyish trick won for us the regard of the king, and we were told that, when our friends arrived, a grand dance and entertainment should be arranged for our amusement.

Curtis pleaded with the king for permission to go at large without a soldier keeping watch over us, and the king, so much delighted with our magic, gave consent providing we declared we would never leave his kingdom without his consent.

This we readily agreed to, for we felt certain we could obtain his permission to depart when we were ready, if only by the exercise of some of our so-called magic.

Lighting our pipes we strolled up and down the street, but for some time we failed to see any of the people. It was a custom for all to remain within the houses when the king was walking, unless special permission was granted. The next day we took advantage of the concession more fully.

We had reached the extreme limit of the village and hesitated whether to go further when a strange creature attracted our attention.

"The devil!" exclaimed Curtis, in English.

I looked, and, as I was rather near-sighted, did not notice anything very peculiar, but the moment I raised my field-glass, I, too, was ready to make the same ejaculation.

A regular, typical devil was in full view of us; horns, tail and hoofs, or, at least, we so thought.

The creature stood upright like a man, and had every appearance of being one, but for the horns and tail.

"Come!" said Curtis, as, with great strides he walked toward the creature.

The man, or devil, stood perfectly still, watching our approach.

It would not have much surprised me if he had vanished into thin air before we reached him, for he had so thoroughly a Satanic appearance that I could scarcely realize his human nature.

But he stood still as though rooted to the spot, but when we were close to him, he fell on his face and muttered some words which neither of us understood.

Curtis bade him stand up, but either he would not obey or did not understand the language, for he still remained prostrate.

I took hold of one of the horns, which I almost expected to come off, and gave the man's head a vigorous pull.

Like a flash he stood erect, with his arms folded over his breast.

The like I had never before seen. Here was something which would interest Fjord, and I quite expected when he saw this strange animal he would wish to take it home with him as a curiosity, a freak of nature.

The horned man stood a little over five feet high. On his head were two horns, very like those of a ram, and about five inches long.

They seemed to grow directly out of the skull, or, rather, they appeared to be a portion of the skull itself, the scalp was covered with a few scanty hairs round the root of the horns, the remainder being entirely smooth.

The upper part of the creatures' abdomen was covered with hair, thick and woolly, and about an inch long. The legs were entirely deficient of the hair or wool.

Another peculiarity we noticed; while the back was shaped like a man's, a thick growth of hair followed the course of the spine and grew in a straight line about two inches wide, terminating in a tuft at the bottom of the back, having all the appearance of a short tail.

A tuft of hair grew on the chin, but instead of looking like a human beard, it more nearly resembled a male goat's chin beard.

Curtis spoke in several different languages to the thing, but to all he was deaf, and we began to think he or it was a mute; when we had finished our inspection however, the strange creature gave utterance to a word the like of which we had never before heard.

I can give but a poor idea of its sound, and as for the spelling, it would tax a spelling bee to the utmost to shape any letters into a word which sounded like a prolonged guttural expletive blended with a genuine nasal snore.

I tried many experiments, and Curtis says I have succeeded pretty well. Here is my idea:

Gwock—gur-r-r—kowpff.

If any one can reduce such a sound to a word intelligible to educated people, they can address me, care of the publisher, if ever this manuscript is given to the world.

I offered the creature some beads, but although he held out his hands, he instantly withdrew them and rushed away like a frightened deer before a hound.

His speed was too great for us to attempt to follow, so we returned to our residence pondering over the mystery we had seen.

Curtis was silent for a long time, and not until we had crawled into our hole did he say anything about the monster.

"I begin to think, Theo.," he said, "that we are on the brink of a great discovery."

"I share that opinion with you," I replied.

"Fjord has the idea that somewhere in Africa we shall find that connecting-link between man and the animal which has puzzled the scientists for years."

"What a glorious discovery that would be, why all the world will honor us."

"Rather say, will call us madmen, they will laugh at our story, deny the facts we testify to, accuse us of being highly imaginative, and then, when all else fails, will declare we are infidels and bad men."

"Yes, that would have been so once, Curtis, but now men are beginning to speculate upon the origin of the soul and the genesis of this wondrous frame of things external to, and surrounding, the spirit which is the real man."

"A few will doubtless be led to investigate, but how few there are who believe that distinct species of animals are not a creation, but a growth; that the mind of man is not a special creation of a spiritual existence, but a result of a long process by which organized matter has slowly worked itself from matter into intellect."

"Do you believe, Curtis, that at some time there was a low form of animal life without intellect?"

"Undoubtedly; and I believe that both with the mental and physical organisms we shall be able to trace everything from the germ to the perfect man, and that even to-day every distinct form, every link in the chain can be found, and when discovered we shall better appreciate the greatness and grandeur of man."

"But will it not tend to so-called infidelity?"

"No, but the contrary, for it will show the greatness of the Supreme Power, which originated the germ and created the forces of nature which produce by gradual evolution the magnificently grand human soul."

"What do you think of the creature we have just seen?"

"That at present I am not able to answer, for he may be only a monstrosity, a *lusus naturæ*, but if he is a representative of others, then we have another link in our chain."

We continued our conversation until the noise of drums and other primitive musical instruments prompted us to put our heads outside the hole, and to our joy we found the commotion was caused by the arrival of Fjord, Good and Umbilla.

Two oxen were yoked together, and on their back we saw our boat carried as carefully as was ever sacred ark.

The warriors who had stayed at home gathered round the new-comers, and especially admired Captain Good and his eye-glass.

He was henceforth "Bougwan"* to them, and he laughingly told us he had borne that name on his trip to King Solomon's mines.

"Kamkivi!"† shouted the king, and the word was taken up by the hundreds of natives who had assembled.

We felt rather jealous, for no shout of welcome had been accorded us; and another reason for jealousy had we—the females turned out to welcome Bougwan and Fjord.

These were the first women we had seen, and candor compels me to confess they were far handsomer than the men.

Good was particularly favored, for one girl fairer—if it is possible to call a black girl fair—than the rest walked round him several times, examined him all over, and then felt his clothes to see if they were artificial or his

* Glass eye.
† Welcome.

natural skin. He wore a very "loud" suit of check, and the varied colors and patterns so pleased all that I was chuckling to myself at the thought that most likely the king would take a fancy to the clothes, and compel Good to strip and give them to him. No such catastrophe, however, happened at the time.

The day was far spent, so we retired through the hole, all preferring for the time to occupy the same house.

Umbilla, however, could not be persuaded to join us; he preferred a house all to himself, as he said he did not wish to presume upon the white Baas.

Curtis could not restrain himself long, so he told Fjord of the strange creature we had seen. That enterprising American at once speculated whether it would not be possible to buy, steal, or kidnap the creature, and take him to America or Europe.

CHAPTER X.
HUSBANDS IN SPITE OF OURSELVES.

The next day we received a summons from the king to attend a grand banquet which was given in our honor.

We followed our guides, and soon found ourselves squatting native fashion in the center of a great circle formed by the natives who were invited to the feast.

We were the only ones permitted to share the seats of honor with the king.

Looking round the circle we counted a hundred men, all well armed with spears and bow, but without shields. No women were present at the feast.

When we had taken our seats with the king a drum was sounded, and from the royal kraal a number of girls, ranging from about fifteen to twenty-five years of age, trooped into the circle. Each girl bore upon her head a kind of jar or vase. As they passed before the king he tapped each on the shoulder, a mark, I heard, of his approval, and they ranged themselves as a sort of inner circle.

When another signal was given the jars were lowered, and each girl singled out a man to whose lips she placed the edge of the jar.

A wonderfully pretty girl was my attendant, and however nauseous the liquid might be, it would be difficult to refuse to take it from so sweet a bearer.

I, at first, took but a sip of the beverage, but it was so good that I took a deeper draught.

It was of the consistency of thin honey, and tasted like a compound of honey and almonds.

Not knowing whether that was to be our only refreshment, I watched the king and followed his example. When he had taken a drink he pushed the jar away, and the girl raising it to her head started back to the kraal with it. There was no need to give the signal to the others, for all the girls immediately followed the attendant on royalty.

Another drum sounded, and the girls reappeared carrying bowls, made apparently from well-burnt clay.

In these primitive basins was some soup, or to be more exact, stew. No spoon or fork was brought with the basins, so we watched the king. The girls knelt in front of us and held the bowls to our lips. Following our royal host's example we drank the soup, and took out the pieces of meat with our fingers.

The meat was tender and nice, the king informing us that it was the flesh of the mehedehet, a species of antelope with rough, brown hair like the Sauber deer of India, and standing about thirteen hands high; the horns are long and twisted, and used as musical instruments by the natives.

THE HORN OF THE MEHEDEHET AS A MUSICAL INSTRUMENT.

After the soup or stew, we were treated to various kinds of fruits and cooked vegetables, more particularly yams.

We had grown a little bolder and more accustomed to the scene, so I ventured to look round and examine the faces and figures of the savages, hoping to notice some of the peculiarities for which we were in search.

The unmarried girls wore anklets, bracelets and armlets made of bright metal, a string of beads round the neck, and another round the loins. The married women had in many cases tattoo marks over their bodies, made generally by their husbands as a proof of ownership.

Women are treated by these people, who call themselves Kasheebars, after their king, as slaves, doing most of the menial work and a great deal of the hardest work of the tribe.

While we were enjoying our fruit, the king graciously declared we were now admitted to all the rights of citizenship, and warned us that once having been received into the tribe of Kasheebars, any attempt to leave or run away, as he termed it, would be punished by death.

The girls who waited on us were given us as wives, and when I commenced to make excuse, I was instantly told I must accept the wife or die.

Again I remonstrated, but the king ordered the drum to be beaten, and a number of old hags whose ages it would be extremely difficult to ascertain, came upon the scene.

Their bodies were nude, but upon their heads they wore chaplets of various dried roots, while some had lizards, crocodiles' teeth, lions' claws, or small tortoise-shells arranged as fantastic headgear.

Curtis, who had become Shakespeare mad, mumbled in an undertone:

"What are these, so withered and so wild, that look not like the inhabitants o' the earth, and yet are on't."

"What say the gods of those who refuse to take to themselves wives of the Kasheebars?" asked the king.

The old witches glowered on us, set up a piercing shriek, and then in a sepulchral voice replied:

"They die."

Good, who had been appropriated by a pretty-looking young girl, remembered the devotion of Foulata, and whispered to me:

"Don't be a fool, Theo., take the girl or we shall get into trouble."

I confess I loathed the idea, but "when in Rome act as Romans," was a good old adage, so for the present I withdrew my opposition and accepted as a present my cup-bearer, whose portrait I drew at the time.

PORTRAIT OF QUEGGA, MY WIFE.

When I presented her with a string of beads, before the king, I thought all the girls round the circle would have torn her to pieces, they were so jealous. The king told me that each of the great braves invited to the feast received the present of a new wife. No one was allowed to choose for himself, and on no other occasion but a feast could a girl be appropriated as the domestic slave or wife of a warrior. Curtis asked innocently whether in case of a second feast another wife would be given, and was quickly answered to our dismay, that such was the custom, and if we continued to please the king with our magic, the feasts should be often.

Umbilla was the most pleased with the prospect, as he was a regular old polygamist, and would have been a credit to the Mormons.

I cannot say I thought much of the wife set apart for him, seeing that she wore a great ring in her nose, and had a wooden skewer pushed through her lip similar to the one worn by old Kasheebar.

The banquet was over. The men rose from their uncomfortable position, and massed themselves at the back of the king and our party, who were the special guests.

A procession of boys passed in front of us. Where they came from I had not noticed. Each boy was beating a drum made similar to that used by the Obodos—a trunk of a tree hollowed out, and over one end the skin of an elephant's ear tightly stretched.

When the music—if so divine a word can be employed to describe the wild, horrible sound of the drums—ceased, the drummers took their places to the right of the king's party.

"Look! great Jupiter!" cried Fjord, as he pointed to the extreme end of the village.

"The Vantackas!" shouted the people in great excitement.

As we looked we saw a score or so of the horned creatures approaching.

They were dressed now with a leopard skin hanging from a strap which passed over the right shoulder and under the left. They were each armed with shield and spear.

As they drew near a cold wave seemed to pass over me, for more unearthly looking creatures I had never seen.

Good wiped his eyeglass, and then stared with all the force of his natural eyes, aided by the pane of glass.

As for Fjord he acted like a maniac; at one moment he was feeling for his revolver, and another would start forward as though he would join the Vantackas, as these creatures were evidently called.

Curtis appealed to the king for an explanation, and he was proud when the request was made, for at last he had something to show us which he rightly imagined was new to us.

His answer was very verbose, but the substance was as follows:

The original inhabitants of the mountain-land now occupied by the Kasheebars, were all Vantackas.

These men were half animal, inasmuch as they had horns, which sprouted from their heads in childhood, growing gradually until the man reached the age of fifty, when the horns fell off and the man died.

At one time, said the king, all Vantackas had long tails; but when the Kasheebars took the country, and put to death all who would not submit to be the slaves of the new people, those who accepted the new order of things formed the habit of sitting down, whereby the tails got rubbed off.

The Vantackas only had the root of a tail left, measuring never more than four inches.

The race seemed likely to die out, because there were no Vantacka women, and the king thought it strange, that although each male had been given a dozen wives, the children were all born without tails, and the horns were very small.

"How many Vantackas are there?" asked Fjord.

"Only ten now," was the answer, which surprised us, as quite twenty were now standing, resting on their spears, awaiting the king's order.

He noticed our surprise, and so told us that, for fear some people should ever leave his country, it would not do for them to say there were only so few Vantackas, so the children born to these strange creatures were trained to all their fathers' ways, and when they appeared in public, had horns fastened to their heads.

All the Vantackas had now long tails, but these were merely cows' tails tied on to the natural stump, where it was long enough, and in other cases fastened by a strap round the loins.

The order was given and the Satanic-looking creatures commenced a war dance so diabolical that it was well in keeping with their appearance.

When the excitement was at its highest pitch these peculiar creatures began pricking each other with their spears.

As the blood trickled down their sides the excitement grew more intense, and the Kasheebars applauded vigorously.

The drums beat furiously and pandemonium seemed to have broken loose.

When the order was given for the dance to cease every Vantacka, real and artificial, was covered with blood.

The creatures, it was hard to call them men, stood in line, and a horrible spectacle was presented. Each Vantacka rubbed his hand over the blood-stained body of his neighbor, and then licked the blood therefrom.

When this sickening scene was over, a live ox was brought on the square.

THE VANTACKA WAR DANCE.

A Vantacka, who had a hunting-knife, which made me dasire to possess it, stepped forward, and with amazing rapidity killed and skinned the ox, draining the blood into a stone jar, from which each Vantacka took a good drink. The body was then cut up, the choice part being given

VANTACKA HUNTING-KNIFE.

to the old witches, and the remainder, including entrails, being divided among the savage Vantackas, who ate it raw and with the warm life-blood still in it.

I felt sick at the horrible sight, and Curtis rose up and turned his back on the inhuman monsters.

The entertainment was over, and the command was given for all to return to their homes.

While the Vantackas and guests were leaving, our party was refreshed by another drink of the almond honey, which the girls again brought and offered us. The drink was delicious, and if intoxicating, it was so pleasant to the taste that it would be hard work to resist its power.

Quegga danced round me with childish glee when the time came for us to go to our residence.

Poor girl, so easily pleased and so delighted, what would be her fate when we had left the Kashcebar country, for we intended our sojourn to be a short one. I had but one hope, selfish it may be, but when was there a time that scientists, explorers, and students were unselfish?

As I look back on my life, how many acts which I committed in the search for knowledge appear now to have been cruel and needless. Yet there was nothing at which I would have hesitated, when the attainment of knowledge was the goal. Like Parrhasius, when torturing the poor old slave to death, that he might the better paint the death dew on the brow of Prometheus, so I felt, that rather than give up my search for the mysterious unknown,

> "Though its crown of flame
> Consumed my brain to ashes as it won me,
> By all the fiery stars, I'd pluck it on me!
> Ah, though it bid me rifle
> My heart's last fount for its insatiate thirst,
> Though every life-strung nerve be maddened first,
> All, I would do it all,
> Sooner than die, like a dull worm, to rot,
> Thrust foully in the earth to be forgot."

And it was this spirit which caused me all through life to accept conditions and live in a way my very soul loathed, all for the sake of that knowledge for which my soul thirsted.

CHAPTER XI.
THE KASHEEBAR HONEYMOON.

WHEN we returned to the houses which had been confiscated by the king and presented to us, whereby he showed how well he understood the custom and practice of monarchs in more civilized countries, I found myself left alone with Quegga.

I could not help thinking that there was something in the female nature more magnetic than mere friendship.

Curtis, Fjord, Good and myself made a most harmonious family. We never quarreled, never had high words, but on all occasions while holding our own opinions perhaps most tenaciously, deferred to the others for the sake of harmony.

Though four houses had been given us, we had declared our positive intention of all sharing the one domicile, that was but a few short hours ago, now without a word of explanation, each of us with the black wife we had just received as a present, chose a separate residence. We were no longer one family, but four.

What had caused the difference? It was not love, for it could not be expected that either of us would or could love the girls whose habits and nature were so opposite to ours.

It was the magnetism of woman.

Wherever I have gone, I have found the same thing. Black and white, savage and civilized, pagan and Christian, all feel the attraction toward the female sex.

When love, pure natural love, is called into play, then the attraction and influence of woman softens and ennobles man more than anything else in creation.

The savage is tamed, the brute becomes gentle, the scoffer grows reverent when touched by the magic wand of the little god of love.

As I crawled into the house after Quegga, for it is the custom of the Kasheebars for the bride or wife to enter first, I could not help smiling to think how thoroughly we were left alone, and I began to speculate on the future, wondering whether my comrades would be ready to continue our researches, or whether they intended devoting themselves to domestic life among the savages.

I felt alone in a greater sense, for I could only understand a very few words of the Kasheebar language, and now I was tied to a wife with whom I could not converse.

Reader, try and realize my position—a householder, yet living on the food supplied by others, a married man, but unable to converse with his wife.

The situation was laughable.

From the time we had left the king, neither Quegga nor I had spoken a word.

We heard Good talking most affectionately to his bride—trust a sailor for accepting the inevitable with good grace.

Fjord seemed to enjoy his *tete-a-tete* with the Venus-shaped beauty by his side.

And even stolid "John Bull" Curtis made the best of the occasion, and was talking quite gayly.

Only I and Quegga were silent. I found the reason later.

I did not understand the Kasheebar language and, therefore, thought it no use to talk to her, for she would not be able to understand me; while Quegga only obeyed the rules of her tribe in not being the first to speak.

We had been in the house for some little time, sitting on the ground quite sulkily, when, to break the monotony, for I was thoroughly tired of it, and felt keenly my lonely position, I started singing, in a low murmur, a few bars of "Home, Sweet Home."

The effect was magical, for Quegga came over to me, seated herself by my side, and, putting her arms round my neck, said:

"Sing again."

She spoke, not in the Kasheebar language, but in the Abyssinian, which I thoroughly understood.

Our tongues were loosened, and she told me she had been waiting an opportunity to speak to me, but I had been so silent that she was afraid of me, and, therefore, rigidly obeyed the custom of the country.

I learned that the king had specially chosen her for my bride, because she could talk several tongues, and then, with a coquettish toss of the head, she said:

"And because——"

"Well, Quegga, because what?"

"I was pretty," was her answer.

I asked her what she thought of us, and so loyal was she, that I could only get from her, at the time, the king's opinion.

Wondering how she knew so much of the monarch, I questioned her, and was told that when a little child, she was stolen by the Kasheebars from a tribe of Abyssinians which had wandered through that country, that she was presented to the king, and was destined to be one of his wives; but when she grew up one of the witches forbade it, and declared she must be the wife of a great magician, and that, when she became such, the king would have great fortune and success.

"So, when the king saw your magic," she continued, I was told I was to be yours, and I was so glad."

"Why?"

"Because I liked you as soon as I saw you," she answered.

So it was evidently a case of love at first sight with Quegga.

Woman-like she had formed opinions of each of us before ever being in our company, but also with feminine tact she gave her ideas as though they came from the king.

"Incubu," she said, "was brave, and could fight, but would not love."

"Bougwan," meaning Good, was no use as a husband, but would make a nice lover; while Fjord she looked upon as cruel and cold.

I almost trembled to ask what she thought of me, but my bashfulness gave way, and I asked her the king's opinion.

"Thou art great and mighty, slow to anger, but of much wrath," was her answer, which was so idiomatic that I scarcely understood her.

Growing bolder, I said:

"And now, Quegga, what is thy opinion?"

She hesitated only for a moment, for there is none of that false timidity and bashfulness among these children of nature which prevails in so-called civilized society.

She rose to her feet, and I followed her example.

Placing her hands on my shoulders and looking up into my face, she sang—or perhaps I should be more musically accurate if I said she gave a recitative, which ran somewhat as follows:

> "I loved thee beloved because thou wast fair;
> Thine eyes were the eyes of truth and of love;
> They flashed like the stars and beamed softly on me;
> Wisdom and prudence, justice and love,
> Belonged to thee, my own, my sweet, for thou art fair;
> The favored of the gods, the mighty magician,
> The wanderer from the lands beyond the big water,
> Thou hast found thy home in my bosom at last.
> Come! nestle down with me, place thy head on my breast;
> No care shall come near thee, no trouble oppress,
> For I am thine, and thine only, through ages to come."

Quegga's eyes flashed brightly as she chanted these lines, her bosom heaved with emotion, and though I knew that every word was extemporized, there was a poetry and ryhthm pleasing to the ear.

What could I do but clasp her to my heart and accept the devotion she so lavishly offered? I am old, it may be, but my spirit is young; and I pray that when I am too old to love and feel its pleasures, when my blood is chilled and I fail to experience the genial glow of the noble passion, when my heart no longer throbs at the approach of the fair, I pray I may pass away to the land beyond, where true love is perpetual and where old age never chills the blood. What is life without love? Tell me what the earth would be without the sun, and you have my answer.

I learned that it was the custom, which all must obey, that the newly married must remain in their dwelling for three days, not going outside to be seen by any one.

Quegga hoped I would obey the law and spend the three days in solitude with her.

It was solitude and darkness, for the only light was that which came through the hole or doorway.

The day following the feast and our nuptials, food of the daintiest was brought and placed outside the house within easy reach, the bearers being young maidens not yet of a marriageable age.

As they placed the food by the door they chanted a kind of epithalamium, which Quegga translated for me, and whose words re-translated into English would read somewhat as follows:

"Greet the happy hour
In pleasant bower
When gentle love is born;
No happier hour,
Kasheebar power,
Could on great man bestow.
Happy, happy man,
Happy, happy maid,
No hour in life can equal this."

The custom was a pleasing one, and Quegga said that no blessing or success ever attended any, unless the maidens chanted this song during the honeymoon.

I have not given any description of the interior of the house which I now shared with Quegga.

The shape was that of a circular tent, the side sloping nearly to the ground, so that it was impossible to stand upright except in the center.

There was no flooring, properly so called, but the ground, which was of a red clayey nature, had been hardened before the house was built by means of great fires being made on its surface.

This had the effect of burning the clay and rendering it hard. The cracks were filled with a waterproof preparation made similar to that used on the grass thatch. Skins of lions and tigers were used in place of mattress, and very comfortable beds they made.

The post of honor, where the husband sleeps—for man and wife among the Kasheebars occupy separate rugs—is just opposite the door on the further side of the house.

The wife lies down just inside the door, on the skins thrown on the floor. No one can enter without waking her, for it would be impossible to crawl over her without contact, therefore she protects her husband.

When I told Quegga that in the country beyond the big water this was reversed, and man protected the woman, she seemed astonished, and could not understand it.

"No Kasheebar," she said, "would ever hurt a woman. They could not harm her, and would not think of doing so. If an enemy entered a house, it would be to injure the man; the woman is always safe."

"But suppose any wished to harm me," I said, "and in trying to get at me woke you, would he not silence you or kill you?"

"No, why should he? Was not his mother a woman, then how could he hurt a woman?" And then Quegga looked at me for a moment in the dim light, and asked, "Do the white men in the country beyond the big water ever kill or hurt women?"

"Alas, Quegga, yes, and if a man was very anxious to kill me, he might not hesitate to get rid of you first."

"Not in Kasheebar," she said quickly. "Oh, I should not like to live in a country where a woman is not safe."

I grew curious, and questioned Quegga about woman's position in Kasheebar, and she told me that a man was always safe while his wife was with him, and that a woman could go anywhere safely; she might carry all her husband's possessions, his beads and skins, everything which he had better than his neighbor, and no one would take them from her.

When I hinted at the terrible outrages sometimes committed on women in civilized lands, she would not believe me, and kept asking, "Were not their mothers women?"

In Kasheebar a girl is safe from molestation. She is given, between the ages of sixteen and twenty-five, to some man as a wife, but although she has but little choice, she can refuse to be given to a man she dislikes. When married, she becomes the slave of her husband, doing everything for him which she is capable of performing, but she is perfectly free from physical violence or injury.

A woman is sacred in Kasheebar, and a man who would lay his hand upon her or attempt to injure her fair name would be at once put to death.

I asked Quegga about the Vantackas, but she shuddered at the very thought of them, and I changed the subject for a time, but later I could not resist asking how it was that any Kasheebar girl would consent to be the wife of a Vantacka.

For some time she remained silent, as though wondering how to frame her answer, and then told me that the women given to the Vantackas very seldom went willingly, they were made to go. If a girl refused the man who had been chosen for her, she was kept in retirement for three months; at the expiration of that time another man was pointed out; if she refused him—of course she only could judge by appearance, as the girls were not allowed to converse with the men until they were married—another season of retirement took place. They could remain unmarried until they were twenty-five, then they were the absolute property of the king, and he gave them to any one he pleased, whether it was to a Vantacka or a Zemeraffe. When a man dies, his widow is given by the king to any one, or she can retire from all publicity as a servant of the king.

Such were the peculiar marriage laws of the Kasheebars. I asked Quegga why a widow could not be allowed a choice, and she answered, that as she had exercised that right once, it was not fair she should do so again, as it would destroy the chances of the girls. I also learned that every one must be married by the time they are twenty-five.

The king had over a hundred wives.

Then Quegga, although only just married, told me that if I pleased the king I should have all the prettiest girls for wives, as not one would ever refuse me.

"But what would you say to that, Quegga?" I asked.

"What could I say but that I should be pleased."

"Pleased!" I exclaimed.

"Yes; why should I not be so?"

I told this strange young woman that where I came from a man was only allowed to have one wife, whereupon Quegga declared she was glad she did not live there, for it must be awful for a woman, and bad for the men.

It was a strange idea, but I found a similar objection to monogamy among the women of nearly all polygamous tribes.

Quegga had mentioned the word *Zemeraffe*, and I asked her what it meant.

"Oh, I cannot tell; I am afraid to describe it. I will show you when I can go out."

Quegga was so thoroughly excited and, it appeared to me, frightened that I forbore to question her further.

When the three days of our enforced retirement had passed, I was glad to again breathe a little purer air than that of the house.

CHAPTER XII.
THE STRANGE ROCK.

As we had all been married at the same time, our honeymoon expired also on the same morning. While I was crawling out of the hole, I laughed heartily at the sight presented to my gaze as I turned my head. The next house was occupied by Good, and I saw him just in the act of emerging, with his eye-glass fixed as usual, but with a collar far from aristocratic looking. Having had no light, he could not perceive how dirty his celluloid collar and cuffs were.

A moment later, and we were joined by Fjord and Curtis, both looking extremely seedy and the worse for the suffocating atmosphere of their respective houses.

It was nearly an hour later before Umbilla left his charmer, and when he did so, though how he managed to get out of his residence with all his war implements on, I know not; but there he was, in full war paint. I was so pleased with his appearance that I asked him to stand still while I sketched his portrait.

His dark-brown skin had been rubbed down, and presented a highly polished appearance.

The feathers stuck in the little tuft of hair showed plainly that feminine fingers had been at work.

On the whole, he was a credit to our party, and "took the shine" out of us, at least so Fjord declared, and he is a great authority on savage costumes.

We related our experiences, and I proposed we should seize the opportunity and explore the part inhabited by the Vautackas.

"No," decisively answered Good. "You can do what you like, but I am not going to neglect the temporary Mrs. Good on the first day out."

"Then let us each get our charmers and we will take a walk; they will be able to show us the way about," suggested Fjord.

"Have you heard anything about the Zemeraffes?" I asked Curtis.

"No, what are they?"

"I don't know; ask the lady."

"What did you call them?" asked Fjord.

"Zemeraffes! What can they be?"

"Confound this language," ejaculated Fjord, "it is such a plaguy mixture, or I should say the word had something to do with the Hebrew *Zemer* and *raffe* a long neck. I have it. By zounds, Zemeraffe will be the long-necked animals we call giraffes."

UMBILLA IN WAR PAINT.

"Not at all," I answered, "they are men or monsters."

"Who told you so?"

"Quegga."

"Oho! A woman has loosened your tongue, has she?"

laughed Fjord. "Here you have been professing not to understand the language——"

"Neither do I?"

"Then how the dickens could you understand Quegga?"

"She spoke Abyssinian," I answered quietly, and turned the laugh on Fjord.

When we could induce the women to emerge from the houses, and summon up courage to face us without blushing—if black girls can blush—we at once suggested that we ramble about and see the neighboring country.

Here another custom was made known to us, the newly married women could go with their husbands anywhere they pleased for ten days after the honeymoon, after that they must not leave home without special permission of the king, except to perform such things as absolutely required their absence for a short time.

We had ten days therefore for exploration with native guides.

"Where are the Zemeraffes?" asked Fjord; but the moment the word was mentioned, the women set up such a scream that we were more perplexed than ever.

We separated, each couple going in a different direction in search of novelties.

Quegga led me toward a high rock on the opposite side of the village to the one by which we entered.

When we were free from the houses, she put her arms round me, and asked:

"Would you like to see the Zemeraffes?"

"I should."

"Come then, I will take you."

I knew she was only doing it to please me, that her mind revolted at the thought, and from the trembling of her body, I was certain she was terribly afraid, yet I was so selfish that I pretended not to notice her emotion.

She clung closely to me, and begged of me not to leave her.

The Zemeraffes were horrible, and if she could take me there, without seeing them herself, she would be glad.

All the way toward the hill, she told me stories of the Vantackas and the Kasheebars, but said little about the creatures we were about to visit.

"Once," she said, "a girl took her husband to see them, and"—here she put her hand over her eyes as

though to press out the very thought of these creatures—
"when she became a mother, the child was a Zemeraffe.
The king was pleased, and took her away from her husband and gave her and the child to a Zemeraffe for wife.

"I would rather die," she said, after an interval, "than be the wife of such or even a Vantacka."

"Well, you never will be," I said, reassuringly.

"I hope not, but if you left me, and went to another country beyond the hills, or over the big water, then the king would make me become the wife of a Zemeraffe."

"I will never leave you, but, when I go away, I will take you with me."

It was a rash promise, but, at the time, I meant it.

After walking about two miles, over a very rough road, poor Quegga's feet being cut with the stones often, we reached a perpendicular rock, with a side as smooth as though it had been polished.

On it there were distinct traces of carvings.

Inducing Quegga to sit down and rest, I took a nearer inspection of the strange rock.

The center was occupied by a very good representation of a monster eye. It seemed, from where I stood, to measure at least ten feet across the iris. It was skillfully carved and was exact in every detail.

The eyelashes and eyebrows were as perfect as anything I had ever seen come from the chisel of sculptor.

On closer examination, I noticed above the eye, and stretching upward a hundred or more feet, lines radiating from the center of the eye and reaching every part of the stone.

Immediately beneath the eye was a *bas-relief* on which various designs of houses, pyramids and columns were carved; these occupied the center of the tablet, while on either side were chiselings representing a cornfield, a man plowing, and a river on which was a boat.

This *bas-relief* measured quite fifty feet long, the rock's polished surface being nearly three times as much.

A little below the level of the monster eye, and on either side of the *bas-relief* a figure stood out prominently.

On one side it represented a man, with a long trumpet in his right hand, in the act of raising it to his mouth.

The figure had a pure, classic face, and was more nearly allied to the white than to the black races of mankind; the only peculiarity about the figure was a monster pair of wings which, rising slightly above his head, yet touched the ground.

On the other side was the gigantic figure of a Vantacka. The face was hideous; the eyes bulged from their sockets; horns, long and straight, grew from the head, and in the monster's arms was a poisonous snake, with the body of a python but the head of an adder.

I sat down by the side of Quegga, and asked her who had cut the figures.

She did not know, but said she had heard the witches say it was done by a race of men who came here ten thousand years before.

It certainly bore marks of great antiquity, and I tried to unravel its meaning.

As I sat there I looked at the rock, but Quegga persistently turned her head away.

Was she tired of looking at what was to her but a piece of stone?

I spoke to her, but she turned her back, and her body trembled with intense fear.

She told me at last that about two hours after noon, as I should judge the time, the eye on the rock suddenly received sight, and glared fiercely at any who dared to look at it.

As noon had passed for over an hour, I determined to wait and prove to the poor girl that the story was but a legend.

"Not so, for I have known people who have seen it," she replied.

It appeared to me that the carvings were symbolic of the world and its Creator. The *bas-relief*, with its husbandmen and cornfield, its rivers and boats, and its cities and monuments, represented the earth; the eye above it, the Supreme Deity, with the flashes of divine light radiating above as well as below; the two colossi seemed to me representative of the spirits of evil and of good; the Vantacka typifying evil and death, while the man with wings was the personification of the angels, or good.

Having solved this to my own satisfaction, I leaned my head on my hands, pondering over such an elaborate piece of sculpture in so strange a place, and wondering who could have been its designer.

I had remained there, perhaps, half an hour or so, when I felt a strange influence pass over me.

I had a desire, a longing, to look up at the eye.

I have often tried experiments with myself, seeing whether I could successfully curb my curiosity, my desire or gratification.

When a great longing took possession of me, I would deny myself, as a test of my power of self-control.

I now wanted to look up at the rock, but, inwardly, I resolved not to do so for ten minutes.

The first sixty seconds passed away easily, though the time seemed long.

The next minute followed it into the eternity of the past; another was joined to its fellows, and then I experienced a very strange sensation.

It seemed that a shaft of fire was directed from the rock straight into the center of my brain.

It burned its way through my head-covering, the hair felt scorched, and my brain seemed to sizzle under the penetrating flame.

I could endure it no longer. All my strength of will was gone.

I had to admit myself conquered by curiosity. The strange feeling, of course, was but a strong imagination, based upon the story told by Quegga.

Was it imagination or reality? Could it be fancy which burned into my brain?

I would not look up yet. I raised my hand above my head, and on the surface of my hand I felt the hot, scorching flame.

I raised my eyes, and saw——

Great Heaven! Never before or since have I seen such a sight.

From the center of the great eye there appeared to come a sharp, red flame, piercing right into my very soul.

I moved my head, and as I looked at the angel, or winged man, I saw the piercing look of two blazing eyes.

I averted my gaze, though the flames of fire seemed to

follow me, and then I encountered the most horrible gaze of the Vantacka.

What rendered this more revolting and repulsive was the fact that the great adder seemed alive, for it had great, staring, green eyes, which sparkled and flashed as I looked upon it.

The heat grew more intense. I felt my skin blistering from its effects, and I fell to the ground terror-stricken.

Where was Quegga?

I raised my head, not daring to look toward the rock, and saw her figure a little distance down the bank, her head buried in her hands.

I laughed hysterically at my fright; more than ever I tried to convince myself that it was all a freak of the imagination, that my mind had got worked up to a high pitch of nervous exaltation by the stories told of the Vantackas and Zemeraffes, which were enough to make any one excited, and then my three days' solitude with Quegga, and I fear the too frequent use of two great stimulants: almond honey as given me by Quegga, and the wonderful leaves I had obtained from Fjord.

Yes, that accounted for it all, I thought, as I lay there. I was delirious, nothing more.

But why this intense burning? Even the grass was scorched up all round the rock. My back, which was toward the carvings, was getting intensely hot.

I remembered I had a lot of powder and cartridges in a pouch on my back, what if that got on fire!

I laughed at myself, and then cursed my folly. I would look up and brave the sight.

I rubbed my eyes, and leaped to my feet, but as I looked at the rock, I saw again the fiery eye with its blood-red flame, the milder eyes of the angel, and the hideous, piercing gaze of the Vantacka and the snake.

I could stand it no longer.

With a piercing shriek which Quegga told me she thought must have been heard by the Kasheebars, I fell to the ground utterly overcome.

When I regained consciousness Quegga was by my side, bathing my temples with water which she had fetched in my hat, and then when she saw my recovery, she sat down and drew my head upon her bosom, chanting at the same time some sweet love melodies.

I fell asleep under the influence, and must have slept for over two hours, but the brave, devoted girl had not moved, she still held my head close to her, though I knew her body must have been stiff with the cramped position.

"The rock!" I gasped rather than spoke.

"It is all right now," she answered, "the time has passed."

I raised my head and looked at the polished surface. It had returned to its normal condition, and no appearance of light or gleam of intelligence was to be found here.

I had received a great scare, and was nothing loath to return home, leaving our visit to the Zemeraffes for another day.

CHAPTER XIII.
THE ZEMERAFFES.

For the first time I shunned the company of Curtis and the others.

I seemed to slink, rather than walk, back to our house, and once inside I threw myself down on the rugs, thoroughly prostrated.

In all my wanderings I had never seen anything like the rock.

When I dared, for I confess my cowardice and fear, I asked Quegga to tell me all about it.

She knew but little, for everybody was afraid to speak of it. All she could tell me was that every day, about that time of the sun's course, the eyes flashed forth fire, and had been known to kill many.

The eye guarded the place where the Zemeraffes resided, and as no one could reach their abode without passing the magic rock, but few ever ventured.

"Was there no other way?" I asked.

"No. Every one who visits these strange people must pass the rock, but," she added, "if they got past before two o'clock they were safe."

I asked Quegga as a favor not to say where we had been, for I knew my comrades would want to go, and I confess I was too much afraid to try the experiment again just yet.

All the next day I remained in the house.

My blood was at fever heat, and I began to think I was in for a spell of sickness.

I took a good, stiff dose of quinine, and ate some half dozen of Fjord's magic leaves, and I felt more comfortable.

Quegga, brave girl, was devotion itself.

I could not help comparing her to Rapa, and as I thought of her who had died for me, and then looked at the dusky form of Quegga, who sat on the floor holding my hand in hers, I felt near loving her.

And why not?

Why should not the white love the colored?

My soul revolted at the thought, and yet I had seen greater devotion, more genuine love shown by naked negresses than was customary in so-called civilized society.

Quegga! my brave girl, who would have endured torture for me, would have willingly given her life, if it would have added to my comfort.

Quegga and Rapa! Two barbarians, as we say in our manner of talking of those who were born under the tropic sun of Africa or the South Sea Islands, yet whether barbarians or civilized, let my pen testify to their purity, their goodness, and their devotion.

Never from either did I hear a word save of love, never had either an aspiration, or hope, or thought but for me and for my happiness.

True, neither wore clothes; both had skins dark and, may be, coarse; but within their bodies dwelt souls as pure and good, as unsullied and white, as any which ever left the Great Master's creative hand.

Yet Quegga had been reared amid scenes of savagery, for the Kasheebars, as I had every opportunity of learning, were a most barbarous people, only one degree removed from cannibalism and the brute kingdom.

Early on the next morning Quegga asked me if I was ready to visit the Zemeraffes.

I hastily prepared my toilet, partook of the breakfast which Quegga had prepared for me, and started out.

We reached the mysterious rock, and such was the magnetic influence it possessed that I had great difficulty in passing. I had a strong desire to again watch its strange manifestation of intelligence.

We began to climb the side of the hill, and my guide left marks all along the track with the blood which flowed from her feet, cut with the jagged stones. She did not appear to mind it, or even to feel the pain.

When we had ascended to about the level of the Great Eye we rested, and I took advantage of the great elevation to look over the surrounding country.

I wondered how it was that the marvelous eye was not seen from the village.

That was now accounted for by the fact that the rock stood really in a narrow pass, so that the light from the eyes could only be carried a short distance to the hills beyond, which formed a natural wall between the group of sculpture and the Kasheebar kraals.

"Come," said Quegga, rising to her feet, ready to continue the journey.

We climbed still higher, and then found ourselves standing on the side of a natural basin with a depth of two or three hundred feet.

The basin was circular, the natural walls or sides being so narrow that in many places it would have been impossible to walk round.

I looked in astonishment at Quegga, and she smiled as she pointed to the bottom of the basin, and said, "They live down there."

"How do you get down?"

"There are steps," was her reply.

She started first, and I expected every minute to see her fall headlong to the bottom, more especially when I found that the steps had only been made by the gradual wearing away of the rock by repeated climbings.

I was always a good hand at ascending or descending difficult places, and had been called the man-monkey by some tribes, but my skill was taxed to the utmost in my descent of that almost perpendicular rock.

Quegga went forward, sure-footed, and with as much ease as if she were walking along a good road.

Every few yards, fortunately, a tree was growing near the steps, and this assisted us greatly, breaking our journey and resting the fingers, which got stiff by the continual grip of the imperfectly formed steps.

When we had got about half way down, my foot slipped and I fell.

Quegga was resting on a tree twenty yards lower down.

Her love-lit eyes were ever on me, and, as she saw me slip, instead of fainting or screaming, she held firmly with her left hand to the tree and caught me by the arm as I fell past her.

The jerk was enough almost to tear my arm from the shoulder socket, but however severe the wrench, it was better than losing my life, which I should have done had not Quegga caught me.

I saw the blood ooze from the fingers which grasped the tree in a grip of iron, and knew that she had endangered her own life in saving mine.

Brave girl, noble, courageous woman, the world shall know how much I honor thee and thy memory.

After resting awhile longer we continued the descent, landing at the bottom in safety.

My arm pained me, but when I saw the swollen hands and strained muscles of Quegga's arms, I felt my trouble was unworthy of mention.

When we looked round no sight of habitation could be found.

Quegga told me the Zemeraffes lived in caves.

We walked round the sides of the basin, and saw several holes, which were evidently the dwelling-places of these creatures, about whom there was so much mystery, and a silence so great that no one, not even my devoted guide, would describe them or their peculiarity.

I suggested that we sit down and wait for some to come out of the caves.

This pleased Quegga, for I could easily see she did not like the idea of crawling into the caves.

We had not waited long before a woman with wild countenance and disheveled hair crawled out of one of the caves.

Her hair had grown very long and hung about in wild disorder.

She was perfectly naked, and so filthy that the very sight of her long unwashed body made me turn sick.

Quegga knew her. She was a Kasheebar who had refused all the men to whom she had been given, and at last for her contumacy the king had given her to a Zemeraffe for wife.

Quegga called to her, and a ray of reason illumined her

ace for a moment, and then it was gone, leaving only a
reature lower than the brutes.

It was horrible, and more so if it was true that three
ears ago she was one of the brightest of Kasheebar
omen, who so prided herself on her good looks and in-
elligence that none but a noble of the tribe was good
nough for her.

Quegga informed me that no woman who had reached
wenty-five and died unmarried could enter the land of
appiness which others of the tribe entered after death.

It was considered that an unmarried woman was a
onster, inasmuch as she did not fulfill the object of her
reation; hence the law which consigned women to a
orced marriage, if their consent could not be obtained.

The woman looked at Quegga, and made some inar-
iculate sound which neither of us could understand.

"And I should have just such a fate if you leave me."

"But I will never leave thee," I said, and I saw the
ears of gratitude well up into her eyes.

The wife of the Zemeraffe set up a howl or shriek and
an across the inclosure.

"He comes," whispered Quegga, nestling so close to
e that she almost pushed me off the stone on which I
as sitting.

A moment later a creature emerged from the hole or
ave.

How can I describe him?

To all appearance he was headless. The shoulders
eemed to be crowned with merely a stump.

The chest and stomach were covered with thick hair,
e foreparts of his legs and thighs were bare, but on the
side and evidently the back, thick hair was growing.

The creature's arms were long and thin, and looked as
ough composed of merely bone and skin. No muscle
as perceptible.

The arms were covered with short, thick hair; the
ands or claws, for they appeared more like the claws of
bird than the hands of a man, were bare, showing dark
rown skin.

The creature seemed oblivious of our presence for a
inute or so, and then suddenly raising his arm above
is shoulder, I saw a face half human, half monkey.

Its eyes glared at me from under the shoulder.

I shuddered at the sight, and Quegga screamed with fear.

Hearing the noise, the strange creature shot up its head above the shoulders, and I then perceived the peculiarity of its formation.

The neck was about sixteen or eighteen inches long, and was very small.

The head being heavy sank over the back, and allowed the forehead to rest upon the shoulder blade.

This peculiar way of carrying the head was apparently the easiest.

Whether the carrying of a head eighteen inches above the shoulders on a long thin neck, or the seeming carrying it under his arm was the most horrible, I know not.

I was transfixed with astonishment, and stared at the Zemeraffe with quite as steady a look as that which he bent on me.

After a moment's examination, he uttered a most horrible shout, which echoed round the inclosure, and made a noise almost like thunder.

Instantly every hole round the place seemed alive, heads protruded from some, and shoulders from others.

I don't think I exaggerate when I record it as a fact that thirty Zemeraffes were dancing around Quegga and me in a few minutes.

Some were old, and covered with hair almost white, others were still in their boyhood's years.

Women appeared, some carrying babies, and in most instances the infants possessed the same hideous peculiarity.

Were they human, or only animal?

Even while the thought crossed my mind I wondered where the line could be drawn which divides the brute from man.

Could it be at the dawn of reason?

No, for I have seen creatures in the shape of men who possessed not the slightest reasoning power, and I have known too many instances of intelligence in animals, to doubt their possession of the great faculty of thought.

Once when traveling over the ice and snow in Greenland, I had with me an Esquimau dog.

I lost my way amid the driving snow. To stay until the storm was over meant most probably death, but to move in either direction was equally dangerous, for so many slides had been made by the ice, that the path was full of pitfalls.

My dog came up to me, and laid his nose in my hand as if bidding me have courage, and then started off at a rapid pace.

Five minutes later he returned and gave utterance to a low growl, then off he started in quite another direction; this he repeated several times until at last he returned, and instead of growling, took hold of my skin-coat and gave it a drag.

I trusted to him, and followed as fast as I could, to find myself half an hour later warmly ensconced in a snow-house, and eating a piece of hot reindeer steak.

Did not that dog show reasoning powers?

No mere instinct, so called, would have been sufficient to explain the conduct of the animal which saved my life.

Once, when in Basutoland, I was cornered by a monster lion.

My horse and myself were utterly exhausted. Unfortunately I had used my last cartridge and had nothing but my hunting knife.

My horse had ridden me all day, could not go any further, and was on the point of sinking to the ground, when I dismounted and bade my faithful steed farewell, for I expected in a few minutes to be torn to pieces by the lion, who was standing ready to make a spring on me.

The moment the horse saw the act, he rushed at the lion, and attacked the monarch of the forest, letting fly with his heels with such rapidity and force that the lion lost all care for me, concentrating its energy on the steed.

This was my opportunity.

The moment the lion had its teeth fast in the flesh of the horse I sprung forward and plunged my knife into its heart.

My life was saved by the self-sacrifice of the horse, which, as it gave its last, expiring breath, looked up into my face and neighed softly.

How many men would have done as much, or have had the same thought?"

Yet there are those who will give an immortal spirit to everything which bears the shape of man, and deny it to intelligent beings of different form.

It required a great stretch of imagination to look upon these creatures as men and brothers, but so we have been taught to consider everything which walks upright on its hind legs.

Quegga drew closer to me, and the poor girl became icy cold with fear.

CHAPTER XIV.
IN CLOSE QUARTERS.

THE creatures danced around us for some time and then began talking in some language which I failed to understand.

Quegga was likewise ignorant, so we knew not what to do, until Quegga saw one of the women who had only resided with the Zemeraffes a year, and she was called to act as interpreter.

She told us, or, rather, told Quegga, in good Kasheebar, which was then translated for my benefit, that after a Kasheebar woman had lived with the Zemeraffes two or three years, they became insane and took no care of themselves.

The Zemeraffes treated them kindly, but only looked upon them as beasts.

They had to live on raw meat and amid the most horrible filth.

These statements had to be given a few words at a time, for fear the Zemeraffes would find out the women were gossiping.

When the palaver had been diluted through the Zemeraffe language into Kasheebar, and then into Abyssinian, and my replies made stronger, I suspect, by the reverse process, the conversation would be something like the following:

"Who is it that darest enter the homes of the great and mighty princes of the Zemeraffes?" asked the oldest of the monstrosities.

"I come from a land afar," was my reply.

"And we are from the stars," the old fellow said, egotistically.

"Tell him, Quegga," I said, "that I have come direct from the sun."

She laughed as she translated it, but when the reply was given her eyes filled with tears.

"Tell the creature from the sun that on the day he sets foot in the Zemeraffe home he surely dies."

Poor Quegga believed such would be my fate, but I told her to be of good courage, I was not afraid. Then to him I asked her to say:

"The men from the stars and the dwellers in the homes of the Zemeraffes have no power to kill the man from the sun."

To which the horrible creature replied:

"It hath been said, and truly, thy flesh shall be eaten, and thy vauquois (wife) shall eat of it before the moon shines."

Poor Quegga trembled as she interpreted the speech to me, and at its conclusion cried bitterly.

Just then a great bird came swooping over the inclosure, and got within pistol shot.

"'Tis the the 'aasvogel' (vulture) that smellest thy carcass," said the Zemeraffe.

I drew my Colt's revolver, took good aim, and fired.

The vulture fell dead at the feet of the monstrosity. Here was new magic.

Even Quegga was astonished, for she had never seen a pistol before.

"Now, Quegga, I said, tell him that as the bird died, so will he, if he lays a hand on either of us."

Whether this was believed or not, I don't know, but a young Zemeraffe threw a long hunting-knife or "tolla" at me, and was within an ace of striking me on the head.

I gave him a forty-four cartridge straight through his right shoulder, which disabled him as a fighter and sent him howling away.

The others had their attention diverted by the dead vulture, for several of the men fastened on it and tore it in pieces, eagerly devouring the still warm and quivering flesh.

Either my prowess as a marksman, or the excellent

flavor of the bird of prey, softened them toward me, for the old spokesman approached, and placing his head conveniently under his arm, asked "the man from the sun" to show some more magic.

Desirous of getting some knowledge of the strange race of monstrosities, I took up the "tolla" and stuck its blade in a cleft of the rock some thirty paces from me.

Raising my revolver I fired, and fortunately the blow was strong enough to break the blade in two.

My skill was now established and I was placed on a good footing with the old chief.

Quegga was almost as frightened now of me as she had been of the Zemeraffes, but I induced her, by various promises, but mostly by telling her how much I loved her, to act still further as interpreter.

By her aid I learned that there were no female Zemeraffes.

In olden times the males would go out and steal wives for themselves, but now, they had a treaty with Kasheebar, the result of a great palaver or council, whereby the old king promised to send each Zemeraffe a wife every year, for these creatures believed in polygamy.

I asked how it was no females were born, the old man shook his head, and then, not willing to confess his ignorance, asked what was the necessity, when they could always obtain women from the Kasheebars.

"Besides, girls," he said, " were a deal of trouble to rear, and so, as they could not fight, they were better without them.

One of the women was here seen to cry violently, and the idea dawned upon me that most likely the female children were put to death as soon as born.

This was afterward confirmed. I further learned that they never buried their dead, but always ate them.

The flesh of the Zemeraffe was good, said the old fellow, but that of a Kasheebar woman better than anything else.

As he spoke he took out his knife and rubbed it several times across his hand, as if to sharpen it, and then looked longingly at Quegga.

She shrank away, and I put my arm round her waist to protect her.

If I had been a cannibal Quegga would have tempted me, for she was plump, and plenty of flesh covered her very small bones, so I should imagine she would make very dainty eating.

But I laughingly told her that if she was to be eaten I would do it myself; she should never be a meal for a Zemeraffe.

The old fellow's mouth watered, and he made me a cool proposal, which was, that I should still further show my skill by shooting Quegga, and then that I should give the body to him for a feast.

When Quegga translated this speech I could restrain myself no longer, but sent out from my left shoulder such a rattler on the old fellow's chest that he fell to the ground stunned.

All thought he was killed, and they gathered round him, intending, of course, to eat him if he was lifeless. I seized Quegga in my arms, and dashed through the crowd to the steps.

I told her to hurry to the top as fast as she could; I would keep the fellows away from her.

We had not got far up the rocks when I saw the old Zemeraffe sit up and look around.

When he saw us escaping his anger was great, and he ordered us to be pursued and captured.

"He says he will eat me," sobbed Quegga.

"Not while I live," I answered; "but mind your steps, for if you fall I cannot save you."

A "tolla" went whizzing over my head, and as I looked round I saw one venturesome Zemeraffe gaining rapidly on me.

Fortunately a tree was near, so I grasped it tightly and fired at the fellow. He fell back to the bottom of the pit dead.

That was our salvation, for all were so anxious to get a share of his flesh that they gave up the pursuit.

We reached the top in safety, and then Quegga sank to the ground exhausted.

While we were resting, I could not help thinking what a wonderful man was Shakespeare. He had not traveled; books at his time were but few and difficult of access, and yet he wrote of

106   "IT."

> "Cannibals that each other eat,
> The Anthropophagi, and men whose heads
> Do grow beneath their shoulders."

These were the very race we had seen, and to the letter they carried out the idea of Shakespeare.

How did he obtain his knowledge? Was it by intuition? It must have been so, for it did not come by travel, and could not have been obtained by research.

Most wonderful and mighty master! At thy feet I lay my tribute, for thou must indeed have been inspired.

CHAPTER XV.
NEWS OF QUATERMAIN.

Just as we were reaching the village we saw several Kasheebars, armed with poisoned spears, and running as though in a race.

A KASHEEBAR NOBLE OUT RIDING,

Quegga explained that they were the body-guard of some noble who was going out riding.

There were ten nobles in Kasheebar, who failing direct issue of the king, stood in the line of succession.

The nobles never deigned to ride on oxen, but made use of slaves taken in war, or purchased from a neighboring tribe.

On the back of one of these the noble would ride, followed by one of his wives, who carried a jar of the almond honey.

Quegga was right, for scarcely had she finished her explanation than I saw a strange sight.

Following the armed men was a naked slave, and on his back sat the noble, riding pick-a-back.

The wife followed, and to show that she was one of the oldest wives, she was not allowed to wear beads, but merely a girdle round the waist.

After her, and at a respectful distance, walked two more armed men.

Quegga told me that she had once been offered to that noble, but somehow she did not fancy him, preferring to wait until the man from the sun came.

I felt flattered, and began to feel that after all there was a consolation in woman's society which could not be obtained in any other way.

We reached our home tired and exhausted. The sun had gone down, and all had retired to rest with the exception of Fjord and Curtis.

They were standing near my house smoking, and at their feet was the head of a magnificent mehedehet antelope, which had fallen before the never-failing shot of Sir Henry Curtis.

"I tell you, Theo.!" he said. "I hope to have this head up at Brayley Hall, side by side with the ivories I got from the elephant which killed poor Khiva down there near King Solomon's mines. I wish Quatermain could see this fellow."

"I want to meet Quatermain," said Fjord, "for I have heard so much about him. He is round about here somewhere."

"How do you know?" asked Curtis.

"Why, when I was with the Obodos, they were talking of him. His name they did not know, but from the description it must have been the same; besides, he left a scrap of paper behind him, which I have somewhere, and which mentions the name of Curtis."

"By Jupiter, you don't mean it?" exclaimed Curtis, excitedly.

"I do, and I will search my pockets for it."

"Do so at once, there's a good fellow. Why, believe me, Fjord, with all respect to you and my old friend Aristo, there isn't a man in the world that I think so much of as I do of——"

"Captain John Good, of Her Majesty's Royal Navy," interposed that worthy, who had come up behind us un-

A MEHEDEHET ANTELOPE.

seen, attracted to us, as he said, by the fragrance of the weed, which for once was stronger to him than his dusky charmer.

"Get out!" exclaimed Curtis; "who cares for you? I was talking about Quatermain."

"What of him?"

"Fjord has some writing of his."

"The devil!"

"No, Good, of Quatermain."

"Why the deuce, then, does he hide it away? Let us have it."

Fjord had been busy searching his pockets, and at last pulled out a piece of paper.

"Ah, here it is! No, confound it, I'm wrong."

It was tantalizing, but we had to wait Fjord's pleasure.

He was a regular American, and it was no use trying to get anything from him until he was ready.

After several ineffectual attempts, he found a scrap of paper which looked like a portion of a leaf out of a memorandum book. It was torn and crumpled and we were compelled to wait until the better light of day before we made any attempt to decipher it.

In the morning we were all anxiety to read the scrap of Quatermain's writing, so after breakfast we got together and Fjord produced the document.

It was but a fragment folded and torn through.

It had the appearance of being a copy of a letter which Quatermain had been going to write. Curtis remembered that the old hunter had a habit of always drafting a letter in his pocket-book and then copying it out.

The writing was in pencil, and nearly illegible, but after a long trial of patience and perseverance we made out the following:

> HARRY
>   By the time this rea
>   have started on another
> from which I may never retur
> In case you don't hear from me
> or at most a year, write or go
> Sir Henry Curtis of Brayl
> find Captain John Good, R. N., his
> easily get from navy
> tell you what I am
> make your name, my boy, immort
> adventure with "glass ey
> since that time I
> Holly who wandere
> woman called *She*, and he
> more remarkable creat

He, She or *It,* I kn
and will find origin of all
I shall pass th
the Gallas and into Sahar
expedition. If
would have got Curtis.

This was all we could read of the fragment. Curtis and Good, who knew the hunter so well, could understand it better than I could, and Curtis took out his pocketbook, unfolded the scrap, smoothed it out very evenly and then took a pencil and endeavored to fill in the missing words and letters.

When he had finished he read off the writing and it seemed to make a very good letter.

This is what Curtis had written:

"DEAR HARRY—By the time this reaches you I shall have started on another expedition from which I may never return

"In case you do not hear from me in nine months, or at most a year, write or go and see my friend, Sir Henry Curtis, of Brayley Hall, and be sure and find Captain John Good, R. N.; his address you can get from navy department, for he draws his pay still.

"I will tell you what I am going to search for.

"It will make your name, my boy, immortal.

"I remember my adventures with 'Glasseye' and Curtis. Since that time I have come across a man named Holly, who wandered about after a woman called *She*, and he told me of a more remarkable creature, but whether named *He*, *She*, or *It*, I know not.

"I shall search and will find origin of all these stories. On my way I shall pass through the Desert of Gallas and into Sahara if possible."

Here Curtis stopped.

"I can't make sense of the last two lines," he said, "but guess the other is pretty accurate."

"Putting things together," said Fjord, "it seems that we are all bent on the same mission, and that the mysterious *It* will be found somewhere to the north of our present location."

"That is my conjecture," I remarked, "and I reckon

if we are going to do anything we shall have to get into Sahara."

"Easier said than done, my boy," remarked Good. "Do you know that from where we now are we have about fifteen hundred miles to march?"

"By Jupiter! that will be pretty stiff," Fjord exclaimed, as he lighted his pipe.

"Wait a moment," continued Good; "don't be so impatient; fifteen hundred miles will only see us on the edge of Sahara, and we may have another thousand to travel before we reach the end of our journey."

"Worse still."

"I don't like the march," said Curtis, who was evidently more inclined to settle down quietly at Kasheebar, and I almost made up my mind that I should have to "go it alone," if the search was continued.

"What would you say if I told you we are now near the dwelling-place of *It?*" I asked.

"Don't joke, Aristo, for the love of Heaven," exclaimed Curtis, testily.

"I am not joking, but seriously I tell you there are wonders here of which you little dream."

I then told them of the strange rock, with its mysterious eyes like flames of fire, and of the Zemeraffes.

They opened their eyes to the fullest extent, and showed very plainly that if any other had told the wonderful story it would not have been believed.

When I asked Fjord, Curtis and Good to give an account of their explorations, they seemed ashamed to confess that they had nothing to tell.

Love and its pleasures had occupied their attention and they had not looked for wonders among the Kasheebars.

That afternoon we arranged to visit the rock and if possible solve the mystery of its eyes of fire.

Leaving the women at home—no doubt well-pleased to get rid of our continued companionship—we started off in the direction I had twice before traveled with Quegga.

When the rock was reached, we carefully examined the carvings.

I looked at my chronometer—and, by the way, I was the most fortunate in the party, for my watch was the only one to be relied on—and found the time to be about a quarter to two.

So confident was I, that the eyes had really given forth fire and would do so again, that I suggested that we walk some little distance, and then return at the regular time for the phenomena.

This was agreed to readily, Fjord rather irreverently saying that no doubt the old boy would like to get his blinkers ready in privacy.

I took Curtis and the others a little way on the road to the dwelling-place of the Zemeraffes, and returned on a lower level, so that when opposite the magic rock we could climb the hill and come full upon it.

Fjord was most eager for this natural or supernatural wonder, and I could scarcely restrain his impetuosity.

He was a few yards ahead of us, when suddenly I heard him shout:

"Great Jupiter!" and had only just time to dodge out of his way, for he had caught sight of the eyes while standing close to the bank up which we had climbed, and the dazzling brilliancy of the rays of light had caused him to fall backward and roll down the bank.

Fortunately, the declivity was not very steep and only a few yards in depth.

Curtis, as stolid and cold as a statue, a regular cold-blooded Englishman, walked steadily up the bank and stared at the rock as unmoved as though it was an everyday occurrence.

Good took one look, and then hid his face. It was really awe-inspiring and frightful.

Curtis maintained his ground, and though the rays of fire seemed to scorch us, he alone was calm and unruffled.

Good and I sat down at some little distance, and were presently joined by Fjord, who laughed at our fears, yet was so overcome himself that he had taken a fall of a few yards in his fright.

He left us, and, taking courage from Sir Henry Curtis, stood beside him.

Curtis, without removing his eyes from the rock, although he dare not look into the eyes, quietly took out his meerschaum, filled it with fine tobacco, and then held it in the ray of light which fell direct from the eye in the center of the rock.

In a moment the tobacco was lighted.

"I thought so," he said, and then, looking round, called, "Come here, you fellows, and I will solve the mystery."

We were both pleased, if a reasonable solution could be found, so listened attentively to Curtis, who thus expounded his theory.

"The very fact that I was able to light the tobacco in my pipe by means of the light from the eye proves that the heat as well as the light is most intense.

"That can be produced by forcing the rays of the sun through a good lens, properly focused.

"Now, the sun cannot penetrate through all that mass of solid rock, therefore the light is caused by reflection.

"The sun shines directly on the polished surface of the eyes, and the light and heat are thrown off.

"It is a clever contrivance, and the old fellow who originated it must have been a great optician."

I had listened very attentively to this long speech, and waited to hear the comment of Fjord and Good.

The naval officer clapped Curtis on the back, and exclaimed:

"Bravo, Curtis."

Fjord put his hands in his trousers pockets and whistled "Yankee Doodle."

I saw that both were convinced with the argument, and all three looked, I imagined, rather contemptuously on me for my fears.

This was my opportunity.

"You say, Curtis, that the sun cannot get through the mass of rock?"

"I do!"

"And that the light is reflected from the eyes."

"Yes."

"In that case the sun has to shine so that its rays fall directly on the rock!"

"That is the case."

"Then look round and show me where the sun is now."

Like many modern astronomers, Curtis had taken

certain things for granted and built up his theory thereon.

I had raised the first doubt in his mind.

He, and in fact all, looked in every direction, and no possible way could be found by which the sun's rays could fall on the surface of that perpendicular rock.

"I'm at sea!" exclaimed Curtis, when he saw his theory so quickly destroyed.

"I wish I was," said Good, "for then I could take my bearings and know just what I was about."

A few moments later the rock was bathed in sunlight, and the glare of the eyes disappeared, looking again a cold, inert mass of stone.

"Was it the sun?" I asked, with almost a sneer, for I sometimes get disgusted with cold scientists who cannot see anything beyond their precise mathematical calculations.

"Yes, it was the sun," answered Curtis, emphatically, "but how its rays were made to fall on the eyes is a mystery."

His theory was gone, but the result he maintained with a pertinacity which has ever characterized the scientific searcher.

I verily believe that these hard, matter-of-fact thinkers would want to apply the acid test to the streets of the New Jerusalem to see whether the pavement was gold or only plated, and would want to weigh and measure the precious stones in their crowns of glory—if scientists ever get to that happy land—to see whether they had their full share.

Neither imagination nor poetry, romance or the supernatural has any charms for them, but all must be judged from the standpoint of solid fact.

We searched round for some time, but could find no crevice or hole through which the sun's rays could penetrate.

Our next move was to examine the eyes, and see whether the mystery could be explained by anything in their composition.

How to reach them was a puzzle, for the head of the serpent which contained the lowest eye was upward of ten feet from the pathway, and the rock was so smooth that it afforded no foothold by which we could climb.

"Oh, for a step-ladder!" exclaimed Fjord.

"Or a good rope, to lower oneself down from the top," said Good.

"I have it," Curtis said.

"What—a rope?"

"No! But you have pretty broad shoulders; let Good, who is a light-weight, stand on them and examine the serpent's eye."

The suggestion was the only feasible one, and as the captain had studied optics while on long cruises with the British war-ships, he was the best qualified for the work.

With the agility of an acrobat, he stood erect on the broad shoulders of the English baronet, and was able to examine closely the eye which emitted the green fire from the serpent's head.

When he returned to *terra firma* he told us that Curtis must be correct as regards the lenses. For he found that the adder's eye was made of a complicated arrangement of lenses, over one of which was a very thin green glass.

The glasses were so arranged that from the road they merely had the appearance of carved stone.

"It is the most splendid arrangement I have ever seen, and, by Jove! the fellow who did it deserves a monument."

Good was quite enthusiastic, but I was still skeptical, for I could not find out how the sun's rays could fall upon the eyes.

It was too late that day for further examination, so we returned.

It was certainly remarkable that in the wilds of Africa, where white men had never been known to travel, we should find such traces of civilization.

The land of the Kasheebars was full of wonders, and I, for one, wished Quatermain was with us, so that we could more fully explore its many curiosities.

I was anxious to get some knowledge of the Vantackas, and again trust myself with the Zemeraffes.

Quegga was weeping when I returned, for she had become possessed with the idea that death had overtaken me because of my folly in tempting the gods.

When I got into our house the warm-hearted girl clasped me in her arms and sang her love-songs, which told of the great pleasure my presence gave her.

CHAPTER XVI.

THE MIRAGE.

IF I were to write down all the adventures through which we passed during our sojourn with the Kasheebars this book would be so long that my publisher would be inclined to wish me at the furthermost parts of the earth, and to exclaim, " Of the making of books there is no end."

Besides, the great discovery which we made later, and after we had left Kasheebar, was the incentive I had in writing this book, for I can handle a rifle better than a pen, and know more about ammunition than I do about ink.

In my young days, when my grand old father used to teach me Hebrew and Arabic, Greek and Chaldaic, mathematics and astronomy, I was considered a quick study, but even then was no great hand at writing; but, after traveling about for so many years, and scarcely writing even a letter, it is not to be wondered at that my style should be clumsy, and that my book would scarcely be read were it not for the truths it contains, the facts of adventures passed through by the writer, and the great discovery which, when its full import is realized, will lead to a clearer conception of man and his origin.

Fjord and Curtis, who are both great enthusiasts, but manifest their feelings in different ways, decided upon a thorough investigation of the Vantackas, and for this purpose resolved to leave their wives and camp for several days with the horned men.

Good preferred the chase, and I cast in my lot with Curtis and Fjord.

A difficulty presented itself in my case. Quegga refused to be left behind.

She had become thoroughly convinced that I intended leaving her, and therefore would not hear of my going without her.

"Didst thou not save me from the Zemeraffes?" she asked. "And shall I leave thee now?"

"But I will come back." I said.

"Nay, how know I that? May not the Vantackas kill thee? And if thou diest thy Quegga will die too."

I pleaded with her, told her of the dangers to be encountered, that perhaps we should be cold and hungry before we returned, but the answer was always the same:

"Where thou goest, so will I. Did I not promise to be thine own, to tend thee when thy limbs are weak, or thy body frail, to bring thee the sweet honey and fruits? Nay, my own, my beloved, I will go with thee."

It was useless to oppose, for I have found through life that:

> "He is a fool, who thinks by force or skill,
> To turn the current of a woman's will."

And so, though I knew Curtis and Fjord would laugh at me, tease and plague, I had to give in, and take the girl along with me.

We had not been away a day, however, before we were all heartily glad that Quegga had insisted on forcing her presence on us, for she found paths through the scrub and brush which escaped our notice, even though we were all old hunters, and never did I know a "spoorer" with keener scent than she possessed.

She waited on each of the party, and was never tired. Of course, her greatest attention was bestowed on me. But her quick perception showed her that none of us had wanted her presence, so she proved her worth as an auxiliary, and made both Curtis and Fjord change their sneers into words of approval and thanks.

Had we been alone we should have looked for the Vantackas at the place where we had seen one before, just after our arrival at Kasheebar, but Quegga informed us that their kraals were nearly two days' march, and if we wanted to see them at home we must go there.

We each carried a Winchester with plenty of cartridges, our revolvers, and hunting-knives.

In addition, Quegga had insisted on us taking some food, while she carried on her head an immense jar of the almond honey.

Umbilla had become so closely attached to Good that he was with him almost inseparably, and naturally preferred the chase to our company.

Fjord pushed on ahead, followed by Curtis, and at an equal distance I walked, Quegga being close behind me.

We adopted this plan to guard against surprises, for we had learned that the natives were very treacherous, and even the king could not protect us when we were out of the village.

When we had gone some miles, a heavy fog came on. It was the first we had seen, but as there were no dangerous roads, and nothing to fear but the natives, we determined to press on through the misty fog.

We could see Fjord, and so long as there was the faintest glimmer of light we were satisfied.

Presently we heard Fjord utter an exclamation and disappear. Then several forms could be seen moving about in the tall grass.

Quegga was frightened, and clung close to me for protection.

Curtis and myself stood still, wondering what had become of Fjord, and scarcely daring to move forward for fear of falling into some hidden hole.

"See!" called out Quegga, and she turned me round to the direction in which she was pointing.

There was Fjord seated on horseback, galloping furiously across the plain, and waving his hand to us to follow.

It was all very well to call on us, but he had the advantage, for while he was traveling at the rate of twenty miles an hour we had difficulty to make three.

A moment later he threw up his arms and then fell to the ground with a dull thud.

At the same time the mists rose and we were able to see clearer.

We ran as fast as the scrub would allow us, and found Fjord sitting on the ground rubbing himself.

He had no bones broken but was sadly bruised.

"What was it? how did it happen?" I asked.

"Well, to tell the truth, I was sold," he answered.

"I was going ahead very nicely in the fog, calling on you fellows to hurry up, when I saw a lot of dim forms lying on the ground.

"I thought they were trunks of trees, and began to imagine we were on the verge of a forest or remains of one. The fog seemed to get denser, and I could scarcely see. So that I might be able to look over the scrub, which was very high, I stood on one of the trees, as I thought, when my foot slipped, but the next moment I found myself on the back of a zebra scampering over the plain.

"My trees were sleeping zebras.

"I thought it was all up with me, and the plaguy thing went so fast that I could not shout, my breath was taken by the wind.

"When it got here the beast got a fit of curiosity, and stood on its hind legs to look over the brush.

"The curiosity was so sudden that I sat down here to wait for you fellows."

We thought Fjord's alighting place would make a very good place for a halt.

We therefore rested a short time, and took some food and a good big drink of the almond honey.

As the mists rose, a very pretty sight was presented to our gaze.

The heavy vapor or fog seemed to gradually ascend, as though it was a thick blanket being raised by unseen hands at each corner.

The sky was obscured just above us, but on a level with our plane of vision there was almost full daylight.

We watched the ascension of the cloud until we sat transfixed with amazement.

Instead of a cloud it looked like a floating island peopled with many forms.

To all appearance there were numbers of people moving up and down.

We could see the tents, or houses made like those of the Kasheebars, then a company of warriors marched up and down the street.

There was some commotion going on.

Messengers were running in every direction.

We saw the king's kraal, and found it surrounded with warriors.

As we gazed on the cloud or picture so full of life, we saw our own forms. Fjord was just in the act of drinking.

I could not resist laughing at the strange figure he cut in the picture.

My laughter was suddenly stopped, however, by the appearance of a great body of men in full war panoply moving toward us.

The clouds broke, and the sun shone forth.

We had seen a mirage, but what did it mean?

"Come!" exclaimed Quegga, jumping to her feet and seizing her jar of almond honey.

We were on the alert, for we had caught the sound of men marching.

Raising my field-glass, which, fortunately, I had with me, I was able to see a large number of native savages marching in our direction.

They were just as we had seen them reflected on the storm-cloud.

Our only chance of escape was to hurry back to Kasheebar, for we knew we should lose our lives if we were overtaken by these savage warriors.

"We stood not on the order of our going," but hurried back as rapidly as our legs could be made to move.

Fjord handed each of us some of his magic leaves, and when we had eaten them all stiffness seemed to leave our limbs, and we had all the vigor of early morning in our muscles.

When we arrived at the village the day was far spent, but we found everything in just the commotion we had perceived in the mirage.

The king, old Kasheebar, was seated on his war-chair, and had gathered in front of him his chosen warriors.

As we approached, a way was made for us, and we were especially honored.

We were glad to find Umbilla and Good ready to receive us.

Good told us that almost as soon as we had gone, swift messengers had brought word that Kasheebar was to be attacked by the nation of the Kagehyis, who were marching in great numbers through the pass and on to the plain.

Umbilla had trumpeted forth our feats of magic and skill, and the king was wishing for our return, as Good was in what Fjord would call "a funk."

He did not relish a fight, and was wishing he could get well out of it.

When asked to show his magic tube, which the Kasheebars had never seen, he refused, and said the king must wait until we came.

He refused to say in which direction we had gone, so the king could not send for us.

Hence his delight at finding us returning so opportunely.

Sir Henry was always ready to take advantage of the occasion, knowing that humbug and bombast went a long way with these people.

He now, in a loud voice, addressed the king and the warriors somewhat in this fashion:

"Most mighty and great Kasheebar, we, children of the land afar, but who have sat with thee, and received from thee wives to cheer us in our houses, we were nearly a day's march away when the stars and the sun did paint in the sky the faces of the warriors who were gathered here, and then we saw the faces of the insects who would make war upon thee. They shall be made to return to their mountains quicker than the zebra can run, and thy servant Fjord can testify to that."

The king was clear-headed, and thought that the speech would have great and good effect on the warriors, but he called us quietly aside and laughed at the good story we had told, but intimated he did not believe it, although he was glad his warriors would.

We felt insulted, and Fjord, raising his voice, and giving his words a regular Yankee twang, which sounded peculiar when applied to the Kasheebar language, said:

"Let my lord, the mighty Kasheebar, send for the woman Quegga, and let her say what she hath seen."

"It shall be done, and if the woman shall tell the same story, verily I will believe thee."

Quegga came with a bearing a princess might envy. In fact I had often thought that she must have been the child of some noble house, for her figure was lighter and more perfect than the majority of Africans whose parents have to work hard.

Her hands were small, the fingers tapering as gracefully as those of a European beauty; her wrists were well-formed, and her ankles were as graceful and pretty as a gazelle's.

She was so classic in her figure that no Venus ever left the sculptor's hand which could claim greater grace, beauty or perfection.

As she walked with stately tread into the king's presence, I felt proud of her.

She, without hesitation told the same story as Curtis, but made it more elaborate, giving it as a recitative.

There was considerable poetry in Quegga, and in her ordinary conversation she spoke with a musical rhythm which was both refined and pleasing.

She had scarcely returned to her house before messengers announced the approach of the enemy, and their encampment for the night.

CHAPTER XVII.
THE COMBAT.

THE sun had scarcely risen the next morning before the drums sounded and the warriors were called to arms.

A council of war was immediately summoned at which the commanders of all the regiments of Kasheebars were present.

It was very evident we were in for a good fight, and we had sufficient experience of African wars to know we should not be considered neutrals.

We would be compelled to take part, and our entire interest was with the Kasheebars.

In the approaching war our people were in the right, for they would be defending their homes against the invader.

The king wanted to separate us, giving each of us command of a regiment, but we objected, and satisfied the old triangle that we could be of more service if we remained together.

I was able by means of my field glass to watch the maneuvers of the invading force and, as I told the king what they were doing he was surprised, and nothing would satisfy him but he must look through the glass.

His amazement knew no bounds as he saw the enemy so close.

He must have the glass. All the honors should be ours if I did but give him the wonderful glass. That I had no intention of doing, so I told that him if once it passed out of my possession, it would be valueless.

"But I can see," said the king.

Fortunately there was a little patent shutter or slide over each lens, so all I had to do was to pass my hand over the top, press down the shutter, and so, of course, obstruct the vision.

This I did, and the king got so enraged that I almost feared I had lost favor.

In a moment, however, he asked me to touch the glass with my magic hands, and I did so, raising the shutters at the time.

The king was delighted.

Two men waving a skin on the end of a spear—a sign that they were heralds from the invading force, approached the Kasheebar village.

The king sent two heralds and Sir Henry Curtis to meet them.

When within a few paces of each other the king's messenger exclaimed:

"Greeting! What would ye with your spears and banners?"

"Greeting!" answered the other. "We have come to the people who are ruled by a jackal, to say that the jackal must die, and the Kasheebars be a part of the Kagehyi nation."

"Never!" answered the Kasheebar herald.

"Then listen! The king of all kings, the ruler of all rulers, the man whose father was the sun, and whose mother was the mighty waters, the giant who ruleth over the Kagehyi nation, and who draweth wisdom from the great and mighty queen whose kingdom stretcheth to the stars, and who is white and comely, and whose people are the great and profound, the first of all humanity who dwell in the earth and on the earth, above the earth and below it, saith:

"That if the Kasheebar people will give up their ruler who oppresseth, together with the men of magic, to be killed and their bodies given to the jackals, my lord my king will let all go free, but will take all the maidens for wives for himself and his warriors."

"We shall not surrender."

"Then listen, vain boaster: thy body and those of all who are gathered in thy camp shall feed the Zemoraffes and jackals to-night."

Curtis had not taken part in the discussion, but as the herald was about to depart he called after him:

"Go, tell thy master, whoever he may be, that there are those among the Kasheebars who can slay with a breath, and woe be to those who come within our gates."

The herald laughed, and went back, I verily believe, pleased at the failure of his mission.

"It will be war stern and pitiless," said Curtis. "And we must do our share. Let each of us have plenty of ammunition for our Winchesters and revolvers. We shall need it."

Umbilla danced with pleasure. War was his recreation and delight, and there was no mistaking his joyous feelings.

As I looked round I could not help wondering how it was that so many really welcomed war, when death was the result.

How was it that man, great, glorious man, the perfection of creation, man with a spirit which would live through the countless ages of eternity, man, given a brain with powers of thought and ingenuity which would enable him to pierce the very sky and snatch the veil from its mysteries, which gave him power to harness the lightning and make fire his servant—this creature Godlike and sublime, yet gloried in scenes of carnage and bloodshed.

The greatest butchers of their fellow men were sainted and enshrined within cathedral walls; poets sung their praises, and statesmen spoke eulogies of their deeds; gentle woman forgot her tenderness and placed laurel wreaths on the brows of the man whose hands were red with his brother's blood. Alas, what a mockery of nature. What a blasphemous commentary on the teachings of the Prince of Peace.

All these thoughts were crowding through my brain as I looked on those men who were so eager for the fray.

That the savage should glory in war was scarcely to be wondered at, when the Christian made wars for as trivial causes as the pagan.

We made no attempt to dress in warlike costume, trusting to our rifles—we each carried two—our revolvers and hunting knives.

Old Kasheebar, however, insisted on our carrying

spears, which were as awkward to us as the guns would have been to the natives.

We looked to the enemy, and saw them slowly, and without any excitement or flurry, march toward the village.

The chief, or king, rode at the head on a quagga. The soldiers were all on foot.

On the right of the king Curtis stood by me, while Fjord and Good were on the left hand of the triangular monarch.

"Theo., my boy," said Curtis, "do you think you could cause that painted savage to dismount."

"I'll try."

The king did not understand one word as Curtis had addressed me in English.

I took my Winchester, and saw plainly I could easily cover the quagga.

When I was ready, Curtis called to the king to look at his royal antagonist.

Kasheebar raised my glass which he still retained and when I knew the old fellow was intently gazing, I drew the trigger.

All the savages saw was a puff of smoke, and they heard a slight report, but the king saw the quagga drop dead, and its rider reduced to the rank of a foot-soldier.

The man who had been so insulting to us while acting as herald, stepped up to speak to his chief.

I could not resist the temptation, so aimed for his head. I for once made a miscalculation, for my bullet struck him in the chest and he fell dead at the king's feet.

This pleased our people so much that they set up a wild cheer for the white man's magic.

Fjord's fingers twitched nervously at the trigger of his Winchester.

Curtis, who led the white contingent in support of Kasheebar, gave orders for us to fire five shots in rapid succession at the distant warriors.

"Crack!" went our Winchesters simultaneously and three warriors lay biting the dust.

Again and again the same result was achieved and with our five shots each, we had laid eighteen dusky braves prostrate.

The enemy could stand this no longer, for they were too far distant to hurt any of us, while we were killing their best men.

An ominous whoop reached us, and at once the whole body of warriors dashed into our village.

We fired many more shots, but did not wish to waste all our cartridges.

On came the Kagehyis charging like infuriated bulls. The shouting and clashing of spears were something fearful to listen to, but they drowned the cries of the wounded and dying.

We were now at close quarters, and the tollas were flashing about on all sides.

The mass of naked humanity surged to and fro on every side, scores of men falling dead or wounded every minute.

Curtis could not resist the temptation, and quickly followed by Fjord he threw himself into the thickest of the fight.

Two forms could be seen towering above that confused mass; they were those of Curtis and Umbilla, who were both fighting like very demons.

One Kagehyi had his spear-point close to the middle of Fjord's back. Curtis saw it, drew his revolver, and the men fell dead.

Good called on me to go with him, and we forced our way through the ranks until the four white men were right in the center of the surging crowd.

We could only occasionally use our revolvers, for we had no desire to shoot any of our own men, so we had to fight with our hunting-knives and short spears.

The Kasheebars had only spears and bows for weapons, in addition to the throwing-knives, while the Kagehyis had battle-axes in addition.

The axes were not very formidable-looking weapons, but very effective.

The haft was a kind of cane, which was twisted round the middle of the ax.

The ax head or blade was about three inches wide, and looked to be exceedingly sharp.

Curtis several times expressed a desire for one, and at last gratified it at the cost of a man's life.

Raising his iron hand, he seized the haft of a battle-ax

held by a sturdy warrior, and with the other hand sent a bullet whizzing through the fellow's heart.

Now came a scene of magnificent butchery.

The ax in the hands of Curtis seemed to be flashing everywhere. At each blow a skull was cleft, and the blows came so rapidly that every warrior tried to get as far from Curtis as possible.

The roll of the meeting shields rose up from that crowd like the noise of thunder.

Good proved himself to be a man of desperate courage. He too had become possessed of a battle-ax, and made many bite the dust.

I felt more like a soldier every minute. At first the sight of human blood was repugnant to me, but now I gloried in it—I actually loved it. My whole nature was changed and I became a savage.

Every man who fell beneath my blows made my heart throb with pleasure and delight.

For several hours the combat raged with fury, and then both sides showed signs of exhaustion.

Gradually the Kagehyis began to form themselves into line, and the Kasheebars followed their example.

The two nations faced each other, hate stamped on every brow.

The fight had stopped through sheer exhaustion, but it was only for a time.

Neither side would admit defeat.

They were well matched, and had both fought with a valor worthy of a good cause.

The signal for renewal of the conflict was given by Kasheebar, and on dashed the two bodies of men.

The Kagehyis had taken some corpses and held them up as shields to receive our spear thrusts.

It was a gallant fight, and Sir Henry performed prodigies of valor, as did also Good and Fjord.

'Tis merciful to be cruel, I thought, and so, acting on the idea, I watched an opportunity, and sent a bullet from my revolver crashing into the brain of the Kagehyi king.

When his soldiers saw him fall, they cried for quarter and began to retreat.

We followed them, spearing right and left, and leaving on our way at every footfall the corpses of the warriors.

Two thousand had started that morning to invade the village of the Kasheebars, and now a miserable remnant of but a hundred or so escaped with their lives.

The bodies of all who had fallen were gathered in a big pile, and then well saturated with some oily substance.

When this was accomplished, the old witches came from their kraal and began dancing round the monster heap of the dead, while one rubbed the fire-sticks and set light to the bodies.

The oil was very inflammable, and soon there was a big blaze. Men and women left the village and gathered the long, dry grass and brush, and threw the armfuls on the fire.

Meanwhile the witches danced as though round their caldron, and, as they danced, chanted a weird funeral dirge. It was a fearful sight, and the odor was sickening.

CHAPTER XVIII.
A FUNERAL DANCE.

WHEN the fire had effectually consumed the dead soldiers, and the stench had somewhat subsided, we were bidden to the great funeral dance.

Quegga had been full of raptures and endearment at finding me comparatively speaking uninjured, for the only wound I had was a small flesh one on the arm.

Quegga, fearing it might have been made with a poisoned spear, put her lips to the wound, and drew from it a quantity of blood and mucus.

She was right, the mucus, we found, contained a deadly corrosive poison, so her devotion and care saved my life.

When the time for the dance arrived we heard the sound of drums beating, horns blowing, and people shouting.

When Quegga and I reached the camp ground, I was lifted up by the people and carried to the king's platform or dais.

A similar honor was conferred upon my four friends.

for I now classed Umbilla in that category; he had proved his faithfulness beyond what we could have expected from a servant.

The dancers were most grotesquely gotten up. About a dozen huge feathers were stuck into a band which was tightly fastened round their heads.

Leopard skins were suspended from their shoulders, and a leather tied round the waist covered a large iron bell which hung on the bottom of the back of each dancer, and looked like one of the old-time fashionable bustles.

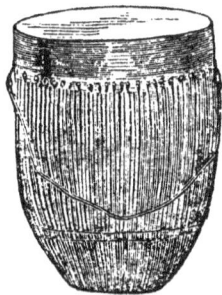

NATIVE DRUM.

A large crowd dressed in this fantastic style, and making a most hideous noise, presented a novel kind of entertainment.

The music was provided by large drums, and each dancer possessed in addition a horn of the mchedehet antelope, which he blew occasionally in his excitement. These instruments made a sound more like the screeching of an owl than anything else I could imagine.

Crowds of men rushed round and round in a sort of infernal galop, brandishing their spears and swinging their bows and arrows.

The women kept outside the line, dancing a slow, stupid step, and screaming a most inharmonious chant, while all the young girls and small children—their heads and necks rubbed with red ochre and grease, and ornamented quite prettily with many strings of beads round their loins—kept a very good line, beating time with their feet and jingling the many iron rings which adorned their ankles.

One woman attended upon the men, running through the crowd with a gourd full of the ashes from the burnt bodies; these ashes she threw by handfuls over the dancers, powdering them very liberally.

This dance continued until the dancers got exhausted, and then, as one by one dropped from fatigue, the drums ceased beating, and the party broke up; only to be again renewed on every day for the next two weeks.

I got into conversation with the medicine-man of the Kasheebars, who could talk several languages with which I was acquainted.

I asked him the meaning of the dance.

His reply was that it kept away the evil spirits.

When asked if his tribe believed in existence after death, he answered:

"Yes, but I have doubts of it."

"What are your doubts?" I asked.

"Existence after death is a farce," he said, "and I don't believe it. How can a man come to life again when his body is burnt?"

"You think then that man is like a beast, and when he dies there is an end of him."

"What is man but a beast? A lion is stronger, but he dies; an elephant's bones are big, but he too dies, while man is weak, why should he be better than a beast?"

"But you, the medicine-man, must know that man is superior to the beast in knowledge."

"No, I don't know that. The ox goes on very well if left alone, gets a good living and never works, but man has to work before he can live."

"But do you not feel that there is something in man which is superior to his body?"

"No."

"When you sleep at night, do you not dream and wander in thoughts to distant places in your sleep, yet your body never moves."

"That is so; but I cannot explain it."

"That is the soul, or mind, which is active when you are asleep; it acts apart from the body, and when the body dies it will live."

"What then?"

"Is not that superior to the animal?"

"No, for I had a dog once that used to dream."

While this philosophic savage, endowed with intelligence far above his fellows, was talking, I could not help recalling Scott's lines:

> "The staghounds, weary with the chase,
> Lay stretched upon the rushy floor,
> And urged in dreams the forest race
> From Teviot-stone to Eskdale Moor."*

I recalled also the many instances I had known of animals dreaming.

I knew that horses neigh and dogs bark and growl in their sleep.

Probably at such times the remembrance of the hunt or chase, or the combat is passing through their minds.

I have known a parrot to talk in its sleep, and utter words which it would never use awake. The mocking bird and raven are both great dreamers, so, after all, my argument in favor of a soul, based upon the capability of dreaming, was a poor one.

I thought I would try and get an advantage over my medicine-man by another question.

"Do you think," I asked, "that the good and bad both die, share the same fate, and perish forever?"

"Of course, what else can they do?"

"But why, then, are some good?"

"Because they are not strong enough to be bad. All men would be bad, as you call it, if they were strong enough. The good people are all weak."

I tried one more question.

"You take some maize," I said, "and put it into the ground. Now, that dies, but it rises again, and you eat the maize?"

"No, white tage, you are wrong; the maize I put in the ground dies, but never rises again; what grows up is but its offspring. So it is with man. I die and am buried, or, if I am killed in battle, I am burned, and there is an end of me, but my children live, and that's all of me which will live after I am dead."

The old man was in earnest and had reasoned well. I was not enough of a theologian to discuss with him, and

---

* "Lay of the Last Minstrel."

I had to admit to myself that I had the worst of the argument.

I was better fitted for talking with the women of Kasheebar than with the philosophers, so I went back to my house and sought consolation for my wounded vanity in the company of Quegga, who would, I verily believe, have worshiped me if I had so allowed.

Later in the day I received a call from Curtis, who managed to crawl into the hole; it was smaller than his doorway, and fitted him tightly.

"See here, Aristo, my boy, we are losing time. I am no coward, but I don't want any more fighting with and for a lot of savages for whom I don't care a brass farthing."

"Well?"

"If we stay here we shall be in for another fight in a few days."

"How so?"

"The Kagehyi people are defeated and their king killed. They will elect a new king, and his first duty will be to thrash us."

"What makes you think so?"

"It is the law of these tribes."

"And then?"

"Why, how obtuse you are! Don't you see we shall have to waste more cartridges, and perhaps some of our blood?"

"What do you propose?"

"That we get back to our wagon, and go up into the Kagehyi country."

"What for?"

"Did you not hear the herald say that the ruler drew his inspiration from a beautiful white queen who ruled over a people who were the first of all things, and who lived in, on, under, and above the earth?"

"I heard all that, but that was a mere African metaphor."

"I am not so sure of that. I have an idea we shall learn something about our mysterious *It*."

"But we have fought against these Kagehyis."

"I know it, but a bit of humbug will overcome all that."

"As you like; I am ready."

"That's right. I have spoken to Fjord and Good."

"What about the women?"

"Why, leave them behind, of course."

"No, Curtis, I shall take Quegga with me; she has saved my life, besides——"

"What?"

"She tells me if a husband deserts his wife she is given to a Zemeraffe."

"Great Harry. That won't do. We are in a mess, for we can't take a lot of women with us."

"I shall take Quegga."

"Please yourself. She is a good creature, and worth all the rest put together. I confess, if Moya was like her, I should be loath to leave her. I have it."

"What!"

"If the women are afraid of the Zemeraffes we will take them until we come to the first friendly tribe where they will be well treated, and then leave them."

"Do as you like, but I shall take Quegga with me."

"To England?"

"Yes, if I ever live to go back, and she is alive."

"What will Dame Powell say?"

"Hang Dame Powell."

"I guess you may have that fate if you take back a black wife."

The conversation ended, but our resolve was taken to leave Kasheebar and get to our supplies as quickly as possible.

When Quegga came in I told her that we were about to leave Kasheebar.

She looked at me for a moment, all the brightness left her face and her hands fell to her side.

"Have you nothing to say?" I asked.

"No. I am my lord's, and he can do with me as he thinks well."

This was said with such a sorrowful voice, showing the keen suffering she was enduring, and yet, such was her love for me that she tried to appear resigned.

Not one word of reproach, not a murmur, though she, the beautiful, would be clasped in the foul embrace of a monstrosity within a few days after I left.

I could see by her face that she had no thought of accompanying me.

My heart bled for her.

"Quegga," I said softly.

"Yes, my lord," was her answer, given in a very meek, resigned voice.

"Come here."

I was sitting on my lion-skin bed, and she came across to me slowly and with her head on her bosom.

I pulled her down beside me, and drew her head on my shoulder, and then gently raising her face, said:

"Are you so sorry at leaving Kasheebar?"

I felt her bosom heave with emotion, and a warm tear trickled down on my hand.

"Quegga," I said, "do you not remember my promise? I will take you wherever I go."

"Do you mean it?" she asked.

"Mean it! Have I ever broken my word to you?"

"No, my own; but——"

"What now perplexes you?"

"The king."

"What of him?"

"There is a law that no stranger who has ever been a resident of Kasheebar can leave it."

"That is all stuff and nonsense. We have magic with us, and the king is not strong enough, nor all his warriors, to keep us if we wanted to leave."

"But will he allow me to leave?"

"He will have to do so. Quegga, I shall take you with me, if you will go."

"Go! oh, my beloved, my own! As the sun shines, so I love you; as the stars twinkle in the blackness of night, so my heart goes out to thee; and when the moon brightly gleams on us, even so, my own, thou art ever in my thoughts. Quegga will brave the mountains, if she can but be near thee; the desert has no terrors, and death will be sweet if it can be in thy arms."

I knew the girl meant every word, and I vowed I would never leave her until death separated us.

Love had come to me. And it was love for a dark-skinned beauty, but for one whose heart was as true as the shining stars.

CHAPTER XIX.

ADIEU TO KASHEEBAR.

THERE was great commotion in the village the next day.

Curtis had obtained audience of the king and had told him of our intention to leave.

The old fellow was furious. Were we not well treated?

"Yes."

"Then what did we wish to leave for?"

Curtis told him that we had a mission to perform, that the gods had bidden us go.

"I care not for thy gods," he answered. "I will slay thee rather than allow thee to go to the lands afar."

Curtis came back and we went in a body to the royal kraal.

When we arrived there old Kasheebar had assembled all his wives and his great army of children, who, with the exception of Koro, were all well formed.

"Why is it that the great tage wish to leave?"

Fjord made reply:

"Because, most mighty monarch, the gods have decreed that unless we leave we lose our magic power."

"If thou stayest, I will give thee each as many wives as thou wantest."

Quegga, who had accompanied me, thought this would surely induce us to stay, but our answer was still the same.

Curtis then tried another strategy.

"Did we not fight for thee, and by magic help to scatter thy enemies?"

"It is true, oh, great Incubu."

"Did we not show thee the magic tubes which sent death to the vermin that marched against thee?"

"Great tage, it is most true."

"Then let thy servants depart into their own land."

"Never! By my royal word I say it. Never shalt thou leave."

"Canst thou prevent it?"

"Ay, and thy body shall be given to the Zemeraffes."

"Hark ye, Kasheebar!" exclaimed Fjord, "unless thou

allowest me to go in peace, then thy body shall feed the aasvogels, and Koro shall be eaten by the Zemeraffes."

"Seize him!" commanded the king.

Two warriors stepped forward and would have pinioned Fjord, but he knocked one down with a sledge-hammer blow from his fist, and the other faced a drawn revolver.

The warrior stepped back frightened, for he had seen the deadly effects of the magic tube.

"Seize him!" again cried the king.

Curtis shouted loud enough for all to hear:

"Great warriors and mighty people. We have fought by your side and used our magic to defeat your enemies. Now hark ye! unless we are allowed to go, the sun shall cease to shine, the moon will be turned into blood, and every man among ye shall march before the death-killing eye of the mighty rock."

The last hit told, for the men would rather face a foe a thousand strong than look upon the burning eye.

The warriors trembled. The king saw he was losing his power over them, so he ordered the drum to be sounded, and then his council drew near.

"Let the magicians show their power. The moon will shine to-night, let it be as blood. Then will the Kashee-burs believe the words of the white men."

"We are in a pretty pickle now," I said, in English, "all through the speech of Curtis."

"Great monarch!" exclaimed Curtis, "the white men will turn the moon as thou directest."

"What do you mean, Curtis?" I asked.

"Look yonder at the horizon," he answered, "and you will see a purple haze, that always is a forerunner of a blood-red moon. Ask Good."

"It is true! By Jupiter! it will be as red as fire to-night."

"Go, then, to thy houses!" commanded the king. "And at moonrise thou shalt have thy answer."

As we left the king's presence, Curtis advised us to get ready to leave at once, for the blood-red color of the moon might only last an hour or so, and the king might repent.

"It will never do," he said, "for our magic to fail now."

We got together our things and prepared for our journey.

Quegga had already well repaid us for our promise to take her, for she was able to tell us the way to our camp without going back through the caves and over the mysterious lake.

She was, after all, the only woman to go with us, for the wives of the others would not consent to leave Kasheebar.

Curtis promised Moya that he would intercede with the king, and get permission for the women to stay as the monarch's servants, a position they might claim if we had died in battle.

A few strings of beads each satisfied them, and I verily believe such was their low natures, that they would willingly have been mated with Vantackas or Zemeraffes rather than go with us, if only we had given them some beads.

With Quegga it was different. She had nothing in common with them. She had received a rude education, and her natural instincts were of a higher order.

I told her that if ever we left the desert and mountains she would have to wear clothes. She laughed, and wanted to put on my trousers and see how she looked. But a grim look of half indignation and yet with a glimmer of suppressed fun, came over her face when I drew for her the appearance of a fashionable beauty, and described the clothes she would have to wear.

"How can they walk?" she asked when I tried to explain to her the skirts; and it was with the greatest difficulty I could make her understand that women were not all deformed.

"Why should they hide their forms in such strange garments," she asked, "unless they wish to hide some deformity?"

It was a picture worthy of a painter to witness her astonishment, when I tried to describe other garments, especially the corset, which seemed to her in her rude, uncivilized way very barbarous.

When I had explained my picture, she laughed loudly and danced about with pleasure, at what she was pleased to call my fun, for I could not make her believe that any one would dress in that strange way.

When Curtis and Fjord told her that the other women preferred to stay, I noticed a shudder of disgust pass over her at the thought of the terrible fate before them.

We had everything ready for our departure, and had purchased from one of the nobles two oxen—we gave three strings of beads and two china dolls for them—on the backs of which we fastened our boat, filled with stores, including plenty of provisions, and two large jars of the almond honey, of which Quegga had quite a large store.

The time for moon-rising was close at hand, and so we went with hearts beating rather rapidly to the king's kraal.

Curtis almost wished that Moya would accompany him, but Fjord and Good were fickle and laughingly said that "there were just as good fish in the sea," and that they did not care to have women with them who were unwilling.

Good sighed, and I overheard him in a low voice murmur, "If it had only been Foulata."

The king and his nobles had gathered outside the kraal, and began as soon as we arrived to entreat us to change our plans and stay.

We were offered wives galore, and promised our choice of all the girls every year, but this was no temptation to us.

Then we were offered nobility, imagine what a bribe that was to Sir Henry Curtis who owned enough wealth to purchase the whole country for many miles, and whose family had held the title of baronet ever since the first creation of that degree of nobility.

When we remained unmoved by these very liberal offers, the king began to storm like a madman; this mood however only lasted a few minutes, for he changed immediately into a coaxing humor, and offered to disinherit Koro and announce Curtis as his successor.

Again his manner changed, and now he wanted us to purchase his permission.

Would I give him my glass?

No! Well then would we leave him a magic tube?

Fjord explained that it was of no use unless he had the

white man's powder which could only be got in the lands afar off.

I gave him several little dolls and we each handed him some beads.

These delighted the old fellow, and he gave his word that we should be allowed to depart in peace if the moon was indeed blood. If not, we must stay.

Good then put in his prayer. He asked that Moya, Beypa, Zoma, and Adera, the wives of himself, Curtis, Fjord and Umbilla might be admitted into his presence as perpetual servants.

To this he readily agreed, and then asked about Quegga.

"She goes with us."

"No, by my great father, she does not; the witches denied her to me before, but now she shall be mine."

The old monster intended having Quegga as his wife.

I asked Quegga if she would accept the honor; for reply she showed me a small spear head, which, she said in a low voice, should pierce her heart if I did not take her with me.

I thanked the girl for her devotion, and just at the moment the moon was seen just rising above the horizon.

No sooner had the natives seen it than they all fell on their faces, the king included, and bade us withdraw our curse.

The moon was redder than I had ever seen it.

The strange phenomenon had scarcely been noticed by the Kasheebars before, and they had their feelings worked up to the highest pitch of excitement because of our threat to produce such effect.

We seized the opportunity, and in less than half an hour were outside the village and on our way to new dangers, and perhaps stranger adventures.

CHAPTER XX.

FJORD'S ADVENTURES IN THE SUBTERRANEAN LAKE.

WE thought it wise to journey some few miles before we camped for the night for fear that "the old triangle," as we always called Kasheebar when alone, should change his mind and send his warriors after us.

After walking a distance of nearly six miles, we found a place which formed a natural camp, and here we rested for the night.

Quegga slept in the boat which we had taken from the oxen; while the men of our party rolled themselves in their rugs and soon were fast asleep.

We kept watch in turns, but were not disturbed once during the night.

The mooonbeams died away, and the gray dawn appeared ushering in the glorious reign of King Sol.

Never had I beheld a more glorious sunrise.

Quegga broke forth in a fit of rapturous poetry, telling of the grandeur of the sun and of man:

"We, like the sun," went the chant, "arise out of nothing, the great dark, and shine for a brief time, going down again into the dark which no man knoweth of, and from which none can return."

This was the morning anthem of the true child of nature, to whom the sun is the greatest mystery, as it really is to us, even though we profess to measure and weigh it, to calculate its eclipses and describe its spots.

It is still a mystery, great and profound, and with all our knowledge we are not so far beyond the savage, who, when asked to describe the Deity, pointed reverently to the great shining orb of day.

We told Quegga of our journey through the mountain, and Fjord described the place where the men had been ordered to encamp with our wagon and oxen.

She was sure she could guide us to the place, so we placed ourselves under her care, and never had travelers a better guide.

Descending the picturesque, rocky hill, which we had crossed on our way from Kasheebar, we entered upon a totally distinct country.

We had now before us an interminable sea of prairies, covering to the horizon a series of gentle undulations inclining from the east to the west.

There were but few trees; those we saw were the dolape palms, and were scattered at long intervals in the bright yellow surface of the high grass.

Our path was narrow, but good.

It had been made by quaggas and zebras, which were very numerous in that part of the dark continent.

All that day we followed the path, only resting for two hours when the sun was at its hottest.

The tsetse fly was a great tormentor, and as its sting was poisonous, we were not very amiable by the time our faces were well stung.

Little blisters filled with water would rise wherever the fly had inserted its sting, and the itching was so great that we had great difficulty in keeping from scratching.

At night we camped by the side of a small stream whose water was refreshing.

The next day we continued our journey through the long prairie grass, which attained a height of ten feet.

Another night passed and then Quegga promised us we should before nightfall be with our men.

It was a weary march, but made worse by the fact that Quegga had lost the road; a large herd of elephants had obscured it by trampling hundreds of paths in all directions. The wind was blowing strong from the south and I proposed to clear the country toward the north by firing the prairies. There were numerous deep swamps in the bottoms between the undulations, and upon our arrival at one of these green dells I fired the grass on the opposite side.

In a few minutes it roared before us, and we enjoyed the grand sight of the boundless prairie blazing like the infernal regions, and rapidly clearing a path for us to the north.

The words of Edgar Allan Poe came to my mind as I saw the magnificent blaze, and I could not refrain from repeating:

" I am Monarch of the Fire—I am Vassal King of Death;
World encircling with the shadow of its doom upon my breath;
With the symbol of hereafter flaming from my fatal face,
I command the 'Eternal Fire'! Higher, higher, higher, higher
Leap my ministering demons, like phantasmagoric lemans,
Hugging universal nature in their hideous embrace."

Flocks of buzzards and the beautiful variety of flycatchers thronged to the dense smoke to prey upon the innumerable insects that endeavored to escape from the approaching fire.

In about an hour we marched over the black and

smoking ground, every now and then meeting dead stumps of palm trees blazing; until at length we reached another swamp. There the fire had stopped in its direct journey and had been driven by the long, green reeds to the east and west.

Again the tedious way of clearing had to be gone through, and the grass was fired on the opposite side, while we waited until the cleared way was cool enough for our march.

We were perfectly black, for the wind brought showers of ashes that fell like so much black snow upon us, making our hands and faces darker than Quegga's or Umbilla's.

The march was exceedingly fatiguing, and took three times as long as it would have done if the elephants had not destroyed our path.

We were tired of our troublesome journey, and wished we had gone through the hills; but even then, as Fjord pointed out, we should have had three days' march round the hill, and would not have fared any better.

It was still early, but having arrived at another swamp, we thought it better to camp on its side for the night than to try another tedious march that night.

The happiest one in the party was the brave woman, Quegga.

She would not burden the oxen, and so marched every step of the way. She was as strong as any man, and felt inclined to be indignant when I suggested she must be tired of walking.

"I wear no skirts," she said in reply, insinuating that the fatigue of the white women and their weakness came, in the estimation of the colored Venus, from wearing clothes.

In crossing the swamp next morning a laughable thing occurred.

Captain John Good, R. N., was terribly afraid of water, and after we had crossed two swamps he insisted on riding over the others on the oxen, so that he might not spoil his boots and trousers.

The water in these swamps was on an average eight or ten inches deep, and the swamps mostly as many yards wide.

The swamp we had to cross had a very soft bottom, and

before the oxen with the boat and Captain Good on their back had gone a yard, they sunk up to their girths.

Good jumped off, and fortunately landed safely, but how was he to get over.

Umbilla volunteered to carry him over on his back, and Good was pleased to accept the offer. It was amusing to see Umbilla with the captain, eye-glass and all, crossing the swamp; but when in the middle the tenacious bottom gave way, and Umbilla sank and remained immovably fixed, while Good, who was so afraid of spoiling his clothes, floundered about, frog-like, in the muddy water.

It required all the strength of Curtis, Fjord, and myself to extricate Umbilla, Good being too much occupied with his clothes to think of helping his devoted servant.

Quegga laughed heartily at the *contretemps*, and I am afraid that had it not been for his natural gallantry she would have made an enemy of the naval hero.

Two hours before nightfall we saw almost close to us the top of our tented wagon, and we hurried forward, glad to find ourselves once more free to roam where we pleased.

Although Umbilla had given his word that our men would not steal our wagon and oxen, I much doubted their honesty, and it was an agreeable surprise to find our property intact, for we had been away nearly three months.

Quegga rewarded the faithful Kaffirs by giving them a good drink of the almond honey, and as the thick liquid glided down their capacious throats their eyes sparkled with delight.

Henceforward the girl was their "kooma" (queen).

The provisions were nearly exhausted, and the men had serious thoughts of going south with the wagon and oxen, of which only three remained alive. I had a pretty strong opinion that some of the oxen had been eaten, but even if so we could not blame the men, for better eat all than run the risk of starving.

Quegga was delighted with the wagon, but absolutely refused to accept its tented part for her bedchamber.

She would take her watch with me, and would not on any account trespass on the comfort of the others.

At first she wanted to roll herself up in a blanket and

camp outside with the men, but that, of course, I would not allow.

We made a compromise with her by hanging a skin across the tent, thus dividing it into two parts, giving her one for her own private use, in which she could sleep on her soft rugs of fur and skins; the other, containing the bed, was reserved for the men.

As there were now four of us, we divided the night so that while two slept, the other two stayed by the camp-fire, and watched.

Fjord elected to share the watch with me, and this suited me exactly, as I had so many things about which I wished to talk to him, and I had a strong desire to recall our adventures in search of *He*, on the island of Rapa Nui.

When the others had retired, we lighted our pipes and soon enjoyed watching the columns of curling smoke which ascended therefrom.

"I have never told you about my dive into that lake," said Fjord.

"No, and although I have been brimful of curiosity, I have scarcely liked to ask you."

"Well, if you would like to hear about it, I will tell you."

"There is nothing I should like better."

"Then here goes, old fellow, but don't laugh at me, there I know you will not, for we have shared so many strange adventures together that I do not hesitate to tell you things which I should expect others to laugh at."

"You can trust me, Fjord."

"I know it. Well, when I jumped out of the boat, I expected to take an ordinary dive, keeping under water for a couple of minutes or thereabouts.

"No sooner did my head strike the surface than I knew it was something different to ordinary water. We had observed its transparency and its luminous nature, but I was not prepared to find that either I could breathe freely under the water, or else be able to live without breathing.

"You open your eyes, I knew you would, but I can only tell you my impression. I went down lower and still lower until I could no longer see the boat above me. That suffocating sensation always experienced in the water by a diver I did not feel, but on the contrary, felt inclined to laugh and talk. Honestly, I don't think I stopped breathing. It seemed that I should never stop, and the lower I went the stranger appeared the water.

"After sinking, for several minutes so it appeared, the water was apparently changed into air, and I opened my mouth and took a good long breath.

"I was refreshed, and regretted that you were awaiting me.

"I was not in sight of the bottom, yet I could walk. Don't laugh, though the idea is, I admit, perfectly ridiculous; but it was real to me, and I walked about for a minute, utterly forgetful of the fact that you were waiting for my reappearance.

"How long I stayed there I have no idea; I suppose it could not have been long, or you would have looked upon me as dead and continued your journey.

"All round me were beautiful flowers and luscious fruits, all apparently growing in the air, or perhaps I had better say water. Every time I turned my eyes about, I saw fresh wonders; then, as my organ of admiration was being worked upon pretty largely, I saw, or thought I did, some mighty pretty girls; their hair was of a greenish golden hue, and hung in long tresses completely over their bodies. I think they were nude, but the hair was so thick, as it divided over the shoulders and hung over the bosom down to their feet, that it formed a very thick and effectual covering.

"These girls seemed also to walk on the air, and as they approached me, sang:

"'Welcome, welcome, stranger,
To our home beneath the waves.'

"The cadence was pleasing, and I moved forward to try to catch the singers, but as I approached near, one would take a quantity of her hair and throw it from her, causing it to fall like a shower over me. It was tantalizing, and I was determined to catch the girls, when they disappeared as suddenly as they had come. I then thought of you, and tried to pass through the water, but could not do it. After each ineffectual attempt a musical, mocking laugh greeted my ears.

"Then, when I was about to despair of ever finding you again the girls reappeared, singing 'Stranger, stranger, follow, follow!" I did so, and a moment later found myself clinging to the rock and calling for you. What think you?"

"I don't know what to say," was my guarded response.

"Well, Theo., I can talk plainly to you; I have done so ever since your father asked me in Madre di Dios to look afer you, so I ask you which is the most probable way to explain the strange phenomenon. Did I when I got into the water become stunned by concussion and dream about the wonders while floating down the river to the rock, or did I really see all I have described?"

I thought for a few moments, and then not liking to express an opinion, I said:

"That is a hard nut to crack."

"I know it; but if it was all a dream, there are some peculiar things which need explanation. Did you dream you saw the submarine fight? Was it a dream of yours and Curtis', ay, and Good too, for I think you told me he was with you, did you all dream, I ask you, about the luminous appearance of the stone thrown into the water?"

"No, Fjord, that was no dream. And I will tell you more; as you descended, your body became equally luminous, and the flesh appeared transparent."

"How then do you explain it?"

"I must give it up, as the clown says in the circus, and fall back on Shakespeare, saying with him:

"But this is wondrous strange!
There are more things in heaven and earth
Than are dreamt of in your philosophy."

"I cannot explain it," said Fjord. "But when I think of it all, I am inclined to look upon it as a phantasm, a conjuration of the imagination."

Our watch had expired, and to the moment Curtis and Good were ready to take our places.

CHAPTER XXI.
THROUGH THE MOUNTAINS.

WHEN morning dawned, we held a council to determine which direction we should take, and what was to be our ultimate aim.

"I tell you, friends, I came to Africa to search for *It*, and *It* I am going to find," declared Fjord with emphasis.

"My dear Yankee," said Curtis, "don't get excited, we are all bent on the same thing; now what we wish to know is, which is the best way, the quickest and easiest way to find the mysterious *It ?*"

"What do you think, Sir Henry?" asked Good.

"Before I give my opinion let me recapitulate. We are explorers, spending our money, risking our lives, denying ourselves comforts and luxuries, for what? Not pleasure, for that we have made but a secondary object, but primarily and principally our object is the discovery of what we have named *It*. The philosophy of the matter resolving itself in my mind somewhat after this fashion: Man is a highly developed animal, formed by a process of natural selection that went on for unknown ages among the individuals of a species called the anthropomorphous apes. A great accumulation of facts is made; following one another in certain order; all those which precede a certain intermediate link are perhaps duly and independently proved, and the same may be the case with those that follow that link. Do you understand me?"

"Perfectly," I answered.

"Go on," said Fjord. "I am deeply interested."

"Then if I make myself thoroughly clear, I will continue by saying that there is no proof of the fact that constitutes the link and makes the complete chain of evidence. We are told very plainly that no one has yet discovered that the intermediate link ever actually existed; that explorations have not yet revealed to us all the specimens of the animal and vegetable kingdom that may have inhabited the world; but that the analogies which lead up and down to that undiscovered link are such that it must have existed, and that we may confidently expect that the actual proof will be discovered. Now, I take our position to be this: We are in search of that missing link—that intermediate between the man and his primordial natural-selection ancestor."

"By Jupiter, Curtis, write that down so that Aristo may get it exact in his book," said Fjord. "It is too good to be lost."

"Have I stated the case?"

"Exactly," answered Good.

"Capitally," was my response.

"It has been ascertained beyond all doubt that two mysterious personages called *He* and *She* undoubtedly lived for several centuries, and found the means of triumphing over decay and death. It was proved that a metamorphosis took place in each case, the one assuming the shape of a goat, the other returning to the form of a wretched-looking ape. These instances show that there is a connection between the animal and human nature. Now, having found so much, it is only reasonable to suppose we shall discover more."

"Excellent, but theory, my friend, won't help us very much," exclaimed Good, who I verily think only joined the expedition for the sake of the sport, and did not care for the scientific aspect of our journey.

"True, my dear fellow, therefore I come to the question of route. We found the Zemeraffes and Vantackas, two very important links in our chain of evidence; is it not natural to suppose that *It* can be found near by? Theo. favors the Sahara, and so evidently does Quatermain; while I am for searching nearer here, and should start among the Kagehyis."

"One advantage of your idea is, that by going through the Kagehyi territory we are on our way north to Sahara," I said.

"Then to Kagehyi let us go, but who can direct the way?"

Umbilla was entirely ignorant of the route as was also the Kaffirs. As for Quegga, I am ashamed to say we had forgotten her, and had carried on our long conversation in English, so the poor girl had not understood one word.

"Quegga, knowest thou the way to Kagehyi?"

"I do, my lord."

"How the deuce does she know her way about so?" asked Good in English.

The same idea had crossed my mind, and so I asked her.

"The witches and wise women can go where they please, and they took me with them."

"Oh."

The answer was satisfactory. We gave orders to get all in readiness to start on our long journey.

All was soon confusion and hurry, and in a couple of hours we were ready to leave the prairie and seek new adventures in the hills beyond.

All that day we marched without meeting with any adventures; at night we camped at the foot of a most picturesque mountain.

This camp was to be our dwelling-place for nearly a month, for the wonderful constitution possessed by Curtis had at length given way, and he was unable to rise from his bed.

A severe fever had attacked him, and for forty-eight hours I despaired of ever seeing him again on the march.

So near death was he, that Umbilla got ready to dig a deep grave for him, so that as soon as death occurred he could be buried before the vultures and jackals scented the corpse.

I used quinine unsparingly, and, at last, was rewarded for my medical skill by seeing Curtis open his eyes and ask what the time was. It was the first gleam of consciousness.

Another trouble overtook us; my arm, which had been wounded by the poisoned spear, began to trouble me, and, so great was the pain, that the arm was really useless. I caught a severe cold, and that and the bad wound prostrated me also, so Fjord and Good had two sick people in camp to wait upon.

I have mentioned the two, but Umbilla was as faithful as any one could be, and as for Quegga, I do not think she ever slept. Her devotion was something marvelous.

By dint of careful nursing and plenty of quinine we recovered, and, at the end of twenty-seven days' encampment, resumed our journey.

When we started, at six o'clock in the morning, we commenced the most lovely journey that I had ever made in Africa.

Winding through the very bosom of the mountains, well covered with forest until the bare peaks towered above all vegetation, to the height of about five thousand feet, we continued through narrow valleys bordered by abrupt spurs of the mountain running up to a height of two thousand feet.

On several of the peaks we could see a village; evidently these impregnable positions had been chosen for security.

Quegga informed us that our journey was now a very difficult one, being entirely up-hill, but that she believed the oxen would be able to make the ascent.

For four hours we toiled up a very steep zigzag pass.

The air was most invigorating, and did Curtis and I more good, I really believe, than all the medicine we had taken.

Beautiful wild-flowers, some of which sent out their sweet perfume on the air, ornamented the route, and innumerable grape vines hung in festoons from tree to tree.

We seemed to be entering a veritable Paradise.

When we arrived at the summit of the pass we had reached an altitude of nearly three thousand feet.

In addition to the grapes and flowers, there was plenty of fruit. We regaled ourselves, and gathered quite a quantity of apples and yellow plums to take with us.

On either side the scenery was very fine, to the east and northeast masses of high mountains, while to the west and south were vast tracts of land as green as any park in old England.

Although the ascent had taken us four hours, the descent on the other side only occupied about half an hour, for we were on an elevated plateau that formed the watershed between the east and west.

Here we experienced a change of climate, for the weather seemed cold compared to that on the other side of the hills, and the rain was falling in such quantities that we were all soaked to the skin, that is those who had not the good fortune to be in the tented wagon.

I called a halt for I was really exhausted, and seeing a house evidently deserted, I sent Umbilla to prospect.

He returned and said it was good and wholesome and that there were no signs of any one having occupied it recently.

We were glad to hear this news, for both Curtis and I were fatigued and wanted rest.

I felt uneasy about Quegga, for I began to fear she was

promising an attack of fever; I gave her some quinine and compelled her to take more rest. Poor, brave girl, she was so grateful to us for allowing her to accompany us, that she would insist on doing more than her strength really allowed.

My forebodings were only too soon realized and our guide and faithful friend was stricken down.

For days she tossed about in delirium, begging us at times not to leave her, and then at others urging us to go forward leaving her to die alone.

She seemed to shrink from all attention, fearing that it gave us trouble.

I had plenty of assistance, but took the burden on myself, for I had seen her devotion and felt that I alone should wait on her.

The house became quite comfortable and we had but one fear, and that was, that the owner might reappear and summarily eject us.

The other members of the party went out shooting and hunting, though there was not much game at such a high altitude.

However they bagged some very fine specimens of the antelope, and several very large gnus.

A very peculiar kind of wild duck came flying over the hills, evidently driven by some great cause from its lake. Fjord brought it down, and it fell close to the house.

It was of a magnificent variety and as large as a muscovy, having a copper and blue colored tinseled back and wings, with a white but speckled head and neck.

This duck had a peculiarity in a fleshy protuberance of the back standing up about an inch and a half high. It looked almost like a cock's comb.

Although very handsome in appearance we thought more about the eating, and found it the most delicious we had ever tasted.

Curtis met with some warriors while he was out one day, and they had seen his prowess with the gun.

"Come along with us," said the chief, "bring all your men and guns and we will attack a village near here and take their molotes (iron hoes) and cattle; you keep the cattle and we will have the molotes."

Curtis asked him if the village was in an enemy's country.

"No, oh, no!" he answered, "it is close here, but the people are rather headstrong, and it will do them good to kill a few and take their molotes."

Curtis declined the offer, and then the chief drew himself up in all the dignity of his position, and said:

"If you are afraid, I will get other allies."

"Why don't you make molotes for yourself?" asked Sir Henry.

"Where is the use, when we can always take as many as we want, and have sport besides?"

With this, to him, very satisfactory answer, the chief and his men walked away, mumbling to themselves of the cowardice of the white men.

Fjord and Good had been away several days, and we began to be uneasy about them, but when they returned we found they had been doing good service.

They had reached a village in the Kagehyi district, and had, by various tricks of magic, worked their way into the graces of the people so effectually that they had learned a great deal that we wanted to know.

Besides, they had secured five Kagehyis as servants, for we were sadly in need of additional men if we had to take a long journey.

CHAPTER XXII.

QUEGGA'S OFFER OF SELF-SACRIFICE.

Fjord told us that the medicine man of the Kagehyis was a most learned philosopher, and talked with the greatest verbosity, especially when under the influence of a good stiff drink of cognac, which Good always carried with him.

The Kagehyis were ruled by a king—so explained the medicine man—who was the direct descendant of the Sun God and the Goddess of the Waters. But even this length of pedigree would not insure constant obedience, so the gods favored the ruler by allowing him to be in constant communication with the Great White Moon.

"The Moon—don't laugh," said Fjord, as he saw the smile gradually appear on my face. "The Moon, I learned, was a woman, white and very beautiful, and she reigned over a country which was very peculiar."

"In what way?" asked Curtis.

"That I can scarcely tell you," answered Fjord, "but the old medicine man said that the people were brave and handsome, but that she had other people who lived in the earth, above the earth and over the earth."

"Those were the same words used by the herald in the late war with the Kasheebars," I remarked.

"Yes, the very same," said Good, "but go on, Fjord, tell our comrades what else was said."

"You are all too impatient," continued Fjord. "This old philosopher after another drink from Good's pocket flask, said that the Moon—that is this ruler, you know—had no soldiers to guard her, but in her kraal she had lions and leopards, and other animals, and the gate was guarded by two elephants, which had a great propensity of killing those who ventured too near."

"Don't you think the old fellow was romancing?" I asked.

"No," asserted Fjord with emphasis.

"I will tell you what I think of it all," said Good, who was not over-pleased about the prospect of a long journey. "I imagine some missionaries or traders have been hoaxing the Kagehyis, and that for purposes of their own have told him of the English Queen, who rules over people in every part of the world."

"That may be so," replied Fjord, "but did not the medicine man say that the late king had seen this queen?"

"Easily said, now that the old fellow is dead."

"You are an awful skeptic, Good. I only report what I found out, and tell of the route we shall have to take if we go to this wonderful country."

"Did he give you a plan of the route?" I asked.

"Not exactly, but he gave such minute directions that I reckon we can find the way."

"Where is it?" asked Curtis.

"From the route recommended, I should say it was somewhere in the unexplored Desert of the Gallas."

"Then Quatermain was on the right tack."

"It seems so," answered Curtis. "And there can be no harm in going that way. One trip is as good as another, I should say."

"It is the best part of Africa for sport," I said, whereupon Good's eyes sparkled, and looking at me, asked:

"Do you mean it?"

"I do, and I imagine that Curtis will agree with me."

"That I do, most cheerfully."

"When do we start?" asked Good, now quite enthusiastic.

"As soon as Quegga is fit to be moved," was my reply.

We were all desirous of leaving our present quarters, although they were really comfortable; but not one of us even suggested going until our patient was recovered and strong enough for the journey.

The days passed and lengthened into weeks, and I began to fear that we should be compelled to make a grave by the side of the mountain for the dear, devoted girl. My heart was sad at the thought.

One morning she opened her eyes, and in a voice soft and sweet, called my name.

It was the sweetest music I had ever listened to from mortal, male or female.

"How long have I been sick?" she asked.

I told her, and the bright eyes filled with tears.

"Why did you not leave me?"

"You would have died."

"Better so, than that you, my own, my beloved, should be compelled to waste your time here."

I soothed her, and was glad to find that from that time she began to improve.

One day, when she was able to walk about a little, she called me to her, and, with low, sweet voice, said:

"I have been thinking that I am a burden to you."

"No, Quegga, far from it."

"But I must be so; when you get to a friendly tribe leave me, or, if you find means to send me to Abyssinia, please do so."

"Quegga, do you mean it?"

"I do."

"Don't you love me?"

"No."

And then the girl burst into tears. I saw this new evidence of her self-sacrificing nature, and could read her better than she thought.

"Oh, Quegga," I said, "why speak falsely?"

"I love you, yes; oh, my dear one, I love you more than my poor words can tell. Thou art the life of my life, the soul of my soul; thou art my all, my sun, my god."

"Then why wish to leave me?"

Again she burst into tears, and I clasped her in my arms, saying:

"Quegga, when you can truly say that you do not love me, then I will listen to thy request. Until then where I am there thou shalt be."

Her recovery was rapid after that, and I could see that her long sickness was in a measure caused by the mental anxiety and the idea of self-sacrifice. I really believe she had wished to die, so that I might be free from the trouble of her presence.

Another week, and we were equipped for our journey.

The five men who had been obtained by purchase from the Kagehyis were horrible-looking creatures, and not such as I cared to have near me, but we were compelled to have more assistance, and only slaves traveling with their owners were allowed to leave Kagehyi; therefore we had to fall into the custom and become slave-owners.

The cost of the five men, strong as elephants, was five pounds of beads and a china doll.

Human flesh has but small market value in that part of Africa.

Although repulsive-looking creatures, they were very tractable and docile, and plodded along apparently without a care or trouble.

We had gone about six miles when we fell in with a score or so of natives who wanted to dispute the right of way with us.

They were insulting and very demonstrative in their opposition, but we parleyed with them, and at last got through their ranks, only to find a shower of arrows sent after us. We returned the compliment by a few bullets from our rifles, and two of the men fell dead. The others were so scared that they ran at great speed down the sides of the hill. We were sure they would be killed by their precipitate flight, but, as far as we could judge, they safely arrived at the bottom—some five hundred feet.

I sent my men back to throw the dead bodies over the cliff, afraid that they would be the means of attracting jackals, and so, perhaps, be a danger to us.

Quegga and Fjord rode in the wagon, for Fjord had sprained his right knee in a leap after some game, and so found walking troublesome.

We reached the entrance to a pass through which the Kagehyis said we must go.

The mountain rose abruptly on our left, while the base was entirely choked with enormous fragments of gray granite that having fallen from the face of the mountains had completely blocked the pass.

Even the oxen had difficulty in getting through, and I wondered how it would be possible to get the wagon over the stones.

After two hours' exertion, we had moved the wagon about ten yards.

What was to be done? We were in a dilemma.

One of the Kagehyis said there was a great chief who would buy the wagon.

It was only about a day's march to the kraal and back.

Curtis and Fjord accompanied the man to the kraal, taking the wagon with them.

The next afternoon, to our joy we found them returning with all our stores loaded on the backs of donkeys.

We had to leave our boat, for no one knew its uses, and it was too heavy to carry.

So once again we tried the pass.

We had two extra donkeys, and on one of these we seated Quegga, while Fjord occupied the other.

We found the pass got more difficult every yard, for in addition to the great rocks which obstructed it, we came across deep ravines formed by the torrents that during the rainy season tore everything before them in their impetuous descent from the mountains.

To increase still further our difficulties many trees and bushes were growing in the interstices of the rocks; these in many cases had to be removed before the donkeys with their loads could get under.

A Kagehyi told us a very pleasing story, and his mouth seemed to water as he related it. He said that, many moons ago, a white man, who wanted to tell the Kagehyis about a new god he had found,* and who brought with him a hundred men who were to carry his stores, gave the people Kagehyis water which set their throats on fire. This the people did not like and so sent the white man home. When he and his men got just here—and the Kagehyi who was telling the story with wonderful dramatic power, pointed first up the mountain and then to the pass on which we were resting a short time—when he got just here, the Kagehyis threw rocks down, "and, why, yes," said the man, "here are some of the bones."

The fellow picked up a bone which, sure enough, was that of a man.

The story was not calculated to make us braver, for we could easily see that if the natives were hostile, they could exterminate us in five minutes without danger to themselves.

The Kagehyi, evidently glorying in the effect his story had produced, began asking questions, and very pointedly asked why we had left the Kasheebars.

Could it be that these savages had lured us into the pass so that we might be destroyed for the part we had taken against them in the recent war?

We began to fear such was the case, for the fellows grew more inquisitive and insulting at every step.

Warning my comrades of the possible treachery, we kept a sharp lookout, and plainly intimated that the first suspicious act would cause the Kagehyi to lose his life.

Bad as the pass was, we had hope before us, for our guides said that beyond this spot there was level and unbroken ground the whole way to the great country, ruled over by the Moon.

After turning a sharp angle of the mountain, leaving the cliff abruptly rising to the left from the narrow path, we descended a ravine worse than any place we had yet encountered, and it was impossible for us to make any headway mounted; all had to get off the donkeys and oxen and walk very carefully. On arriving at the summit a lovely view burst upon us. The valley was about five hundred feet below, and only a mile distant.

* Evidently a Christian missionary was meant, though it is hard to believe that any missionary would give fire-water to the savages.—ED.

Beautiful mountains rising in all their grandeur until their summits pierced the clouds walled in the narrow vale; while the landscape of forest and plain was bounded some fifty miles distant by the blue mountains of the north.

Below us in the valley I observed some prodigious trees growing close to a ravine, in which was running water, and the sides of the valley under the mountains being, as usual, a mass of crumbling pieces of rock.

I noticed quite a number of villages strongly fortified with strong bamboo palisades. The valley was very thickly populated.

Curtis drew me on one side.

"What think you," he asked, "are we in for treachery?"

"I am afraid so."

"Then we may bid good-bye to our hopes, for if we have to fight a way through a valley a quarter of a mile wide, hemmed in by walls of rock, and bristling with lances and poisoned arrows, there is not much chance for us."

"No, and we shall have to be on the constant look-out."

Fjord and Good did not share our fears; but both were in high spirits over the chances we should have, not only for exploration, but for sport. And Fjord had become almost as great an enthusiast on the subject of game as the naval officer himself.

CHAPTER XXIII.
THE KING OF AAGANDA.

WE passed through the valley safely, meeting with neither treachery nor hostility, and we were able to breathe more freely when we were on the open plain.

Day after day we marched through scenery so grand that the pencil of the most skillful artist could scarcely do justice to its wonders.

Quegga had become to all of us a *Kooma*,* we had got to look upon her as our good fortune. Her health was entirely restored and now she was assiduous in her efforts to make us all comfortable.

* Good fairy.

As for the Kagehyis they were almost ready to prostrate themselves before her. She was so gentle and kind.

On the tenth day after leaving the narrow pass we met a runner from a tribe which we had reason to consider hostile.

When he saw us, he began talking in several languages so that at least a few words might be understood.

It was a peculiar way of proceeding, but perhaps a good one. We selected a language, and then the real dialogue commenced.

He invited us to the village beyond the palms, and promised us a welcome.

This we knew but to be the African custom, so we asked why so good a messenger needed his spear and shield.

His answer was plausible, he might meet enemies.

But we knew if we parleyed long enough we should make him commit himself.

We had only to wait, and in a few moments he asked, did we want ivories (tusks).

"No," I answered, "we only desired to pass on our way. We were not traders."

"But the ivories are good."

"Yes," answered Curtis, "but all the ivory in Africa would not tempt us to become traders."

"Then why travel through the valleys and over the plains."

While the man had been asking the last question, we saw he was uneasy, this put us on our guard, but hardly quick enough, for we were instantly surrounded by over a hundred of the dirtiest-looking creatures we had ever seen.

They showed their hostility so clearly that I knew we should have a hard struggle, but as oftentimes a little ready wit is best, I turned to the runner who had so beguiled us, and evidently signaled his tribe to annoy, if not to attack us, and asked:

"Is not the country large enough for us all? Take us to your ruler so that we may give the presents we have brought."

"And why should we escort you there? Give us the presents and we will take them to the king."

"No, for we are commissioned to see your king, and to none other can we talk."

"What if I am the king?"

"That would not surprise me," said Curtis, "for you look better than most kings I have seen."

This pleased the fellow, and he consented to take us to the king's kraal.

It was the best for us under the circumstances, for it was useless to fight at such long odds unless we were absolutely compelled.

The natives, strong, powerful fellows, but wretchedly dirty, kept dancing round us, and felt inclined to take greater liberties than were pleasant.

This we had to rebuke and check rather sternly.

It is lamentable, but easily understood, that the natives look with suspicion upon any who invade their land, feeling that the only object of strangers is that of robbery.

For several hours we marched, but made very slow progress, for the savages, through the fear that we should escape, kept so close to us that it was with difficulty we moved at all.

At length a village strongly fortified was seen, and we held a quiet council in English as to our mode of procedure.

Fjord and Curtis were both of opinion that if we entered the bamboo fortification we should be held as prisoners, and should stand a very poor chance of escape.

I had confidence in Quegga's judgment, and asked her what would be best to be done.

"Let my lord," she always spoke in this formal way when in the presence of others, "let my lord send a messenger to the king that presents will be given if he comes from within his village."

Acting at once on the suggestion, I said to the runner:

"Go tell thy lord and king that the men who have come from afar have brought him presents, which shall brighten his eyes and make his cheeks flame like the sun."

The man objected, and insisted that we should enter the village, but we were equally firm, so, fearing that the king might blame him unless the message was delivered, he started off at a quick trot to the village.

The savages danced and shouted, and then growing bold, demanded that we should give them some presents.

"IT." 161

We refused to do so until after the king had seen our treasures.

One fellow went up to our pack donkey and was about to open one of our bags.

Good gave him such a slap on the ear—just such a one as is often given to a child, that the fellow jumped back, startled and afraid.

We laughed heartily at the episode.

Nearly an hour elapsed before the messenger returned, and then almost immediately appeared the king.

THE KING OF AAGANDA.

He was a pleasing contrast to his subjects, and was quite a good-looking savage.

He had disfigured his lip by piercing it and sticking the wooden skewer or spike through the flesh. His form was well-knit and muscular. The dress he wore consisted of several rows of beads round the neck, another row round his waist. He had armlets and anklets of polished iron on his limbs.

That he was a brave man could easily be seen, inasmuch as he approached us unarmed and unattended.

The savages who acknowledged him as king fell back as he approached.

"What would the men from afar with the people of Aaganda?" he asked in a voice which I thought exceedingly musical.

Curtis stepped forward and told him that we were going north to the country of the Gallas, and claimed the pleasure of giving him some presents as we passed his village.

I motioned to Umbilla to bring forward some iridescent beads, the like of which had not before been seen in Africa.

When a few of them were placed in his hand, he was as delighted as is a child with a new toy.

They sparkled in the sunlight, and nothing would do but he must have them threaded. This we did for him at once, taking care to put a few big glass beads covered with gold and silver foil in with the others.

Curtis placed the necklet over his head, and without a word the king ran back to the village as fast as his strong, powerful legs could carry him.

What was in the wind now?

Was it friendship or war? Had we offended him or pleased his kingship?

The question was soon settled, for a few minutes later he was seen with several of his people leading a goat, which, when they arrived near us, was presented to Curtis, and killed immediately as a peace-offering.

The king carried a live fowl, holding it by the legs, with its head downward. Curtis had accepted Quegga's advice and mounted a donkey. The king walked up to Curtis and stroked the donkey's forefeet with the fowl, and then made a circle round it by dragging the fowl over the ground. Curtis next had his feet stroked in a similar manner, and when that ceremony had been performed, he was requested to lean forward so that the king might wave the fowl over his head.

When this performance had been gone through, the fowl was waved over the donkey's head, which showed its appreciation by kicking out behind at such a rate that the natives fell over one another in their desire to give it a wide berth.

All these ceremonies meant that we were to be welcomed as the king's guests; and as the blood of the fowl was spilt after the welcome had been gone through, so would the blood of any who offered us molestation or insult.

The village was strongly fortified, and resembled all the natives we had seen, with the solitary exception of the king—in being miserably dirty.

Being built on an eminence, it gave its inhabitants a splendid view of the picturesque landscape.

Although desirous of reaching our journey's end as early as possible, yet a few days' rest did not come amiss.

We were well treated and at a very slight expense, for we had only to give a few rows of beads to insure us the possession of everthing of the best.

The king was a man of a higher order of intellect than most of the Africans, and he told us much that was of interest.

We made no secret of the fact that we were going to explore the Gallas desert.

"It is a great treasure country," he said, "for a mighty queen who once ruled there stored up ivory, and beads, and stones that glitter, and placed a flaming sword to guard them."

Here was some information for us, so we questioned him further.

"I know not of myself, oh, most wise men, but the medicine man of my father did often tell me the stories when I was young."

"What were the stories?" asked Fjord.

"One I well remember," said the king. "He told me how long years ago, before the people of Aaganda left the mountain caves to live in houses, there lived a mighty man whose fame went to the uttermost parts of the earth, so that even the white people heard of it.

"This mighty man lived in a country across the big

waters, but his fame was so noised abroad that all were ready to pay him tribute. In the Gallas land there lived at the same time a queen whose face shone like the sun upon the waters. She was altogether comely. Her brow was like the white polished stone, and her eyes like sharp knives; her bosom was fair to look upon, and many had tried to lie upon it, but all she had turned away.

"When she heard of this mighty man in the great country across the big waters, she gathered together a hundred camel-loads of ivory, and a hundred camel-loads of gold and silver, and the same quantity of ophir wood, and went to see the great king. She crossed the big waters and laid the presents at his feet. He was so lovely to look upon that she offered herself to him, and a happy pair they made.

"Now this mighty man was building a great kraal in which to offer sacrifices to his gods, and the queen returned to her own country to gather up the treasures for him.

"She sent out to all her people to bring gold, and silver, and ivory, and this she hid away from the people in some cave of the mountains, putting a sword of fire to prevent any one ever taking the treasures. And then she died."

The king had told the story remarkably well, but the ending was very abrupt.

As we talked it over among ourselves, we came to the conclusion that the queen was known as Queen of Sheba, and that the great king was Solomon.

If so, was there any truth in the story of the treasure-caves?

And was the wonderful creature *It* a resident of the same land?

The king was rewarded for his story by an additional present of beads and dolls.

These dolls which cost less than one penny each had proved a "great draw," and many a welcome they secured.

The king was so pleased with us, or our presents, that we had great difficulty in getting away.

He offered us each some wives, and then when we excused ourselves, he said we could have a hundred slaves.

This generous offer was refused, although the slaves, if they could be relied upon, would form an excellent body-guard in case of attack, but we had two objections to the slaves: the first was their utter unreliability, and secondly, the difficulty of feeding them; although this latter was easily got rid of when we used it as an excuse to the king, for he said the slaves he would give us could steal enough to keep themselves and us as well.

Bidding him adieu at the end of the week we resumed our journey.

CHAPTER XXIV.

WE ENTER THE DESERT.

FOR days we wandered through valleys and over mountains, and then entered a prairie whose boundary seemed to be the horizon. As far as the eye could reach, we saw nothing but a dead level.

The Kagehyi guides warned us to be careful of elephant pitfalls.

I learned that the natives of that part of Africa generally hunt the elephant for its flesh, the tusks being considered as almost worthless.

The death of an elephant is a great feast for the natives, and is always a red letter time.

It supplies them with flesh which lasts a long time for a good number of people.

If the elephant is fat, so much the better, as the grease is much prized for external ornamentation.

Mixed with red ochre the fat of the elephant makes an elegant pigment for painting the skins of the women. In civilized society fashionable beauties are satisfied with putting red paint (*rouge*) on their cheeks, white powder on their foreheads and necks, cherry paste on the lips, and dark cosmetic liberally applied for the arching of the eyebrows; but in the land of which I am writing the beauties take the red ochre mixed with elephant grease and smear their body all over with it, or else, as on state occasions, paint various devices and designs on different parts of their persons.

Herein we see the wide difference between civilized and barbarian.

The natives employ various methods of killing the elephants.

Pitfalls are the most common, but the wary old bull elephants are not to be caught in this manner.

The position chosen for the pit is almost without exception in the vicinity of the drinking-place, and the old hunters show considerable cunning in felling trees across the usual run of the elephants, and sometimes cutting an open pit across the path, so as to direct the animal by such obstacles into the way of the snares.

The pits are generally about twelve feet long and three feet broad, having a depth of nine feet; the sides slope down to a width of only a foot at the bottom.

The usual path to the drinking-place being diverted by the obstacles, the animal takes the next nearest way, and meets with several of these pits artfully concealed by grass and straw, the latter often strewn with the elephant's dung to give it a more natural appearance.

If an elephant during the night falls through the deceitful surface, and his foot gets so jammed in the narrow space at the bottom that he cannot extricate himself, the remainder of the herd, thoroughly scared by the accident to one of their number, beat a hasty retreat, and generally one or more are also trapped.

The elephants are then easily killed by lances.

These pitfalls abounded on the prairie on which we had just entered.

Day after day we traveled, camping at night by the side of a running stream or a swamp, but meeting with no adventures worthy of note.

Three weeks passed away since we had left Aaganda, and we were weary of our march.

One morning—having camped late at night when it was too dark to see far forward—we looked ahead, and saw that at last we had reached the outpost of fertility.

Beyond us for miles, hundreds, it may be thousands of miles, stretched the great sea of waterless sand.

The desert across which but few, if any, white men had ever crossed.

The very sight was enough to appal the stoutest heart.

We were entering on a journey which might be our last. In all probability we should not all return alive, even if any did.

On all sides nothing but sand. As far as the eye could

reach there was no sign of a tree or anything but the Karoo shrubs which seem to thrive without water.

I felt for Quegga; how would she endure the intense blistering heat; what would she do when water gave out, and we found our tongues swollen and our throats parched.

I had grown accustomed to consider her comfort first, forgetful that many of the discomforts and dangers we felt were as nothing to her hardy nature.

We were by the side of a little spring of water, and we determined to stay there for a few days so that we might get the moon favorable for our journey across the desert; it being our intention to rest during the heat of the day and march at night.

We met with a greater misfortune, for we found that the donkeys were of no use for the desert.

Where could we obtain camels?

The Kagehyis assured us that the nearest place was distant ten days' march, and even then we were not sure they could be obtained.

Ten days, perhaps fifteen, meant a whole month wasted.

We held a council, and, as had been our custom, we left the matter for Quegga to decide.

With her usual wisdom, she suggested leaving the donkeys and surplus stores at the camp we were then occupying, and carrying what we could with us over the sands.

"Will you stay at the camp?" I asked her.

"No, not if my lord will allow me to go with him."

"But the heat—can you bear that? And then think of the dangers."

"My lord, Quegga's heart beats strong, her limbs are good, and her will is, that where her lord goes, so should she."

"My faithful one, I fear for thee; we may be without water, the fever may attack us, and our lives may pay the forfeit."

"Even then, in death, we could be united. Now hear me, my beloved, whose words are those of wisdom, and whose thoughts are of me. Hear me: on the day that thy spirit soars to the stars, and leaves thy body to the aasvogels, on that day and at that hour, thy Quegga will bid farewell to all and join thee in the land thou hast told me of, where all are white, and live forever."

It was no use trying to change her determination, she would go with us.

We arranged our stores, so that each should have the lightest amount to carry.

We made up our kit as follows:

Each man carried a Winchester repeater, with one hundred cartridges; two revolvers, with plenty of ammunition; a water bottle holding five pints of water; five pounds of biltong; two pounds of beads, for gifts; and in addition we had a blanket for each.

This was our outfit, with the exception of some quinine, and a few small surgical instruments, a pocket-filter, our hunting-knives, and two express rifles to be carried as a reserve.

I had taught Quegga how to use a revolver, and she had become quite expert.

Accordingly she carried one, and a long hunting-knife; her outfit was, in addition to these weapons, a blanket, water-bottle, and various sundries which she insisted on carrying.

When we were ready to start, we took with us Umbilla, our Zanguebar driver, and three of the Kagehyis, leaving behind, to guard our stores and donkeys, two Kagehyis and one Zanguebar.

We, to make the men more cautious, loaded the guns we left behind, and told them that if they attempted to leave, the guns would go off. The men believed this fully, and would just as soon have thought of flying as deserting their post of duty.

The moon rose beautifully above the horizon and the pale moonlight flooded the treacherous desert with silvery beams.

There is a beauty in moonlight wherever seen, but if one wishes to see it in all its grandeur, then go to the African desert, and as the beams of silvery light fall on the light-purple Karoo shrubs and the almost silvery sand, an effect is produced which charms the beholder.

The signal was given for the march, and we went forth on our perilous journey.

It was hard walking, and our feet soon became blistered.

Quegga had been induced to wear some sandals which Good had made out of some thick skin, but we had not gone far before she removed them, and declared the walking far better.

I felt inclined to try it, but Curtis and Good dissuaded me.

By the aid of my field-glass I had seen at a distance of about fifteen miles, or so it seemed to be, a little oasis, and we resolved to push on and camp there the following day.

If there was water it would save the supply we were carrying, and the coolness would also assist us to rest.

But fifteen miles over sand, with the little tufts of bushes or scrub constantly getting round our feet, was a different thing to the same distance across well-kept fields or good roads, and so we began to feel weary before we had got half way.

By strong resolve we pushed on, but no sign of the oasis. The light was not strong enough for us to see far in the distance; but when the sun's rays began to flood the dreary waste with light, we saw what made our hearts heavy and our feet grow weary.

The oasis appeared as far away as ever.

Could we have gone wrong? No. There in our rear was the place we started from, and we had taken a beeline toward the cool-looking green spot.

When we sat down to eat our morning meal we were the most despondent party that had ever crossed the desert. Even Quegga's morning anthem, rich and sweet, which had been to us of such comfort on our journey, now failed to rouse us.

When she had finished her chant she came across to where I was sitting, very despondent, my head resting on my hands, my heart heavy as lead. Placing her hands on my shoulders, she said cheerfully:

"Why so heavy? Didst thou not know of the trials of the desert? Art thou weary so soon?"

I deserved the reproach, for she had walked as far, and was bright and cheerful, while I—— But there, I am getting old, I must be, and yet I would cut a friend who told me so. No, I will not admit it. I am not old, I am but in the prime of life. Why, all my theories have been that my years should reach over a hundred, and yet with a long, vigorous life before me, I talk of being old.

"But, Quegga," I said, "I thought we should have reached yonder green oasis."

"I am glad we did not," was her answer.

I looked at her in amazement, my tongue refused to form any words. What could be her motive for such an expression?

"Yes," she continued, noting my silence: "is it not better to know that in the distance, when our water-bottles are empty, and the sun more powerful, we should reach shade and the springs?"

I saw the wisdom of the reply, and my heart became lighter.

We slept well rolled up in our blankets, which we carefully pulled over our heads, to protect them from the sun.

When we woke, we found our party smaller, for one of the Kagehyis had started back to join his fellows.

One night's journey was enough for him.

If only he had left the water-bottle; but then we had each as much as we could carry.

When the sun's fury had abated, we resumed our march, and by easy stages reached before morning the oasis.

It had been over thirty miles distant.

We stayed there two days, replenishing our water-bottles, and living upon some birds which we shot. They had been tempted to the water like ourselves, and lost their life, but perhaps were the means of prolonging ours.

I scanned the wide expanse of desert with my glass; nothing but sand met my gaze for many miles. In the far distance I saw what appeared to be a mountain; when all had looked and were of the same opinion, we asked the Kagehyi about it.

"The wonderful land to which thou wouldst go, lies beyond its gates," was his reply.

Many nights we walked, and rested during the day.

The sun had now got the mastery over the elements, and came down upon us with a power which we had never before realized.

One Zanguebar was taken sick with the fever, and in less than two hours was dead.

We all set to work to dig, with the poor tools we possessed, a grave in the sand for his body.

This led us to make holes for ourselves in which to rest during the hottest part of the day.

It afforded some shelter, but was very uncomfortable.

We had but one more small draught of water left, and our food was getting very scanty.

Quegga never murmured, but I could see that she was getting thin; her flesh began to look flabby and lose its solidity, and I much feared she too would perish.

The next day I found out the cause.

We had been sweltering in the heat for several hours, our bodies so dry and hard that the skin began to crack, when Quegga crawled up to me, and placing her water-bottle to my lips, bade me drink.

I found that it was nearly full. Here, then, was the secret; she had starved herself, saving both food and water for me.

We had been blind or we must have noticed it, but she kept up the pretense of eating and drinking so well that her self-denial was unperceived.

How could I be angry, yet I felt such admiration for her that I was inclined to be severe.

I refused to drink until she had first done more than wet her lips. I literally forced some water down her throat, and made her eat some biltong and other food.

Another night's journey without any sight of water or food.

The day passed like the others only that our agony was getting intense.

I felt guilty in drinking out of Quegga's bottle, while the others were so parched, but I could not rob her for any one, and my own drinks only amounted to a moistening of the lips.

The monotony of that march will never be forgotten.

The time came when the supply of water entirely gave out, and we were reduced to about one ounce each of food.

The mountain stared at us in the distance, but seemed a hundred miles away.

I failed to discover a blade of grass or the slightest sign of water.

What could we do?

We had now been entirely without water for three days, and as we laid ourselves down on the hot sand, we presented most pitiable objects.

Our tongues were so swollen that we were nearly choked.

The skin on our bodies cracked and broke as though it was so much burnt parchment.

We had lost almost the power of speech.

Quegga rolled about on her blanket uneasily; I thought she was dying, but she was only trying to reach me.

She could not walk, but after several ineffectual attempts, she managed to roll close to me, and then before I knew what she was doing, she pricked her arm and let her life-blood run into my mouth.

Great Heaven! I never believed such devotion, such love possible.

Now I felt the immensity of love, and I realized that it was stronger than all else in the world.

The few drops refreshed me.

Poor girl, she would have drained every drop of her heart's blood into my mouth if I had let her, but I bound up the wounded arm, and pressed a kiss on her face.

The report of a gun startled me.

I turned over and saw what gave us all the greatest happiness—lying on the sand near by was a splendid duck.

Curtis had seen some flying over us, and had just sufficient strength left to fire.

The bird gave us hope and renewed life, for as we drank its blood and ate its raw flesh we got new energy, and in addition knew that there must be water near.

The duck was a very large one, and was more than sufficient for our pressing needs.

We waited no longer for rest, but followed the flight of the ducks, hoping to find water.

After several hours' tramp across the terrible desert we saw unmistakable signs of water.

CHAPTER XXV.

A LOSS AND A GAIN.

WE forgot our pains and agony.

All we knew was that there was water near.

I felt ready to cry with joy, and down Quegga's cheeks the tears did roll copiously.

Fjord was the coolest of us all, and very fortunate was it for us that we had some one with us who was calm and collected.

"Hark!" he whispered, for we none of us could speak above a faint whisper, "what do you hear?"

"Ducks, as I'm a sinner!" exclaimed Curtis.

"True," said Fjord; "now get your guns ready, and crawl up as near as possible to the water, and let us bag as many as we can."

The advice was sensible, but I hardly knew whether I had strength enough to fire.

When we got pretty near the water we crawled along as quietly as possible, fearing to alarm the birds before we got within good range.

Our eagerness to get at the water was near spoiling our chance of food, for Umbilla, in crawling along, cut his hand, and gave a shriek with the pain which he endured.

This started the birds, and about twenty-five ducks rose from the water.

Having repeating-rifles we were able to fire two shots each before the ducks got beyond range, and by this means bagged seven birds only one shot out of the eight missed.

We were so delighted with the sight of water, that we all stripped and rushed into it.

We lay down in the shallow part, and let our skins drink in the precious liquid.

We opened our mouths and let it run down our throats.

It was brackish stuff, but wretched as it was, two hours before I would have given all the wealth I possessed for a single bath in it, nay, I would have given all for one drink.

When we left the water we started to prepare our birds,

or at least two of them, so that we could have a good meal.

We had fire-sticks with us, so were able to make a fire with some of the karoo shrubs. They burned so fast that we had to mix them with the green reeds from the small pool, and then put plenty of sand on the top.

There out on that desert, far removed from habitation, we had a glorious repast of roast duck.

Our beverage was water, so thick that we could not force it through our filter, but we cared not for that, it was the best and most welcome drink I had ever swallowed.

We determined to camp for a few days by the water so as to regain our strength, and very glad we were to have such a chance.

Trouble was in store for us, however, for we had to bury our faithful Umbilla.

He got a severe attack of fever, and very unwisely drank too much water.

For several hours he was delirious.

When the first gleam of reason returned he looked at us all intently.

He muttered something, but we were unable to catch the words. I drew nearer to him and raised his head.

"Kooma," he said, and Quegga kneeled down and placed her hand upon his burning brow.

"Kooma, adieu!" he muttered, and then, throwing up his arms, his head fell back.

He was dead.

As faithful as any black could be, we mourned his loss. I felt it as much as if he had been a brother, and "Kooma," as he called Quegga, wept as though her gentle, loving heart would break.

We commenced to dig his grave by the side of the water, knowing that if his spirit could see he would prefer that place to the hot, burning sands of the desert.

We made a valuable discovery by digging his grave, for when we had hollowed out a hole about two feet deep we saw water bubbling up.

We had struck a spring.

We lay down on our stomachs and lapped up the water. It was delicious—as pure as any water we had ever tasted.

In our joy we forgot poor Umbilla. It was but the work of a moment to empty our water-bottles, which we had filled with the brackish stuff, and refill them with the pure, fresh fluid.

Not until we had done this did we return to our work of burial.

We succeeded in shooting some more ducks, and then prepared for our continued march.

We had not got more than five miles across the desert before we came to an object lying on the sand, which we found to be a human being

It was the simultaneous thought of us all to dig a grave for the body, which was that of a white man, or at least so we supposed, for it was dressed in hunter's clothes.

We turned it over and found it still warm.

As Good, who was helping me with the body, looked at the now upturned face, he cried out:

"Great Heaven! It's Quatermain!"

Curtis suspended his digging and came across.

It was true. Allan Quatermain, the old hunter, was there, dead or dying.

We poured some water between the clinched teeth, and it seemed to sizzle as it went down the parched throat.

The sign was good, for the ability to swallow was still there.

I found my pocket-flask, and to my great joy saw that there was about a teaspoonful of brandy still there. This I let drop carefully, so as not to waste one drop, into Quatermain's mouth.

The result was splendid. He opened his eyes, and as he met the clear orbs of Curtis, he exclaimed:

"Why, Incubu." And then fell over, as though dead.

We bathed his face, and wetted the scanty hair on his head.

This refreshed him, and then we resolved to go back to our last resting-place, and nurse Quatermain back to life.

We made a bed of the blankets, and, as both Umbilla and the Kagehyi had spears, Umbilla's being carried since his death by the sole remaining guide—our Kagehyi having absconded the night before—we fastened them to the blankets as bearers, and carried the old hunter back to the pool.

Arrived there, we took off his clothes and let him lie in the shallow water so that his parched skin might get refreshed.

We were rewarded for our efforts very quickly, for Quatermain opened his eyes and looked round.

As his eyes fell upon Good, he put out his hand.

"Bougwan!" he said. "Am I dreaming?"

"No, old boy, I don't think so."

The next day he had so far recovered that he was able to converse with us.

His joy bordered on positive rapture as he found that Curtis and Good were once more with him.

Curtis took from his pocket-book the torn scrap and asked him if he remembered it.

"Why, of course; but how did you get it?"

Fjord told him its history, and then Curtis read what he had written.

"Yes," said Quatermain, "in the main it is correct. It was a letter I wrote to Harry."

When he found we were all bound for the same place, he was still more delighted.

"I thought I was on the right track," he said, "but I fell short of water and food, and died, or thought I did so."

Quegga received his thanks for her very careful nursing.

A week later, armed with more ducks and all our water-bottles filled, we recommenced our journey.

The heat was intense, and the nasty flies worried us so that we could scarcely sleep, but food and water we still had, so we were able to keep up our spirits.

At the end of twenty days' marching, or rather that number of nights' journey, for we always rested during the day, we found ourselves weak and exhausted at the base of the mountains.

We had been for four days without other food than a skin-coat which we slashed up with our hunting knives and devoured, and for two days our water supply had run out.

More miserable-looking objects were never seen than we were when we reached the mountains.

Quegga was the best of us all, and I often look back with wonder at her power of endurance and pluck.

On the other side of the hills lay the country to which we were directed, but we began to feel like Moses, in view of the promised land but not permitted to enter it.

We should surely die of hunger and thirst unless we found both food and water quickly.

The mountains gave us but little promise, for they were almost bare, scarcely any signs of vegetation were discernible.

Quegga for the first time in our wanderings left us. She had been absent two hours, and I grew alarmed. No one seemed to know in which direction she had gone. But half an hour or so later we saw her walking very slowly dragging some heavy object.

We hurried to meet her, and found her pulling a young antelope.

She now explained her absence.

Instinct told her that there must be water somewhere near, if only a little pool made by the trickling down the hills of the last rain shower.

As she searched for water, she saw some animal in front of her. Cautiously she moved forward, intending, if possible, to get round it and drive it toward us, so that we might shoot it.

When she got very near, she perceived that it could not get away.

It had got a leg caught in a crevice of the rock and was a prisoner.

She had the revolver with her, so going as close as possible for fear of a mishap, she fired and shot her first antelope.

We were not long before a portion of it was prepared for our refreshment, and in absence of other liquid we drank its blood.

Our last guide was dying, and before we were ready to climb the hills, we were alone.

Five white men—that is, if Allan Quatermain could be called white, for the residence for so many years under the African sun had pretty well tanned him—and one woman.

How were we to climb the hills? We could see no

path, neither could we discover trace of any one having ever ascended the steep rocks.

Quatermain told us he had heard of a road somewhere, so we resolved to skirt the mountains for some little distance and try and find a place easier to ascend.

CHAPTER XXVI.
THE MYSTERIOUS CAVE.

AFTER skirting the mountain for some distance we perceived a trail which was so much like that made by hunters, that Quatermain exclaimed:

"By Jove, boys, there's sport somewhere near."

Following the trail up the side of the hill we found the ascent easier than we had expected.

About half-way up, or perhaps a matter of eight hundred feet from the desert, we found a cave, and its cool shelter was agreeable.

We were so exhausted with our long journey and want of food that the distance we had traveled was as much as we could manage in a day.

Quatermain entered the cave to make search. There is always a danger that a cave may contain a lion, or mayhap a leopard, and these are far from pleasant companions for a weary party of travelers.

Only a few minutes' elapsed before the hunter returned and announced that it was quite safe to venture.

We entered, and were at once struck with the pure air of the cave. Generally, there is a foul atmosphere about subterranean passages and caverns far from pleasant.

Arranging as we thought a watch, we fell asleep.

Fjord enjoyed the honor of the first watch, and after an hour had passed I took his place.

I set out to write a true and faithful history, or I should omit this paragraph, and not allow the world to know my shame, but as I am pledged to write the truth and nothing but the truth, I will confess my failings and admit that I fell asleep.

How long I slept I know not, for I was so confused when I awoke that I never noticed the time.

Curtis was to follow me, and so I roused him, and

rolled myself up in my blanket and lay down by the side of Quegga.

The afternoon passed, and we enjoyed ourselves so much, and the sleep was so refreshing that we agreed to sleep the night through, and resume our journey on the following day.

About five o'clock in the morning it was my watch, and I still felt heavy with sleep.

I paced up and down the cave until I got tired of the monotony, and I squatted, native fashion, on the floor at the mouth of the cavern.

I was nearly asleep when I fancied I heard voices.

I listened, and became more positive.

Where could they come from? I was wide awake now, and went outside, but no sign of human being could be seen.

I returned to the cave and walked past my sleeping friends and to the extreme end, but still no trace of any one.

I felt annoyed with myself, for I became now convinced I had been dreaming, when a merry laugh startled me.

That was no dream. There was something very real about it; but whence did it proceed?

It was a woman's laugh, and Quegga was asleep.

I grew timid. My legs began to tremble, and I was actually nervous.

I stumbled forward and roused Curtis.

"Incubu," I said, softly, for I often called him by that name, "come here, quietly."

"What is it?" he asked, in a whisper.

"I don't know, but come here."

He followed me to the mouth of the cave, and then I said:

"I have not been dreaming. Listen."

For a few moments "the beating of our own hearts was all the sound we heard," and then a merry laugh joined in by two or three was heard.

"The devil!" ejaculated Curtis. "Where are they?"

"That is what I cannot find out. But hark!"

We distinctly heard several people in conversation, but search all we could, there was no sign of any one alive but ourselves.

"Must be spirit voices," said Curtis.

"Perhaps so," I replied, "but I don't like them any the better for that."

Curtis went forward and roused Fjord.

He, too, heard the voices, so we were convinced that the sounds had a better basis than imagination, for it was not likely that all three would, or could, imagine the same thing without prompting.

Fjord expressed his astonishment, and then we roused Quatermain and Good.

They were equally astonished and we were still in the dark as to whence the sounds proceeded, when a sudden ray of light pierced the gloom of the cave.

On the side opposite to where Quegga was still sleeping, we saw a crevice which had not been noticed when we searched the cave.

Through this the light proceeded.

We were about to look through the crevice when we observed it grow larger. The rocks seemed to open, and slide, like folding doors, leaving a wide space in the center.

We stood in the angles of the rocks on the opposite side, desirous of seeing all we could without the chance of being discovered.

A scene of picturesque beauty was disclosed to our gaze.

We saw a garden most beautifully laid out. In the center was a fountain, made either of crystal or alabaster. The basin into which the water fell was transparent and through it we could see fishes swimming about and disporting themselves in the pure and clear water.

Flowers which seemed to be of every color of the rainbow made the beds look beautiful and even gorgeous. While every time the wind stirred, sweet perfumes were wafted to us.

Birds were singing sweetly, and as they flitted from tree to tree, their wings seemed to give forth prismatic rays of light.

We stood looking at the scene in breathless astonishment.

Had we got to fairy-land or was it only a dream?

We were anxious to wake Quegga, but feared to do so, lest the beautiful vision should vanish.

I had never seen anything like it in Africa.

Quegga turned over uneasily, and as the light fell on her upturned face, she opened her eyes and gazed on the bright and dazzling scene.

After looking round to convince herself that she was really awake, she got up and then we began to whisper among ourselves as to what the scene really meant.

Quegga said in her quaint way that we were all dead and that heaven had opened to our gaze.

Quatermain was more matter-of-fact, and declared he was not going to stay fooling round long, for he was thirsty, and the water in the fountain looked very inviting.

"What say you to entering?" I asked.

"Let us go," said Good, and his answer was agreed to by the others, so we stepped across the cave and through the mysterious crevice, which we were positive had only opened a few minutes before.

When we got inside the garden our astonishment was still greater, for we saw a most beautiful country stretching as far as the eye could reach, and only separated from the desert by the rock through which we had passed.

The garden was not a very large one, but the whole country appeared equally luxuriant.

The houses were of different styles of architecture, some were built after the fashion of civilized people, while others were bell-shaped, like those of the Kasheebars.

While we were standing in an attitude of rapt admiration, twenty warriors came marching toward us.

They were naked, but wore very fine breast-plates, which were so highly polished that it dazzled one to look at them.

These men were armed with a very peculiar battle-ax and spear.

The spear was shaped very much like the ace of spades, but it looked quite formidable as it flashed in the sunlight, it being made of polished metal.

The battle-ax was smaller than any I had before seen, and both weapons seemed capable of doing good service in the hands of strong men.

These warriors, without a word, surrounded and took us prisoners.

I verily think that had they ordered us to execution, we should have gone without a word of protest, so utterly amazed were we.

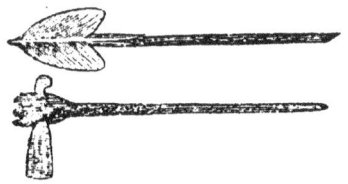

OPHITE BATTLE-AX AND SPEAR.

When we asked a little later where we were to be taken, the head man of the warriors answered by pointing to a building on the outside of the garden.

I thought it a good opportunity to say how hungry we were, but before I could shape my speech we had arrived at the building, which was made of bamboos and was very strong. Inside the building there was a very appetizing perfume of cooked meats, and we hoped to be invited to the repast at the earliest possible moment.

The room was a long one, and neither table nor seat was in it.

A nude woman entered it through a door in the extreme end, and walked over to us, carrying a bowl of some most savory soup in her hand.

This she handed to Quegga, and with it a command to drink.

Quegga waited to see if I was to get any before she partook of the soup.

A few minutes elapsed, and each of us was served with a bowl of the soup.

Considering the privations of the past few months, one can easily imagine the ardor with which we swallowed so savory a liquid.

Our attendants would not enter into conversation with us, but brought dish after dish, until we had partaken of a most substantial repast.

"This is a queer go," remarked Fjord, when he had swallowed the last morsel of a very dainty dish.

"They can't be very hostile," said Quatermain, "or they would not feed us so well."

To which Curtis replied:

"Of that I am not so certain, for they may want to fatten us for their own tables."

"Great heavens! you don't think they are cannibals?" exclaimed Good, dropping his eye-glass in his excitement.

When the repast was over we felt much refreshed, and wondered what our next adventure would be.

We had not long to wait, for the warriors again marched in and ordered us to follow them.

It was no use disobeying orders, for the least attempt at rebellion would, we felt sure, have meant an unpleasant prick with the spears.

We left the building and returned to the garden.

Across this we went, preceded by some of the guards and followed by others.

We entered a gate in the rock which opened in a similar way to the one through which we had gained access to the garden.

Passing through a long, narrow passage we reached another gate or opening, and then found ourselves in a square or garden.

On a little raised dais sat a woman, and round her, on the ground, a number of girls and young warriors.

We were ordered to stand immediately in front of the dais.

"We are in for it," murmured Quatermain, while Fjord, with the same nonchalance which he ever manifested, began to whistle to himself very softly.

The woman was evidently waiting for something, for she moved about uneasily, and kept looking at the doorway through which we had entered.

"I am tired of this," said Curtis, "and shall soon ask where we are."

"You are here sure enough," said Good; "better ask how we can get out."

Quegga stood motionless and as cold as a statue. Her countenance was unruffled, and her bosom heaved and fell as regularly as if we were not in a most trying predicament.

CHAPTER XXVII.

THE DEPUTY RULER OF OPH.

THE woman who sat on the dais was no ordinary individual.

Whatever her rank in her tribe, she was one that would command attention everywhere.

Her garments were of the usual nature of native women, consisting of beads, of which she wore several rows or strings round her neck.

Over each eye lines were carefully drawn, and either fixed by paint or tattooed. These lines seemed to radiate from the eye over the forehead.

OPHITE WOMAN.

Her mouth was ornamented with the skewer. I have forgotten the native name for the unsightly ornament.

Quegga, knowing my dislike of the fashion, hinted to me in a side whisper that she would have her lip pierced.

"If you do I will never kiss you," I said. Notwithstanding the tattooed lines and the lip skewer, the woman was not bad looking.

A few minutes later two drummers came in and set up the most horrible row on their drums that we had ever heard.

We were glad to put our hands over our ears to try and drown the sounds.

When the drumming had ceased—the woman asked in a loud voice, which was not near so pleasant as her appearance.

"Who art thou that darest pass through the cave into the land of Oph?"

"We are travelers from afar, most mighty one, and have come across the great desert," answered Curtis.

"Not so," she answered, "for no one could live in the desert."

"Yet it is true, most mighty one, and some guides of the Kagehyi nation did show us the way."

"The Kagehyis are ungrateful, and the great ruler of this mighty land of Oph shall know of their treachery. But who is the woman?"

"She is my wife," I answered.

"Nay, thou mistakest. Light cannot wed with darkness, the sun does not mate with the night. She may be thy slave, but thy wife—never."

I thought it bad policy to contradict, so I let it pass unheeded.

"We come in peace," said Curtis.

"It matters not," said the woman. "It hath been written that the stranger that passeth over the mountain shall surely die."

"But why should we die, seeing that we bring thee presents, and are many-headed men."

The last expression was the Kagehyi way of expressing the fact that we knew much or possessed wisdom.

"Then let the many-headed men go back to their own country, for the mighty ruler of this great land has heard that wherever the white man has entered he has brought ruin and misery with him."

"Thou talkest wisely, most mighty one," said Curtis,

"but we are most humble people who desire only to see thy greatness."

"Ay, so says my ruler, that white men will see our greatness and will send their warriors to slay us and take our treasures."

"Not so; but thy servants will stay with thee and teach thee many things."

"How canst thou teach the Queen of Oph, the mighty ruler who is the Moon, any things, seeing she knows all things?"

I was pleased to hear this deputy call the ruler "the Moon," for by this token we knew that we were at our journey's end.

"Take us to the mighty ruler then," said Curtis.

Whereupon our hostess and all the warriors set up such an unearthly screech that we thought our ear-drums would be split.

"What have you done now, eh, Curtis?"

"Goodness only knows," he answered. "I am tired of the palaver."

"So am I," was my reply.

"And here is another," responded Good.

"Good, take out your teeth and show the old girl that trick," said Quatermain. "You know how well it took with the Kukuana people."

"There can be nothing lost by trying it," said Good, with resignation.

The naval officer stepped forward and stared at the august person who seemed to have power over our destinies.

And when he had succeeded in fixing her attention, he relaxed the muscles of his face and allowed his eye-glass to fall.

The woman raised her hands in wonderment, and sat as though her gaze was riveted on Good.

He grinned, and showed two splendid sets of ivories, teeth which had been the envy of so many; and then, when all were wondering what would be the next piece of fooling or impudence, Good raised his head and quickly withdrew his teeth, slipping them into his pocket.

Again he opened wide his mouth and grinned.

Nothing but two rows of gums, destitute of the slightest sign of teeth, appeared.

The woman was captured by this last trick, and was just as ready to treat Good as a supernatural being as were the people of Kukuanaland.

"Bravo. Good," exclaimed Fjord. "I shall go to my dentist before I venture among savages again."

Good had by this time replaced his teeth, and the astonishment of the warriors and their ruler was so great that all hid their faces.

"Go! go! go!" shrieked the woman on the dais. "I will tell the Mighty Moon, the ruler of Oph, of thy wonders, for peradventure she may wish to rebuke thee and mayhap give thy body to the aasvogels.

We were escorted back to our long dining-hall, and were as effectually secured as if bolts and bars were on the door, for two soldiers stood at the entrance with spears pointed therein.

As we had no desire to feel their sharp points, we squatted on the ground and waited.

"This is evidently a great country, Theo.," remarked Good, "for a woman is the ruler and no one can see her but by the consent of her deputy."

"That's true, but who can this ruler be? Is she white or black, yellow or bronze?"

"I have a notion; how I got it I don't know, but I fancy this queen is white, or nearly so," answered Curtis.

"I hope so, for we shall stand a better chance," I said.

"No, no, a thousand times no," emphatically declared Quatermain. "The whites who get power in Africa are very devils. Give me a jet black nigger, one whose only dress-suit is a string of brass beads hanging from his neck, and I will get on better than with any of the white people I have seen here for thirty years."

"You give your own color a bad character."

"I do, for I hate the resident whites. They came to Africa, saw its vastness, witnessed the strength of its men, and then seized the men and sold them for slaves, robbed the natives out of their gold and diamonds and ivory, and if the poor savages as much as made a protest, the strong white man made war upon them and killed thousands."

"England has sinned everywhere," said Fjord.

"I am not talking of England alone; you, Fjord,

know well that if England for years stole the Africans, you Americans bought them. Nay, if you feel so much pride of your land and its people, tell me, have you not for many generations robbed and killed the Indian, driving him from his lands and killing him if he objected?"

"That is so. I guess it is human nature," responded Fjord.

We continued our conversation for some time, and then found ourselves invited to another feast.

We made no objection.

It was very pleasant to be waited on, and we had endured so many privations that a little attention now was pleasing.

Quegga had remained unusually silent, and I drew her on one side and asked the reason.

Instead of replying at once she burst into tears.

For some minutes her emotion was so great that her sobs could be heard all over the room.

I cared not for the opinion of others, or what remarks might be made, so I drew Quegga's head to my shoulder, and whispered endearments in her ear.

When she was able to overcome her emotion, she said:

"Light cannot wed with darkness."

I saw she was hurt by the unfeeling remark of the ruler from whose presence we had but just come.

"It is so," she continued: "take me as thy slave, call me not by the dear name of wife."

"Nay, Quegga, I shall own thee ever as my own wife, slave thou shalt never be, and when we leave this country—if we ever do—I shall take thee over the big water, and ever be proud of thee as my wife."

"I shall never see thy land," she sobbed.

"Yes, dearest, together we will see its wonders."

"Nay, my own, my beloved, I have something here," placing her hand on her breast, "which tells me that before many suns have arisen I shall be in the dark grave, and my spirit shall await thee in the land where all are white."

"Say not so, Quegga. I could not bear to lose thee. Stay with me, for thou art my comfort, and together we will go through life, happier than thou canst ever imagine."

"'Tis sweet to hear thee talk so, but, my own, it will not be. My body will never leave this land."

"Quegga, thou art weary with thy trials and travels, when thou art rested, different thoughts will fill thy mind."

She smiled, and pressed me to her heart, but I could see under the smile a sorrow which was deep and real.

I hoped her presentiment would not come true, for I had grown to love her, and life to me would be a dreary waste without her dear presence.

White reader, laugh not at my infatuation, despise me not for my choice of a dark wife. If you could have known Quegga, you would have agreed with me, that on the whole earth there lived not a brighter, better, dearer girl than she.

Her presentiments had so often been a foreknowledge of events that her words filled me with sadness, and a strange fear chained my soul in iron fetters.

My heart seemed like lead, and all joy had left me.

Curtis, who had heard part of the conversation, expressed his sympathy, and tried to cheer us both, but it was of no use.

We both felt sad and low-spirited, and nothing which others could say would lighten our grief.

Much as I dreaded parting with Quegga, I did not know that when the time came it would be under such painful circumstances, and that the parting would rend my very soul, until all joy and gladness would be banished from my life.

CHAPTER XXVIII.

MORE MYSTERIES.

For three days' we were kept prisoners in the large hall or room.

Our food was brought to us with a pleasing regularity and promptitude, and we really wanted for nothing but liberty.

How strange it is that the moment we are deprived of freedom we value it most.

We may have every comfort, have good food, the company of friends and every luxury, yet, if our liberty is restrained, we at once put such value on freedom that we had never done before.

We chafed at the restraint, and longed for our freedom.

On the fourth morning we heard the noise of drums and other instruments discoursing music sweeter than we had heard for many months.

Rushing to the door to see from whence the sounds proceeded, we were surprised to find our sentry absent, our jailor gone.

We waited for no further invitation to escape, but gathered up our blankets and walked forth.

The sun was shining brightly and the birds sang sweetly.

All nature seemed in gala or holiday attire.

We were puzzled about the absence of people.

We had seen but few, and they had disappeared the moment their services were dispensed with; even the warriors seemed to vanish most mysteriously.

We walked about the well-kept paths of the garden, and watched the frolics of the fish in the fountain.

It was sweet to be free, and even though we starved, I think all would have preferred death rather than a deprivation of liberty.

We left the garden and wandered about under the trees.

Quegga seized my arm, and with nervous fear pointed to some object in the distance.

It was a strange-looking creature, and had we seen it in the desert or on the prairie, would most certainly have shot at it, but here we were ourselves in danger, and so restrained ourselves.

How shall I describe the strange creature?

It walked upright like a man, and had a strange, human face.

But there its resemblance to man seemed to end, for its breast and body was covered with shaggy hair.

Its arms were long, and seemed as if they would touch the ground, and I noticed that the fingers were strangely shaped.

Our first impression was that it was a man clothed in a shaggy, tight-fitting dress made of bearskin, but as it came closer we saw that the creature was entirely nude.

Quegga sank to the ground, frightened at its appearance, and said that it was more horrible than a Vantacka or a Zemeraffe.

In this I differed, for there was more of the human in the creature we were gazing at than in the hideous monstrosities we had seen at Kasheebar.

No sooner had the creature seen us than it sounded an alarm, and instantly there appeared a hundred or more creatures of all sizes, but of the same species.

They evidently were intent on criticising our appearance, and were very curious to know who we were, but a certain fear came over them, and so prevented their near approach.

Fjord put his hand on his revolver as though he was itching to fire at them and have an opportunity of examining the creature's strange frame at his leisure.

We noticed that the faces of the animals or men, we knew not which to call them, were much whiter than those of the native soldiers we had seen.

Fjord wanted to try an experiment, and seeing a bird flying at long range over our head, he raised his rifle and fired.

The bird dropped down dead, and the hairy creatures ran away with an agility and speed which we had never seen in a man.

Curtis stood leaning against the trunk of a tree, intent on some meditation.

His eyes were closed, and he might have been asleep for all we knew.

I did not care to disturb his reverie, but Good was not so thoughtful, so going up to Curtis he slapped him on the shoulder, and exclaimed in a cheery voice:

"A penny for your thought, old boy."

"My good Good"—Curtis often liked to tease the naval captain by the use of his name coupled with the same word as a qualifying adjective—"a pipe of tobacco would be worth far more than a penny to me."

"Haven't you got one?"

"Not a smoke."

"Poor fellow! No wonder you looked glum."

Good felt down in his capacious pockets and brought up an old leathern bag, which he handed to Sir Henry.

The gift of food to the starving was nothing compared

with the pleasure which that pipe of tobacco was to Curtis, it was to him

"As welcome as the haven
To the tempest-driven ship."

When he had lighted the fragrant weed, he asked Good what he thought of the creatures we had seen.

"Shiver my timbers! I don't know. I never saw such animals in my life."

"They are not animals, but men."

"You don't mean it!"

"Yes. They are the aborigines of this country, just as the Vantackas were the original inhabitants of Kasheebar."

"What makes you think so?"

"Intuition if you like."

"I hope we shall not have to live much with them."

"No, they would be far from pleasant companions, but I am going to study their habits a bit if I get the chance."

"Count me in."

"All right."

"What secret conspiracy are you plotting?" I asked as I joined the couple.

Curtis told me, and I was very much of the same opinion about the creatures, and was just as anxious to learn more about them.

Quatermain was gloomy and heart-heavy. He had not been the same since we entered Oph.

Had he, too, a gloomy foreboding of evil, or what was it which weighed so heavily on his spirits?

A few minutes afterward he grasped Sir Henry by the hand, and in almost a whisper said:

"If I die, give a look at Harry sometimes."

"Of course I will; but what is the matter with you, old fellow? Are you down in the dumps?"

"I don't feel very bright, and I dreamed of my dead wife last night."

"Oh, is that all? Why, no wonder you should have such a dream when you have witnessed the spooning of old Theo. and his pretty wife."

"She too will never leave this confounded country alive," said Quatermain, in a voice evidently intended to reach Sir Henry's ears alone.

I overheard them, and turned on the old hunter and asked why he should make such a remark.

"That's more than I can tell. I have had a sort of feeling that way, that is all."

I looked at Quegga, who was standing watching some birds feeding on the grass, and I prayed that she might be spared to me in my old age.

We were in close conversation about the country and its inhabitants when Quegga gave a little scream and came running toward us.

We turned to see the cause of her alarm, and found she was pursued by one of the creatures we had before seen.

The poor girl was badly frightened, and as she threw herself in my arms, cried almost hysterically.

The creature withdrew when he saw our close proximity, and that we were ready to protect Quegga, even at the expense of our lives.

Once more we were alone, and thought it better to return to the place where we had been so hospitably treated.

In very truth we began to experience some of the pangs of hunger.

When we got back we found the old woman who had been our attendant in great excitement about us.

After a good repast she gave us a message to the effect that the most mighty ruler Shoara had organized a great feast for us, and that we were to be in readiness to attend at any time when the signal drum was sounded.

We asked where the festival was to be held, and all the answer we could get was, that we should find the way by following the natives.

CHAPTER XXIX.
THE FETE.

AFTER we had got thoroughly refreshed, we waited with impatience for the beating of the drum, and wondered what savage scenes we were to witness.

After an hour's speculation and thought, the discordant noise of the drum was heard, and we left the building.

The garden was now black with people—black both as to number, which was so great that the flowers and grass were hidden from view, and also the definition was true as regarded the color of the people, for the natives running, rushing, falling over each other and acting like school-boys released for an hour's romp, were the blackest crowd I had ever seen.

We fell into line, following at a safe distance. Through the garden with its beautiful flower-beds and fountains, so out of harmony with the savages who were now scrambling along its paths, and into the open country we went.

Before us was a large field, fashioned almost like a race-course. For on one side was a raised platform, made of bamboos artistically strung together; on the other, about a hundred yards' distance, a railing of bamboos, fastened to uprights firmly planted in the ground, kept back the surging crowd.

At one end was another inclosed space.

"Are we at Epsom?" asked Good.

"Not exactly, but I guess we will see more sport," was Fjord's rejoinder.

When we entered the field we were led by the warriors to the grand stand or platform, and were shown the posts of honor.

There were no seats, and we found later that only the ruler or the deputy was allowed to sit in public.

Shoara, the woman we had previously interviewed, was carried in state to the grand stand.

Her chair or throne was made of elephant tusks and buffalo horns, while over the seat were thrown several lion and leopard skins.

She sat European fashion on the throne and looked highly amused at the vast crowd gathered.

Then she very graciously bade us welcome, and said that Shebina, the sovereign ruler—the great and mighty Moon—had ordered this sport for our amusement.

When Shoara raised her hand, the drums beat furiously, and a herald, or messenger—perhaps it would be better to call him the ringmaster—entered, and fell on his face before Shoara.

She bade him rise, and then we saw a fine and handsome specimen of a young native of Oph.

His hair was dressed and arranged in a peculiar manner.

There is little difficulty in describing the toilet of the natives of Oph—that of the men being simplified by the sole covering of the head, the body being entirely nude.

We were highly amused to observe among these wild savages the consummate vanity displayed in their head-dresses.

As we looked round the circle we saw several tribes, and perceived that each tribe had a distinct and unchanging fashion for dressing the hair. So elaborate is the *coiffure* that hair-dressing might almost take rank as a science.

The ringmaster was one of the inner circle of Oph life. He was, *par excellence*, an aristocrat.

The ladies who read this story of adventures will be surprised to learn that to perfect the head-dress of one of these aristocrats requires a period of from eight to ten years.

However tedious the operation, the result is extraordinary.

The Ophites of the inner circle of society wear most exquisite helmets, all of which are formed of their own hair, and are, of course, fixtures.

AN ARISTOCRATIC HEAD-DRESS.

At first sight it appears incredible, but a minute examination shows the wonderful perseverance of years in producing what must be highly inconvenient and uncomfortable.

The thick, crisp wood is woven with fine twists of fibre from the bark of the palm-tree, until the hair presents the appearance of rough felt. As the hair grows through this woven mass, the new hair is subjected to a similar process, and so on every year for eight or ten years.

A strong rim of about two inches deep is formed by sewing the twists of hair together with thread, and the front part of the helmet is protected by a piece of polished copper; while a piece of the same metal, shaped like the half of a bishop's mitre, and about twelve inches in length, forms the crest.

The framework of the helmet being completed, it must be perfected by an arrangement of beads, should the owner of the head be sufficiently rich to indulge in the coveted distinction.

The most fashionable beads with the aristocracy of Oph are red and blue porcelain, about the size of peas. These are sewn on the surface of the felt, and so beautifully arranged in sections of blue and red that the entire helmet appears to be formed entirely of beads, while the shining crest of copper, surmounted by ostrich plumes, gives a most dignified and martial appearance to the elaborate head-dress.

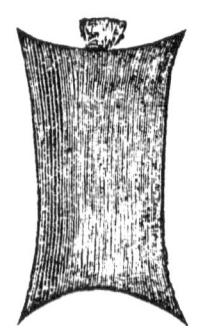

ELEPHANT-SKIN SHIELD.

This herald rose to his feet, and, turning his face toward Shoara, said, in a loud voice:

"Great and mighty one, the day is now here; the sun fulfills its course and shines on the great people of Oph, and we, thy servants, ask thy great pleasure."

Without awaiting any reply, he turned away and ran

across the open space, shouting and gesticulating like a maniac.

As soon as he retired about fifty warriors of another tribe came rushing into the arena.

They were perfectly naked, their bodies being painted in various patterns with red ochre and white chalk; their heads were adorned with ornaments of cowry shells, surmounted with plumes of ostrich feathers, which drooped gracefully over the back of the neck.

They carried shields and spears.

The shield most prized was made of elephant-skin, stretched over a framework of bamboo; at the top was a wristlet composed of the hair from a horse's tail, when the owner of the shield was rich enough to buy a tail.

Horses' tails are much prized, and any trader who penetrates the Gallas district or the southern part of the Soudan will have no difficulty in getting a cow in exchange for a good, long tail. For two tails, of medium length, he can purchase a camel.

The spears carried by this tribe were long, like the Zulu assegai, and the blade, in war-time, was poisoned.

When Shoara raised her hand, as a signal, the drum commenced to beat, and the tribe amused us and exercised themselves by a war-dance.

The scene was picturesque and characteristic of a savage people.

The dancers got so excited that a savage fury seemed to take possession of them, and there is no doubt the dance would have ended in a free fight, had not Shoara risen from her throne.

That instant the drum ceased to beat, and the dance ended.

Many other sports took place of a similar nature, each tribe, which made up the Oph nation, contributing something to the amusement.

When we thought all had been exhausted, and our eyes had become heavy with the ever-varying scene, we were surprised to find a number of the strange creatures, whose natures appeared to be half-human and half-animal, enter the arena.

I ventured to ask Shoara who they were, but she replied by the use of one word which, as I never saw it in print or writing, I can only spell phonetically. To me it sounded like Homono.

These Homonos, when they had prostrated themselves before the presiding beauty, rose to their feet, and went through a very creditable gymnastic performance.

They ran and leaped over one another, walked about on their hands, and seized one another with their feet, which were shaped almost like hands.

OPHITE WAR-DANCE

Every conceivable gymnastic and acrobatic performance was given by the Homonos, and then they stood, or, rather, crouched on all fours, and sang very harmoniously. The words were strange to me, but the music was delightful.

They retired, and the *fete* closed.

We returned to our abode more than ever determined to find out something about the nature and habits of the Homonos.

Before the day waned a fresh surprise was in store for us.

The aristocratic herald entered our residence and looked at each one of us keenly for awhile.

Having satisfied himself with the inspection, he tapped Curtis and myself on the shoulder and bade us follow him.

I refused unless he would tell us our destination.

It took him ten minutes to tell us, so profuse was he in the use of adjectives, that "the great and mighty Moon, the lovely Shebina, the mistress of the world, ruler of the universe, at whose wish the sun shines and the moon gives forth its light; who orders the stars to twinkle and the rain to fall."

And a host of other attributes too numerous to remember, the sum total of all which was that Shebina, the mysterious queen, wished to see us.

I bade Quegga farewell, and shook hands with each of the others. Curtis followed my example, and then, with hearts rather heavy, we went forth with our escort to solve some more mysteries, and gaze on this much-vaunted queen.

I had a lurking feeling that we were to encounter some great danger, but Curtis laughed at my fears.

CHAPTER XXX.
QUEEN SHEBINA.

Our guide led us to the rock through which we had gained admission into the land of Oph.

Instead of entering our cave, however, he walked a little distance along the side of the hill, which towered above us a thousand feet or so.

Giving a signal, made with his feet and hands, the rock seemed to part and we entered a dark passage.

"Follow," he said, and we were quite ready to do so for the mysterious doors had reclosed and escape was impossible.

He led the way along the vault-like passage, which was not illumined by a single ray of light and then we passed into a large cavern which was dimly lighted by a lamp suspended from the arched roof.

It was a spacious room, and entirely destitute of any furniture or adornment.

On the opposite side was another passage. This was lighted by means of lamps, so that we were able to see the way we were going. We next ascended at least a hundred steps; our legs got weary before we reached the top, but we were well repaid for we emerged on a plateau overlooking the lovely garden and picturesque country.

Here we had again another passage to traverse, and after walking along in the semi-darkness, stumbling often, and climbing more steps we once again saw the blue sky.

But what a scene of dazzling brilliancy was presented to our bewildered eyes.

If we had been charmed with the garden below, we were enchanted now.

Never have I seen anywhere a garden to equal the one in which we now stood.

Flowers of every sort and color, breathing out rare perfumes on the air, trees bearing most luscious fruit, their branches being weighted to the ground with their beautiful burden, and fountains with jets of water forced upwards through colored glasses which gave varied tints to the spray.

Our guide would not allow us to tarry in the garden, but hurried us forward to a little bamboo gate, which we had perceived as we emerged from the cave.

This gate opened most mysteriously, and we followed our barbaric guide into a cave or room fashioned out of the solid rock, which was replete with luxurious splendor.

Rugs and skins were thrown in profusion on the floor, and a soft, mellow light pervaded the room, the rays coming from a suspended lamp.

It was difficult to believe that we were only an hour's distance from the scene of savage sports so recently witnessed.

If we had suddenly been aroused from sleep and found ourselves starving in the desert, we should not have been surprised, for our eyes fell on a scene so grand and so different to anything we expected to find that we could not imagine it was other than a dream.

Our guide, a native, naked as he was born, was out of place amid such barbaric splendor.

He left us, and we were alone.

Curtis asked me what I thought of it all.

I could not give my opinion, for words refused to come at my bidding.

I was dazzled and mystified.

Sir Henry felt at home in all places, but he said afterward that he had never felt so strange in his life before.

After standing for a few minutes we perceived the approach of some one with light step.

The room was filled with the famed perfume of Arabia, and the next minute we were so overcome with surprise that it was a wonder we kept our feet.

A girl—she could not have reached twenty years—entered. She was dressed in Persian fashion.

Her limbs draped with a gauzy material, through which the pink flesh was plainly visible. The upper part of her body was clothed in a tunic of the same material.

Was she dressed?

If dress is intended to conceal the form, figure, and tint of the body, covered then, indeed, she was not. For every line, every crease of the fair, plump form, every dimple showed plainly through the gauzy dress.

Yet she had obeyed the fashion and wore clothes.

Her eyes were as black as coals, the eyebrows of the same color, but her face was of so fair an olive tint that made the extra blackness of her eyes only the more fascinating.

And this was Shebina—the Moon—the ruler of Oph.

The mystery was all the greater, for she too, seemed out of place.

A merry laugh burst from her lips as she saw our surprise.

Having taken her seat on a pile of skins, she asked us in the language of the country from what lands we came.

When we told her she seemed pleased, and then very downcast, for as she subsequently told us, she feared the English and their power.

She bade us be seated, and then having lighted a cigarette which she rolled up daintily while talking, she told us her story.

"When I was a baby, a little wee thing, my mother left her own land——"

"Which was?" I asked.

"Persia," she replied, and then continued.

"And came here. She crossed the desert, and nearly died with hunger and thirst.

"She came here, because it had been handed down to her from preceding generations that she was the lineal descendant of that Queen of Sheba, who sent the great offerings to the Jewish Solomon.

"Fond of adventure, my mother came, and so far proved the truth of the stories, by describing these caves and treasure-chambers.

"The wise men hailed her as queen, but kept her prisoner here.

"There are but two means of entrance; one is guarded by lions and savage elephants, the other is the one through which you entered, and no one but you has ever been allowed to live, if they discovered the cave and secret door.

"When my mother died, I was chosen to fill her place, but have never been down the mountain since. In fact, I have never seen the outside world since I was carried here an infant."

Shebina paused, and then as we were too much amazed to question her, or even to express an opinion, she continued:

"The nation of Oph is a peculiar one. It has a history many thousand years old, and the original people believe that it was the first place upon which man lived."

"But," I said, "there are various tribes in your country."

"Yes, I told you the nation was a peculiar one. People have come here at times, but whenever they reached our rocky fastness they were never allowed to leave, therefore we have very many different tribes. Now you," and she looked at Sir Henry, "you will stay here and have a wife, and in course of time your descendants will form another tribe in this strange land."

Curtis was about to show his John Bull nature by

asserting his intention of leaving, but I stopped him by asking what seemed to be a most impertinent question:

"How did you get these things," I said, pointing to a modern pipe, a lamp, and a miniature fountain which was standing in an alcove.

"Your curiosity is natural," she answered, sweetly, "and it shall be gratified. I have some faithful servants who carry for me messages to an agent in Abyssinia. He in turn sends to Europe, and by this means I am able to get everything I want."

"But are you not afraid of being discovered?"

"How can I be? My servants never say where they are from, and the agent in Abyssinia is therefore ignorant."

The scheme was a good one, and by its success Shebina was enabled to surround herself with luxuries.

"May I deign to ask you other questions?" I inquired.

"Certainly; why did I allow you to come if it were not that we might talk together?"

"I am afraid I should weary you."

"That you cannot do. It is so nice to have some one to talk to, for it is, oh, so long since I was able to converse."

"Then may I ask something about the Homonos?"

"Hush!" she said, and she put her finger on her lips.

After a short pause she came across from the pile of skins to where I was seated, and threw herself on the floor by my side, and then raising her sweet mouth so that its breath fanned my ear she whispered:

"Take care! I am afraid of them myself."

"But who are they?"

"I know not. Only they say that they were the first people who lived here, and that they have strange power; they know all that goes on, and can read what one is thinking about."

Her voice had fallen to a very low murmur, so soft that it would be nearer correct to call it a zephyr sigh rather than a whisper.

I was inclined to laugh at this idea, but seeing it she drew my head down, and pointing to the gate through which she had entered said, very softly:

"*It* is there."

"What?" I asked.

"*It.*"

"You promised to answer my questions, and now rebuke my curiosity," I said almost angrily.

"No, no, I have answered;" and I could see that the subject was a painful one. "I am afraid," she continued, "for *It* may know I am talking about its people, and then—— oh! I shudder to think what I shall have to endure."

"May we ask whom you mean when you speak of *It?*" asked Curtis.

"I will answer, even though it cost me my life."

"Surely there is no danger?"

"Hush! *It* is the king of the Homonos, and is ever near me. Oh, how I loathe *It!*"

Shebina rose to her feet and stood as dignified as a queen, while she tapped her fingers on a small gong. A female, black as ink, and as ugly as could be found, appeared in answer to the summons.

"Show these great tage to the chamber of the faithful."

The woman beckoned and we followed, knowing it was useless to attempt to prolong the interview.

The chamber to which we were shown was situated some distance from the one in which the interview had taken place. It was a cave like the other, and was furnished with a plentiful supply of skins.

The woman left us, and we knew we were prisoners for the night.

Sir Henry was charmed with our fair and lovely hostess, and I began to think that his heart had been taken captive.

My thoughts were with Quegga, and I wished she had been with me. I don't understand why, but I began to be apprehensive that I should lose her.

When I suggested the thought to Curtis, he answered brusquely that, though she was a rare good girl if we were going to stay here, it would never do to take her to England.

"My dear fellow," I answered, "I hope to have her presiding over my English table at Rapa Cottage when you honor me by dining there."

He only laughed, and then facetiously made a remark which many times recurred to me afterward.

"One great charm of Quegga is her perfect figure,

Nude, she is a queen among women, but to take her to England and dress her fashionably and the charm of her figure is lost, and she is only a colored woman."

"But it is her mind, her goodness, I admire."

"No doubt. But mark my words, Theo.: if you take her there, you will live to regret it."

"If you love me, Curtis, never breathe such an idea to Quegga."

He gave his word, and that was ample security, for Sir Henry Curtis was one of those men who never say a thing without weighing the consequences. Once his word pledged, and no power could move him from his impregnable position.

I dreamed all that night of Quegga, and somehow she and Rapa became associated together in my mind, so that at times I saw Rapa where I expected to find Quegga.

Both were the very perfection of womankind, as regards the spirit which occupied their dark-colored bodies.

We were awakened in the morning by a fierce roaring, as it seemed, in the very room we were occupying; but after listening a few minutes we knew the noise proceeded from the lions of which Shebina had told us.

CHAPTER XXXI.
SHEBINA'S LOVE SONG.

THE woman who had shown us to the chamber entered soon after we were roused by the roaring of the lions, and beckoning for us to follow, left the room.

Desirous of knowing all we could, we followed and found ourselves in a spacious cave, in which was a large pool of water.

We were pleased at the prospect of a bath, and enjoyed it to the fullest extent.

When we got back to our room, we found an excellent breakfast awaiting us.

Everything seemed to be performed by signaling, for, scarcely had we finished our repast, than we were beckoned again by the woman, and led to Shebina's apartment.

She was dressed the same as on the preceding evening, and looked more lovely than ever.

She asked us how we had slept, and whether we had received all the attention we desired.

And then, addressing Sir Henry, she asked if he was fond of music.

With the greatest gallantry, he answered in the affirmative, although I knew he dreaded native music, as he often said, worse than yellow fever.

Shebina motioned him to sit on the highest pile of skins, and then she retired to an inner room, bringing with her, when she returned, a musical instrument, constructed somewhat on the principle of the harp.

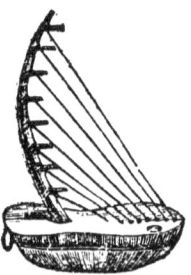

SHEBINA'S HARP.

She threw herself on a single lion-skin at Sir Henry's feet, and leaned her head against his knee.

Her fingers passed lightly, several times, over the strings, and then, in a voice melodious and sweet, she sang an extemporized love song, accompanying herself on the harp.

The words, as near as I can remember them, ran somewhat as follows:

> " Oh, give me thine heart, to be mine! Mine only,
>   Mine alone!
> Choose me for your love, for I am lonely,
>   All alone!
> The earth is fairer when thou art near, and the
>   Stars above you
> Are more brilliant for the shining of your eyes—
>   And I love you.
> My love for you is tender, true, and sweet,
>   And divine;

> Let us, then, unite our lives—
>   Yours and mine;
> And I take you as a gift the gods have given,
>   For I love you."

With every line she gazed most bewitchingly up into the face of Curtis.

How it must have made his heart-strings thrill!

It made even my blood course madly through my veins.

Shebina was lovely, and the beautiful pink of her skin, as seen through the gauze, seemed to make her far more fascinating and charming.

If, however, Curtis was to have the whole of Shebina's attention, I felt I should be in the way, and hoped I would get a chance to retire.

Her moods, however, like the ways of all beauties, were variable, and she cast aside her harp, rose from the skin, and came across to me.

"Wouldst thou like to see the lions?"

"I should."

"Come, then; and thou, my king," she said, turning to Curtis, "wilt thou come likewise?"

"It will afford me pleasure," was his courteous reply.

Shebina led the way past the chamber which had been ours the preceding night, and through a long, narrow passage.

At the end of this way was a very slight bamboo gate.

I started back, startled, for on the other side of the gate crouched a lion.

It was a veritable king of beasts, for a larger one I had never seen.

It was chained, but its chain was long enough to enable it to reach any part of the cave.

"That is the only other way to get out of this place," said Shebina, as she pointed to a passageway on the other side of the lion's cave. "Whoever wishes to leave my apartments this way must pass through here."

"They might enter there," I said, "but would they get out again?"

"No."

"And yet I could."

"You?"

"Yes, I could," said Curtis.

"How?" she said, in surprise.

Curtis drew his revolver from his belt, and said, that by pointing that at the lion, he could kill it.

"And would it kill me?"

"It would kill anything which has life."

"Come away."

She led the way back to her room, evidently reflecting on what we had told her.

A moment only did she remain there, for she beckoned us to follow her to the garden.

"Kill something," she said to Curtis.

Curtis looked round and failed to perceive anything large enough to kill.

A buzzard was perched on the rock, about thirty yards away. This he pointed out to Shebina, then, raising his Smith & Wesson, he fired and the bird fell dead.

"It is awful," was her only response, as she left the dead bird and re-entered her cave.

"You asked about the Homonos," she said. "What do you wish to know about them?"

"Everything."

"Explain yourself."

"Why, then, are they different to the others? Why are they covered with hair, and what is the reason their arms are so long?"

"You had better see some of them, and ask, for I cannot tell you."

"Can they talk?"

"Of course, that is, some can."

"May I see the king—*It*, as you called him."

"Not now."

A few moments later she came to me and asked if I wouldn't like to go back to the city of Oph and question the Homono.

I replied I would like to do so.

"Then you shall. My king shall remain with me."

I could see Curtis did not like the prospect, but I whispered to him in English that he might coax her to show him this wonderful King of the Homonos.

That reconciled him somewhat to the situation.

I had a shrewd idea that the charming Shebina had fallen in love with Sir Henry, and it would be his own fault if he did not become King of Oph.

"I will pass thee back to Shoara, who rules for me,

below," said Shebina to me, "and when thou art tired of thy questionings thou canst return."

"May I bring my friends with me?"

"Friends! I thought thou wert alone?"

"No, most mighty ruler, for we have a great hunter from afar, a wonderful magician with a glass eye, and a mighty traveler."

"Oh!"

Why did I not mention Quegga?

Was I getting ashamed of her because I had seen a white woman?

I felt ashamed of myself, and yet had not the courage to add her name to my list.

"We shall see," she said later, in reference to my request.

The day passed away pleasantly; Shebina singing and playing most beautifully, and doing her utmost to ensnare the heart of the swarthy Briton.

When my watch registered six o'clock the herald appeared, and I was conducted back to the valley beneath, and found my friends in a state of great excitement at our absence.

Quegga became hysterical, which was an ususual thing for a child of nature, but as she rested in my arms, she told how she had suffered at the thought of losing me.

When later I told them of the wonders of the queen's residence, and the evident intention of the beautiful woman to keep Curtis, they all opened their eyes with astonishment. Quegga crept close up to me and asked:

"Is she beautiful?"

"Very."

"Is her skin white or dark like mine?"

"It is fair, and so clear and lovely that never was bright marble more beautiful."

A shudder passed over Quegga, but she quickly recovered herself, and asked:

"Was she dressed?"

"Yes."

"Did she wear those funny things, those bags—what did you call them—oh, I remember, skirts?"

"No!"

"What then?"

I described Shebina's dress, and then Quegga crept closer to me and whispered:

"Wouldst thou have thy Quegga dress so?"

"No, my own dearest, I like my Quegga as she is."

"Did you mention me?" asked Good, who was a regular lady-killer.

"I mentioned you all."

"What did she say about me?" asked Quegga.

For the first and only time, I told her a falsehood, for I had the audacity to say that Shebina hoped to see her soon, for she knew she must be a dear, loving girl.

Great Heaven, forgive me! And thou sweet spirit of Quegga, if thou seest what is transpiring, and if thy fair eyes can watch me as I write, then thou knowest that I regret the falsehood and my cowardice, and that in my inmost soul I would rather have thee as my wife than any white-skinned beauty I ever saw.

Alas! Thou wast taken from me and I was left desolate, but the world shall know of thy devotion and thy great love.

Taking Fjord with me the next day, I went to the part of the city occupied by the Homonos.

Quatermain and Good took their guns and started off in search of game.

We were full of speculation as to Sir Henry, and Fjord was ready to back his opinion with any amount of money, that Curtis would be king of the Oph when next we saw him. I could not blame him, for Shebina was lovely and I have no doubt as good as she was charming.

CHAPTER XXXII.

THE TRADITION OF THE HOMONOS.

We reached the Homono quarters and found ourselves to be objects of great curiosity with these people.

The nearer view we got of them the more repulsive they really were.

I had neglected to ask Shebina in what language they could converse, so we had to find out by actual experiment.

We spoke in several different dialects, but could not

make ourselves understood; at last one of the Homonos grunted out something and started to run.

Although these creatures walk upright, I noticed that whenever they desired speed they went on all fours.

The Homono returned after a short time, bringing a very venerable-looking friend with him.

Let me describe this new arrival.

His face was nearly white, he had a good shaped forehead, a long nose, slightly inclined to the African width, a firm upper lip, but such a mouth—it seemed to reach right across his face. There was no hair growing on his face, but over all the other parts of his body the hair was about three inches long, growing quite thick on his back, but thinner on his chest.

His arms were very long and the hands were in the same proportion. The feet were shaped almost similar to the hands, the big toe answering very well as a pedal thumb.

Such was this Homono.

He asked us in good Abyssinian what we wished to know.

Telling him we came from afar, and that we were guests and friends of the great and mighty ruler, Shebina, we naturally wished to find out all about the ancient people—the Homonos.

Our curiosity, he said, was natural, and he asked us to pay him a visit at his house.

We entered a room in which we found for the first time rude tables and stools.

Noticing our surprise our host said:

"You may well be astonished, for the savage ophites squat on the ground, instead of using a stool. We sit in our old way."

Suiting the action to the word he sat down on the stool in a manner thoroughly civilized.

Then the old gentleman got very loquacious, and told us that long before any of the tribes which we saw now had lived the Homonos possessed the earth.

In fact, no white men nor badly-formed black men lived then.

But one Homono brought a curse on the race.

A female Homono gave birth to a monstrosity. It had feet which were so short that it could not hold by them;

its arms were short, and there was no hair on its back to cover it.

The Homonos gathered round the mother and wanted to kill the monster, but she clung tightly to it, and when night came, ran away and hid the horrible creature.

The deformed Homono was a girl, and when it got to be a few years old it came back with its mother.

What a difference! The mother was a fine-looking Homono, well covered with hair, but her offspring was always cold, for it had nothing by which it could be shielded from the wind.

It could not climb trees to get the nuts, and so would have starved, had it not been for a young male Homono, who took a fancy to the strange-looking female, and got the food for it.

The Homonos gathered together and warned the young fellow not to do it, but he said that not only would he find the food, but he was going to take the bare female for a wife.

Then there was commotion among the Homonos. And the wise one of the family, who got his ideas from some great power of which he knew, cursed the Homonos, and said that if he dared to marry the female, that he should be condemned to live until all other Homonos were killed by the offspring of himself and the monstrosity.

He only laughed, and had his way.

He still lives and must live for a long time yet, for there are many Homonos living.

We listened to the tradition with great interest, and then asked how we could discover the descendants of the Homono and the monstrosity.

"All the Ophites, the Kaffirs, and the people from afar are his offspring," he answered.

"Where is this wonderful Homono living?"

He pointed with his finger to the castellated rock where dwelt Shebina, and the thought occurred to us that the Homono there must be the great *It*.

"What name does this aged Homono bear?" I asked.

"That I know not, we have all been too afraid to speak about the subject; but whenever we desire to mention the Homono, we use no name—simply '*It*.'"

We had been well repaid for our visit to the Homonos,

and as we returned we reduced the old tradition to this argument:

The Homono, who had lived through all the ages, was the father of the human kind. Therefore he was evidently the missing link between the Homonos and man, just as the Homonos must have at some time been descended from a lower order of intelligence.

We must by some means see *It*, and find out the basis for the tradition.

Fjord was deep in contemplation all the way back.

The great mystery was to be solved, and our names would be mentioned as those of the greatest benefactors of our kind.

We were elated with pride, and gave no heed to the threatening looks of some of the war dancers who glowered on us as we passed.

We made our way to the dwelling of Shoara, and found that lady quite willing to receive us and bestow her thanks on us for a present of beads which we made her.

We asked her to tell us the tradition of the Homonos, so that we might compare her version with that which we had heard from the Homono philosopher.

For a long time Shoara hesitated, but the additional present of some beads of a larger and finer nature softened her heart, and she told us the story, which coincided exactly with the one we had already listened to, and which was now verified.

"But how long is it since this wonderful Homono married and received as a wedding present the eternal curse?" asked Fjord.

"That is impossible to say, but *It* has said that those hills were under the big waters and only the mountains of Kilimandjaro were dry."

This set us thinking, for certain geologists have declared that in the table-land on the Atlas range they found shells and other proofs of the sea having washed over there, and that these shells must have been there ten or twelve thousand years.

This statement found a strong corroboration in the remarks of the woman Shoara.

"But will you tell me that *It* has lived several thousand years?" I inquired.

"Hush! he knoweth all things, and I will say no more. Ask him if thou wouldst learn more."

Shoara positively refused to answer any more questions, so we left her presence minus a few beads, but plus the story of the Homonos, which harmonized so thoroughly with that told us earlier in the day.

Quatermain met us on our return, and told us that he had met a strange-looking man, a native of Oph, who declared that no one need die, if they did but use certain things which he could give them.

"I offered him some beads, but he said they were of no use to him, unless he had the means of getting one ingredient for his compound.

"I inquired what that was, and the old man hesitated for a long time, and then told me it was a woman's blood. If he could get a white woman, he would kill her at once, and so live forever, and give his friends some of the mixture, so that they too might have perpetual life. I looked upon him as being a lunatic, but he was awfully in earnest. Then I said he would have to wait a long time before he found one in Oph. He expressed his fear that such would be the case, and then a sudden thought seemed to strike him, for he said if he could not get a white woman, a white man's wife would do as well. Great Jupiter, Theo., take care of Quegga, for he must have referred to her."

I was thoroughly alarmed, though I had not thought of Quegga until Quatermain mentioned her name.

We hurried back, and our fears were allayed for the time by finding Quegga safe and well.

We thought it best not to alarm her, so said nothing about the strange adventure.

However, we determined to keep watch over her, and, at all hazards, save her life from enemies or cranks.

"Poor Kooma!" said Good. "Will she, too, die, like my Foulata?"

"Not if I can help it, Bougwan," I replied.

"Watch her well, Aristo, for she is worth it, even if she is colored. I would not have exchanged Foulata for the best white woman that ever lived."

And Good said it with an earnestness which showed he meant what he said.

We spent the evening in the gardens, watching the

fishes and birds, and wondering how so much water could be obtained at that altitude, while only on the other side of the hill there stretched a wide expanse of dry desert, with scarcely a well or spring to refresh the weary traveler.

CHAPTER XXXIII.

SHEBINA'S LOVE-MAKING.

Sir Henry Curtis handed me a very carefully-written account of his adventures after I left him, and I have thought it best to insert a portion of his narrative in this place, letting him use his own words as far as possible.

Let it be understood, then, that I, John Theodosius Aristophano, am only responsible for this chapter as editor, and not as author. With this preface I leave Curtis to tell his own story:

I promised to write a full account of all that took place after Aristophano left me, so must do so, although I detest writing.

No sooner had Theo. gone than Shebina left me in the room alone, and was away for several minutes.

When she returned she had changed her apparel, and now wore the same kind of costume, but of pure white, whereas the other was tinted.

The effect was startling. The gauze was of the very finest silk and shone in the lamplight with a sheen which was remarkably pretty.

But it was no protection against the weather, neither was it of use to hide the natural charms of the young queen, for the white gauze only brought out into greater relief the dark pink of her form.

Seeing me notice her appearance, she herself explained her costume:

"I would prefer not wearing anything," she said, "for the natives with a string of beads must be far more comfortable than those who are clothed; but I gave a promise to my mother that I would always dress. But here came a difficulty, for the people hold it as a part of their religion that no one would hide their bodies with clothes unless to cover some deformity. "Now gaze on me," she said, "and say am I deformed?"

Shebina stood up with her arms stretched above her head, and bade me answer.

"Deformed?" I exclaimed. "no, you are the most perfect woman I have ever seen, and it would be a shame and a wrong to hide so much beauty."

I am afraid I said more than could have been uttered in a London drawing-room, but when a wonderfully pretty woman, with skin like wax, and cheeks like peach-bloom, stands revealing her natural loveliness which would have made the fame of a sculptor, if copied in marble, what could I say other than what I did?

She was pleased with my remarks, and then sounded the gong for refreshments.

I drank some most delicious nectar, which set my pulses aglow with rapturous pleasure.

Fruits and confections, which I never expected to find in a barbarous African nation, were next served, and I don't think I ever enjoyed a repast so much as that one.

When the remains of the fruit and nectar had been removed, Shebina drew near me, and asked:

"What is thy name?"

"Henry Curtis, when I am in the land of my birth," but here they call me Incubu."

"Stand up!" she commanded.

"Yes, Incubu, thou art," she said, as she looked at me, "but why wear all these clothes?"

I told her it was the custom of my country.

"I know it, but how you must hate it! I like to look upon a well-knit frame, such as that of the herald who brought thee hither. What would he be if he was all covered with clothes like these? Methinks it is the dress which attracts in thy country; here we spurn that, and look to the muscles and the skin."

I laughed and said that while there was a great deal of truth in what she said, yet in my country there was so much cold weather that the body needed to be shielded.

Then she changed the subject and said:

"They call thee Incubu. I will call thee ma koom (my king)."

I began to feel uneasy.

She came and threw herself in a half-reclining position on the pile of skins.

"Is it not a shame," she said, "that I have no husband?"

"It is," and then I regretted the very moment I had let the words escape me. I asked: "Why don't you get one?"

"Oh, my king! be thou my beloved," she said at once. I pretended that I did not understand her meaning.

She remained silent a few moments and then said:

"I have only a few moons wherein to get a husband."

"Why? I don't understand you."

"It is the law. Unless I have a husband within six moons from now the chiefs of Oph will find me one of their number, and then I shall be the mother of a colored child. No; I want a white husband, and I will buy one."

"Buy one?"

"Yes. I will send to my agent in Abyssinia to find me a poor man who shall be handsome as thou art, tall, broad shoulders, strong arms"—and here she pinched my arms—"good skin, and healthy, and I will buy him."

"But what if thou dost not like him?"

"I can kill him. The lions are always ready for a good meal."

"A pleasant prospect, truly, and then thou wouldst buy another?"

"No, for I should have obeyed the law, and my child would succeed me, and it would be white."

I pleaded that I was weary, and would retire to rest.

But she drew me to her and pressed her lips against mine, calling me her king, her beloved, and then very pointedly declared:

"I sent for thee to be my husband."

"No, thank you, I should only be given to the lions in a few days."

"No, no, no, no!" she repeated, over and over again. "I only said if I bought a husband and did not like him. I love you, and choose you for my own."

Again I declined the honor, and she seized me by the arm, and passionately exclaimed:

"Come, be my love and I will smother thee with kisses, and thy lips shall cling to mine, until the long, long day shall be but an hour spent in such pleasant work."

I was incorrigible and, with all her entreaties, could not be moved.

Don't give me too much credit. She was lovely enough to tempt a mortal, but I had coolness sufficient to weigh the consequences.

Consent to be hers and I should never be allowed to leave the caves, and even though I should have pleasures beyond the power of man to describe, I felt that,

> "When liberty is gone,
> Life grows insipid, and has lost its relish.
> A day, an hour of virtuous liberty
> Is worth a whole eternity of bondage."

I left Shebina, but not without a scene, hard to describe and still more difficult to realize.

She put her arms round my neck, and pulled my head down to hers. She smothered me with kisses, promised me all the wealth that was stored up in the treasure chambers, and then, as a last bid, offered to let me kill the lions and effect our escape with the treasures.

All, she would give all, if I would but consent to be her husband.

She sobbed and bedewed me with tears, until I told her that in my land men despised women who asked a man to marry them.

"What sort of a land can that be?" she said in surprise. "Is not a woman allowed to choose who shall be her companion for life?"

"No. It is a man's duty to propose, a woman has the right to accept or decline."

"But what if the one she loves never asks her?"

"In that case she does not get him."

"Oh, most unhappy country," she exclaimed.

I broke away from her, and found the chamber which had been assigned me, and was soon asleep, fearing every minute though, that Shebina would appear and renew her entreaties.

But I was undisturbed, and determined that on the next day I would find out what she knew about the Homono and their mysterious king.

Shebina next morning, however, was cross and pouting, and had thrown a lion skin round her form as I entered her room.

I was not sorry, for I scarcely could stand a second attack like that of the previous night.

I reminded her of her promise to tell me of the Homonos. Instead of replying, she tossed up her pretty, shapely head, and looked in an opposite direction.

I felt for her, for I don't think there are many women who can say that they have been refused.

I therefore coaxed. Would she show to me the treasure-chambers?

She cast a hurried glance at me, and then off went the skin-rug, and she stood in all her glorious perfection, as I had seen her the night before.

"I will show my king, my Incubu," she said.

Perhaps she thought the sight would cause me to relent, and that I should for the sake of the treasures, take her.

Taking a small lamp in her hand, she motioned me to follow her.

I did so, and as we passed the lions, who were roaring furiously, she looked at me and laughed.

"And so you would not have a wife for fear she gave you to the lions. Why, Incubu, I wish you would kill them for me."

I would like to have done so, but to tell the truth I was rather afraid of the consequences. The whole tribe might avenge the death of the lions, and what would it profit me to kill two lions and lose my own life?

She called to the lions, but they took no heed.

"They, too, have had a disappointment," she murmured.

Throwing open a door at the top of some stairs, a sudden gust of wind came with such force against us that we both staggered, and Shebina would have fallen had not I been there; as it was she was saved by my arms.

"Oh, my brave Incubu," she said, "how good and great thou art."

I don't know what there was particularly good or brave about preventing a woman from falling, more especially when that woman is young and lovely; however, if it pleased her to call me so, I was not going to cavil with her about it.

We descended the stairs, and when we had reached the bottom, we opened another gate and passed into a large cave, which presented to our view a strange sight. Every portion of it was filled with some treasure.

Piles of ivory, which were worth a king's ransom; sheets of polished copper, which, even after the lapse of ages, were bright as a mirror; cowry shells by the bushel; stones of all kinds, rubies, diamonds, sapphires and emeralds being plentifully besprinkled about.

I stood aghast, for never before had I beheld so great an assortment of beautiful and costly things.

"All these we could take away if we got rid of the lions," she said.

"Shebina," for the first time I called her by name, instead of using the customary titles, "Shebina, I am wealthy in my own land. I have more money than I can possibly use, why, then should I take these from you?"

"From me, nay, but with me, and we will be the richest people in all the lands beyond the waters. We will visit the land where my mother lived, and, if I am not a queen, I will be a happy wife."

I let her talk on until she got tired, and then I asked her if she would take me to the dwelling of the great Homono.

"No," she replied, emphatically.

"Will you tell me about him?"

"No."

"A queen should never break her word."

That speech brought down a torrent of wrath upon my head.

"A queen should never break her word," she repeated. "You are a fine man to tell of a monarch's duty. If I am not your queen, what matters it whether my word is broken; but if I am your queen, then it is your duty to obey. Do you hear, sir, a queen commands, a subject obeys."

We returned to her apartments, and as she stood with the lamplight falling on her shapely figure, I thought she looked sublimely beautiful.

She took her harp and twanged the strings rapidly, breaking out into a wild, weird melody, which at times sounded like the wailing of the wind through the forest trees, at others one could imagine the tornado's wrath, again the sweet lullaby of the mother would give place to the wild song of the warrior on his way to the battle. Then as she finished her improvisation she gave vent to a passionate outburst of tears terrible to witness, and agonizing in the extreme.

Who could resist soothing when beholding such a scene?

I went to her and drew her head upon my bosom and wiped away her tears.

She had for the time conquered, but only for a few moments, for my better self asserted itself, and I knew that our places in life lay far apart and that there would be no real happiness in such a union.

Her tears were dried and I left her to herself.

Later I again appealed to her to take me to the Homono.

But to all my prayers she was alike deaf and immovable.

"Tell me at least all you know about *It*," I said.

"Come with me, beloved, and thou shalt hear."

CHAPTER XXXIV.
SIR HENRY CURTIS' STORY CONTINUED.

SHEBINA led the way to a smaller cave which I suppose might be termed her boudoir.

When we had entered, she gathered all the skins together and made one pile.

I was then requested, or rather commanded, to sit at one end. Shebina reclined full length upon the rugs, resting her head on my knee.

"You wish to know about Homono?"

"I do."

"I will sell the information," she said, laughingly.

"Then I am afraid I am not a purchaser."

"You hard-hearted man! Well, I will tell you. When I was little, about so high," holding her hand on a level with my knee, "my mother used to tell me never to pass a certain door, for it opened into a series of caves occupied by the greatest personage in the world. I was curious, and asked who it could be, for I had no idea that any one could be greater than my mother, who was a queen. For a long time she refused to tell me, but my importunities won the story from her.

"The narrative may appear to be strange, and the philosophy—I think that is what you would call it—very extreme, but I tell it as I heard it, although I do not understand the subject even yet. But here is what my mother told me. At one time most of the land was under water, and the countries were all small, but no one resided on them but Homonos. Now, one of the great Homonos offended the gods, and brought down the wrath upon him. Homono wanted to be the father of a child, but although his wife had been with him for many, many moons, yet she bare him no children. At last Homono swore a great oath, that he would offer no more sacrifices to the gods until his wife bare him a child. 'A child thou shalt have, but through it thy race shalt end, and thou shalt live to see it.' So spake the gods. Homono laughed, and waited. In due course the child was born, but it was of a different species to the Homonos. It had no hair upon its body, and its hands and feet were shaped differently. It grew, however, and thrived, and to it were born children, as no Homonos. The father of the first strange child can die while any of the Homonos live. When they die out and give place to a different order of being, then this great mystery we call *It* will die also."

That was the story Shebina told me concerning the great Homono.

I thought over the subject, and this is how it resolved itself in my mind.

From a germ came the first life, from that one life others were developed until from the jelly-fish arose the first boned animal, and so on through countless ages, a constant progression until the ape was reached; the ape was improved upon until it became so nearly human that it wanted but one link to complete the chain of evidence. According to Shebina, the Homono was the link which stood between the animal and the human, between the monkey and the man.

Under the legend or tradition which had been told me by Shebina, I thought I recognized the missing link.

It was found. If such should be the case, what a glorious work we should have achieved. And what benefit to science the result would prove.

I thanked Shebina for the story, but was all the more desirous to see the wonder.

To all my entreaties she had but one answer. It was plain and explicit.

"She would have given me all, but I insulted her by refusing her hand when she offered."

I asked what good it did to refuse so small a request, but she only laughed and declared that when she was my wife it would be her place to obey.

"Come," she said, and she put out her hand for me to take.

Like children hand in hand we walked out into the garden and sat beneath the fruit festoons looking at the beauties of the place.

As Sir Henry's manuscript goes on to deal with other subjects, at this point I again take up the story and narrate the events as they occurred. It will be seen that there is a great divergence in the story told me by one of the Homonos and that told by Shebina.

Both, however, have as the central idea the fact that through the Homonos a superior animal came into the world, but whether that animal was man remains to be proved.

That Curtis must have an interview with *It* even if he has to marry Shebina we were all agreed upon, and a long discussion took place on the right and wrong of refusing the liberal offer made by Shebina.

While we were talking, a noise outside attracted our attention, and we went to see what had caused the commotion, when to our horror we saw quite a number of the Homonos gathered round our door.

They commenced jabbering and chattering in a peculiar language.

We did not understand them in the slightest, but had to trust to the signs they were making.

From what we could learn, they desired our revolvers.

Good thought it would be good practice to shoot a few of them, while Quatermain declared that he was getting rusty for want of exercise.

What to do with them we did not know.

If they had been hostile natives we might have tried

to buy their friendship by a gift of some beads, but the Homonos never wore them, so that would not answer.

They were evidently not inclined to be antagonistic, for they made no attempt to touch or in any way molest us.

We all tried to satisfy them, but still we were on the wrong tack.

Quegga, with her ready wit, searched round and found our old attendant, who came forward, and after a confab with the Homonos told us that we were highly honored, that the tribe had prepared a banquet to which we were all invited and that this was our escort.

I was in no humor for the adventure, but as the others would not go without me, I accompanied them.

The banquet was at the house of the old philosophic Homono, who had told me the tradition of his race.

This was pleasing to us, for we should have at least one who could converse with us.

What a strange sight was presented in that dwelling in the city of Oph.

I have dined with princes at state banquets, have sat as a guest at the table of the Lord Mayor of London, have hobnobbed with scientists and philosophers, but never before or since have I seen such a banquet.

Over a score of men or animals, each with long, shaggy hair over their bodies as the only clothing, waited upon by women or female animals—truly it was a strange spectacle.

The first course consisted of a liquid which, while not near so good as the Kasheebar almond honey, reminded me very much of it.

As we all drank out of the same jar, there was no danger of us being specially singled out for poisoned drinks.

The drink was followed by some broiled antelope, which was very good.

Then followed a dish which we left entirely to the Homonos.

It was an antelope's head, which had been buried until putrid and full of maggots. The head was then taken up and partially cooked, care being taken not to make it so hot that all the maggots would be killed.

As this horrible dish was placed on the table and the fleshy parts began to move and quiver with the live stock contained therein, the Homonos smacked their lips and expressed great delight at the, to them, most savory joint.

We declined the pleasure of partaking, but every Homono ate it as though it was the rarest gastronomic treat.*

This was followed by a course which we thoroughly appreciated. Nuts of nearly every kind, together with various sorts of fruits, were served up by the females, and enjoyed by all present.

When the dinner was over, singing and dancing were the order of the day, thus showing that the Homonos knew how to enjoy themselves.

We understood from the Philosopher that we were pitied by them, for man was looked upon as being an inferior creature in every way to the Homono.

Before we separated the old philosopher offered us pipes to smoke; but, much as we should have enjoyed a pipe of tobacco, the fact that the principal recommendation of the pipes was their age debarred us from the pleasure.

We had learned that the homono sat at the table in a more civilized manner than the native African, and that his habits were cleaner than his supposedly far more favored brother.

CHAPTER XXXV.
THE DEATH OF QUEGGA.

THE next afternoon was a sad one for me. If I ever find that elixir which gives perpetual life, and should live to see a thousand summers flit into eternity, I shall never forget it.

I had learned to love Quegga with an intensity which I thought I could never feel for any one. She had been very downcast of late, which I attributed to the fact that she had been in the house more than was her former custom.

That afternoon I devoted to her. The others were all exploring in different directions, and Curtis was still with Shebina.

* Dr. Livingstone says this was a favorite dish of various tribes in the interior of Africa, and that he was considered uncivilized because he refused to partake of the putrid stuff.

Quegga resumed a little of her animation when she found I was staying with her, and some of the old brilliancy came back to her eyes when I praised her form and said I thought she was pretty.

"My lord, my own, my beloved, canst thou say thou art glad I came with thee?" she asked.

"Quegga"—I placed my arm round her waist as I spoke—"Quegga, I love you, and were I offered all the gold and precious things in the world to give thee up, I would prefer thee to all."

"I am so glad."

"Yes, Quegga, and whether we go to my own land or stay here, my only hope is that thou wilt be by my side."

"If it is my lord's wish; but oh, Theo., I feel that I shall not live long."

"Haven't you got rid of that feeling yet?"

"No; it grows stronger every day; and I would like you to kiss me, Theo., and tell me again that you love me."

I pressed her to my heart, and the hot breath fanned my cheeks. Her blood was like a lava tide of passion.

We experienced in that close embrace all the exaltation of true love, and felt that, though all beside were hostile, our love would be strong enough to ward off the attacks of the enemies.

We strolled out into the country beyond the town, and alone rambled almost like children enjoying an hour's freedom.

I was examining some rare plants which had attracted my attention, when I heard a scream from Quegga. I turned instantly, to find her in the powerful grasp of the maniac, of whom Quatermain warned me a few days before. The man who wanted Quegga's blood to make some compound for life preservation.

I sprung across to the man and struck him a heavy blow on the head, causing him to relinquish his hold. I then pushed Quegga, who, fortunately, was unhurt, behind me, while I waited for the attack which I knew I had to face.

I was too chivalrous to use a pistol on a man only armed with a hunting-knife; so, drawing my own knife, I closed with him.

Our knives clashed, and the sparks flew from them; we were well matched.

He, though a savage, had been well drilled in the use of a hunter's knife, so there was strength and science on both sides.

Quegga watched the combat, wishing intently that I might come out of the fray uninjured.

The man, whose name was Jocko, fell. Instead of seizing my opportunity and driving my knife right home, I waited for him to rise.

The man now became savage in his fury, and pressed me hard.

I got my foot against his, and our knives rattled and clashed together like sweet martial music.

I got pricked two or three times, and gave him just as good as he sent.

Quegga looked on with interest; though she regretted the risk I was running, she would not have had me withdraw; she was far too good a child of nature for that.

We both fell and held each other in an iron grip, while each struggled to get free.

I held on for dear life, for I knew if Jocko got his arm free for one moment, I should never raise a hunting-knife again.

He felt in the same way, so it resolved itself into a struggle for freedom.

Seizing a favorable opportunity, I raised myself on one knee, and then, with a desperate push, tried to throw him over, and thus both get free, but though he fell over again, his hold was so tight that I went over with him.

We were both beginning to feel exhausted, and yet neither would give in. It was "war to the knife."

After several more rolls on the green sward we succeeded in getting to our feet.

Our hands were again free, and we fought like tigers.

Quegga saw that I was getting the worst of it, so kept her eyes fixed on me.

She saw Jocko draw some powder from his belt, and rub it on the blade of his knife.

"Theo., take care, the knife is poisoned."

The sudden calling out caused me to fall back just in time to escape a blow from the poisoned weapon.

Had I been wise, I should then have used my revolver,

for my adversary was taking an unfair advantage; how often I wish I had done so, and yet, perhaps, it is all for the best.

Jocko rushed at me now, with hate gleaming from his eyes; never did knife move quicker through the air than it did in his hand. His figure seemed like elastic, it bent and twisted in every imaginable shape in order to get the point of vantage against me.

I had to be extra careful, for I knew that the simplest scratch with a poisoned blade would prove fatal, so my whole attention had to be devoted to dodging his blows, I was entirely on the defensive.

I was driven back and stumbled, that moment was an opportune one for Jocko, and he was quick to seize it; but scarcely sharp enough, for Quegga glided close up to me, and before I knew what she was doing, had drawn a revolver from by belt.

Jocko's knife was raised to strike me to the heart, and I was powerless to stop it. I felt weak and exhausted, and resigned myself to my fate.

The knife was in the act of descending when the lithe figure glided past me, and a report rang out on the air.

The girl had shot Jocko, but alas, she had not been in time to escape the blow intended for me.

The very moment that she fired, the knife was in the act of descent, and she had thrown herself in my way. The blow cut her left breast and laid bare a terrible gash.

I remembered how, when my flesh had been poisoned, she had sucked the venom from the wound; I did the same now, but it had gone too deep. The heart's blood was oozing rapidly way.

In despair I seized her in my arms, trying to stanch the blood all I could, and ran home with my brave, devoted Quegga.

I took out my small case of instruments, and, after bathing the wound and washing it out with a little antiseptic cotton, I stitched it up.

Quegga remained unconscious all the time, but when the blood was stanched she opened her eyes and looked up at me.

I saw death plainly written there, and my heart was heavy.

"My own! my beloved!" she murmured.

I raised her head to my shoulder, and pressed my lips to hers.

I felt her arms tighten round my neck, and then in a faint, feeble voice she gasped:

"My beloved, oh, how I love thee!"

"Dearest, my own Quegga," I replied, though I could scarcely form a word; my heart was full, and I felt like choking.

"I—oh, Theo., I am dying—I will—meet thee—beyond—— Kiss me."

Again I kissed her, and my whole soul seemed to have gone out to her in that one kiss, for her face brightened, and looking up at me she said:

"It is for the best. Good-bye."

For a moment the brave, devoted girl lay in my arms motionless. I thought the vital spark had gone, but the lips began to move, and the eyes opened slightly.

I stooped down to catch the words she was trying to utter, and heard the faint murmur:

"Kiss me."

Our lips met. I felt the arms tighten round my neck, one embrace; our lips seemed glued together, so fervent was that kiss.

I feared the excitement would be too much for Quegga, so I moved her away.

Alas! she was dead.

Her spirit had left the body when her lips met mine.

Quegga, the devoted, was but a memory.

She had given her life for me, and at the sacrifice of her own young career she had saved me.

May Heaven reward her. She was a pagan, but never had Christian a purer soul or more lofty mind.

Never did any mortal woman live more purely and with more love for her fellows than did my pagan Quegga.

She must be in the realms of glory, or heaven itself is but a mockery.

I have seen the beauties of Rome and Paris; have danced with the stately dames and blushing daughters of Berlin and London, but even now, though the scenes have changed and no sight of colored people recalls to me the life on the Dark Continent, I would give up all, and go back to a kraal in the wildest and most uncivilized part of that land, if I could have Quegga to share my life.

When I found she was really dead, I went out to dig a grave for her.

No one but myself should do it. She was mine, and as I had closed her eyes in death, so would I cover her body with the earth.

I dug the grave as deep as my tools would allow me.

It was a work of a long time, but I wanted to take no chances. She was precious to me, and no vulture or jackal should pray upon the body which had been so often warm in my embrace.

At last the grave was ready, and I was in the act of rolling Quegga in her blanket, when Good and the rest came in.

They looked at the body, and I could see the tears trickle down Good's cheeks.

He said not a word, but in English fashion put out his hand and clasped mine silently.

The others did the same, and then sadly and silently we carried Quegga to the new-made grave, and in a few moments her body was hid from sight forever.

I walked away, wandered for miles to and fro on that lovely plateau. I saw neither flower nor shrub. I noticed neither native nor Homono. My eyes were blinded by the sorrow of my heart.

I should see her no more!

Great Heaven, be merciful! Let me in the great beyond be reunited to her who loved me with so great a love that she hesitated not to give her life for me.

As I write I feel her gentle influence, and it seems as if Rapa and Quegga were near me, one and the same individuality.

Could it be? Why not? Did not Rapa say she would be ever with me, did not she tell me that her spirit would seek possession of some other body and would be guided to me?

Was Quegga Rapa reincarnated?

Enough years had relapsed since the tragic death on Rapa Nui.

Could it be that the unseen Eternal power had sent the spirit of Rapa to take possession of the body of the

Abyssinian baby, and then directed its steps to Kasheebar, reserved the girl from the king's evil desires, and placed her in my arms.

It may have been so. Much I saw in Quegga reminded me of Rapa—but there, I dare not think, or madness would overtake me.

Had I been convinced to a certainty that my spirit would have joined that of Quegga, I should that day have died a suicide.

The uncertainty made me pause, and made me rather "chose those ills we have, than fly to others we know not off."

The darkness had covered the earth with a heavy pall before I returned to our house.

I found my blanket, and rolling myself in it, slept on Quegga's grave.*

CHAPTER XXXVI.
INCUBU'S SURRENDER.

WE had not heard anything of Sir Henry Curtis for ten days, and began to feel alarmed.

We had found unmistakable evidence that the strange being who lived near the rocky palace of Shebina, was the undoubted *It*, the missing link, the one necessary to complete the chain of evolution from the germ to the jelly-fish, the jelly-fish to the monkey, the ape to the man.

It was our great desire to see *It*, to learn whether it possessed the power of thought and language, to study its anatomy, and compare it with that of the monkey, the Homono and man.

But how could he gain access to this marvelous creature?

Shoara refused to even send a message to the queen, so we were powerless.

That evening, just as we were about to roll up in the blankets for a night's rest, the queen's special messenger entered and walking up to me, handed me a letter.

When the messenger retired I opened the missive and read, in English, as follows:

DEAR THEO. AND THE REST,—After all my resolves, after the promises I have made, the vows registered in the recording angel's ledger, I am at last, by the laws of this strange country, a married man. I am no longer Sir Henry Curtis, Bart., of Brayley Hall, Yorkshire, England, but I would have you understand I am King Incubu of the Oph nation. I will tell you how it came about, or I shall not like to look you in the face again; but first let me ask you all to come and see me to-morrow. The herald will conduct you all to my august presence—for I am not allowed yet to leave the palace—don't fail to bring Quegga."

How my heart throbbed when I read that line, Sir Henry little knew that the dear one was moldering in the cold grave.

The letter continued:

"For I have told my wife all about her, and she is desirous of seeing her. Of course you will all come. Remember I am your king, and if you don't come at once I will have to send my warriors to fetch you. I must fulfill my promise and tell you how I became a married man. I think the best way will be to send you a page or two of my diary, so that you can read as the events happened."

I looked for the diary, but it was not with the letter. Had Curtis been so engrossed with his new cares that he had forgotten it? That was the most probable thing. With a sigh I turned back to the letter and read:

"I am the richest man in the world, but of what value are my riches, for I cannot leave these caves, that is at present, but I am very well content, and if I don't change my views I may remain king of the Oph nation all my life, and spend my days in the royal palace.

" But come and see me, and we will talk over all events and have a good smoke, for I discovered a lot of real Turkish tobacco. Although your king, I shall ever be your sincere friend, CURTIS."

Scarcely had I finished reading the letter when the herald returned with many apologies, bringing with him the missing diary.

" What have you got?" asked Fjord.

" A letter from King Incubu," I replied.

" Who the deuce is that?" inquired Good.

" Here, you fellows want to know too much, take the

letter and read it," I said as I handed over Sir Henry's letter.

While they were reading it, I looked over the diary and found the explanation of the marriage to be as follows—I quote now entirely from Sir Henry's writing:

After Shebina had told me the legend of the Homono, I was the more desirous of seeing the first person who broke through the custom, and by that means constituted the missing link so long looked for. Though Shebina insisted that the creature was alive and had existed through all the thousands of years, I did not believe it, but thought when seen it would turn out to be a mummy or perhaps some old piece of carved stone.

But entreat as I would I could not get her consent, so I had to try other means, for I was fully resolved to settle the question before I left the caves—or I suppose I ought to call it, the palace.

The day passed like the preceding one.

Shebina changed her costume at least a dozen times—of course with the evident intention of charming and tempting me.

Before the day had gone I began to feel pity for and sympathize with Shebina. Pity is akin to love, it is said, but that I cannot help, for it is true I pitied her.

She was most lovely, but a prisoner. She saw no one but the repulsive natives, with the exception of the herald, who was really good-looking, but he was of low rank.

By the laws of the Oph nation unless she was married in six months the chiefs of the tribes would meet together and select a husband for her.

Shebina told me that the most popular chief would get all the votes, and he was a man she hated; besides, he had fifty wives already. I remembered the chief she referred to. He was a giant in stature; his nose was pierced for a huge ring to hang therefrom, and his cheeks were tattooed. He was one of the most repulsive creatures I had ever seen. "And this man," said Shebina, with a shudder, "will take possession of me in six months. Think of it. Is it not horrible?"

"Is there no escape?" I asked.

"Yes," was the answer; "I have told you I can marry

any one I please during the next six months, and if my husband leaves me a week, nay, a day after, I am free forever. I shall have been married, and that is all the custom requires."

Who would not feel sorry for a girl so young and lovely, placed in such a terrible position?

I thought of Captain John Good, and tried to fancy him King of the Oph nation, and even suggested sending for him, but Shebina kept saying: "To-morrow, do so," so that the invitation got delayed.

That evening the lamp was burning low, when Shebina came to me as I was sitting on the cushions, and leaned over my shoulder; her face was close to mine, her breath passed like a zephyr over my cheeks, her hair, which had been fastened up in some way, escaped from its fastening and fell like a veil over my head.

Shebina had most wonderful black hair. It was long enough to touch the ground as she walked, yet as soft as silk.

As the hair covered our faces, she leaned her head forward and pressed a warm, passionate kiss on my lips.

That instant she jumped away, her cheeks flaming with maidenly blushes, and she exclaimed:

"I could not resist; it was all the fault of my hair."

My blood was at fever-heat — who could wonder? Everything tended to make me captive to the little love-god.

The room was warm, and a subtle perfume filled its every niche; the light was dim, and with me was one of the most beautiful women I had ever seen, dressed not as the fashionable belles of London or Paris, neither was she nude like the natives, but her gossamer clothes showed the purple veins as they filled with her heart's blood, and every light and shade of her form was fully revealed.

My senses grew dim, and I nearly lost consciousness in the excitement of the time.

Then Shebina seized her harp, and in a low, plaintive, but winning voice, sang:

> "Am I hard-favored, cruel, or very old,
> Ill-shaped, or crooked, coarse in voice?
> If so, pray tell me that I may know
> Thou lovest not me."

When the last words died away, she quietly laid aside

the musical instrument, and drew herself close to me and nestled in my arms.

Her sweet lips were uplifted, and as I looked down I caught the flash of her eyes as they looked straight into mine

What conjurations or what mighty magic she used I know not, but a dreamy feeling came over me and my senses were lulled into a voluptuous repose.

Before we separated that night I had promised to be hers.

The morning sun had scarcely risen before I heard the love songs of Shebina floating on the breeze.

I soon joined her, and asked what time she had risen from her couch.

"Sleep! and didst thou sleep?" she asked.

"Yes, dear one; why not?"

"Oh, you men! I could not sleep, I was too happy."

She had not been to bed all night, but had passed the hours in a kind of ecstasy bordering almost on frenzy, as she thought of her coming life.

The ceremony of marriage in Oph is a strange one, but all that was necessary in the case of the queen was to say in the presence of witnesses: "This is my husband."

When the early meal was being served, and two black waiting-women were in the chamber, Shebina raised her lovely head, and turning to the women, said:

"Women, this is my husband."

That was all.

I was a married man, and am to be declared King of Oph, under the title of King Incubu.

What will they say in England when the society papers have a paragraph something after this fashion:

"*On dit*, that Sir Henry Curtis, of Brayley Hall, Yorkshire, who has been so extensive a traveler, has at last settled down by marrying the queen of one of the savage tribes in the interior of Africa. Will Sir Henry, or we suppose we should say—will King Curtis bring his black bride to England?"

How my friends will laugh, but some day when I take Queen Shebina to England, won't they open their eyes about my bride when they find her more beautiful than any of their fashionable society ladies, and with a skin which European beauties might envy.

I am afraid, though, I shall have a difficulty about dress, for Shebina holds the same views as Quegga addressed to Theo.: "Dress," says Shebina, "should not conceal, but only bring into prominence the perfection of the figure."

I am afraid she will need educating before she goes to England.

Here, Sir Henry's diary ended, and when the others read it, they all agreed they would have succumbed quicker than did Curtis.

CHAPTER XXXVII.
KING INCUBU.

THE sun was some hours above the horizon the next morning before we received the summons to attend the herald to the court of King Incubu and Queen Shebina.

We had all tried to look as aristocratic and courtly as possible.

Good had shaved himself with a very blunt razor, had polished his eyeglass, and made his celluloid collar as white as a linen one could be. He was the swell of the party undoubtedly.

We followed the guide up the stairs and through the passages which I had traversed with Sir Henry on that night when he was so cleverly taken in the net.

When we arrived at the royal cave we found Curtis waiting for us, looking handsome and great.

His face was covered with a genial smile, and if appearances went for anything he was wondrously happy.

He shook hands with each of us, and looked round.

"Where is Quegga?"

I could not speak, my feelings were too excited, and my emotion too great.

Quatermain told him the story briefly, and I saw Curtis put his hand to his eyes and dash away a tear.

Sir Henry walked across to where I was standing at a little distance from the others, and putting one hand on my shoulder, he grasped my hand with the other and shook it silently.

It was more expressive than words.

When the conversation began to slacken a bit, Curtis looked at us quizzically for a moment, and then said:

"Come boys, and I will introduce you to the queen."

Although I had described the furniture of the royal caves, and tried to paint the loveliness of Shebina to my comrades, they stepped back almost aghast at the sight which met their eyes.

On the pile of cushions reclined Shebina, dressed as I had seen her on that first night, in the gossamer Persian tunic and pantaloons, tied round the bare ankle.

As we entered the stood up, revealing to the gaze of us all a vision

"Of youth, and love, and beauty."

all combined.

Not one could speak. All were completely dumfounded. When I had said the queen was white, they expected to see a mulatto, but they looked upon one whose skin was as beautiful as that of any aristocratic lady.

She bade us welcome, and as I was considered the principal friend of the new king, so she was pleased to tell me, she kissed me on the cheek.

Good whispered later to me, that he would have forfeited a year's pay for that one kiss.

Shebina was pleased with Good, and had pleasant words for all.

"At twelve o'clock," said Curtis, "the chiefs will be here and I am to be introduced, you will all be created chiefs at the same time."

Shebina whispered to Curtis for a moment, and then she left the room.

"My wife, the queen, wished me to apologize for her forthcoming appearance. It is the law of Oph, that on all state occasions, and there are only about half a dozen in a generation, the monarch must appear dressed as the natives—in other words, we shall have to appear before you in beads and feathers. Until we are ready, adieu!"

"Well, I'm blest!" exclaimed Good. "Is Curtis going to strip?"

"It seems like it," I said.

"Well, I wouldn't," said Good, emphatically.

"What, not to have so lovely a wife as Shebina and be declared king?" I asked.

"Not for all the kingdoms in the world," he replied; "but I'm blest if I wouldn't do more than that for such a woman as Shebina."

The hour of twelve was near at hand.

The drums were beating and horns were blown.

Six gigantic fellows, dressed with helmet of hair, and beads, shield and spear, but otherwise nude, entered the chamber where we were standing.

These were the chiefs of the Oph nation. The signal was given, and we followed the chiefs into the large council chamber and beheld a sight which was worthy the pencil of an artist.

Curtis stood on a raised dais at the end of the room or cave; round his head he had a black band, in which were placed some splendid ostrich feathers.

Round his neck hung several rows of beads, and round his loins he had a girdle made of lion skin, and thickly sprinkled with jewels.

By his side stood Shebina, nude with the exception of the beads, and a leopard-skin girdle about eight inches deep round her waist.

But her hair was down, and acted like a veil, covering her lovely form even down to her feet.

When the drums ceased Shebina declared that, as queen of the nation of the Ophs, most mighty ruler of all rulers, and many other attributes too wearisome to remember, she had bestowed herself upon Henry Curtis, who would forever be known as King Incubu of the Oph nation.

The chiefs bowed their heads very low, kissed the spear which their new king took in his hand, and then retired to the back of the room.

We were then called forward, and each became a chief with a new and distinctive title. Curtis had told Shebina about the Kaffir names of Quatermain and Good, and they were elevated to the position of chiefs with the names of Bougwan and Macumazahu. Fjord was called the Fox, and I received the name of the Lion.

We went through the form of kissing the spear, and the ceremony ended.

The chiefs went back to their tribes well pleased at the turn things had taken, while we were specially retained as guests of the royal and newly-wed pair.

The royal couple retired, and a little later returned dressed in a little more respectable—as we thought—manner.

A sumptuous repast was served and a right jolly time we had.

My heart was sad at the thought of Quegga, but with that exception, the twelve days we spent in the caves were replete with happiness and pleasure,

Each day Shebina devised some new amusement, and each night we all retired to rest intoxicated by gazing on her wondrous beauty.

It was not until the last evening that we spent in the caves that the subject for which we had traveled so many miles, and endured so many privations was mentioned.

Curtis said that he had been thinking much over the question, and he was more than ever convinced that the facts in the physical organization and mental manifestations of the animal called man, when viewed historically through all the conditions in which we know anything of this species, lead up to his supposed ancestor, the ape. And the facts in the physical organization and instinctive habit of the ape, when viewed in the light of history, show that he too was evolved by the process of natural selection out of a very low form of animated organisms through countless periods of time.

"I agree with you," said Fjord, "but intermediate between the man and the monkey, and also between the monkey and his primordial natural-selection predecessor, there are links missing."

"Say there *were*, not *are*," said Curtis with emphasis, "for the link has been found."

"Are you sure?"

"Certainly I am."

"Please explain," I said.

"With pleasure. Now look at these creatures called Homonos, what are they? They are not monkeys, are they?"

"No, and yet——"

"That is just it. That *yet* is just the point I was bringing out. They are not monkeys, yet their feet are shaped nearly like their hands, their arms are larger than in the purely human, and they have hair growing on their bodies. At the same time these Homonos, have the gift of speech, can adjust themselves to the wants of society, can fight like men and act so. Now are they not intermediate between the monkey and the man?"

"It looks very like it, and the tradition of the Homonos would bear out the idea, for the first monstrosity which was born without hair was a female human child."

"But will not that destroy the idea of creation and undermine religion?" asked Quatermain.

"Not at all," replied Curtis, "but on the contrary, for it gives us a God who evolved out of his own nature the first germs, and sent them forth to be ruled by immutable laws, and by the changes they undergo to evolute into various forms, until the great perfection of the angel-world is reached."

"Don't you stop at death?" I asked.

"No," responded Curtis, "for death is but another link in the chain. It is but the evolving process by which the human becomes purer, freer from gross defects, and in its ethereal or spiritual form nearer to perfection."

"Have you seen the great Homono yet?"

"No, but we will all go together and see it before you leave, for I suppose you will not be content with your chieftainship?"

"No," I answered; "will you?"

To our great astonishment Curtis replied that he would most likely stay there some years, and enjoy the society of his beautiful Shebina, when he hoped to return to England and introduce her to English society.

Curtis gave each of us as many gems of the first water as we cared to carry, and then after showing us Homono our paths in life would separate.

It was so, for a few weeks after we sailed for England, even Quatermain having had enough of Africa. I occasionally get a letter from King Incubu, and he is enjoying the kingship so much that he makes no promise of a speedy return.

To resume then my story, it was resolved that on the next day we should visit this wonderful Homono, which we believed to be the veritable *It* of which we were in search.

CHAPTER XXXVIII.
"IT."

ACCOMPANIED by Shebina, the whole party of us, each carrying lamps, wound our way through interminable passages, corridors and caves, until we reached another plateau, higher than the one in which the royal caves were situated.

Instead of flowers there were trees of various kinds and shrubs growing, some bearing nuts and others a kind of red berry bitter to the taste.

Two priests, dressed in the sacred vestments prized by the Oph nation, guarded the entrance to the caverns to which we were bound.

We explained that it was our pleasure to see the king of the Homonos.

To this they replied, that his majesty, on account of his great age, did not receive visits.

The queen approached and handed a beautiful row of beads to the priests; King Incubu gave them a splendid tusk of ivory, and we each made them a present, whereupon we were at once admitted to the royal presence.

In a room, large and comfortable, seated on a chair in front of a table, was a very respectable-looking old gentleman. He wore spectacles of a European shape and design.

These be carefully removed from his eyes, wiped them, and again settled them on the bridge of his nose.

We entered, and he uttered the one word signifying welcome, and shook each of us by the hand.

The priests explained to us the legend, which declared that this monarch of the Homonos had existed for many thousands of years, and that he would live until all the Homonos were dead.

He would be the last of the line, and was hoping soon to rest in the quiet of his grave.

I could not help wondering whether there was not some trickery about the age. That was the only doubt I had, for that he was a genuine link between the monkey and the man I had not a shadow of doubt. The proofs were too plain and palpable. Had the Homono kept his seat I should have almost believed that he was altogether human, but when he left his seat, and in a moment of forgetfulness crossed the floor, using his hands as well as feet, I knew there was some of the monkey in his nature.

We were speechless with astonishment, and though we left Oph the next day, and made our way across the desert, having plenty of servants to carry food and water for us, and arrived three months after safely in England, I shall never forget the wonderful *It*.

Many doubt my story, but in the last letter I received from Sir Henry Curtis, he tells me he had studied the Homono more closely, and that it was truly the missing link. As I had a great respect for my primordial, natural-selection ancestor as I saw him, and conversed with him in the wonderful kingdom of Oph, ruled over to-day by King Incubu and Queen Shebina, I sketched his portrait and respectfully submit *It* to an admiring public.

THE END OF "IT."

LOST RACE AND ADULT FANTASY FICTION

An Arno Press Collection

Ames, Joseph Bushnell. **The Bladed Barrier.** 1929

Anderson, Olof W. **The Treasure Vault of Atlantis.** 1925

Arnold, Edwin Lester. **Lepidus the Centurion.** 1901

[Atkins, Frank]. Frank Aubrey, pseud. **The Devil-Tree of El Dorado.** 1897

[Atkins, Frank]. Frank Aubrey, pseud. **King of the Dead:** A Weird Romance. 1903

Bennet, Robert Ames. **Thyra:** A Romance of the Polar Pit. 1901

[Bennett, Gertrude Barrows]. Francis Stevens, pseud. **The Heads of Cerberus.** 1952

Blackwood, Algernon. **The Fruit Stoners.** 1935

[Boëx, Joseph-Henri]. J.-H. Rosny aîné, pseud. **The Xipehuz** *and* **The Death of the Earth.** Translated from the original 1888 and 1912 French editions by George Edgar Slusser. 1978

Bruce, Muriel. **Mukara.** 1930

[Burton, Alice Elizabeth]. Susan Alice Kerby, pseud. **Miss Carter and the Ifrit.** [1945]

Carew, Henry. **The Vampires of the Andes.** 1925

Chambers, Robert. **The Slayer of Souls.** 1920

Channing, Mark. **White Python:** Adventure and Mystery in Tibet. 1934

Chester, George Randolph. **The Jingo.** 1912

Clock, Herbert and Eric Boetzel. **The Light in the Sky.** 1929

Coblentz, Stanton A[rthur]. **When the Birds Fly South.** 1945

Constantine, Murray, pseud. **The Devil, Poor Devil!** 1934

Cook, William Wallace. **Cast Away at the Pole.** 1904

Cowan, Frank. **Revi-Lona:** A Romance of Love in a Marvelous Land. [c. 1890]

Day, Bradford M., compiler and editor. **Bibliography of Adventure:** Mundy, Burroughs, Rohmer, Haggard. Revised edition. 1978

de Comeau, Alexander. **Monk's Magic.** 1931

[de Grainville, Jean Baptiste François Xavier Cousin]. **The Last Man, Or, Omegarus and Syderia.** Two vols. in one. 1806/1806

Dunn, J. Allan. **The Flower of Fate.** 1928

Eddison, E[ric] R[ucker]. **Styrbiorn the Strong.** 1926

Fleckenstein, Alfred C. **The Prince of Gravas.** 1898

Fyne, Neal, pseud. **The Land of the Living Dead.** [1897]

Gillmore, Inez Haynes. **Angel Island.** 1914

[Gompertz, Martin Louis Alan]. "Ganpat," pseud. **Adventures in Sakaeland Comprising Harilek** *and* **Wrexham's Romance.** Two vols. in one. 1923/1935

Green, Fitzhugh. **Z R Wins.** 1924

[Gregory, Jackson]. Quien Sabe, pseud. **Daughter of the Sun.** 1921

Griffith [-Jones], George [Chetwynd]. **The Romance of Golden Star....**1897

[Guthrie, Thomas Anstey]. F. Anstey, pseud. **Humour & Fantasy.** 1931

Haggard, H[enry] Rider. **The Mahatma and the Hare.** 1911
Haggard, H[enry] Rider. **Wisdom's Daughter.** 1923
Haldane, Charlotte. **Melusine or Devil Take Her!** [1936]
[Harris-Burland, John Burland]. Harris Burland, pseud. **The Princess Thora.** 1904
Hartmann, Franz. **Among the Gnomes.** 1895
Hodder, William Reginald. **Daughter of the Dawn.** 1903
Knowles, Vernon. **Sapphires: Here and Otherwhere** and **Silver Nutmegs.** Two vols. in one. 1926/1927
Kummer, Frederic Arnold. **Shades of Hades: Ladies in Hades** and **Gentlemen in Hades.** Two vols. in one. 1930/1930
Large, E. C. **Asleep in the Afternoon.** 1939
Le Queux, William [Tufnell]. **The Eye of Istar.** 1897
Leroux, Gaston. **The Bride of the Sun.** 1915
Lindsay, David. **Devil's Tor.** 1932
Linklater, Eric. **A Spell For Old Bones.** 1950
London, Jack. **Hearts of Three.** 1920
[Lunn, Hugh Kingsmill]. Hugh Kingsmill, pseud. **The Return of William Shakespeare.** 1929
Marshall, Sidney J. **The King of Kor; Or, She's Promise Kept.** 1903
McHugh, Vincent. **I Am Thinking of My Darling.** 1943
Menville, Douglas and R. Reginald, editors. **Dreamers of Dreams: An Anthology of Fantasy.** 1978
Menville, Douglas and R. Reginald, editors. **Worlds of Never: Three Fantastic Novels.** 1978
Merritt, A[braham]. **The Fox Woman and Other Stories.** 1949
Morris, Kenneth. **Book of the Three Dragons.** 1930
Murray, G. G. A. **Gobi or Shamo.** 1889
Owen, Frank. **The Purple Sea.** 1930
Potter, Margaret Horton. **Istar of Babylon.** 1902
Reginald, R. and Douglas Menville, editors. **King Solomon's Children: Some Parodies of H. Rider Haggard.** 1978
Reginald, R. and Douglas Menville, editors. They: Three Parodies of H. Rider Haggard's *She*. With an Introduction by R. Reginald. 1978
Rolfe, Frederick [William] and [Charles Harry Clinton Pirie-Gordon]. Prospero and Caliban, pseuds. **Hubert's Arthur.** 1935
Savile, Frank. **Beyond the Great South Wall.** 1901
Scott, G. Firth. **The Last Lemurian.** 1898
Sheldon-Williams, Miles. **The Power of Ula.** 1906
Sinclair, Upton. **Prince Hagen.** 1903
[Smith, Ernest Bramah]. Ernest Bramah, pseud. **Kai Lung Beneath the Mulberry-Tree.** 1940
Todd, Ruthven. **Over the Mountain.** 1939
Vivian, E[velyn] Charles. **Aia: Fields of Sleep** and **People of the Darkness.** Two vols. in one. [1925]/1924
Vivian, E[velyn] Charles. **A King There Was--.** [1926]
Wells, H[erbert] G[eorge]. **The Wonderful Visit.** 1895

www.ingramcontent.com/pod-product-compliance
Lightning Source LLC
Chambersburg PA
CBHW020045190426
43199CB00042B/33